What Research Has To Say About Reading Instruction

second edition

S. JAY SAMUELS
University of Minnesota

ALAN E. FARSTRUP
International Reading Association

Editors

International Reading Association
Newark, Delaware 19714

The International Reading Association attempts, through its publications, to provide a forum for a wide spectrum of opinions on reading. This policy permits divergent viewpoints without assuming the endorsement of the Association.

Director of Publications Joan M. Irwin
Managing Editor Romayne McElhaney
Associate Editor Anne Fullerton
Associate Editor Karen Goldsmith
Assistant Editor Kate Shumaker

Library of Congress Cataloging in Publication Data

What research has to say about reading instruction/S. Jay Samuels, Alan E. Farstrup, editors. — 2nd ed.
    p. cm.
Includes bibliographical references and index.
    1. Reading. 2. Reading—Research.
I. Samuels, S. Jay. II. Farstrup, Alan E.
LB1050.w435 1992 91-34558
428.4—dc20 CIP
ISBN 0-87207-495-1

Second Printing, February 1993

Cover Design Boni Nash

Contents

Foreword   v

Preface   vii

1 The Role of Reseach in Reading Instruction   1
       Wayne Otto

2 Home and School Together:
       Helping Beginning Readers Succeed   17
       Lloyd O. Ollila and Margie I. Mayfield

3 Whole Language Research: Foundations and
       Development   46
       Kenneth S. Goodman

4 Assessing Literacy: From Standardized Tests
       to Portfolios and Performances   70
       Elfrieda H. Hiebert and Robert C. Calfee

5 The Role of Decoding in Learning to Read   101
       Isabel L. Beck and Connie Juel

6 Reading Fluency: Techniques for
       Making Decoding Automatic   124
       S. Jay Samuels, Nancy Schermer, and David Reinking

7 Developing Expertise in Reading Comprehension   145
       P. David Pearson, Laura R. Roehler, Janice A. Dole,
       and Gerald G. Duffy

8 Improving Reading Instruction in the Content Areas   200
       Stephen Simonsen and Harry Singer

9 Text Structure, Comprehension, and Recall   220
       Barbara M. Taylor

10 Metacognition and Self-Monitoring Strategies   236
       Ruth Garner

11 Teaching the Disabled or Below-Average Reader   253
Jeanne S. Chall and Mary E. Curtis

12 Reading and the ESL Student   277
Joanne R. Nurss and Ruth A. Hough

13 Teaching Adults to Read   314
Thomas G. Sticht and Barbara A. McDonald

Author Index   335

Subject Index   343

Foreword

I am delighted to see this volume. Those of us engulfed in day-to-day school operations have little time to sit back and take a scholarly perspective on our craft. This volume makes our scholarship easier by pulling together many of the issues that confront us daily in school systems.

Most school districts are trying to figure out what to do about assessment. The discussion of this issue by Hiebert and Calfee could not be more timely. The authors provide us with a historical perspective on testing and describe alternatives that hold great promise for changing assessment practices.

The chapters reviewing research on comprehension, content area reading, text structure, and metacognition thoroughly investigate how students learn and what we as teachers can do to ensure that learning occurs in our classrooms. The authors pull together a rich store of information that documents our advances in knowledge. I especially applaud our progress in understanding comprehension. These reviews provide clear testimony that we know far more today than we did 20 years ago.

A never-ending issue in primary education is decoding. Should instruction be explicit or implicit? Beck and Juel grapple with this issue in their chapter, which examines the research on decoding and presents suggestions for helping children acquire decoding skills early on. Goodman, on the other hand, approaches phonics from a whole language perspective. While the two chapters present different views on how phonics should be taught, the authors agree that an understanding of sound/symbol relationships is essential. Reading these chapters will help us make better informed decisions.

Many of us use repeated reading to improve children's fluency. We know it works. Samuels, Schermer, and Reinking explain why in their chapter on reading fluency. Their comprehensive review and explicit teaching suggestions provide us with additional incentives to continue this practice.

Readers will welcome the reviews of home and school partnerships and the discussions of special populations—struggling readers, bilingual children, and adult readers. As schools and teachers take on ever-expanding roles, the issues discussed in these chapters will be of growing relevance to many of us.

This volume provides us with a single, up-to-date resource on reading research and instruction. The authors, representing the best in our field, provide a unique combination of breadth and depth of knowledge. Their contributions help us all stand back and examine what we know about literacy. From this stance we can gain clearer insights about the future.

Carol Minnick Santa
Kalispell, Montana, Public Schools

Preface

What Research Has to Say About Reading Instruction has had a long run. The first edition of this book was published in 1978, but many of the chapters in that volume were papers presented in 1975 at the Association's annual convention. The original volume was an outgrowth of an idea that Constance McCullough had when she was president-elect of the International Reading Association. She had observed that many of the papers given at previous annual conventions were either overly prescriptive (telling teachers what to do without explaining the rationale) or overly theoretical (giving rationale without explaining the practical applications in sufficient detail).

As organizer of the 1975 convention, it was McCullough's idea to devote prime program time to papers that offered a balance between theory and application. The exclusive research format for the convention was very popular, and Harry Singer, one of the presenters, suggested that the papers be preserved in the form of a book. These papers, along with several others, became the first edition of *What Research Has to Say About Reading Instruction*.

This second edition maintains the balance between theory and application while updating the contents to keep up with changes in reading curriculum. For example, this volume has chapters on text structure, metacognition, and home background factors influencing reading that were not found in the earlier edition. If you have an opportunity to compare the chapters of the authors represented in both editions, you will find that they, too, have new ideas and have refined their old ideas.

We close this introduction on a sad note. Dr. Harry Singer, the person who originally suggested that the 1975 IRA research presentations be published in book form, has died. In fact, his last writing is found in this volume. For the past quarter of a century he had a major impact on reading theory, reading practice, and public policy.

His honors were many, ranging from the presidency of the National Reading Conference to recognition for distinguished teaching and research. To many of us in the reading profession, he was not only a valuable resource we could call on when needed, but a friend as well. We will miss him.

SJS

AEF

Contributors

Isabel L. Beck
University of Pittsburgh
Pittsburgh, Pennsylvania

Robert C. Calfee
Stanford University
Stanford, California

Jeanne S. Chall
Harvard University
Cambridge, Massachusetts

Mary E. Curtis
Father Flanagan's Boys' Home
Boys Town, Nebraska

Janice A. Dole
University of Utah
Salt Lake City, Utah

Gerald G. Duffy
Michigan State University
East Lansing, Michigan

Alan E. Farstrup
International Reading Association
Newark, Delaware

Ruth Garner
Washington State University
Vancouver, Washington

Kenneth S. Goodman
University of Arizona
Tucson, Arizona

Elfrieda H. Hiebert
University of Colorado
Boulder, Colorado

Ruth A. Hough
Georgia State University
Atlanta, Georgia

Connie Juel
University of Virginia
Charlottesville, Virginia

Margie I. Mayfield
University of Victoria
Victoria, British Columbia

Barbara A. McDonald
San Diego State University
San Diego, California

Joanne R. Nurss
Georgia State University
Atlanta, Georgia

Lloyd O. Ollila
University of Victoria
Victoria, British Columbia

Wayne Otto
University of Wisconsin
Madison, Wisconsin

P. David Pearson
University of Illinois
Champaign, Illinois

David Reinking
University of Georgia
Athens, Georgia

Laura R. Roehler
Michigan State University
East Lansing, Michigan

S. Jay Samuels
University of Minnesota
Minneapolis, Minnesota

Nancy Schermer
St. Paul Public Schools
St. Paul, Minnesota

Stephen Simonsen
College of the Desert
Palm Desert, California

Harry Singer
University of California
Riverside, California

Thomas G. Sticht
Applied Behavioral and
   Cognitive Sciences
El Cajon, California

Barbara M. Taylor
University of Minnesota
Minneapolis, Minnesota

CHAPTER 1

The Role of Research in Reading Instruction

WAYNE OTTO

The author's main purpose here is to remind teachers who are attempting to improve instruction that they must approach the vast and varied literature of reading research with a clear purpose and a realistic perspective. Otherwise, they are likely to be inundated by the mass of material—sometimes with conflicting results and often out of step with specific local realities—that is available. Research is not a collection of ready-made answers to instruction-related questions, waiting to be claimed by eager and trusting teachers. It is a resource that can provide direction and substance for making instructional decisions when it is approached with purpose and with caution. The author offers three suggestions to teachers: (1) approach the research literature with well-conceived queries that are sensitive to local concerns and realities, (2) view research as a source of alternatives rather than definitive answers to local questions, and (3) make use of the full range of publication vehicles in vogue for disseminating research results.

I wish I could start out with Snoopy's standard opening line, but it wasn't a dark and stormy night. It was a cold and snowy afternoon. I was sitting in my big leather chair, staring at the TV, thinking about the topic of this chapter. I wasn't sure what my opening line should be because I wasn't sure how to approach the topic. Should research drive instruction? Would research results ever be comprehensive and definitive enough for that? Or should instruction drive research, with attention given to perceived flaws in and limitations of instructional practice? Would the scope of research be sufficient, then, to yield new insights and new directions? After a while I decided not to get bogged down in such abstract issues but to think instead about the role of research in teachers' day-to-day efforts to provide their pupils with effective reading instruction.

Soon there were new questions to bog me down. Should teachers rely on books like this one to tell them what the research says? Or should they be taught to extract what they need to know directly from research reports? What *do* they need to know? Would it be more effective to prepare and encourage teachers to conduct their own action research in order to resolve problems and choose among alternative practices and materials? How could they best focus such efforts? What's the best fit between existing research and action research? How would busy teachers pick and choose from library shelves filled with research related to reading? On the TV screen I saw teachers sinking in a quagmire of research reports while their pupils waited to be taught.

Then, among the fancied images I saw a familiar face; I heard lines that I know and love. It was Jimmy Stewart as Elwood P. Dowd in a PBS rerun of *Harvey*. Soon my thoughts were with Elwood and his sister.

Remember the part where Elwood's sister is trying to get him committed to an asylum? Elwood's niece takes up with one of the asylum attendants and her life turns from simple to complex. That's when her mother (Elwood's sister) says to her, "Young lady, you have a lot to learn, and I hope you never learn it." And that's when I knew what I wanted to say to teachers about the research related to reading instruction.

Teachers, you have a lot to learn... The proliferation of research related to reading presents any number of dilemmas for teachers. For example, they might read broadly and deeply from original reports, attempting to draw valid inferences and strike reasonable balances; read more selectively, seeking ways to approach and resolve local issues; ignore original sources and rely on reviewers, translators of research, for suggestions and direction; or simply throw up their hands in despair. The problem is that already there is more reading research than a busy practitioner can sort out in a lifetime, and much more is generated each month.

...and I hope you never learn it. Like Elwood's sister, I'm genuinely concerned, and I'd like to be helpful. I'm not at all sure what to offer by way of advice, but I'm convinced that learning all that might be relevant could be painful and, in the long run, not very rewarding.

It seems to me that teachers have reason to ask some fundamental questions about the role of research in reading instruction. For example, how does—and how *should*—research figure in the process of making instructional decisions? Should teachers be producers as well as consumers of research? As a consumer, how can a teacher approach the vast literature of reading research with much hope of finding information that will be useful in improving instruction? These are tough questions that deserve answers, but the best answers are ones that fit unique situations and suit specific needs. The purpose of the discussion that follows is not so much to provide those answers as to suggest ways to seek them.

Making Instructional Decisions

Educational decisions are based on four main factors (Borg, 1981): personal experience, expert opinion, the research literature, and action research. Each has its pros and cons; together they provide solid cornerstones for planning and improving reading instruction.

Personal Experience

Like most people, teachers are inclined to base most of their decisions on their personal experience. One reason is that they tend to be comfortable with the familiar. Witness the common observation of teacher educators that teachers in the field are more likely to teach as they were taught than as they were taught to teach. Another reason is that personal successes have more credibility than do the success stories of others. Not only that, but when instant decisions must be made daily, personal experience is the most readily accessible basis for action. Alternatives may be too time consuming to pursue.

Yet, there are serious entries on the debit side of the ledger. First, personal experiences are accumulated in a haphazard fashion; to assume that what worked with a unique group of children in a unique situation will work with other people in other places is risky. Second, memories of past experience may be faulty. The human inclination is to recall successes and other experiences that bolster biases and to repress failures and experiences that contradict cherished beliefs and practices. Finally, decisions based strictly on personal experience ignore the accumulated knowledge and experience of others.

Thus, although personal experience is a powerful and pervasive basis for decision making, it is necessarily limited in both scope and vision. Borg (1981, p. 5) sums up: "A basic rule in decision making is that the more relevant information the decision-maker has, the more likely it is that she [or he] will make a sound decision."

Expert Opinion

Expert opinion is based not only on the expert's personal experience but also on the shared experiences, judgments, and research findings of others. When opinion is restrained by balance and common sense, this broader view can contribute substantially to the decision-making process. In the schools, reading specialists are generally seen as the main purveyors of expert opinion regarding reading instruction. If the reading specialists are well experienced and informed, this is as it should be. However, the experts' interpretations are nearly certain to be influenced by their own experiences—and perhaps prescribed by selective viewing of evidence that supports preconceived notions.

The reading specialist who best fills the role of expert is the one who functions as a broker between a large cohort of experts (practitioners, researchers, scholars) and local teachers. That function is well served as long as the specialist remains objective in weighing and interpreting evidence and unbiased in offering recommendations.

The Research Literature

Practitioners—including both reading specialists and teachers—who have the skills needed to read and evaluate research reports have access to a resource that goes far beyond personal experience and expert opinion. Teachers who go directly to the literature have the advantage of knowing their own situation better than any outside expert and the assurance that their search will be as comprehensive as they care to make it. Omissions and distortions can be minimized, information can be as timely as this month's journals, and the search can be focused precisely on problems as they are perceived in the classroom.

The disadvantage of a personal literature search is that it requires hard, time-consuming work. This is one of the main reasons that, more often than not, the search is delegated to the reading specialist. Delegated or not, a diligent literature search is an important requirement for informed decision making.

Action Research

If a literature search fails to yield information that is on target for solving a given problem, an action research project may be in order. The main features of action research are its relative informality and its focus on day-to-day problems. The main goal of more formal educational research is to test theory and to advance scientific knowledge. To obtain results that can be applied beyond a particular sample, researchers carefully design studies to meet rigorous standards of external validity. Action research employs the scientific method, too; but because practitioners are not usually interested in generalizing beyond the local situation, many of the rigorous criteria of regular research can be relaxed. Selecting a sample of students, for example, would be easier in an action research project because practitioners would be interested in generalizing only to, say, the tenth grade students in their own school or district. Furthermore, since practitioners are mainly interested in practical significance, there is no need for inferential statistics. If statistical tests are used at all, nonparametric techniques usually suffice.

Action research is in order when local practitioners are looking for a specific answer to a local question rather than results that can be generalized to other locales. By bringing the scientific method to bear in action research, practitioners can avoid the limitations of personal experience and expert opinion and, at the same time, put the realities of home in sharp focus. Above all, action research is an active alternative to using the research of others that may or may not be on target for a particular application.

An Example

In the example that follows all four of the bases for making instructional decisions are brought to bear.

Imagine a scenario in which teachers have read and discussed Chall's (1983) *Stages of Reading Development*. (Chall argues that the beginning reader's main task [Stage One] is to learn to associate letter forms with letter sounds, or to become "glued" to print. At Stage Two, the main task is to get unglued from print, to develop the fluency needed to shift attention from getting the words to getting the meaning.) The teachers agree that the movement from Stage One to Stage Two is important to positive reading development. They decide to seek ways to ensure a smooth transition from Stage One to Stage Two in order to provide for appropriate instruction in their program planning. The reading specialist agrees to do a literature search.

The search yields evidence to support the importance of a smooth transition from decoding to fluency in developing reading competence, as well as suggestions for easing the transition. The planning group decides that repeated reading is a particularly promising technique for developing fluency (Otto, 1985). Two members of the group volunteer to prepare directions for implementing the technique for distribution to teachers. In the course of their work, they come upon a study by Rashotte and Torgesen (1985) that makes them wonder about an important aspect of implementation. While most writers on the subject suggest repeated reading of the same material, Rashotte and Torgesen's results suggest that *shared words* among different practice passages may be more important than repetition of the same passages. The subcommittee plans an action research study to help them get a better grasp of the issue and to guide their recommendations.

Research-Based Decision Making

Sensible instructional planning and improvement calls for well-informed decision making. The siren song of personal experience as a basis for decisions is particularly seductive because everyone likes to believe that what worked once will work again (besides, it's comfortable). For on-the-spot decisions, personal experience points the way to go.

When the limitations of personal experience are recognized and acknowledged, the tendency is to reach out for the experience of others by seeking expert opinion. While such a move can be productive if the consultant's role is clear and understood by all concerned, consultants are as likely as anyone to be selective viewers of reality and, therefore, purveyors of their own limits and biases.

Well-directed searches of the literature by people who are in touch with local realities (that is, members of a local program planning group) can establish a broader base for making decisions and, at the same time, remain sensitive to local constraints and possibilities. The words *well directed* are the ones that establish perspective for approaching the reading research literature. A comprehensive search is certain not only to take more time than most teachers have available but also to yield a blooming, buzzing profusion of facts, implications, and conclusions that have little relevance to specific planning. Selective searches—ones that zero in on important issues identified by local practitioners—will produce much more useful results. Such searches often can be delegated to the reading specialist. Then, if equally attractive alternatives are identified, action research can help determine what is best for us.

Breaking into the Research Literature

The vast and varied literature related to reading can be intimidating. As a result, many practitioners are inclined either to approach the literature in a helter skelter way or to avoid it altogether. They grab a bit here and a bit there in an effort to find the pieces that suit their needs, or they withdraw and rely completely on "experts" to tell them what the research says. In either case they're almost certain to get a distorted view; and, more important in the present context, they are unlikely to get the information they need to make specific instructional decisions that are right for them and for their students.

What's needed, then, is a way for practitioners to direct attention to matters of particular interest at different times. One step in the right direction is to develop a clear sense of priorities, to decide what comes first in addressing concerns. Emphasis on models and theories of the reading process would be appropriate when definitions and directions are being set for the overall reading program. Programs that are well grounded in clear concepts and agreements regarding basic processes are more likely to stand up to scrutiny and to retain support than programs that simply respond to short-term needs. Then, when it is time to seek information for making instructional decisions, the emphasis can shift to instruction-oriented research.

A related step is to recognize that there are subthemes, or research thrusts, in the literature. Pursuit of recognizable subthemes can help to bring focus to a search. Of course, different people may acknowledge different thrusts in the current reading research literature, but I'll offer a couple of examples that may be useful.

Two Research Thrusts

Kamil (1984) has identified two definable thrusts in recent reading-related research. The first is directed toward a clearer understanding of basic reading processes. It involves the generation and refinement of models and theories of the reading process as well as basic research. To demonstrate his point, Kamil cites Davis (1971) and Singer and Ruddell (1970, 1976) for their summaries of earlier work in modeling and theory construction; Carver (1977), Gough (1972), Gough, Alford, and Holley-Wilcox (1979), Gough and Coskey (1975), Herndon (1978), Rumelhart (1977), Singer and Ruddell (1986), and Stanovich (1980) for evidence of current interest in theories and models; and LaBerge and Samuels (1983) for their continuing efforts to extend and refine the modeling of the reading process.

The second thrust is a continuation, but with renewed vigor and intensity, of the traditional quest for better methods of teaching reading in order to improve education and reduce illiteracy. The renewal can be attributed, at least in part, to (1) greater emphasis on the reader as an active seeker of information, (2) the availability and application of improved techniques for discourse analysis in reading research, and (3) increased interdisciplinary cooperation in translating research into practice. Work that emanates from the Institute for Research on Teaching at Michigan State University and from the Center for the Study of Reading at the University of Illinois at Urbana-Champaign exemplifies the systematic nature of current attempts to identify and improve instructional practices in reading.

The point to be stressed is that practitioners will have reason to direct their attention to basic process research and to instruction-oriented research at different times and for different reasons. By and large, attention to process-oriented research will enhance practitioners' understanding of the reading process, but it will not yield much in the way of specific instructional techniques and procedures. On the other hand, attention to instruction-oriented research will yield ideas about techniques and procedures that may or may , not be appropriate for local application. Practitioners who approach the literature with an awareness of and an appreciation for these two discrete thrusts are less likely to be distracted in their search— and less likely to be disappointed with what they find.

Three Broad Areas of Concern

Members of the Commission on Reading draw on three broad areas of reading research in their report, *Becoming a Nation of Readers* (Anderson et al., 1985). Two of the areas are more or less in line with Kamil's analysis: the reading process and the teaching techniques, tools, and testing. A third area, environmental influences on reading, reflects a sensitivity to the importance of cultural and other contextual factors in the acquisition of reading proficiency. Together, the three areas offer another way of focusing a literature search to pursue a particular line of interest.

The reading process. In his foreword to the Commission's report (Anderson et al., 1985), Glaser says that research on the reading process has provided researchers and practitioners with a fuller understanding of how children can learn basic decoding, the importance of fluent word recognition, and how the structure of text influences the meaning drawn from it. He even goes so far as to say that process research has not merely "uncovered the roots of proficient reading" but also "described how the development of well-practiced skills in beginning reading fosters comprehension of complex texts" (p. v).

Whether or not one is inclined toward full agreement with Glaser's and the Commission's rather exuberant conclusions (see, for example, Davidson, 1988), there is good reason to examine recent research into reading processes. As researchers continue to clarify basic processes and the complex relationships among those processes, practitioners continue to gain evidence to confirm certain of their intuitions and actions and to sort out others that are less useful or out of touch with current evidence.

Environmental influences. By giving explicit attention to environmental influences, the Commission acknowledges the importance of contextual factors in teaching/learning to read. Practitioners, too, must make this acknowledgment in order to plan instruction that recognizes and takes advantage of the myriad factors of home and family, the larger social/cultural milieu, and the school itself that set the stage and enable (or hinder) students' acquisition of the competence to tackle reading tasks of increasing complexity. A good deal of literature is available to help clarify (1) the role and nurturing of early habits and motivation; (2) the systematic teaching of foundation skills for decoding words, developing vocabulary, inferring meaning from sentences, and enjoying stories; and (3) the development of special strategies for comprehending and interpreting textbooks in the subject matter areas.

Teaching techniques, tools, and testing. Research in this category helps make clear the role and importance of professional knowledge. Examples include approaches to pacing, adapting, and grouping for instruction; guidelines for designing textbooks, practice exercises, and self-study materials; and techniques for directing reading instruction, assessing pupils' progress, and evaluating their reading performance. As Glaser says, "In teaching, as in other professions, well-researched methods and tools are essential" (p. vi). Fortunately, the research literature is sufficiently broad and sophisticated to serve as a useful resource to practitioners as they make decisions that will guide the day-to-day teaching of reading.

A Word of Caution

Teachers could, of course, think of many other promising subthemes or research thrusts. The purpose here is not to offer a comprehensive list, but to suggest that the reading research literature may be less formidable when practitioners approach it on their own terms. This body of literature is a rich resource for people with inquiring minds; it is not a storehouse of definitive answers to teachers' questions. Practitioners need to see it for what it is rather than for what they hope it might be.

Developing Perspective

Venezky's chapter on the history of reading research in the *Handbook of Reading Research* (1984) is a good resource for developing a realistic perspective on approaching the research literature. Among other, more serious points, Venezky likens the task of organizing the published research on reading instruction to the twelve labors of Hercules. The collection of works, he says, includes "over 15,000 books, pamphlets, articles, and occasional records of educational verbosity," which amount to "an enduring testimony to the patience of the American printer and the vulnerability of American forests" (p. 17). Venezky concludes that "to read, comprehend, and evaluate even 1 percent of it is a staggering and not entirely enjoyable task."

Teachers may take some comfort from Venezky's words and feel a bit less guilty for not having read and digested all the literature. They also may take comfort in his observation that although many studies were poorly executed, the real problem is discerning why many of them were done at all. Once again the advice is that those who select carefully from a well-stocked smorgasbord will be better nourished than those who try to swallow all of it.

Venezky also offers some thoughts on the chasm between research results and actual reading instruction and why it is so difficult to build bridges between the two. First, adults, not children, continue to be the favored subjects in reading process studies. Consequently, more is known about the performance of practiced readers than about how readers acquire the ability to perform. Research still does not clarify the basic question of whether poor readers develop word-recognition abilities through different stages than do good readers or whether the process is simply slower.

Second, experimental psychologists who work on reading rarely get involved in curriculum design and classroom practice. Consequently, the focus of much research is on matters with little or no application to instruction. Investigations of learning processes do not necessarily address instructional questions. Acknowledging this simple fact will spare practitioners much of the disappointment they may feel when they see no application for certain research results.

Third, funding agencies often assume, erroneously, that support of basic research will lead directly to improved reading instruction. Basic research may serve its own purpose, but to justify the support of such research under the guise of instructional improvement leads to false expectations and disappointment. Venezky cites basic research on letter discrimination as a case in point: the research offers worthwhile insights into visual processing, but letter discrimination is not a source of any major instructional problems.

The perspective that comes from a consideration of points like these should help practitioners see that the chasm between research results and instructional practice is not one of their making, and that bridging that gap is not something for which they can or should take ultimate responsibility. Spared false or unrealistic expectations, teachers will be in a better position to approach the research literature as critical and selective consumers.

Finding the Latest Research

While professional journals—ranging from reading-specific ones like *Reading Research Quarterly* and the *Journal of Reading Behavior* to more general ones like the *Journal of Educational Research*—continue to publish most of the current research reports related to reading, book chapters have emerged as a common forum for publishing research results, syntheses of lines of research, and expositions of models and theories. A few examples are works edited by Guthrie (1981), Kanowitz (1974), Mackinnon and Waller (1981), Pflaum-Connor (1978), and Resnick and Weaver (1979). Kamil (1984) suggests that the shift toward book chapters—along with a shift away from using formal models to describe and discuss reading processes—may be setting authors free from some of the constraints of journal publication. Because the rules of argument and method that must be observed for successful journal publication may be less stringent for book chapters, authors seem freer to offer more speculative conclusions and conjectures. As a result, they may offer more interesting and provocative notions to guide further research and tentative application.

This is not to suggest that authors are likely to produce work of inferior quality when they write chapters instead of journal articles. The point is that when authors are freed from certain folk expectations, they may be more inclined to deal with larger chunks of information in more ecologically valid settings. When this is so, book chapters may be a better source of useful information for planning and improving instruction than the tightly focused and controlled studies typically reported in journals. Some researchers (as well as some practitioners) argue that refereed journals are, and should remain, the prime purveyors of research results. They maintain that the rigorous review process is the best means for ensuring quality and balance in reporting on research studies. Most agree, though, that communication between researchers and practitioners would be enhanced if implications for practice were always treated as an integral part of the report rather than as an afterthought.

One obvious drawback to book chapters as information sources is the longer delay in publication. Journals generally offer shorter turnaround times than books. Fortunately, research institutions usually make technical reports and working papers available as they are produced. Since these reports and papers often become book chapters, practitioners may be able to get previews of coming attractions. Many research institutions maintain regular mailing lists to keep their constituencies informed of works as they become available, and most of the works are entered in the ERIC system. Teachers should not neglect this important source of current, usable, and often creative and forward-looking information.

Published conference proceedings and yearbooks are other important sources of timely research-related discussion. Many institutions, agencies, and professional organizations sponsor conferences on selected topics and publish the proceedings, which tend to be state-of-the-art synthesis, reaction, and application papers.

Conference yearbooks typically are the collected papers from the annual meetings of professional organizations. Increasingly, these papers are selected by a review process similar to that employed by scholarly journals. While a given annual meeting may have a theme, yearbooks generally are not as finely focused as volumes of conference proceedings. An attractive feature of the yearbooks is that they may include reports of work in progress and even plans for future work, as well as more traditional research reports and syntheses. Teachers who are aware of work in progress and in planning may be able to establish contacts with others who are tackling problems similar to theirs in order to explore possibilities for collaborative efforts as well as to share insights and findings as they become available.

Summary

Teachers who are interested in improving instruction must approach the vast and varied body of reading research literature with a clear purpose and a realistic perspective or be inundated by the mass of available material. One suggestion offered here is that approaches to research literature ought to be directed by well-conceived queries and tempered by an abiding sensitivity to local realities and concerns. Action research can help secure the bridge between researcher and practitioner by bringing local concerns and conditions into sharp focus.

Another suggestion is that teachers need to develop a realistic view of the research in reading. The research is not a collection of ready-made answers to instruction-related questions, waiting to be claimed by eager and trusting teachers. It is a resource which, when approached with purpose and caution, can provide direction and substance for making instructional decisions.

A final suggestion is that teachers ought to be aware and make use of the full range of publication vehicles in vogue for disseminating research results and synthesis. Just as participation in action research efforts can help teachers keep the focus of research on local views and realities, awareness of what is current can help teachers develop and maintain a sense of involvement in the larger research community. The role of research in reading instruction then becomes active rather than passive.

References

Anderson, R.C., Hiebert, E.H., Scott, J.A., & Wilkinson, I.A.G. (1985). *Becoming a nation of readers.* Washington, DC: National Institute of Education.

Borg, W.R. (1981). *Applying educational research.* White Plains, NY: Longman.

Carver, R.P. (1977). Toward a theory of reading comprehension and rauding. *Reading Research Quarterly, 13,* 8-63.

Chall, J.S. (1983). *Stages of reading development.* New York: McGraw-Hill.

Davidson, J.L. (Ed.). (1988). *Counterpoint and beyond: A response to Becoming a Nation of Readers.* Urbana, IL: National Council of Teachers of English.

Davis, F.B. (Ed.). (1971). *The literature of research in reading with emphasis on models.* New Brunswick, NJ: Rutgers University, Graduate School of Education.

Gough, P.B. (1972). One second of reading. In J.F. Kavanagh & I.G. Mattingly (Eds.), *Language by ear and by eye.* Cambridge, MA: MIT Press.

Gough, P.B., Alford, J.A., Jr., & Holley-Wilcox, P. (1979). Words and contexts. In M.L. Kamil & A.J. Moe (Eds.), *Reading research: Studies and applications.* Clemson, SC: National Reading Conference.

Gough, P.B., & Cosky, M. (1975). One second of reading again. In J. Castellan, D. Pisoni, & G. Potts (Eds.), *Cognitive theory* (vol. 2). Hillsdale, NJ: Erlbaum.

Guthrie, J.T. (Ed.). (1981). *Comprehension and learning: Research reviews*. Newark, DE: International Reading Association.

Herndon, M.A. (1978). An approach toward the development of a functional encoding model of short term memory during reading. *Journal of Reading Behavior, 10,* 141-148.

Kamil, M.L. (1984). Current traditions of reading research. In P.D. Pearson (Ed.), *Handbook of reading research*. White Plains, NY: Longman.

Kanowitz, B.H. (Ed.). (1974). *Human information processing: Tutorial in performance and cognition*. Hillsdale, NJ: Erlbaum.

LaBerge, D., & Samuels, S.J. (1983). A critique of "Toward a theory of automatic information processing." In L. Gentile, M.L. Kamil, & J. Blanchard (Eds.), *Reading research revisited*. Westerville, OH: Merrill.

Mackinnon, G.E., & Waller, T.G. (Eds.). (1981). *Reading research: Advances in theory and practice* (vol. 3). San Diego, CA: Academic.

Otto, W. (1985). Research: Practice makes perfect—always, sometimes, never. *Journal of Reading, 29,* 188-191.

Pflaum-Connor, S. (Ed.). (1978). *Aspects of reading education*. Berkeley, CA: McCutchan.

Rashotte, C.A., & Torgesen, J.K. (1985). Repeated reading and reading fluency in learning disabled children. *Reading Research Quarterly, 20,* 180-188.

Resnick, L.B., & Weaver, P.A. (1979). *Theory and practice of early reading* (vol. 2). Hillsdale, NJ: Erlbaum.

Rumelhart, D.E. (1977). Toward an interactive model of reading. In S. Dornio (Ed.), *Attention and performance* (vol. 6). Hillsdale, NJ: Erlbaum.

Singer, H., & Ruddell, R.B. (Eds.). (1970). *Theoretical models and processes of reading*. Newark, DE: International Reading Association.

Singer, H., & Ruddell, R.B. (Eds.). (1976). *Theoretical models and processes of reading* (2nd ed.). Newark, DE: International Reading Association.

Singer, H., & Ruddell, R.B. (Eds.). (1986). *Theoretical models and processes of reading* (3rd ed.). Newark, DE: International Reading Association.

Stanovich, K. (1980). Toward an interactive-compensatory model of individual differences in the development of reading fluency. *Reading Research Quarterly, 16,* 37-71.

Venezky, R.L. (1984). The history of reading research. In P.D. Pearson (Ed.), *Handbook of reading research*. White Plains, NY: Longman.

CHAPTER 2

Home and School Together: Helping Beginning Readers Succeed

LLOYD O. OLLILA
MARGIE I. MAYFIELD

The authors emphasize that research has shown that the foundation for learning to read begins in the home and is nurtured as the child grows and goes to school. This "nurturing" of emergent literacy covers the spectrum from minimal assistance to a rich literacy environment in both home and school. The first half of the chapter reports on research showing characteristics and strategies of homes where children have many positive opportunities to engage in emergent literacy activities. The remainder of the chapter describes examples of effective school programs that have formed successful partnerships with parents in fostering children's literacy development. In light of the growing body of research evidence, the authors stress the importance of home and school working together for the greatest positive influence in helping children become successful readers.

For a long time reading researchers explored children's success or failure at beginning reading by looking at what happened at school. This focus has broadened and researchers now are finding that home environment also influences reading achievement (Jacoby, 1988; Laminack, 1990; Rasinski & Fredericks, 1991; Sutton, 1985; Teale, 1986). Some research even suggests that home factors may be more influential than school-related factors in determining children's achievement (Coleman, 1966; Mosteller & Moynihan, 1972). Numerous studies of emergent literacy conclude that environmental factors as diverse as exposure to reading, general physical well-being, mental health, and parents' interest in and expectations for their children's academic work can play major roles in young children's success as readers (Clark, 1976; Durkin, 1966; Larrick, 1988).

Reading instruction begins informally at home and continues at school with a more formal approach. This chapter highlights the research on how parents can help their children become successful readers and how the home and school can work together to influence children's initial reading success, including examples of home-school programs.

The Parent's Role in Promoting Experiences with Print

Creating a Literacy Setting

Educators and researchers have looked at the environments, values, beliefs, and actions of young children who began to read before going to school. They have found that these children's homes have many books, easy access to print, and lots of writing materials (crayons, pens, pencils, paper) available for creating print (Clay, 1980; Harste, Burke, & Woodward, 1981; Taylor, 1983; Teale, 1982). In addition, these homes featured labeled items such as records, games, room decorations, and clothing (Schieffelin & Cochran-Smith, 1982). Many of the parents were readers themselves and thereby modeled reading behavior to their children (Smith, 1988, 1990).

Researchers have found strong positive correlations between early reading ability and the number of books in the home (Durkin,

1966; Malmquist, 1958). However, having books and other reading materials present in the home does not necessarily ensure that children will use them. As several researchers have pointed out, not all experiences with print are of equal worth (Harste, Burke, & Woodward, 1981; Teale, 1984). A child who absentmindedly flips through a book alone may not learn as much about reading, print, and books as a child sharing a book with a parent or another adult.

Encouraging Reading Through Writing

Children learning how to read make three discoveries: (1) everything has a name you can hear—a spoken word; (2) everything can be represented visibly—by drawing; and (3) every spoken name of a thing can be drawn—with writing (Vygotsky, 1978). Many children who learn to read before school develop an interest in writing and begin writing before reading (Bissex, 1980; Chomsky, 1971; Clay, 1987; Haley-James, 1982). In the homes of children awakening to literacy, a variety of writing materials (note pads, loose paper, chalkboards, pencils, crayons, felt pens) are available. These children have many opportunities to watch others write and are encouraged to use writing materials themselves. Researchers have seen much experimenting with writing—scribbling, copying names and other meaningful words, inventing spellings—as children grow in their writing skill (Anderson, 1985; Bissex, 1980; Deford, 1980; Harste & Burke, 1980; Taylor & Dorsey-Gaines, 1988).

These studies indicate that parents can help children ease into reading by making writing materials available, by modeling writing, and by encouraging their children to experiment with writing (Shook, Marrion, & Ollila, 1989). However, parents should not expect well-formed handwriting or correct punctuation, spelling, capitalization, and grammar as children begin to write (Haley-James, 1982). Neither should they expect children to be able to spell before they begin to write. Temple, Nathan, and Burris (1982) suggest keeping models of print at children's height for them to copy and use as aids for letter formation. Dyson (1984) advises parents to "accept whatever writing the child produces, respond to any written messages, answer the child's emerging questions, and through sensitive questioning, focus the child's attention on specific print features, thus promoting the development of more sophisticated encoding strategies" (p. 270).

Reading Aloud to Children

In addition to access to a variety of interesting print, children need someone to orient them to the print (Gibbs, 1987; Rasinski & Fredericks, 1990; Taylor, 1983). Parents do this by reading aloud to children regularly (Feitelson & Goldstein, 1986; Jones, 1981). Studies have shown that early readers enjoy being read to by an adult or sibling (Clay, 1979; Doake, 1982; Holdaway, 1979). Jones (1981), Dudley-Marling (1989), and Smith (1988) suggest that parents make family read-aloud sessions a special daily time in which they emphasize the fun and enjoyment of reading. Siblings, other relatives, and friends also can be involved. Children should be sitting next to the reader so they can follow the text if they want. In this way, they learn about handling books and the order in which the text is read. They also learn to listen, to focus attention, and to concentrate for a period of time. Most important, children discover that print communicates a message.

Other benefits arise from reading aloud to children and discussing stories with them. In many homes, for example, story time takes place when the children are tucked in bed. In other homes, children sit on the storyteller's lap. The warm, shared, close feelings that are part of enjoying the companionship of caring persons tend to favorably color children's attitudes toward books and reading. Many adults who like to read still recall with pleasure being read to when they were young. Children also learn book language (literary conventions and story structure) and become familiar with the way people talk about books (Heath 1982; Strickland & Morrow, 1989; Teale, 1984; Tierney & Cunningham, 1984). Terms such as *word, letter,* and *sentence,* which are used in reading instruction (Downing, 1969; Olson, 1984; Reid, 1966), can be highlighted naturally as parents read to their children.

For reading aloud and other introductory reading activities, parents need to know that the value comes not only from the activity itself but also from the way it is done. Simply reading aloud to children has merit; however, reading and discussing the story may be more valuable in helping children develop reading skills.

Numerous researchers note the importance of interacting with children when reading aloud (Flood, 1977; Gibbs, 1987; Smith, 1971; Snow, 1983; Thomas, 1985). Many suggest holding pre- and post-reading discussions and asking a variety of different types of questions (e.g., detail, predictive, inferential) about a story as effective ways of interacting during read-aloud sessions. However, questions should enhance the story and should not be overdone (Sansone, 1988). Some specific questioning techniques include asking for the child's version of the story, allowing the child to fill in characters' lines, asking the child to look at an illustration and describe that part of the story in detail, asking the child about personal situations similar to an event in the story, and encouraging the child to draw and write his or her version of the story and share it with other family members.

An interactive approach increases the depth of knowledge processing and imbues the story with purpose and meaning. Children come to enjoy reading as a process of self-exploration (relating their own experiences to others through stories) and learning concepts introduced in the story, making them meaningful in terms of their own experience and developmental levels. Jones (1981) concluded:

> Where books are a part of the daily life of a home, where parents read lots of books themselves and share children's books by devoting time and attention to the matter, children acquire incidentally and effortlessly skills which are necessary for reading (p. 29).

Becher (1983) found that parents were surprised at the many benefits derived from reading aloud to children and urged teachers to emphasize these benefits when talking to parents.

Providing Literacy Activities

Much of the home's influence in helping children achieve literacy success is more indirect and subtle than the factors mentioned previously (Hall, 1987; Mason & Allen, 1986; Moffett & Wagner, 1983; Teale, 1982). Parents' literacy activities with their children—how they talk with their children (Rasinski & Fredericks 1989), what they have to say, how they interact with them socially—play a vital function in developing children's literacy (Mason & Allen; Taylor, 1983; Taylor & Dorsey-Gaines, 1988). The home can help by leading children to understand that written language plays an important role in the daily life of the family (Mavrogenes, 1990). Many children who become good readers come from a family or home orientation that values and uses print (Clay, 1982; Schieffelin & Cochran-Smith, 1982). Taylor (1983) described how children in this type of home learn:

> Growing up in an environment where literacy is the only option, they learned of reading as one way of listening, and of writing as one way of talking. Literacy gave the children both status and identity as it became the medium of shared experience; it facilitated the temporal integration of their social histories as the highly valued artifact of family life became the prized commodity of the schools. Clearly, children from such literate environments have an enormous advantage in learning to read and write (p. 87).

Children need to be included in the "natural, logical ways of going about the business of the day" (Harste, Burke, & Woodward, 1981, p. 6). For example, children can be given paper and a pencil to make their own shopping list as a parent makes one. Children can "write" their own letters as parents write letters, or include their own written message as part of the adult's letter. Children can receive a portion of the junk mail to read as parents read their mail.

Parents can help make literacy meaningful and functional for their children in a variety of ways. They can point out signs; encourage children to read; discuss instructions for playing with toys and games (Heath, 1983; Loveday & Simmons, 1988); and focus on literacy in entertainment, religion, schoolwork, daily living routines, interpersonal conversations, read-aloud time, and work (Ninio & Bruner, 1978; Snow, 1983; Teale, 1986; Wahl, 1988).

Developing Effective Language Interactions

Oral language ability plays a crucial role in a child's success in reading (Logan & Logan, 1981; Petty, Petty, & Salzer, 1989). Parents can help their children learn about language and books by providing "quality" time to pursue language activities with them (Glazer,

1990; Heath, 1982; Teale, 1986). Taylor (1983) reports that the parents of literacy-oriented children stress the importance of talking and listening to their children as they learn to read. Researchers have identified some characteristics of this social interaction between parents and children (Bloome, 1983; Snow, 1983; Sulzby, 1985; Thomas, 1985; Zubrick, 1987). For instance, parents can practice "semantic contingency," which involves continuing a topic their children have introduced, answering questions they've posed, or adding new information to a statement they've made (Snow). During reading time, parents might read aloud when asked, talk with their children about the book's text, and answer children's questions about the text, pictures, or print (Thomas).

Another effective procedure is "scaffolding." With this technique, parents structure discussions of language or reading tasks to make it easier for children to arrive at an answer or to complete a task (Snow, 1983). For example, as a mother and her toddler look at a page in a picture book, the mother points to the picture and asks, "What's that?" The child replies, "Bow-wow." The mother exclaims, "You're right, that's a dog." Then she points and says, "Look what he's wearing on his head." The child answers, "Hat!" "Yes," says the mother, "it's a cowboy hat. You have one too." Or, after reading *Miss Nelson Is Missing* by Harry Allard and James Marshall (a story about a teacher who disguises herself as a mean substitute to teach her class a lesson), a father asks his six year old, "What really happened to Miss Viola Swamp [the substitute]?" The child replies, "It was Miss Nelson dressing up." The father expands, "She disguised herself so the boys and girls wouldn't recognize her. Why did she do that?" The dialogue continues as the father helps his child to understand the story and further develops language concepts in an informal conversational manner.

With scaffolding, parents help their children understand the meaning of the text by using prereading, during-reading, and post-reading questions. Parents of early readers report that after a while, their children begin to take over this scaffolding/questioning process (Thomas, 1985). Parents also help by insisting that one language literacy task be accomplished before the child goes on to something else; following the child's lead in play situations; encouraging appropriate speech patterns; and rereading books on request, even if it's for the tenth time.

Teaching Reading Skills

Some parents of good readers help their children by giving them direct instruction in reading skills. These parents actively and deliberately guide their children's literacy development. Researchers have noted that these parents often instruct their children in the mechanics of reading, teach them specific techniques and reading subskills, guide them to library activities, help them set goals and select reading materials, aid them in looking up words and topics, and regularly take time to listen to them read (Cuckle & Hannon, 1985; Hansen, 1969; Hewison & Tizard, 1980; Silvern & Silvern, 1990; Teale, 1978; Wells, 1978). Some studies of early readers indicate that older siblings, grandparents, and other relatives can help teach reading skills effectively (Clark, 1976; Durkin, 1966). Although many educators maintain that formal reading instruction is the school's business, in her review of the literature, Becher (1985) stated:

> The fact remains that many parents are instructing their children and those children are benefiting as indicated by their higher achievement scores and more positive attitudes toward reading. Enhancing existing parental activities and assisting other parents in developing appropriate and effective "reading instruction" skills are critical means of contributing to the development of reading achievement and excellence (p. 49).

Motivating Children

Parents once were school children themselves, and they have definite views and feelings about their experiences in school. These views, in turn, color their expectations for what they want their children to gain from school. Seginer's (1983) review indicates that parents' expectations seem to have a major effect on their children's academic achievement. Children who are good readers and have more positive attitudes toward reading often are found to have parents who highly value education and the ability to read well (Downing, 1987). For some parents, the idea of their children growing up illiterate is unthinkable (Taylor, 1983).

Although most parents want their children to have a good education, some are more effective than others in passing these values on to their children and in helping their children develop the tools necessary for school success. Parents of good readers clearly state their expectations to their children, and they praise and reward reading achievement. In contrast, children who are overly pressured by their parents and punished for reading poorly tend to have more negative attitudes and lower reading achievement (Hess et al., 1979; Wells, 1978).

White's (1982) review of 200 studies showed that early reading achievement can be attributed more directly to family characteristics—such as availability of reading materials, home conversations, attitudes toward education, parents' aspirations for their children, academic guidance, and cultural activities—than to socioeconomic status. Researchers have found that underclass socioeconomic parents, whose children tend to perform below the norms of middle class students in school, do hold positive views of education (Brantlinger, 1985; Cloward & Jones, 1963; Roberts, 1980). Goldenberg (1984) notes that while much research has concentrated on explaining this difference in achievement, it has tended to overlook the beneficial role minority and underclass parents can play in educating their children, if they are taught how. In Goldenberg's study of at-risk but successful Hispanic grade 1 readers, several of the parents played a key role in helping their children improve in reading by teaching them directly and by motivating them to do their work. All the parents in the study (even those whose children experienced reading failure) expressed interest and were willing to help in their children's academic achievement. However, many of these parents either didn't realize that their children were having difficulties or didn't know how to help. A few parents who tried to help were irregular in their instruction or taught something that didn't tie in with the school's reading program, so the effect of their instruction was minimal.

What Parents Can Do—A Summary

Parents who wish to have a positive influence on their children's beginning reading success can learn much from the research just discussed. Parents or caregivers should create a rich reading-readiness setting in which printed materials and writing activities are valued, varied, and readily available. Parents should include their children as they go about their daily literacy activities. They can model their reading and writing behavior and take time to read aloud to their children. A number of studies have stressed the importance of parent-child communication and different ways parents can develop effective language interactions. Parents can set clear expectations for their children's reading, stress the importance of reading well, and reinforce progress toward this goal. In addition, some parents may provide their children with direct instruction in various reading skills.

Parents and Home-School Programs

The research evidence suggests that parents play an important role in encouraging their children's reading development; the school is also an important component, providing more formal instruction. Home and school working together will enhance the efforts of both in developing children's reading attitudes and abilities.

Why Involve Parents?

One characteristic of successful school reading programs is parent involvement (Becher, 1985; Office of Educational Research and Improvement, 1986; Samuels, 1988; Topping & Wolfendale, 1985). After reviewing the research, Becher reported that "informational and training programs designed to instruct parents about the teaching of reading and to encourage their active participation have resulted in significant increases in the reading attitudes and achievement of their children" (p. 49).

Numerous educators worldwide (e.g., Berger, 1981, 1991; Fantini, 1980; Goodlad, 1984; Gordon & Breivogel, 1976; Greenwood & Hickman, 1991; Hymes, 1974; Karim, 1981; Nedler & McAfee, 1979; Sartain, 1981; Tizard, Mortimore, & Burchell, 1981; Walberg, 1984) have recommended a partnership between the home and school. This concept of partnership is not new; it has been advocated for many years (e.g., National Society for the Study of Education, 1929). As Epstein (1990) notes, however, "increasingly, schools are changing their laissez-faire practices concerning the family by designing and conducting programs to help more families become 'knowledgeable partners' in their children's education" (p. 99).

Parents want to be involved in the education of their children, and they want to be informed about what their children are doing and what they can do to help (Cleve, Jowett, & Bate, 1982; Epstein, 1990; Galinsky, 1990; Mayfield, 1990). Surveys have found that most parents help their children at home; many reportedly do so on a regular basis (Epstein; Hannon & Cuckle, 1984; Newson & Newson, 1977). However, parents often wonder if they are doing the right things when it comes to reading; many desire more information about the field. Good home-school literacy programs can help parents foster their children's literacy development in partnership with the school.

An effective home-school literacy program can be developed through a variety of approaches and strategies. For example, a program may involve parents as teachers of their own children at home, as volunteers or paraprofessionals in the classroom, or as policymakers on school advisory committees (Gordon & Breivogel, 1976; Greenwood & Hickman, 1991; Olmstead, 1991). The program might target the parents in one classroom, in one school, or in an entire school district. The goals of the program can be few or many. Some examples are to encourage parents to read to their children, to increase the number of family visits to the library, to reinforce specific reading skills taught in the classroom, to foster a positive attitude toward literacy, to provide information to parents about children's literacy development, or to promote the sharing of information between parents and teachers.

The following examples of successful home-school partnerships illustrate the importance of variety and flexibility. The variety among these programs supports the idea that there is no one best model for home-school reading programs. It is important that the needs and wishes of the children, their families, and their schools be matched effectively.

Parents Helping Children at Home

In-home programs teach parents about children's literacy development and provide specific materials or suggestions for them to use at home with their children. Research has demonstrated that parents can be effective teachers of their own children (Epstein, 1990; Lazar & Darlington, 1982; Slaughter, 1983). Moreover, parent involvement with one child in the family can have positive effects on siblings (Bronfenbrenner, 1974; Karnes & Teska, 1980).

The home-based literacy activity teachers most often recommend to parents is reading with their children—either reading aloud to them or listening to them read. Giving such advice, when combined with specific help and guidance by teachers, can be an effective strategy because "most parents need help to know how to be productively involved in their children's education at each level" (Epstein & Dauber, 1991). Also, when teachers offer specific guidance, parents may respond by spending more time helping their children (Dauber & Epstein, 1989). In addition to reading to children or listening to them read, other options such as educational games have been used effectively in the home (Loveday & Simmons, 1988). This section describes successful programs for working with parents to help their children at home.

The Haringey Reading Project compared the effects of three methods for fostering the reading achievement of children aged 5 to 11 in a multicultural area of north London (Hewison, 1985; Hewison & Tizard, 1980; Tizard, Schofield, & Hewison, 1982). One group of children took books home three or four times a week; their parents listened to them read and recorded their progress. Another group of children received extra assistance from a reading teacher at school. The control group received no special reading instruction, either at home or at school.

On a standardized test, children who received extra practice at home showed significantly greater improvement in reading levels than the control group. The home-trained children also improved more than those who received extra help at school. Hewison (1985) reported that the parents who participated in this study were willing, able, and effective. Also, the teachers in the home partnership group found working with parents so worthwhile that they continued to involve parents after the original project ended (Tizard, Schofield, & Hewison, 1982). The gains the children made in this project were reportedly still in evidence several years later (Hewison).

Another London-based program, the Parents, Children and Teachers (PACT) Project, used multiple strategies to encourage more than 90 percent of innercity parents to help their children with reading. Griffiths and Hamilton (1984) reported that "where parents help consistently with reading, their children gain in both reading age and in the quality and enjoyment of their reading" (p. 13). Some guidelines for parents that proved useful in the PACT Project follow:

- Listen to children read regularly, at least three times a week if possible.
- Keep reading sessions short (10-15 minutes).
- Praise children as often as possible.
- Talk about the book.
- Make the sessions enjoyable for both parents and child.

The program developers also recommend that individual teachers or schools explain how parents should respond when a child makes a mistake.

Other activities of the PACT Project included providing book bags for children to carry books home, helping children get library cards at the local public library, encouraging parents to write comments about the books and their children's reactions to the stories, increasing the number of books in the school library and making it more accessible to parents, and welcoming parents into the classroom.

Effective parent-child literacy programs also have used games and other materials. The Preschool Readiness Outreach Program (PROP) used 26 weekly 3-hour workshops to help parents make educational games, learn about how to use the material through role playing, and participate in informal discussions in order to foster their 3- to 5-year-olds' literacy development (Vukelich, 1978). In addition, program members distributed nine monthly pamphlets with ideas for materials and activities to develop reading and language skills. Parents' response to the workshops and home visits was reportedly enthusiastic. Vukelich noted that the children's beginning reading skills improved in general, and that "the children whose parents participated actively in the program achieved significantly greater gains than those whose parents participated minimally" (p. 526).

For older elementary school children who are having difficulty with reading, parents can be effective as tutors at home. Teachers can help parents by providing workshops, courses, or educational materials. In Parents Encourage Pupils (PEP), innercity parents tutored their children (grades 3-5) using selected books, games, word lists, and poetry, along with individualized homework activities (Shuck, Ulsh, & Platt, 1983). The children's completed activities were tallied on individual progress charts and then translated into points. An interesting feature of this program was that the children could exchange their points each month for a prize from the "reading laboratory store." Most of these prizes were donated by local toy stores, civic groups, and parents. Other programs, in which parents in Australia and New Zealand help their learning-delayed children, also have reported improvements in children's achievement in and attitudes toward reading (Butler, 1987; Kemp, 1985, 1987; Mundell, 1989).

Individual classroom teachers can do a lot to help parents work with their children at home. As Griffiths and Hamilton (1984) state, "teachers have a large body of knowledge, gained through their training and experience, which would help most parents" (p. 118). Some teachers help parents by sending home (1) weekly or monthly newsletters with general ideas for promoting reading in the home, such as tips for telling stories or for choosing a book (Asheim, Baker, & Matthews, 1983; Taylor & Walls, 1990); (2) booklists related to subjects the children are studying (Fredericks & Rasinski, 1987); (3) "TV Picks of the Week" for families to watch and discuss (Rich, 1988); (4) descriptions of "Reading Families of the Month" (Fredericks, 1987); or (5) calendars of activities and holiday packets (Fredericks & Rasinski, 1990a, 1990b).

In addition, individual teachers have demonstrated that children's language and reading skills can improve when a teacher provides materials for parents and young children to use at home during the school year and over the summer holidays. Such materials may include games (Cooknell, 1985; Loveday & Simmons, 1988; Poy, 1985), activity sheets (Probst, 1986), book kits (MacCarry,

Ollila & Mayfield

1989), or activity packets (Children First, 1980; Duncan & Von Behren, 1974).

The Children and Parents Enjoying Reading (CAPER) program in Wales combined several components, including an initial information meeting, five parent workshops, individual parent reading clinics, and daily teacher-parent contact via comment booklets. Results of this program included increased use of children's books, increased use of book language by children, gains in children's reading levels, and increased parent participation in a range of school activities (Branston & Provis, 1986). This successful program served as a model for other schools in Wales and has been replicated elsewhere.

The programs we have described represent a variety of ideas and strategies for helping parents work with their children at home. Many of the researchers and program developers involved in these programs commented on the importance of communication with parents: explaining the significance of their role in their children's literacy development, encouraging them to participate in the home learning program, and providing initial and ongoing support.

Parents Helping Children in School

Many schools provide one or two evening sessions for parents each year to explain the school's reading program and to suggest ways that parents can encourage their children's literacy development. Some schools go further and provide opportunities for parents to help children with literacy activities in the school. One example is the Fox Hill Reading Project in England, which encouraged parents to work on reading with their five- to six-year-old children for one hour a week at school. The parents participated in a variety of activities, including "listening to their child read, playing reading games together, helping with a sound sheet, talking about books and pictures and looking at books" (Smith & Marsh, 1985). Both teachers and parents reported improvement in the children's reading abilities, increased social interaction for the parents, and a more positive attitude toward reading.

Another example of parent participation in schools was the reading club for parents and children sponsored by the City College of New York and a local elementary school. The Parents Assistance Program was designed to improve the reading abilities of second and third graders (85 percent Hispanic) through weekly meetings with parents. At these meetings, parents made instructional materials which they used in school with their children with the guidance of a reading teacher. An end-of-year comparison of standardized reading scores indicated that each child "had held his/her own, and half of them were closer to grade level than when the program started" (Raim, 1980, p. 154). Teachers also reported improvement in specific skills and increased motivation for classroom reading on the part of the children, as well as improved reading skills on the part of the parents.

Many teachers lack the time or resources to initiate the types of programs described here. In such cases, a schoolwide initiative might be more efficient. The school staff could get together and develop some of these activities or programs, thus sharing their expertise and experience as well as reducing the amount of time and work required of the individuals.

District-Sponsored Programs

Many of the programs described so far have been developed and implemented by individual or small groups of teachers. District-initiated home-school programs involve the expanded, cooperative efforts of teachers, school administrators, and district office personnel. Such efforts usually have access to more resources and expertise than one individual teacher or one school would have.

A school district in Wisconsin began a workshop program for the parents of preschool children based on the belief that if parents knew the "background and techniques which would enable the children to have an extremely positive first experience with reading," the result would be children who wanted to read when they came to school (Lautenschlager & Hertz, 1984, p. 18). The reading teachers, district reading consultant, and elementary school principals presented workshops for parents throughout the school district on the benefits and techniques of reading aloud to children. They also used videotapes, a bibliography of children's books, reprints of articles, book excerpts, bumper stickers, and displays. In written evaluations, a third of the parents said they had gained new ideas that they planned to use with their children. Nearly all participants wanted the workshop series to continue. These results support the idea that parents want more information and ideas to help them help their children, even when most of the material presented reinforces their existing knowledge.

The New Haven (Connecticut) School District developed a comprehensive approach to home-school reading that included a reading advisory board (including four parents), parent resource rooms in six schools, "make and take" parent workshops, two 10-week courses for parents about reading, a series of articles in the local newspaper on what parents can do to help children read, a program for parents to tutor intermediate grade students, parent activity sheets (K-8) to reinforce classroom instruction, a book bank, and a talent bank of parents interested in being classroom resource people. In addition, the district developed and distributed several written guides for parents: *Read to Succeed* (for parents of kindergartners), *Reading Recipes* (64 activities to reinforce reading in the home using common household materials), *Homework Resource Activities* (for primary and intermediate levels), and *Questions Parents Ask About Reading* (Criscuolo, 1982, 1984, 1986).

Districtwide programs can be used in combination with school or individual teacher-sponsored efforts. For example, school district personnel could provide workshops for parents on reading and how the home can foster children's reading development. Then individual teachers could provide suggestions appropriate for their own classes and for specific children. Teachers could communicate these suggestions to parents by newsletters, telephone calls, conferences, workshops, group meetings, and informal contacts at school.

Other Home-School Programs

The possible options for home-school literacy programs are varied and wide ranging. These programs need not be limited to parents; other adults or older siblings also can participate.

A program for Cantonese-speaking children in Vancouver, British Columbia, recruited volunteers to read to the children twice a week for 40 minutes in Cantonese or English. In addition, books written in Chinese were placed in the classroom libraries. As a result, library checkouts increased, and the children "made significant gains in English reading over the three-month period" (Walters & Gunderson; 1985, p. 68). Through this program, non-English-speaking members of the community could contribute to their children's learning in school. In another program, teenage girls trained as home visitors read to young children (Smith & Fay, 1973); and in others, senior citizens and other volunteers from the community worked with young children in homes, schools, libraries, and senior citizen centers (Dowd, 1988; Rich, 1988; Smith, 1991; Wabigoani, 1986; Ziemba, Roop, & Wittenberg, 1988).

What Teachers and School Administrators Can Do

A successful home-school reading program requires the enthusiasm of all school personnel and a commitment to foster parent involvement and promote language and literacy. Teachers, schools, and district staff need to consider the following points when planning and implementing these programs.

In identifying areas where parents can participate, recognize their requests for help and consider their suggestions. Educators need to assess rather than to assume what parents want and need. If the program fits the needs of the parents, more and longer participation is likely. This, in turn, can increase the program's effectiveness. However, the available time, expertise, and resources of the staff and school also must be taken into account in identifying possible areas to be addressed. If the home-school partnership is to be a meaningful one, parental input is necessary (Cochran & Dean, 1991; Comer & Haynes, 1991).

Plan the program with the children's abilities, the school's program, and the parents' ability to participate in mind. For example, an at-home program might be more appropriate if a high percentage of the parents work. Not all parents are able or willing to attend activities at school on a regular basis. Parents differ in the type and degree of involvement they prefer; some prefer working with their own child at home, while others may want to be a classroom volunteer or help plan the home-school literacy program.

Provide a variety of activities for parents to do with their children and explain why these activities are valuable. Doing the same one or two activities repeatedly can become boring both for children and for parents. When parents understand an activity, they are better able to modify it to suit their children. Parents also need information on how children learn to read and on what they can do to help.

It is important to make advice to parents specific enough to be useful. Advising parents to "read to your child" or "talk with your child" may not convey sufficient information. Parents appreciate information about what and how much should be read, how long each reading session should last, what to do when their child encounters difficulties, what kinds of discussions to have, whether their child should read orally or silently, and how to keep the activity a positive experience. Given specific knowledge and suggestions, parents will feel that they are able to help (Smith, 1988).

There are many sources of ideas for appropriate home-school activities to share with parents. For example, Wahl (1988) lists 26 ideas, including discussions, cooking, grocery shopping, book sharing, and television time. Strickland and Morrow (1989) suggest reading to children, responding to and supporting children's literacy activities, and visiting the library. Teachers may want to lend parents such articles; besides providing ideas, the articles add weight to teachers' suggestions. In addition to these resources, both the International Reading Association and many of its local chapters produce booklets and brochures for parents who want to help their young children with reading and writing development. Examples include *Helping Your Child Become a Reader* (Roser, 1989), *How Can I Prepare My Young Child for Reading?* (Grinnell, 1989), *You Can Help Your Young Child With Writing* (Baghban, 1989), *Creating Readers and Writers* (Glazer, 1990), and *Beginning Literacy and Your Child* (Silvern & Silvern, 1990).

Encourage parents to use school resources whenever possible. For example, teachers should offer parents access to the school library, informal drop-in sessions to discuss their questions related to reading, and a chance to contribute to the regular school or class newsletter. Joint school/parent fund-raising projects can help provide more books, equipment, and materials that can be used to foster children's literacy.

Monitor programs or activities, provide positive reinforcement, and request feedback from parents. After a program has been in operation for a while, it is a good idea to assess its status, give participating parents support and positive feedback on their efforts with their children, and consider how other parents might be included. Ongoing and final evaluations provide information needed to help fine-tune or modify the program to better achieve its current objectives and to plan for the future. Program developers can evaluate progress by sending written questionnaires to the participants, conducting telephone or in-person interviews with the parents, or holding focus-group discussions (Epstein & Dauber, 1991).

Good sources of more detailed information on planning and implementing reading programs include Branston and Provis (1986), Fredericks and Taylor (1985), Griffiths and Hamilton (1984), Samuels and Pearson (1988), and Topping and Wolfendale (1985).

Summary

Although parents' involvement in their children's education is not a new idea, it has received a great deal of attention and interest in the past 15 years. Educators, administrators, policymakers, and parents themselves have become more aware and accepting of the idea that a home-school partnership can be successful and rewarding for children, their families, and the schools. This concept of partnership recognizes that the child's world includes much more than the time and experiences in school.

The home-school partnership can be developed by diverse strategies and program models that accommodate the children's diverse needs, the needs and interests of the parents, and the needs, resources, and goals of the school. A program that has achieved success in one classroom, school, or district may not necessarily be appropriate in another situation.

Successful parent involvement in school literacy programs can have far-reaching effects. Both the children in the program and other family members can benefit; for example, preschoolers often will listen to stories or participate in the games or activities of their older siblings and thereby improve their language and reading skills. For some parents, participation in these types of programs presents an opportunity to have a successful experience with the school system, to develop a stronger commitment to education, and to become more aware of and confident in their role in their children's learning. In addition, effective home-school literacy programs can generate increased parental and community support for education in general and the school in particular.

Conclusion

In this chapter, we have described the importance of the home in children's literacy development and how the home and school can work together to foster this development. A major portion of a child's waking life is spent in the home, not in the school (Walberg, 1984). Parents are their children's first teachers, and usually the home environment is a crucial determinant of children's attitudes and motivation.

It is important to help parents become involved during their children's formative years. Parents want to know what their children are doing in school, how the children are progressing, and what they can do to help. Most parents are willing to become involved with the school in meaningful ways to foster their children's literacy development. And one of the most meaningful ways is to work with their children at home.

Teachers and schools can encourage and facilitate a home-school partnership in many ways. The initiation, development, and implementation of successful home-school programs require time, effort, and knowledge—but we think it's time and effort well spent.

References
Anderson, K.F. (1985). The development of spelling ability and linguistic strategies. *The Reading Teacher, 39*(2), 140-147.
Asheim, L., Baker, D.P., & Matthews, V.H. (Eds.). (1983). *Reading and successful living: The family-school partnership.* Hamden, CT: Library Professional Publications.

Baghban, M. (1989). *You can help your young child with writing.* Newark, DE: International Reading Association.

Becher, R.M. (1983). *Problems and practices of parent-teacher school relationships and parent involvement.* Unpublished manuscript, University of Illinois, Urbana, IL.

Becher, R.M. (1985). Parent involvement and reading achievement: A review of research and implications for practice. *Childhood Education, 62*(1), 44-50.

Berger, E.H. (1981). Parents as partners in education. St. Louis, MO: C.V. Mosby.

Berger, E.H. (1991). Parent involvement: Yesterday and today. *Elementary School Journal, 91*(3), 209-219.

Bissex, G.L. (1980). *GYNS AT WRK: A child learns to read and write.* Cambridge, MA: Harvard University Press.

Bloome, D. (1983). Reading as a social process. In B.A. Hutson (Ed.), *Advances in reading/language research* (vol. 2, pp. 165-195). Greenwich, CT: Jai Press.

Branston, P., & Provis, M. (1986). *Children and parents enjoying reading: A handbook for teachers.* London, UK: Hodder & Stoughton.

Brantlinger, E. (1985). What low-income parents want from schools: A different view of aspirations. *Interchange, 16*(4), 14-28.

Bronfenbrenner, U. (1974). *Is early intervention effective? A report on longitudinal evaluations of preschool programs.* Washington, DC: U.S. Department of Health, Education, & Welfare.

Butler, S.R. (1987). The RAT Pack: An early intervention program. *McGill Journal of Education, 22*(2), 93-100.

Children First. (1980). *Promising practices for administrators in pre-elementary Right-to-Read programs.* Washington, DC: U.S. Department of Education.

Chomsky, C. (1971). Write first, read later. *Childhood Education, 47*, 296-299.

Clark, M.M. (1976). *Young fluent readers.* Portsmouth, NH: Heinemann.

Clay, M.M. (1979). *Reading: The patterning of complex behavior.* Portsmouth, NH: Heinemann.

Clay, M.M. (1980). Early writing and reading: Reciprocal gains. In M.M. Clark & T. Glynn (Eds.), *Reading and writing for the child with difficulties* (Educational Review Occasional Publication No. 8, pp. 27-43). Birmingham, UK: University of Birmingham.

Clay, M.M. (1982). *Observing young readers: Selected papers.* Portsmouth, NH: Heinemann.

Clay, M.M. (1987). *What did I write?* Portsmouth, NH: Heinemann.

Cleve, S., Jowett, S., & Bate, M. (1982). *And so to school: A study of continuity from preschool to infant school.* Windsor, UK: NFER-Nelson.

Cloward, R., & Jones, J. (1963). Social class, educational attitudes, and participation. In A.H. Passow (Ed.), *Education in depressed areas* (pp. 198-216). New York: Bureau of Publications, Teachers College, Columbia University.

Cochran, M., & Dean, C. (1991). Home-school relations and the empowerment process. *Elementary School Journal, 91*(3), 261-269.

Coleman, J. (1966). *Equality of educational opportunity.* Washington, DC: U.S. Office of Education. (ED 172 339)

Comer, J.P., & Haynes, N.M. (1991). Parent involvement in schools: An ecological approach. *Elementary School Journal, 91*(3), 271-277.

Cooknell, T. (1985). An inner-city home reading project. In K. Topping & S. Wolfendale (Eds.), *Parental involvement in children's reading* (pp. 246-254). London, UK: Croom Helm.

Criscuolo, N.P. (1982). Parent involvement in the reading program. *Phi Delta Kappan, 63*(5), 345-346.

Criscuolo, N.P. (1984). Parent involvement in reading. *Childhood Education, 60*(3), 181-184.

Criscuolo, N.P. (1986). Ways to foster a home-school partnership in reading. *Reading Horizons, 26,* 278-282.

Cuckle, P., & Hannon, P. (1985). How far do schools involve parents in the teaching of reading? *Reading, 19*(3), 155-160.

Dauber, S.L., & Epstein, J.L. (1989). *Parent attitudes and practices of parent involvement in inner-city elementary and middle schools* (CREMS Report 33). Baltimore, MD: Johns Hopkins University, Center for Research on Elementary and Middle Schools.

Deford, D. (1980). Young children and their writing. *Theory into Practice, 19,* 157-162.

Doake, D.B. (1982). Learning to read: A developmental view. *Elements, 13*(7), 4-6.

Dowd, F.A. (1988). Latchkey children in the library. *Children Today, 17*(6), 5-8.

Downing, J. (1969). How children think about reading. *The Reading Teacher, 23*(3), 217-230.

Downing, J. (1987). Comparative perspectives on world literacy. In D.A. Wagner (Ed.), *The future of literacy in a changing world.* New York: Pergamon.

Dudley-Marling, C. (1989). The role of parents in children's literacy development: Collaborating with parents of exceptional children. *The Pointer, 33*(4), 16-19.

Duncan, L.J., & Von Behren, B. (1974). Pepper: A spicy new program. *The Reading Teacher, 28*(2), 180-183.

Durkin, D. (1966). *Children who read early.* New York: Teachers College Press.

Dyson, A.H. (1984). "*N* spell my Grandmama": Fostering early thinking about print. *The Reading Teacher, 38*(3), 262-271.

Epstein, J.L. (1990). School and family connections: Theory, research, and implications for integrating sociologies of education and family. In D.G. Unger & M.B. Sussman (Eds.), *Families in community settings: Interdisciplinary perspectives* (pp. 99-126). New York: Haworth.

Epstein, J.L., & Dauber, S.L. (1991). School programs and teacher practices of parent involvement in inner-city elementary and middle schools. *Elementary School Journal, 91*(3), 285-305.

Fantini, M.D. (1980). The parent as educator: A home-school model of socialization. In M.D. Fantini & R. Cardenas (Eds.), *Parenting in a multicultural society* (pp. 207-222). White Plains, NY: Longman.

Feitelson, D., & Goldstein, Z. (1986). Patterns of book ownership and reading to young children in Israeli school-oriented and nonschool-oriented families. *The Reading Teacher, 39*(9), 924-930.

Flood, J. (1977). Parental styles in reading episodes with young children. *The Reading Teacher, 30,* 864-867.

Fredericks, A.D. (1987). Recognizing parent participation. *The Reading Teacher, 40*(8), 818.

Fredericks, A.D., & Rasinski, T.V. (1987). Five good ideas for sharing the reading experience. *The Reading Teacher, 40*(9), 923-924.

Fredericks, A.D., & Rasinski, T.V. (1990a). Whole language and parents: Natural partners. *The Reading Teacher, 43*(9), 692-694.

Fredericks, A.D., & Rasinski, T.V. (1990b). Factors that make a difference. *The Reading Teacher, 44*(1), 76-77.

Fredericks, A.D., & Taylor, D. (1985). *Parent programs in reading: Guidelines for success.* Newark, DE: International Reading Association.

Galinsky, E. (1990). Why are some parent/teacher partnerships clouded with difficulties? *Young Children, 45*(5), 2-3, 38-39.

Gibbs, C. (1987). What do beginner readers say when they 'read'? *Australian Journal of Reading, 10,* 159-170.

Glazer, S.M. (1990). *Creating readers and writers.* Newark, DE: International Reading Association.

Goldenberg, C.N. (1984). *Roads to reading: Studies of Hispanic first graders at risk for reading failure.* Unpublished dissertation, University of California, Los Angeles, CA.

Goodlad, J.I. (1984). *A place called school: Prospects for the future.* New York: McGraw-Hill.

Gordon, I.J., & Breivogel, W.F. (1976). *Building effective home-school relationships.* Boston, MA: Allyn & Bacon.

Greenwood, G.E., & Hickman, C.W. (1991). Research and practice in parent involvement: Implications for teacher education. *Elementary School Journal, 91*(3), 279-288.

Griffiths, A., & Hamilton, D. (1984). *Parent, teacher, child.* London, UK: Methuen.

Grinnell, P.C. (1989). *How can I prepare my young child for reading?* Newark, DE: International Reading Association.

Haley-James, S. (1982). When are children ready to write? *Language Arts, 59,* 458-463.

Hall, N. (1987). *The emergence of literacy.* Portsmouth, NH: Heinemann.

Hannon, P.W., & Cuckle, P. (1984). Involving parents in the teaching of reading: A study of current school practice. *Educational Research, 26*(1), 7-13.

Hansen, H.S. (1969). The impact of the home literary environment on reading attitude. *Elementary English, 46,* 17-24.

Harste, J.C., & Burke, C.L. (1980). Examining instructional assumptions: The child as informant. *Theory into Practice, 19,* 170-178.

Harste, J.C., Burke, C.L., & Woodward, V.A. (1981). *Children, their language and world: Initial encounters with print* (National Institute of Education Final Report). Bloomington, IN: Indiana University Press.

Heath, S.B. (1982). What no bedtime story means: Narrative skills at home and school. *Language in Society, 11*, 49-76.

Heath, S.B. (1983). *Ways with words: Language, life, and work in communities and classrooms.* New York: Cambridge University Press.

Hess, R.D., Holloway, S., Price, G.E., and Dickson, W.P. (1979). *Family environments and the acquisition of reading skills: Toward a more precise analysis.* Paper presented at the Conference on the Family as a Learning Environment, Educational Testing Service, Princeton, NJ.

Hewison, J. (1985). Parental involvement and reading attainment: Implications of research in Dagenham and Haringey. In K. Topping & S. Wolfendale (Eds.), *Parental involvement in children's reading* (pp. 42-53). London, UK: Croom Helm.

Hewison, J., & Tizard, J. (1980). Parental involvement and reading attainment. *British Journal of Educational Psychology, 50*(3), 209-215.

Holdaway, D. (1979). *The foundation of literacy.* Sydney, Australia: Ashton Scholastic.

Hymes, J.I. (1974). *Effective home-school relations.* Sierra Madre, CA: Southern California Association for the Education of Young Children.

Jacoby, S. (1988, April/May). Roots of success. *Family Circle Survey*, 1-8.

Jones, J.R. (1981). Advising parents on reading. *Reading, 15*, 27-30.

Karim, Y. (1981). Opportunities to use family resources for reading in developing countries of Southeast Asia. In H.W. Sartain (Ed.), *Mobilizing family forces for worldwide reading success* (pp. 35-43). Newark, DE: International Reading Association.

Karnes, M.B., & Teska, J.A. (1980). Toward successful parent involvement in programs for handicapped children. In J.J. Gallagher (Ed.), *New directions for exceptional children: Parents and families of handicapped children.* San Francisco, CA: Jossey-Bass.

Kemp, M. (1985). Parents as teachers of literacy: What are we learning from them? *Australian Journal of Reading, 8*(3), 135-140.

Kemp, M. (1987). Parents as teachers of literacy: What more are we learning from them? *Australian Journal of Reading, 10*(11), 25-31.

Laminack, L.L. (1990). "Possibilities, Daddy, I think it says possibilities": A father's journal of the emergence of literacy. *The Reading Teacher, 43*(8), 536-541.

Larrick, N. (1988). Literacy begins at home. In M.P. Douglass (Ed.), *Fifty-second yearbook of the National Reading Conference* (pp. 1-17). Claremont, CA: Claremont Reading Conference Center for Developmental Studies.

Lautenschlager, J., & Hertz, K.V. (1984). Inexpensive, worthwhile, educational—parents reading to children. *The Reading Teacher, 38*(1), 18-20.

Lazar, I., & Darlingon, R. (1982). Lasting effects of early education: A report from the Consortium of Longitudinal Studies. *Monographs of the Society for Research in Child Development* (Serial No. 195), *47*(2-3).

Logan, L.M., & Logan, V.G. (1981). Readiness for reading: A shared responsibility. *Reading-Canada-Lecture, 1*(1), 73-77.

Loveday, E., & Simmons, K. (1988). Reading at home: Does it matter what parents do? *Reading, 22*(2), 84-88.

MacCarry, B. (1989). Helping preschool child care staff and parents do more with stories and related activities: A pilot joint venture between a Florida public library and local child care centers. *Young Children, 44*(2), 17-21.

Malmquist, E. (1958). *Factors related to reading disabilities in the first grade of the elementary school.* Stockholm, Sweden: Almqvist & Wiksell.

Mason, J.M., & Allen, J. (1986). *A review of emergent literacy with implications for research and practice in reading.* Paper presented at a conference on the process of reading acquisition, University of Texas, Austin, TX.

Mavrogenes, N.A. (1990). Helping parents help their children become literate. *Young Children, 45*(4), 4-9.

Mayfield, M.I. (1990). *The roles and perceptions of parents participating in three early childhood education programs.* Paper presented at the Canadian Society for the Study of Education annual conference, Victoria, BC.

Moffett, J., & Wagner, B. (1983). *Student-centered language arts and reading, K-13* (3rd ed.). Boston, MA: Houghton Mifflin.

Mosteller, F., & Moynihan, O.P. (Eds.). (1972). *On equality of educational opportunity.* New York: Random House.

Mundell, P. (1989). Parents help with reading. *National Education, 71*(2), 60-63.

National Society for the Study of Education. (1929). *Preschool and parental education.* Chicago, IL: University of Chicago Press.

Nedler, S.E., & McAfee, O.D. (1979). *Working with parents: Guidelines for early childhood and elementary teachers.* Belmont, CA: Wadsworth.

Newson, J., & Newson, E. (1977). *Perspectives on school at seven years old.* London, UK: Allen & Unwin.

Ninio, A., & Bruner, J. (1978). The achievement and antecedents of labeling. *Journal of Child Language, 5*, 5-15.

Office of Educational Research and Improvement (1986). *What works.* Washington, DC: U.S. Department of Education. (ED 263 299)

Olmstead, P.P. (1991). Parent involvement in elementary education: Findings and suggestions from the Follow Through Program. *Elementary School Journal, 91*(3), 221-231.

Olson, D. (1984). "See! Jumping!" Some oral language antecedents of literacy. In H. Goelman, A.A. Oberg, & F. Smith (Eds.), *Awakening to literacy* (pp. 185-192). Portsmouth, NH: Heinemann.

Petty, W., Petty, D., & Salzer, R. (1989). *Experiences in language* (5th ed.). Boston, MA: Allyn & Bacon.

Poy, C.A. (1985). *The effects of a parent-child game program on readiness of kindergarten children.* Unpublished master's thesis, University of Victoria, Victoria, BC.

Probst, A.M. (1986). *The effects of parent involvement on the learning of kindergarten children.* Unpublished master's thesis, University of Victoria, Victoria, BC.

Raim, J. (1980). Who learns when parents teach children? *The Reading Teacher, 34*(2), 152-155.

Rasinski, T.V., & Fredericks, A.D. (1989). Working with parents: Dimensions of parent involvement. *The Reading Teacher, 43*(2), 180-183.

Rasinski, T.V., & Fredericks, A.D. (1990). The best reading advice for parents. *The Reading Teacher, 43*(4), 344-345.

Rasinski, T.V., & Fredericks, A.D. (1991). The Akron paired reading project. *The Reading Teacher, 44*(7), 514-515.

Reid, J. (1966). Learning to think about reading. *Educational Research, 9*(1), 56-62.

Rich, D. (1988). Bridging the parent gap in education reform. *Educational Horizons, 66*(2), 90-92.

Roberts, K. (1980). Schools, parents, and social class. In M. Craft, J. Raynor, & L. Cohen (Eds.), *Linking home and school: A new review* (3rd ed.). New York: HarperCollins.

Roser, N.L. (1989). *Helping your child become a reader.* Newark, DE: International Reading Association.

Samuels, S.J. (1988). Characteristics of exemplary reading programs. In S.J. Samuels & P.D. Pearson (Eds.), *Changing school reading programs: Principles and case studies* (pp. 3-9). Newark, DE: International Reading Association.

Samuels, S.J., & Pearson, P.D. (Eds.). (1988). *Changing school reading programs: Principles and case studies.* Newark, DE: International Reading Association.

Sansone, R.M. (1988). SKWL DAS: Emerging literacy in children. *Day Care and Early Education, 16*(1), 14-19.

Sartain, H.W. (1981). Research summary: Family contributions to reading attainment. In H.W. Sartain (Ed.), *Mobilizing family forces for worldwide reading success* (pp. 4-18). Newark, DE: International Reading Association.

Schieffelin, B.B., & Cochran-Smith, M. (1982). *Learning to read culturally: Literacy before schooling.* Paper prepared for University of Victoria Symposium on Children's response to a literate environment: Literacy before schooling, Victoria, BC.

Seginer, R. (1983). Parents' educational expectations and children's academic achievements: A literature review. *Merrill-Palmer Quarterly, 29*(1), 1-23.

Shook, S.E., Marrion, L.V., & Ollila, L.O. (1989). Primary children's concepts about writing. *Journal of Educational Research, 82*(3), 133-138.

Shuck, J., Ulsh, F., & Platt, J.S. (1983). Parents encourage pupils (PEP): An innercity parent involvement reading project. *The Reading Teacher, 36*(6), 524-528.

Silvern, S.B., & Silvern, L.R. (1990). *Beginning literacy and your child.* Newark, DE: International Reading Association.

Slaughter, D.T. (1983). Early intervention and its effects on maternal and child development. *Monographs of the Society for Research in Child Development* (Serial No. 202), *48*(4).

Smith, C.B. (1988). The expanding role of parents. *The Reading Teacher, 42*(1), 68-69.

Smith, C.B. (1990). Involving parents in reading development. *The Reading Teacher, 43*(4), 32.

Smith, C.B. (1991). Family literacy: The most important literacy. *The Reading Teacher, 44*(9), 700-701.

Smith, C.B., & Fay, L.C. (1973). *Getting people to read: Volunteer programs that work.* New York: Delacorte.

Smith, F. (1971). *Understanding reading.* Orlando, FL: Holt, Rinehart, & Winston.

Smith, H., & Marsh, M. (1985). "Have you a minute?" The Fox Hill Reading Project. In K. Topping & S. Wolfendale (Eds.), *Parental involvement in reading* (pp. 255-259). London, UK: Croom Helm.

Snow, C.E. (1983). Literacy and language: Relationships during the preschool years. *Harvard Educational Review, 53*, 165-189.

Strickland, D.S., & Morrow, L.M. (1989). Family literacy and young children. *The Reading Teacher, 42*(7), 530-531.

Sulzby, E. (1985). Children's emergent reading of favorite storybooks: A developmental study. *Reading Research Quarterly, 20*(4), 458-481.

Sutton, W. (1985). Some factors in preschool children of relevance to learning to read. In M. Clark (Ed.), *New directions in the study of reading* (pp. 54-63). London, UK: Falmer.

Taylor, D. (1983). *Family literacy: Young children learning to read and write.* Portsmouth, NH: Heinemann.

Taylor, D., & Dorsey-Gaines, C. (1988). *Growing up literate: Learning from inner-city families.* Portsmouth, NH: Heinemann.

Taylor, D., & Walls, L. (1990). Educating parents about their children's early literacy development. *The Reading Teacher, 44*(1), 72-74.

Teale, W.H. (1978). Positive environments for learning to read: What studies of early readers tell us. *Language Arts, 55*, 922-932.

Teale, W.H. (1982). Toward a theory of how children learn to read and write naturally. *Language Arts, 59*, 555-570.

Teale, W.H. (1984). Reading to young children: Its significance for literacy development. In H. Goelman, A.A. Oberg, & F. Smith (Eds.), *Awakening to literacy* (pp. 101-121). Portsmouth, NH: Heinemann.

Teale, W.H. (1986). Home background and young children's literacy development. In W.H. Teale & E. Sulzby (Eds.), *Emergent literacy: Writing and reading* (pp. 173-206). Norwood, NJ: Ablex.

Temple, C.A., Nathan, R.G., & Burris, N.A. (1982). *The beginning of writing.* Boston, MA: Allyn & Bacon.

Thomas, K.F. (1985). Early reading as a social interaction process. *Language Arts, 62*(5), 469-475.

Tierney, R.J., & Cunningham, J.W. (1984). Research on teaching reading comprehension. In P.D. Pearson (Ed.), *Handbook of reading research* (pp. 609-655). White Plains, NY: Longman.

Tizard, B., Mortimore, J., & Burchell, B. (1981). *Involving parents in nursery and infant school.* Ypsilanti, MI: High/Scope Press.

Tizard, J., Schofield, W.N., & Hewison, J. (1982). Collaboration between teachers and parents in assisting children's reading. *British Journal of Educational Psychology, 52,* 1-15.

Topping, K., & Wolfendale, S. (Eds.) (1985). *Parental involvement in children's reading.* London, UK: Croom Helm.

Vukelich, C. (1978). Parents are teachers: A beginning reading program. *The Reading Teacher, 31*(5), 524-527.

Vygotsky, L.S. (1978). *Mind in society.* Cambridge, MA: Harvard University Press.

Wabigoani, W. (1986). Support programs meet needs. *Education Manitoba, 13*(4), 13-14.

Wahl, A. (1988). Ready...set...role: Parents' role in early reading. *The Reading Teacher, 42*(3), 228-231.

Walberg, H.J. (1984). Families as partners in educational productivity. *Phi Delta Kappan, 65*(6), 397-400.

Walters, K., & Gunderson, L. (1985). Effects of parent volunteers reading first language (L1) books to ESL students. *The Reading Teacher, 39*(1), 66-71.

Wells, R. (1978). Parents and reading: What fifth graders report. *Journal of Research and Development in Education, 11,* 20-25.

White, K. (1982). The relation between socioeconomic status and academic achievement. *Psychological Bulletin, 91,* 461-481.

Ziemba, J., Roop, K., & Wittenberg, S. (1988). A magic mix: After-school programs in a nursing home. *Children Today, 17*(6), 9-13.

Zubrick, A. (1987). Oral narrative in young children: Implications for early reading and writing. *Australian Journal of Reading, 10*(2), 97-105.

CHAPTER 3

Whole Language Research: Foundations and Development

KENNETH S. GOODMAN

Goodman argues that whole language puts research where it belongs, at the foundation of sound practice. In whole language, he believes, practice derives from the research of Piaget, Vygotsky, and those who have studied the reading and writing processes. The usual experimental research is inappropriate because it reduces whole language to what it has in common with traditional programs. Research to evaluate whole language must approach the method from its own premises and principles and show whether it is consistent with them and whether it reaches its own objectives. Goodman further argues that the innovative nature of whole language classrooms makes them fertile ground for innovative research on the teaching and learning of literacy.

Note: From K.S. Goodman, Whole language research: Foundations and development. *The Elementary School Journal, 90*(2), 205-219. © 1989 by The University of Chicago. All rights reserved. Used by permission of The University of Chicago.

The practice of whole language is solidly rooted in scientific research and theory. While it owes much to positive, child-centered educational movements from the past, it goes beyond them in integrating scientific concepts and theories of language processes, learning and cognitive development, teaching, and curriculum into a practical philosophy to guide classroom decision making (Y. Goodman, 1989).

In a very real sense, whole language represents a coming of age of educational practice, a new era in which practitioners are informed professionals acting on the basis of an integrated and articulated theory that is consistent with the best scientific research and the theories in which it is grounded. The consistencies of practice across whole language classrooms come from this shared scientific theory. The differences in whole language classrooms come about because teachers are not relying on gurus and experts to tell them what to do. They make their own decisions and build their own implementations based on their own understandings.

There is a tradition for educational research to be atheoretical, particularly as it deals with classroom practice. A trial-and-error kind of experiment has been popular in which the acceptability of school practice is studied by contrasting an experimental instructional methodology or set of materials with an alternative considered to be a control. Most often gain scores on a test, usually a published standardized test, are used to judge the effectiveness of the "treatment." It has become common to argue in support of methods, materials, or techniques by citing evidence from such studies that they "work" (i.e., produce better gain scores than the control treatment), though it is difficult to draw conclusions from such research that could provide useful knowledge about *why something "works."*

It is not the intention of this chapter to review or criticize the large body of such experimental research. But often whole language teachers and advocates are asked for evidence that whole language "works." This demand reflects the common acceptance of this trial-and-error research. Appropriate research to judge whole language, because it has a base in research and theory, can deal with much more important and productive questions. It can examine the extent to which whole language practice is consistent with its scientific base; it can study what happens to learners and teachers when the philosophy is implemented. And whole language classrooms can provide authentic settings for studying some basic research concerns, such as how cognitive and language processes develop. Research in whole language classrooms can test the underlying theory and contribute to its development.

Any research designed to examine whole language must start by considering what whole language is, the goals of whole language teachers, and how whole language can be studied without destroying or distorting it in the research design. As Rich (1983, p. 165), says, "Whole language...goes beyond the simple delineation of a series of teaching strategies to describe a shift in the way in which teachers think about and practice their art."

Whole language starts with the premise that the whole is more than the sum of its parts; it cannot be studied or evaluated by reducing what happens in whole language classrooms to what also happens in skill-based classrooms. Controlled studies that compare whole language to traditional classrooms by using scores on standardized tests do just that. They reduce whole language to posttest skills gains. Whole language teachers are trying to do more than that.

I begin this chapter with a simple summary of what whole language is about, where it comes from, and what teachers and pupils in whole language classrooms do. In doing this, the theoretical views of learners, teachers, language, and curriculum that whole language incorporates are explicated. Then I discuss the strong research base for whole language. Finally I suggest some of the rich research whole language classrooms make possible.

Key Characteristics of Whole Language

Whole language is a dynamic, evolving grassroots movement. For that reason there is considerable variability among views of whole language held by its advocates and among whole language classrooms. Furthermore, most whole language teachers and advocates are themselves in transition from more conventional subject and skill paradigms. So traditions hang on in their minds and actions. A further complexity is that, particularly in the United States, whole language teachers often find themselves limited by unsympathetic administrators, inflexible and restrictive policies and decision making, and mandated inappropriate materials.

Whole language teachers operate from an examined theory of how language, thought, and knowledge develop holistically and in support of each other. These teachers regularly use this theory to make teaching decisions. They are constantly collecting a wide range of data from their classrooms to make their decisions and examine and develop their operational theory. Whole language teachers do not attribute the learning of their pupils to published programs, prescribed behaviors, and preset outcomes. They believe that they play key mediating roles in facilitating the learning of their pupils. Most adherents of whole language recognize the key tenets that follow (K. Goodman, 1986; Newman, 1985).

Key 1

A Positive View of Human Learners

Whole language takes seriously Dewey's statement about starting where the learner is. It views learners as strong, capable, and eager to learn. It is child centered in that it accepts the responsibility for helping every child to grow as much as possible in whatever directions are most useful (Dewey & Bentley, 1949). At the same time that whole language sees common strengths and universals in human learning, it expects and recognizes differences among learners in culture, value systems, experience, needs, interests, and language. Some of these differences are personal, reflecting human variability, and some of them are social, reflecting the ethnic, cultural, and belief systems of the social groups pupils represent.

Thus teachers in whole language programs value differences among learners as they come to school and differences in objectives and outcomes as students progress through school. They view the goals of education as expansion on the learners' strengths and maximum growth, not conformity and uniformity. In whole language classrooms learners are empowered. They are invited to take ownership of their learning and are given maximum support in developing their own objectives and fulfilling them.

Redefining the Teacher's Role

Vygotsky (1978) offered a view of teachers as mediators who facilitate learners' transactions with the world. Whole language teachers accept that view of their role. They are professionals who know children, learning, and teaching. They support learning but they do not see themselves as controlling learning. They reject the definition of teachers as technicians administering a fixed technology to learners (Goodman, Shannon, Freeman, & Murphy, 1988). Whole language teachers accept responsibility for facilitating growth in their pupils but they also expect power and authority to plan, organize, and choose resources.

Whole language classrooms are communities of learners. Teachers learn with and from their pupils. Teachers share what they know with their pupils but collaborate with them in defining and solving problems and seeking answers to questions. Whole language teachers reject restrictive models of effective teaching because they view teaching as much more complex and comprehensive than do these models.

Language as Central to Learning

Language exists for two reasons. First, humans are capable of symbolic thought, that is, they let things represent other things—they can create semiotic systems. The second reason for language is that humans are social beings, dependent at birth and interdependent throughout their lives. Social communication among people is necessary. So language is central to human communication and human thought. Language, as Halliday (1978) describes it, is a social semiotic. It is also the medium of human learning and makes human learning quite different from the learning of other species. Humans can share their experiences and insights through language and thus pool their intelligence.

Vygotsky (1978) has shown that people internalize language from social interactions. Halliday (1975) calls language learning "learning how to mean" because in the process of learning language people learn the social meanings language represents. Halliday (1984) describes three kinds of language learning that happen simultaneously: learning language, learning *through* language, and learning *about* language.

In school and out of school, both oral and written language are learned best and most easily in authentic speech acts and literacy events that serve real functions. So whole language programs reject part-to-whole views of literacy development, insisting on *real* reading and *real* writing from the very beginning. Whole language builds on the base of print awareness that children growing up in a literate society bring to school. Ferreiro and Teberosky (1982), Piagetians, have shown that even children in the barrios of Mexico City are seeking to make sense of print in their physical environment. Yetta Goodman (1984) and others have shown in their research how widespread a developing knowledge of print is among American preschoolers. So reading and writing in whole language classrooms start where learners are and help them build their own literacy.

Miscue research by Goodman and Goodman (1978) and many others provides an understanding of the reading process and how it develops. The work of Graves (1975, 1981) and of Britton (1977) and other researchers in England offers similar insights into writing. Whole language incorporates this knowledge into a holistic program to support and sustain written language development. Literacy is seen as a major part of the language expansion that pupils achieve during their school years.

Traditional school concerns—spelling, handwriting, grammar, and usage—are integrated in whole language classrooms into authentic language experiences. Reading, writing, speaking, and listening are not isolated for instruction but rather are integrated.

A Dual Curriculum

Halliday (1984) concludes that we learn through language while we learn language. The whole language curriculum builds on this conclusion. It is a dual curriculum; every activity, experience, or unit is an opportunity for both linguistic and cognitive development. Language and thinking develop at the same time that knowledge is developed and concepts and schemas are built.

Whole language teachers plan thematic units to provide opportunities for both curricula. They are kid watchers who monitor language development while pupils solve problems and pursue the answers to questions they have generated. None of this is new in education. Whole language reestablishes Dewey's (Dewey & Bentley, 1949) learning-by-doing views and the project method of Kilpatrick (1918). But it does so with a new base in theory and research. In this dual curriculum, integration, authenticity, learner choice, and collaboration are all of basic importance. The term whole language itself draws on two meanings of *whole*. It is undivided, and it is integrated and unified.

Theory, Research, and Practice

All research requires a theoretical base, and there must be a harmony between theory, research, and related practice. Since whole language teachers operate on the basis of well-developed theory and use it to plan their teaching, one cannot, therefore, usefully study or evaluate whole language classrooms outside of the theoretical context whole language derives from. Reductionist, experimental paradigms are of limited utility in studying whole language classrooms. It is possible to conduct experiments using traditional designs in whole language classrooms, but researchers must fully understand the relation of what they are studying to the theoretical premises of whole language. To study *time on task,* for example, researchers would need to define *task* to fit the concepts of dual curriculum, of learner choice, and of integration around problem solving. It probably would be necessary to replace the concept of *time on task* with a term like *learner commitment and involvement.*

Research in whole language classrooms may well require redefinition of usual research roles. Pupils and teachers in whole language classrooms will be found in a wide range of activities, locations, and ways of relating to each other. So it will not be easy to define role structures. The researcher, too, may not be able to maintain the role of dispassionate outsider coming in to give a test or two or gather data quickly. To research the whole language classroom adequately the researcher may need to be present and participate. Teachers and pupils may themselves need to become part of the research team.

Goodman

Seeing for Ourselves, a compilation of case study research by teachers, underscores this change:

> The classroom becomes a place of inquiry, where questions are explored in meaningful contexts and teacher and students collaborate to seek answers. No longer dispensers of curricula designed by "experts" from universities, textbook companies, or their school districts, these teachers become experts themselves, bringing knowledge and confidence to their teaching and showing that they are professional educators to be respected within schools and without. By becoming researchers, these teachers take control over their classrooms and professional lives in ways that confound the traditional definition of *teacher* and offer proof that education can reform itself from within (Bissex & Bullock, 1987, p. xi).

Case study and ethnographic research fit well for the study of whole language. However, other methodologies also are appropriate. Whatever methodology is used, researchers must be able to study what happens in whole language classrooms without restricting it, changing its nature, or isolating features from their natural contexts.

Relating Research and Practice

The relationship between research and practice is never simple, never an isomorphic, one-to-one correspondence between a research finding and an application in practice. Too often researchers, particularly experimental researchers, conclude their reports with brief sections in which they recommend direct application of a particular finding in classrooms, like a shot or a pill to be administered. In any practical situation, even the most useful insights must be considered within particular contexts.

Research will be most applicable to whole language classrooms if it draws on the same theoretical base as the whole language practice and if it is conducted in the real world rather than in laboratories. Even then, the concepts or ideas drawn from research must be integrated within a unified theory and translated into practice.

Consider, for example, the concept of invented spelling (Read, 1971). Read's actual interest was the sense of the phonology young children have. He discovered, incidental to his intent, that children begin representing, in invented spellings, the sounds they hear in oral language. In this they show a remarkable sensitivity to actual sounds of speech, in contrast to adults, who tend to impose their adult knowledge of the phonemic system and the orthography (the spelling system) on what they perceive.

Teachers and researchers closer to the classroom recognized that this was an important developmental insight: children invent the spelling system just as they do other language systems. The concept fit well with the holistic view that language control develops in the context of its use. Furthermore, it supported the intuition of many teachers that pupils learn spelling without direct instruction if they read and write. Subsequent research by classroom teachers such as Milz (1982), who studied her own first-grade pupils, and researchers such as Y. Goodman and S. Wilde (1985) went beyond Read's work to study the evolution of spelling in children's writing in school. They demonstrated the remarkable development toward conventional spelling over time that children achieve without explicit instruction. Thus theory, research, and practice come together, and whole language teachers gain confidence in teaching spelling in the context of meaningful reading and writing.

Out of Goodman's miscue analysis came a transactional, psycholinguistic theory of the reading process (K. Goodman, 1984). A key insight is that readers predict as they read and use cues from their reading to confirm or disconfirm their predictions. For whole language teachers, this is a more useful and powerful concept than the concept of readability, a largely atheoretical attempt to measure potential text difficulty. The problem for whole language teachers is that readability leaves the reader totally out of the estimation. What whole language teachers saw was that texts, any kind of coherent and cohesive reading material, were hard or easy for particular readers to the extent that they were predictable. They realized that books beginning readers found easy to read had this characteristic predictability. Successful writers for children, showing a sense of

Goodman

audience, had been creating predictable children's literature. Teachers were able to collect numerous predictable books that facilitated their pupils' reading development. In turn, they communicated this to publishers and authors, who produced more predictable books.

While contemporary psychologists were discovering that the past experiences and schemas of readers strongly influenced what they understood from what they read, insightful teachers responded, "Yes, of course. We start where the learner is." As whole language teachers are finding their voices, the communication between researchers, theorists, and teachers is no longer one way. Academics are finding that they have much to learn from practitioners.

Interdisciplinary Research

The current period of research relating to language and literacy can best be characterized as multidisciplinary. Important research is being done in psychology, linguistics, literary criticism, semiotics, composition, rhetoric, ethnography, artificial intelligence, and education. But there is not nearly enough interdisciplinary work. The net result is that it is left to practitioners, with the support of a small number of synthesizers and disseminators, to integrate new information into practical theory and theory-based practice.

In fact, a dynamic international literature is developing to support the integration and practical implementation of new ideas. It involves Canadians, Britons, Americans, Australians, and New Zealanders. It is collaborative with groups of teachers in Nova Scotia, Manitoba, New England, the U.S. Southwest, England, and Australia. It involves teachers writing for teachers.

So dynamic is the whole language movement that innovative practice is leaping ahead of research and rapidly expanding and explicating the fine points of theory. This is as it should be. There is sound, scientifically based theory underlying whole language practice. Teachers need not wait for research findings before innovating within their classrooms. When skeptical administrators and colleagues say to such innovative teachers, "Where is the proof that what you are doing works?" teachers have a right to answer that the proof is in their classrooms and their pupils.

In another recent compilation, *The Whole Language Evaluation Book* (Goodman, Goodman, & Hood, 1989), a wide range of teachers report how they have gone far beyond testing in finding creative ways of evaluating learning and teaching in their classrooms. This evaluation is a part of the ongoing activity in their classrooms. It involves learners in reflective self-evaluation and makes it possible to continually improve what happens in their classrooms.

Young children, given the opportunity to read and write in holistic, authentic, and functional contexts, are learning faster and producing more than their teachers thought possible. In classroom after classroom, at a wide range of grade levels, students are far exceeding in their productivity and in the scope of their learning what schools have traditionally expected. It is up to researchers to find ways of documenting and explicating these classroom events. They can perform a useful service for teachers by helping them understand the processes at work so they can be used in other classrooms and so teachers can expand on what is working. There is also much in these dynamic whole language classrooms for researchers to learn about language learning and language teaching when neither is constrained by sequenced textbooks or narrow curricula.

Bringing Science and Humanism Together

For three-quarters of a century, American education has been split between a science/technology view on the one hand and a humanistic, child-centered view on the other. These views have a common history. At the end of the last century, as scholarship in education began to emerge, there was a movement to replace tradition and the personal views of text writers with practice more solidly based in theory and research. In the beginning there were studies centered around understanding language and learning and school practice. There was concern for both scientific understanding and humanistic practice.

Rice (1893), whose research spanned several decades, reported the conclusion of his studies of the extent to which contemporary school practice reflected the best knowledge:

> In schools conducted upon the principles of unification, language is regarded simply as a means of expression and not as a thing apart from ideas. Instruction in almost every branch now partakes of the nature of a language-lesson. The child being led to learn the various phases of language in large part incidentally while acquiring and expressing ideas.... And, strange as it may seem, it is nevertheless true that the results in reading and expression of ideas in writing are, at least in the primary grades, by far the best in those schools where language, in all its phases, is taught incidentally (pp. 223-224).

Rice's comments sound as if they could have been written today as an endorsement of whole language. Teacher education was emerging in places like Cook County Normal School under Francis Parker. Dewey was beginning to raise key philosophical concerns about the purposes and issues of education. He had started the laboratory school at the University of Chicago, which began initiating experimental programs.

However, in 1914 Rice published his second book, *Scientific Management in Education*. Key educators and researchers had been swept up in the American fascination with the efficiency of the assembly line. They saw science as a new synonym for technology. Recognizing that teachers of the time were minimally educated, they believed they could ensure that students received the benefits of scientific learning theory if the theory were incorporated into tightly constructed materials with detailed teachers' manuals to guide teachers step by step in their use.

In a National Society for the Study of Education yearbook, Gray published the "Principles of Method in Teaching Reading, as Derived from Scientific Investigation" (Gray, 1919). Gray enunciated the key criteria on which basals are still constructed. These principles, together with Thorndike's laws of learning, have dominated reading instruction through the basal reader ever since (Cuban, 1984).

Science was seen as represented by the texts and tests that proliferated over the ensuing decades. A separate movement that was humanistic, child-centered, holistic, and focused on meaningful experience was perceived as emotionally based and unscientific or even antiscientific. The humanistic tradition was represented by the new education, progressive education, open education, and in reading by such approaches as language experience and individualized reading.

Reconceptualizing Science

The dichotomizing of educational belief and practice was never valid. However, while educational research and curriculum were dominated by behavioral psychology and narrow experimental views of what constituted acceptable research, the theory and research of the humanistic movement in education were not valued. Simultaneous with the emergence of whole language, however, education has been broadening and reconceptualizing its necessary scientific base.

Research on reading and writing and related issues in the several disciplines mentioned above is producing useful knowledge. It is foundational knowledge that must be integrated to produce practical applications in classrooms. That is what whole language does. It recombines the scientific and humanistic traditions in education. It builds solidly on Dewey's epistemology, his philosophical theories of how knowledge develops, how we learn by doing what is functional and relevant. It also expands on the psychological research and theories of Piaget and Vygotsky. Whole language incorporates the concepts of language as social semiotic and language learning as "learning how to mean" from the theory and research of Halliday (1975). It builds on and contributes to the research on reading and writing from print awareness, miscue analysis, process writing, schema theory, discourse analysis, literary criticism, and artificial intelligence. It draws on ethnography and descriptive and collaborative research in building curriculum and methodology that support natural language learning.

In doing this, whole language shifts school literacy programs away from technology. It gives to teachers the power to make decisions and provides them with the knowledge necessary to do so. Thus it shifts power from teachers' manuals to teachers. The curriculum is no longer the texts and the tests. Now it becomes a network of authentic experience in which language is developed. Teachers, supported by informed administrators who see themselves as facilitators of classroom teaching, translate scientific knowledge in the context of humanistic theory. It is the teachers who bring science and humanism back together for the service of their pupils.

Whole language teachers read broadly and deeply because they recognize that they have undertaken the responsibility for translating theory and research into practice. Atwell, an exemplary researcher, reported her own development in a presentation to the National Council of Teachers of English in November 1987:

> All the while my activity in the classroom changed, my professional activity outside was changing, too. I read all the writing theory and all the relevant research I could lay my hands on. For me, as for many other classroom teachers, "relevant" meant process-observational studies of young writers, readers and speakers.... These studies were in every way unlike the experimental design research I had read in English education courses. Context was so fully explained and explored I could understand why teachers and learners were teaching and learning...these were explorations of principles underlying practices (pp. 3-4).

The energy and innovations these empowered teachers are generating are producing a new base of practical knowledge for teachers and researchers to draw upon. A good deal of this development is passed from teacher to teacher in personal contacts, in teacher support groups, and in local conferences. Teachers are not only sharing their classroom innovations, they are collaborating with researchers and conducting their own research as they teach.

Atwell (1987) cites reports of a number of studies by teacher-researchers. The data in these studies are not only carefully gathered and richly described, they are supported by authentic vignettes and examples of young people reading and writing in the real world of the classroom. That is why teachers find the research so easily applicable. It is also why it is so full of insights for researchers.

Politics, Economics, and Traditions

If American education existed in a rational world, it would be clear that whole language brings together and is based in modern research in language, learning, and teaching. However, American education is being pulled by several forces that make it less than rational.

One force is the politics of fundamentalism, which underlies the back-to-basics movement. In all fields this fundamentalism tries to reduce complex phenomena to simple ones. In reading that means insisting that direct teaching of a reduced and inaccurate set of letter-sound relationships, phonics, is necessary and sufficient to develop readers. It would be easy to dismiss such a view in light of modern research on language and language learning, but this misconception has so powerful a political base that even reports by authoritative research groups find it politic to endorse early direct instruction in phonics as essential to reading development. The authors of *Becoming a Nation of Readers* (Anderson, Hiebert, Scott, & Wilkinson, 1985) proclaimed that the research literature had proved that early direct instruction in phonics is essential. That put a scientific seal of approval on simplistic phonics programs that the *Reader's Digest* and the Reading Reform Foundation hastened to broadcast, most conspicuously in a full-page ad in the *New York Times*.

Whole language does support the learning of phonics, to the extent that phonics is the set of relationships between the sound system and the orthographic system of written language. That is shown in the invented-spelling research and in the studies of developing readers. However, there is abundant research to show that direct instruction in phonics is neither necessary nor desirable to produce readers. Since the studies Rice reported in 1893, it has been clear that learning to make sense of print in reading or express sense in writing does not require learning letter-sound relationships in isolation. Now researchers are providing evidence that phonic relationships develop consistently and most usefully as pupils write (Goodman & Wilde, 1985) and read (Goodman & Goodman, 1978).

Another tradition interfering with the objective pursuit of truth is the remarkable status that basal texts and standardized tests have achieved. Shannon's (1983) research showed that both teachers and administrators believe that basal readers incorporate the best knowledge from research and that they should therefore be carefully and mechanically followed by all teachers and learners. It is not simply that they have a scientific base, but that everything in them is in a specific place in the sequence for scientific reasons.

Publishers succeeded so well in equating science with technology that local and state authorities frequently require by law or edict that teachers must use basals in prescribed ways. Specific published tests are mandated by law in several U.S. states as the key basis for pupil promotion and program evaluation.

Most recently the State Board of Education in Georgia ruled that scores of kindergarten children on a mandated test must be given serious consideration in deciding whether the children may enter first grade. This decision is not based on research but on the belief that research strongly underlies both the test and the text-based phonics curriculum mandated for Georgia kindergartens. Many Georgia children will experience failure and defeat even before they enter first grade because state policymakers are convinced that the children have been scientifically shown to be inadequate.

The National Association for the Education of Young Children has gathered substantial research evidence to show that curricula and promotion criteria based on skill hierarchies are developmentally inappropriate for young children (NAEYC, 1987).

The scientific aura around basals is so strong that researchers are reluctant to suggest that dropping basals may be necessary. Duffy and Ball (1986) studied how teachers use basals: "the data suggest that teachers do not rely upon rational models to make decisions, but instead focus on procedural concerns regarding classroom organization and management...which encourage teachers to follow the prescriptions of the instructional materials in a technical rather than a professional manner" (p. 173).

When Duffy, Roehler, and Putnam (1987) attempted to help teachers become substantive (make their own decisions about how to use the substance of the lessons rather than the explicit directions) in their use of basals, they achieved no long-term effects because "neither the content nor the instructional design offered much structure for decision making" (p. 360). Yet the researchers decided that "the solution does not lie with abandoning basal textbooks" (p. 362).

It will be difficult to find American school systems willing to replace textbooks completely, particularly basal readers, with trade books and resource materials so that research evidence can be accumulated to show that students can learn in whole language classrooms without controlled and controlling textbooks. Schools spend almost 10 times as much on basal readers as they do on trade books (Goodman et al., 1988). Researchers need to support teachers and schools who have the courage to teach without basals. The more research there is that shows readers succeeding without basals, the less irrational will be the enforced dependence on basals in our schools.

Potential Research in Whole Language Classrooms

This article has shown that the theory and practice of whole language are solidly based on fundamental research on language, learning, literacy development, and the relationship of teaching to learning. No movement in education has ever been so comprehensively based on scientific theory. Further, it has shown that there is a growing tradition of research in whole language classrooms.

There is much to be learned in whole language classrooms, not only in evaluating whole language in concept and practice but in studying teaching, learning, language and literacy development, curriculum, and other aspects of education. Some fundamental questions can be studied in whole language classrooms in ways that were not possible before because of the authenticity of the language transactions and the integration around themes and problem solving. Vygotsky believed that spontaneous and scientific concepts were learned differently, but he did not consider how they might be learned similarly if schools changed. If learning in schools is more like learning outside of school, then what does that mean for the development of scientific concepts?

Dewey talked about learning by doing, but this and other concepts of progressive education never developed a grassroots constituency comparable with the whole language network of teachers. Research in classrooms that operationalize learning by doing can explore the potential of Dewey's concepts.

Smith (1986) has argued that those who are successful in becoming literate in school become members of the "literacy club." In whole language classrooms researchers can explore the validity of this concept. What happens in classrooms that includes or excludes pupils from this club? Here is a research concern that may profit from the comparison of whole language and skills-based classrooms. Does whole language do a better job of making more pupils feel like members of the literacy club?

It would be interesting to explore how pupil and teacher roles change as transitions are made to whole language from more traditional classrooms. Studies of the success of pupils and teachers as it relates to the evidence of their empowerment would also be valuable.

These studies will require research methods from a wide range of disciplines. Discourse analysis, drawing on functional grammar, might look at the language teachers use in inviting students into the literacy club. Ethnography would be appropriate for studying access to and use of resource materials. Schema theory could be combined with cohesion analysis in examining children's choices of topics in their writing. Small-group methodology from social psychology would be appropriate to studying participation in literature study groups. Case studies of individuals—teachers, learners, or administrators—would help to examine the pupils' development as readers, writers, and problem solvers. Piagetian research methodology, as Ferreiro and her colleagues have developed it (Ferreiro & Teberosky, 1982), could be useful for studying transitions into literacy. In whole language classrooms, Vygotsky's "zone of proximal development" can be studied in authentic problem-solving situations.

Just as teaching and learning have broken out of the constraints of an outmoded technology in whole language classrooms, so educational research needs to break the behavioristic ties that bind it. That means learning how to do real world, naturalistic research without controlling the variables in what we study so that we destroy it. It also means researchers raising their sights, broadening their perspectives, and asking new sets of questions about the potential of teaching and learning that whole language programs make possible. Next I identify five of many such areas of focus.

Invention

Whole language classrooms empower learners to invent language and conceptual schema. Researchers and teachers have been aware for some time, as we indicated above, of the role of invention in children's spelling development. But invention is present in all aspects of linguistic and cognitive development. In the research on writing of Y. Goodman and her colleagues (Goodman & Wilde, 1985), for example, there was evidence of invention in narrative, in report writing, in grammar, in punctuation, and in concepts. Research could use the right evidence of invention in whole language classrooms to fully explore the process. More understanding is needed on how invention follows similar and different directions among groups of learners. Teachers will appreciate insights from research on how mediation supports and extends invention without stifling or misdirecting it. Studies of the social, personal, cultural, and classroom resources that pupils draw on in their inventions would also be useful. For example, in a study that was a part of the Goodman research, Bird (1987) looked at how Native American learners drew on their own life experience in their written expression.

Convention

All learners need to come to control a wide range of social conventions in order to communicate successfully. These social conventions become internalized and play a vital role in thinking and learning. Whole language teachers share the concern of other teachers that learners come to control these conventions, but they recognize that traditional attempts to teach conventions directly distort them, often suppress invention, and do not ensure that pupils will usefully internalize the conventions. There is evidence from the Piagetian research of Ferreiro and her colleagues of how the conventions of written language develop. Halliday has shown how linguistic conventions of grammar and texts develop. Whole language teachers monitor development as they work closely with pupils. They understand that conventions are inferred as learners engage in functional, meaningful, authentic social transactions. They understand the importance of encouraging risk taking as they help pupils deal with the tension between their inventions and social convention.

Research is needed to document the development of the conventions of various oral and written language genres. How do pupils build a sense of written sentences? How do they learn the pragmatic conventions of personal and business letters? How do they develop a sense of audience in oral and written presentations? What kinds of experiences enable readers to read like writers and learn the conventions of written language to use in their own writing? Research should examine the tension between personal invention and social convention in developing reading, writing, thinking, and problem solving.

Organizing for Whole Language

Traditionally teachers have organized around the teachers' manuals of textbooks, around discrete subjects, or around specific activities. Whole language integrates language and its use in learning. Thematic units are planned to last several weeks and integrate social studies, science, language arts, mathematics, and the arts. So there is long- and medium-term planning as well as daily planning. Whole language teachers use flexible, ad hoc grouping rather than relatively permanent ability grouping of pupils. Furthermore, different pupils and groups of pupils may be doing different things at the same time. All this makes developing facilitative organizational procedures very important. This is a very dynamic area now as whole language teachers move away from traditional practice and create holistic alternatives. Research can help teachers while knowledge is developed about how innovative uses of time, space, materials, and social transactions facilitate teaching and learning. Practice is leading theory in this area, and both can profit from creative research.

Resources for Whole Language Classrooms

It is relatively easy to set aside basal readers and use real children's literature to develop reading in whole language classrooms. But what other materials do whole language classrooms need to facilitate literacy development, problem solving, question answering, and researching for thematic units? Commercial publishers and governmental and quasigovernmental groups have developed whole language resource materials such as big books, predictable books, writing portfolios, kits of trade books, and teaching units for use with literature sets. And the whole language label is being used by commercial publishers on materials that appear to have little in common with the principles discussed in this article. Development of resources is another dynamic area in whole language classrooms. Many teachers feel quite comfortable with their own ability to assemble enough authentic real world resources to meet the needs of their pupils. They enlist parents in finding resources and scavenge from their homes and communities. But they often have a good sense of resources that would be useful that do not exist, such as factual resources for use by pupils of various ages, abilities, and language backgrounds.

Research on materials for supporting whole language is another broad area that could be opened up. Research might also help whole language teachers to fight off the "basalization" of literature by superimposing skill packages on the reading of stories. Research could document for teachers their innovative use and development of unconventional resources. Teachers and administrators need research help to establish criteria for evaluation of available materials and specifications for new resources.

New Roles for Teachers and Learners

There are no teachers today who were themselves learners in whole language classrooms. As teachers move away from the conventional, limited roles to new and broader ones, and as they open the range of roles for learners in their classrooms, they are moving into unexplored territory. Even when they become comfortable, confident, and highly effective in these new roles as kid watchers, mediators of learning, and liberators of learners, they encounter resistance, skepticism, and sometimes hostility from colleagues, administrators, and the community. Besides their own careful documentation of the success of their new professionalism, they need the support of research. They need the insights that systematic research can provide to continue their innovation in desirable directions, to modify their practice to better achieve their goals, and to help doubters to understand what is happening. Teachers and learners need to be partners with researchers in these studies.

In places where whole language has become policy on national, state or provincial, and local levels, research is needed on ways of supporting teachers and learners as they make transitions from traditional to holistic schooling. Preservice and staff-development programs have been developed, particularly in New Zealand and Australia, for dissemination of whole language philosophy and practice. As these and other programs are implemented in North America, their effects need to be carefully researched.

A Message for Teachers, a Challenge for Researchers

I hope the message has come through to teachers from this discussion that they ought not to be defensive about their whole language programs. There is a solid research base to whole language. Whole language teachers incorporate this into a philosophy they use in making instructional decisions and planned innovations. What they are attempting is different and much more ambitious than the objectives of traditional classrooms. Whole language teachers and administrators need to document what they and their pupils are doing. Many of them do research in their classrooms themselves or with researchers. They need to resist the attempts of researchers and evaluators to make them restrict or modify what they are doing to fit conventional research designs and evaluation instruments, such as standardized tests.

Whole language offers a challenge to researchers. They need to understand that whole language is a major step forward. It involves bold new innovative programs and settings for teaching and learning. The professionals participating in this grassroots movement are eager to have research support. But it is up to the researchers to demonstrate their ability to do useful, relevant research. The practitioners will move ahead, with or without this support.

Note
Many of the quotes and ideas in the section "Bringing Science and Humanism Together" come from Patrick Shannon's contribution to *Report Card on Basal Readers* (Goodman et al., 1988).

References

Anderson, R.C., Hiebert, E.H., Scott, J.A., & Wilkinson, I.A.G. (1985). *Becoming a nation of readers: The report of the Commission on Reading.* Washington, DC: National Institute of Education.

Atwell, N. (1987, November). *"Wonderings to pursue": The writing teacher as researcher.* Paper presented to the National Council of Teachers of English, Los Angeles, CA.

Bird, L.B. (1987). *The reflection of personal experience in the writing of Papago Indian children.* Unpublished doctoral dissertation, University of Arizona, Tucson, AZ.

Bissex, G., & Bullock, R. (Eds.). (1987). *Seeing for ourselves.* Portsmouth, NH: Heinemann.

Britton, J. (1977). Language and the nature of learning: An individual perspective. In J.R. Squire (Ed.), *The teaching of English* (pp. 1-38). Chicago, IL: University of Chicago Press.

Cuban, L. (1984). *How teachers taught.* White Plains, NY: Longman.

Dewey, J., & Bentley, L. (1949). *Knowing and the known.* Boston, MA: Beacon.

Duffy, G.G., & Ball, D.L. (1986). Instructional decision making and reading teacher effectiveness. In J.V. Hoffman (Ed.), *Effective teaching of reading: Research and practice* (pp. 163-180). Newark, DE: International Reading Association.

Duffy, G.G., Roehler, L.R., & Putnam, J. (1987). Putting the teacher in control: Basal reading textbooks and instructional decision making. *Elementary School Journal, 87,* 357-366.

Ferreiro, E., & Teberosky, A. (1982). *Literacy before schooling.* Portsmouth, NH: Heinemann.

Goodman, K. (1984). Unity in reading. In A. Purves & O. Niles (Eds.), *Becoming readers in a complex society* (pp. 79-114). Chicago, IL: University of Chicago Press.

Goodman, K. (1986). *What's whole in whole language?* Portsmouth, NH: Heinemann.

Goodman, K., & Goodman, Y. (1978). *Reading of American children whose language is a stable rural dialect of English or a language other than English* (Final Report). Washington, DC: National Institute of Education.

Goodman, K., Goodman, Y., & Hood, W. (1989). *The whole language evaluation book.* Portsmouth, NH: Heinemann.

Goodman, K., Shannon, P., Freeman, Y., & Murphy, S. (1988). *Report card on basal readers.* Katonah, NY: Richard C. Owen.

Goodman, Y. (1984). The development of initial literacy. In H. Goelman, A. Oberg, & F. Smith (Eds.), *Awakening to literacy* (pp. 102-109). Portsmouth, NH: Heinemann.

Goodman, Y. (1989). Roots of the whole-language movement. *Elementary School Journal, 90,* 113-127.

Goodman, Y., & Wilde, S. (1985). *Writing development: Third and fourth grade*

O'odham (Papago) students (Occasional Paper No. 14). Tucson, AZ: Program in Language and Literacy, University of Arizona.

Graves, D. (1975). An examination of the writing process of seven-year-old children. *Research in the Teaching of English, 9,* 227-241.

Graves, D. (1981). *A case study observing the development of primary children's composing, spelling, and motor behaviors during the writing process* (Project NIE-G-78-0174). Washington, DC: National Institute of Education.

Gray, W. (1919). Principles of method in teaching reading, as derived from scientific investigation. In C. Seashore (Ed.), *Fourth report of committee on the economy of time* (pp. 26-51). Chicago, IL: University of Chicago Press.

Halliday, M.A.K. (1975). *Learning how to mean.* London, UK: Arnold.

Halliday, M.A.K. (1978). *Language as social semiotic.* London, UK: Arnold.

Halliday, M.A.K., (1984). Three aspects of children's language development: Learning language, learning through language, and learning about language. In Y. Goodman, M. Haussler, & D. Strickland (Eds.), *Oral and written language development research: Impact on the schools* (pp. 165-192). Urbana, IL: National Council of Teachers of English.

Kilpatrick, W.H. (1918). The project method. *Teachers College Record, 19,* 319-335.

Milz, V. (1982). *Young children write: The beginnings* (Occasional Paper No. 5). Tucson, AZ: Program in Language and Literacy, University of Arizona.

National Association for the Education of Young Children. (1987). *Developmentally appropriate practice in early childhood programs serving children from birth through age 8* (Publication No. 24). Washington, DC: author.

Newman, J. (1985). *Whole language: Theory in use.* Portsmouth, NH: Heinemann.

Read, C. (1971). Preschool children's knowledge of English phonology. *Harvard Educational Review, 41,* 1-34.

Rice, J. (1893). *The public school system in the United States.* New York: Century.

Rice, J. (1914). *Scientific management in education.* New York: Hinds, Noble & Eldridge.

Rich, S. (1983). On becoming teacher experts: Teacher researchers. *Language Arts, 60,* 892-894.

Shannon, P. (1983). The use of commercial reading materials in American elementary schools. *Reading Research Quarterly, 19,* 68-85.

Smith, F. (1986). *Insult to intelligence.* New York: Arbor House.

Vygotsky, L.S. (1978). *Mind in society: The development of higher psychological processes* (edited by M. Cole, V. John-Steiner, S. Scribner, & E. Souberman). Cambridge, MA: Harvard University Press.

CHAPTER 4

Assessing Literacy: From Standardized Tests to Portfolios and Performances

ELFRIEDA H. HIEBERT
ROBERT C. CALFEE

As standardized tests become more influential, curriculum and instruction planning are increasingly driven by test content. This chapter begins with a review of the impact of tests and the efforts that have been directed at bringing large-scale assessment more in line with a view of reading and writing as the construction and communication of meaning. The chapter then moves beyond tests to consider alternative forms of assessment that involve teachers in gathering and interpreting measures of students' progress toward critical literacy goals. The authors examine the benefits and pitfalls of alternative methods such as performance and portfolio assessment. They conclude by identifying the issues that require attention if educators and policymakers are to use multiple indicators of student progress, and if schools are to focus on the critical goals of literacy.

Classroom teachers have daily access to information about their students' literacy development. Teachers gather information from sources such as the book authored by the student who disdained writing at the beginning of the year, or the youngster who chooses to spend free time in the library. When a district, province, or state emphasizes standardized tests, teachers discuss how their data compare with these external sources.

Standardized tests are a fixture in most U.S. schools, but they evoke widespread misgivings among both teachers and researchers. Shepard (1988) describes the harmful consequences of allowing test content and format to dictate the curriculum. Cannell (1988) reports inflated test scores, which he attributes to "teaching to the test." The causes are more complex (Koretz, 1988; Linn, Graue, & Sanders, 1990), but increased emphasis on standardized achievement clearly has led to instruction driven by test content and format (Mehrens & Kaminski, 1988), as well as to neglect of both "thoughtful" and higher-level literacy (Brown, 1989). As Applebee, Langer, and Mullis (1989) note, U.S. students perform adequately on low-level tasks, but they do poorly on higher-level tasks.

Recently, attention has moved to alternative assessment methods (Johnston, 1984, 1989; Linn, Baker, & Dunbar, in press; Morrow & Smith, 1990). One aspect of the discussion is the need to return control of classroom assessment to the teacher as an informed professional. The argument here is that the narrowness of standardized paper and pencil tests threaten the quality of a school's curriculum and instruction. A second facet of the discussion raises the possibility that alternative assessment measures better serve policymakers for accountability purposes.

In the U.S., states are the focus of accountability since they have primary responsibility for public schools. Although most states and districts have testing programs, educators worry that standardized instruments measure only low-level basic skills. Some states have responded to these concerns with new tests designed to tap advanced skill and knowledge. Several states, for example, now assess "real writing" (a technique that has implications for reading assessment, although policymakers seldom connect the two). A few states have departed completely from standardization. Vermont's experiment relies on classroom portfolios of student work (Brewer, 1989); California has opted for gathering writing samples and assessments that integrate reading and writing (Claggett, Cooper, & Brenneman, 1989); and Connecticut calls on teachers to design alternative assessment approaches around actual classroom projects (Moses, 1990).

Although proposals for alternative assessment are springing up all over, other developments mean a stronger role for standardized tests. The National Assessment of Educational Progress (NAEP), which until now has summarized results by geographic region, will report state-by-state results in 1992. At the same time, NAEP's assessment measure is being redesigned to emphasize higher-level comprehension processes, with many open-ended items added (Reading Consensus Planning Project for 1992 NAEP, 1990).

What are classroom teachers to make of these developments? Here we describe the emerging field of alternative assessment: performance-based, classroom-based, teacher-based, and portfolios. We report research where available, although we've found more suggestions than solid findings. We also attempt to place recent developments in the context of the continuing evolution of norm- and criterion-referenced tests, because these instruments will continue to influence classroom education for some time.

Externally Mandated Tests

In this section we look at standardized testing in local classrooms and at the national level. Most of these instruments are designed by experts, either for accountability (How is the nation, state, district, or school achieving?) or for decision-making purposes (Has this school, class, or student completed a particular objective?). Standardized methods, the foundation of present practice, have been challenged by a range of alternatives. To understand the alternatives, we begin with current practice.

Current Use and Effects

With few exceptions, U.S. states conduct large-scale assessments in reading (Afflerbach, 1990); many also perform some form

Hiebert & Calfee

of writing assessment (Freedman, 1990). Large districts conduct their own standardized testing programs, often in response to federal or state mandates.

These large-scale programs rely on either norm- or criterion-referenced tests. In norm-referenced tests, student performance is compared to statistical criteria (e.g., above the state average). In criterion-referenced instruments, performance is gauged against a fixed standard (e.g., 80 percent correct). The two types employ similar formats and some instruments can serve either function. The emphasis is on efficiency and ease of reporting; tests must be cheap to design and score, and simple to aggregate and display.

Standardized reading comprehension tests have several shortcomings. Passages tend to be inconsiderate, and the questions often are tricky (Drum, Calfee, & Cook, 1980; Hill & Parry, 1988; Langer, 1987). In addition, criterion-referenced tests from state departments of education and textbook publishers seldom undergo the reliability and validity procedures of norm-referenced tests (Foertsch & Pearson, 1987). And the tests embedded in basal reading series often determine student placement on the basis of limited information.

Serious problems also arise from misinterpretation and misapplication of tests. The psychometric concepts that undergird test construction often are unknown to test users (Linn, 1990). Ruddell (1985) found serious misunderstandings of test purposes among legislators, administrators, and teachers—groups that use test data for decisions ranging from funding and program evaluation to placement and retention of students in special programs.

Does the value of test data warrant the current expenditures of time and money on standardized measures? For classroom decisions, evidence shows that it does not. Teachers downplay test scores and rely on information gained by observing students and sampling student work (Crooks, 1988; Dorr-Bremme & Herman, 1986; Salmon-Cox, 1981; Stiggins, Conklin, & Bridgeford, 1986). Teachers consider standardized data only when a test score is considerably higher or lower than their estimates of student achievement; even then, they view the test simply as a cue that something is amiss either in the student's work or in their own judgment.

Standardized testing is driven not by teachers' needs but by the need to hold schools accountable.

Nonetheless, standardized tests often influence school curricula. At one extreme, Popham and colleagues (1985) have proposed "measurement-driven instruction" in which a curriculum is explicitly designed to match tests. Mehrens and Kaminski (1988) found that test taking strategies are a major element of the curriculum in many locales. Instruction in test taking ranges from pedagogically sound techniques ("Think about the sources of questions") to direct instruction on specific test content or format. The latter guidance is of dubious value to students; also, it invalidates the test (Shepard, 1988).

In one example of this trend, teachers changed their classroom instruction in response to pressure for higher test scores. McNeil (1988) describes how top-ranked Texas teachers altered instruction after the state required classroom monitoring of test-related objectives. Some lessons remained unchanged, with students discussing the broad meaning of historical events or scientific explanations. In other lessons, however, teachers switched to decontextualized activities involving core vocabulary or key equations. They told students to memorize the material by rote because it would appear on the tests.

Shifts in Large-Scale Assessment

The past decade has seen enormous shifts in educators' views of reading comprehension, from a focus on specific skills and objectives toward a definition of reading as the reconstruction of meaning. The latter view moves curriculum and instruction toward strategic, high-level outcomes. Several states have redesigned their testing programs to reflect this new perspective. Tests in Illinois and Michigan differ in several ways from previous tests (Greer, Pearson, & Meyer, 1990; Roeber & Dutcher, 1989; Valencia & Pearson, 1987; Wixson et al., 1987). Test passages are five to ten times longer and resemble materials encountered in trade books, textbooks, newspapers, and magazines. Most questions address higher-level comprehension. The Illinois test requires students to evaluate each choice rather than scan for the right answer. These new tests also include

Hiebert & Calfee

questions about students' prior knowledge, reading strategies, and reading habits.

The effects of these new instruments on teachers' practices and children's learning are under investigation. For now the projects demonstrate that large-scale assessment can be more compatible with a view of reading as a constructive and strategic process.

Several other states are exploring variations on existing practices. In addition, as noted earlier, NAEP has proposed major revisions in the 1992 reading test, extending the range of formats and the scope of questions. We foresee a parallel shift in textbooks as pressure for change increases from professional organizations (Goodman et al., 1988) and state departments of education (California Department of Education, 1987). The pipeline between reading research and test publishers seems less open at present; popular tests of reading comprehension have not changed much over the past decade.

Performance and Portfolio Assessment

Alternative literacy assessment has a history almost as long as that of standardized tests. However, alternative techniques received little attention until recently, when the work of both evaluators and curriculum specialists brought them into the spotlight (Stiggins, 1985, 1987; Stiggins, Conklin, & Bridgeford, 1986).

Current proposals distinguish between performance and portfolio assessment. Performance assessments document students' efforts in particular situations, the way that Boy or Girl Scout merit badges do (Wiggins, 1989). Sizer (1990) describes the idea as "the public expression by a student of real command over what she's learned" (p. 1). In some cases, the switch to performance assessment has meant simply using passages from magazines or trade books (Maine Department of Education, 1987; Massachusetts Department of Education, 1987). More in the spirit of the concept are events such as dramatic readings of poems or formal debates over contrasting themes in a novel.

Portfolios provide an ongoing record of student accomplishments in a variety of settings. In the arts, candidates select from their best works; in other areas the usual practice is to gather representative samples. "Process-folios" include information about strategies as well as the products, and student reflections as well as teacher evaluations (Wolf, 1989).

Performance and portfolio assessment grew out of the needs of individual classroom teachers, but educators are now exploring its application to large-scale assessments for policy purposes. In the ideal scenario, the two purposes are fulfilled through common measures grounded in curriculum and instruction planning; but this ideal has proved difficult to attain even in theory, much less in practice (Calfee & Drum, 1979; Cole, 1988). Even so, performance-portfolio techniques offer more promise than standardized tests as a bridge between these domains (Calfee, 1988).

Alternative Assessment for Policy Purposes

"What is tested is what is taught." This statement by Resnick and Resnick (1990) captures an important reality of school reform in the 1980s, which equates learning with higher test scores (Pipho, 1985). What might assessment look like if the phrase were reversed: "What is taught is tested"? A variety of projects are moving in this direction at the national, state, and district level.

National assessment. Although schooling falls under state jurisdiction in the United States, Congress in 1965 mandated national periodic assessments of American students through NAEP. As originally conceived, this program was to be descriptive rather than prescriptive. In 1988, however, Congress passed legislation allowing state-by-state NAEP comparisons, raising the specter of high-stakes national testing. Plans for the 1992 assessment have generated considerable debate (Point/Counterpoint, 1989-1990).

Concern about the implications of statewide reporting has led NAEP to initiate several alternative assessment projects to measure ability in reading and writing. One of these projects uses an "Integrated Reading Performance Record" (Educational Testing Service, 1990). Students bring a book they are reading to an interview, review their reasons for the choice, interpret personal responses to the text, and read a portion of their choosing. Finally, they will discuss several works typical of their reading experiences (for example, literature logs, notebooks with semantic maps).

Burstall (1989) describes preliminary results from a similar plan designed for Great Britain in 1992. Students are assessed in groups of three to six under teacher guidance. The tasks integrate language arts, science, and mathematics. In one prototype, students test the malleability of different substances. After experimenting with substances like tinfoil and paper, students record individual conclusions, and teachers add their comments about students' abilities.

In the Primary Language Record (Barrs et al., 1988), also from Great Britain, the emphasis is on teachers' judgments, based on systematic analysis of student work samples. The PLR was developed in 1985 by the Centre for Language in Primary Education for the Inner London Education Authority as part of a program to improve literacy instruction for at-risk youngsters. Unlike other portfolio models that use students' work samples, the PLR relies heavily on teachers' decisions. The PLR provides detailed advice about collecting and maintaining portfolio information, including examples of parent reports. Unfortunately, attention has not been paid to ways in which this information can be summarized so that patterns of students' literacy accomplishments are clear.

State assessment.   At least 13 U.S. states assess student writing samples (Freedman, 1990), the most basic type of performance-based testing. Aschbacher (1990) reports that many of these programs also are developing alternative approaches to reading assessment. The reading-writing connection is difficult to bridge, however; while writing projects move toward alternative forms of assessment, reading tests often are limited to changes in format, with longer passages, higher-level questions, and more open-ended responses (as in Illinois, Maine, Massachusetts, and Michigan).

Vermont's assessment project (Brewer, 1989; Rothman, 1990b) is the most ambitious effort to employ classroom activities for statewide accountability. As now designed, the project follows a model proposed by Valencia (1990). All students complete a standardized task (not involving multiple choice questions), teachers collect samples of day-to-day classroom writing in a portfolio, and each student contributes a "best piece" from his or her year's work. The standardized instrument, still under development, will probably parallel NAEP plans. Selected data will be aggregated for reporting at the state level, but plans also call for a school "town meeting," where parents and other citizens can view displays of local students' work.

Another innovative state effort is California's language arts assessment program (California Department of Education, 1990). An outline directs the classroom teacher through the process, but the context resembles a typical classroom interaction. On the first day, the teacher engages students in a topic-related discussion. Students then read a passage and discuss it in small groups. On the second day, students write individual reactions; the writing-to-source technique is designed to mirror real life tasks in high school and college (Spivey & King, 1989). The California program, still under evaluation, shows that literacy assessments can move beyond multiple choice tests toward an integrated reading-writing model.

District assessment. In many parts of the United States, districts are developing their own performance and portfolio assessment programs. Documenting these endeavors is difficult because small district staffs must handle the immediate needs of school boards, administrators, and teachers, and are less likely to worry about preparing research reports. Nonetheless, the Northwest Regional Educational Laboratory clearinghouse has collected several district case studies (NWREL, 1990) from locales as diverse as Juneau, Alaska (McLain, 1989), Pittsburgh, Pennsylvania (Eresh, 1990), and Orange County, Florida (Mathews, 1990). Standardized writing assessment is the first step for many districts, but the broader potential is illustrated by the Orange County project. Portfolios for grades K-2 include a comprehensive array of entries from checklists for word identification and comprehension strategies to a list of books students have read. In this endeavor, as in most other projects, the emphasis is on formats and routines; issues of aggregation, reporting, and use of information remain unresolved.

In our final example, Simmons (1990) worked with a New Hampshire consortium to develop a performance-based prototype. The information includes a standardized, timed writing exercise, along with three compositions chosen by students from their year-long portfolios. Students keep notes on how long they take to complete each composition, as well as critical reflections about portfolio entries. A teacher team analyzes each collection for such elements as mode and range of discourse, length, and completion time. Simmons reports that the timed-composition and portfolio assessments produced similar rankings, but writers who scored lowest on the timed composition achieved the greatest (untimed) portfolio gains. This group also spent the most time on their portfolio entries, suggesting that motivation was less important than opportunity in determining their performance level.

Alternative Assessment in the Classroom

Most teachers routinely gather performance data during instruction; the process is intuitive and automatic. The focus in this section is on making classroom assessment systematic. Methodology textbooks have long discussed observational checklists and informal reading inventories, but the literature in these areas has burgeoned recently. Entire volumes of practitioner-oriented journals have been devoted to this topic (Brandt, 1989; Calfee, 1982; Dillon, 1990), along with numerous articles and books (Edelsky & Harman, 1988; Flood & Lapp, 1989; Goodman, Goodman, & Hood, 1989).

Early measures. What happens when teachers do turn to alternative assessments? Some evidence comes from the use of an alternative assessment that has a long history in reading instruction, the informal reading inventory, or IRI (Gray, 1920). In this approach, teachers use text similar to that in classroom materials to assess students' reading proficiency. The technique can be flexible and interactive; rather than offering a fixed set of questions, IRIs often encourage the teacher to experiment and explore the conditions that lead to student success or failure.

Elementary teachers are generally familiar with IRIs through preservice or inservice sessions, but little is known about how they use the method. In one of the few published studies, Harris and Lalik (1987) report that teachers trained in informal reading inventories actually made little use of them. Teachers explained that administrators made the decisions about reading instruction. Further discouragement comes from Gil and colleagues (1980) who found that teachers' interpretations of IRI data were idiosyncratic unless guided by explicit training in the requisite skills.

Although IRI techniques vary considerably, fluent oral reading often is an important element. Allington (1986) reports that performance on this task outweighs other considerations when teachers judge student competence. In Clay's (1985) Reading Recovery program, teachers keep daily records of students' oral reading.

An innovative perspective on this type of assessment comes from the concept of *situated learning* (Collins, Brown, & Newman, 1989). The key idea here is to combine testing and teaching in meaningful contexts. In a related development, *dynamic assessment,* the aim is to assess learning rather than competence. With this technique, according to Lidz (1987), "the examiner is an active intervener who monitors and modifies the interaction with the learner in order to induce successful learning" (p. 3). Stiggins (1987) notes that "No other single specification contributes more to the quality of your performance assessment than this one....Place yourself in the hypothetical situation of giving feedback to someone who has performed poorly on the task" (p. 36).

Assessment conditions. Recommendations that teachers take greater responsibility for assessment are undercut by threats to their autonomy. Johnston, Weiss, and Afflerbach (1989) found that when a district removed external mandates, teachers turned to more innovative curriculum materials (e.g., children's literature and other trade books) and developed assessment methods to match the curriculum. In contrast, teachers in a large urban district that mandated textbook use and stressed standardized tests focused on students' skills.

Even teachers in the same school may interpret conditions differently. Hiebert, Hutchinson, and Raines (in press) conducted a case study of two teachers in a school where portfolios were encouraged but not mandated. The two teachers expressed similar opinions but differed considerably in how they approached practical matters such as documentation, interpretation, and decision making. The second grade teacher used checklists and anecdotal records, and could clearly articulate the manner in which assessment informed instruction. The fourth grade teacher was less clear about the connections between assessment and instruction. For example, when the fourth grade teacher evaluated work from the folders where students kept compositions and literature logs, the emphasis was on evaluating the current "final" product with no reference to earlier work or to students' development of particular dimensions of composing or responding to literature. Alternative assessment modes were in place but were not being used to inform students or parents about progress toward critical literacy goals.

Classroom experiments. Complementing the studies of small-scale alternative assessments are a few experiments in which researchers introduce the practice in a classroom and track the results. Often these investigations prove successful, although sometimes hard data are needed. For instance, an elementary teacher observed by Carter and Tierney (1988) became more systematic in gathering and summarizing performance assessments. Use of similar tasks and summaries of information allowed the teacher to make comparisons of students' performances over time in a way that had not been possible before.

Reports of experimental portfolio projects also have emerged from the National Writing Project (Camp, 1990; Howard, 1990; Murphy & Smith, 1990). These projects are from junior and senior high English classes, but two conclusions are worthy of note for all teachers. First, portfolio activities vary with the school context. In one setting portfolios emphasized research reports and subject matter topics, while in another instance portfolios included personal letters from students to teachers about their writing. Second, teachers generally ascribe substantial benefits to the portfolio process; according to Murphy and Smith, teachers particularly note improvement in student writing.

Further supportive findings come from a study designed for different purposes, the Elementary Literacy Study of the Stanford Teacher Assessment Project. This project, which explored alternative approaches to teacher certification, included a substudy in which 25 elementary teachers gathered portfolios to document literature-based reading instruction (Shulman, 1988; Wolf, in press). Project assistants periodically visited each teacher to discuss portfolio entries; a guidebook gave direction to the process. Portfolio entries included lists of books read and students' responses to the books. Teachers documented student progress with interviews, surveys, and work samples such as story graphs and semantic maps.

At the year's end, master teachers and university researchers reviewed the material to assess teachers' planning and use of the portfolios. Results showed that teachers from diverse school contexts could assemble student information in ways that were meaningful to review teams from equally diverse settings. Mechanical aggregation of the data would be difficult to imagine; expert judgment was an essential feature of the process.

Another important finding was the strong professional impact of giving teachers guidance in setting up a portfolio system. State and district personnel aiming to implement portfolios might find the details of value because portfolio efforts without similar support structures have yielded disappointing results (Freedman, 1990). Unfortunately, the Stanford project did not study whether teachers continued with portfolios once the support was gone.

Succeeding with Alternative Assessment

In an insightful essay on portfolios, Bird (1989) noted that practical application is moving far in advance of model building, and warned that overemphasis on practice and disregard for theory could undermine the idea's potential. Linn, Baker, and Dunbar (in press) lay a theoretical groundwork by suggesting several criteria for alternative assessments:

- Are the consequences for schooling an improvement over present practice? Do teachers respond to the innovations with broader, more meaningful, and fairer instruction?

- Is the content of the assessment an improvement over present practice? Is it high quality, cognitively complex, and related to students' backgrounds and to the tasks they will encounter in life after school?

- How do the new methods match up against the criteria for today's tests: reliability, validity, cost, and efficiency?

Hiebert & Calfee

These are hard questions that deserve answers. Our review of the literature suggests that if performance and portfolio assessments are to have a positive impact at the classroom and policy levels, four issues require attention: clarity of purpose, use of multiple performance indicators, attention to student diversity, and support for professional development.

Clarity of Purpose

Why the need for alternative assessments in reading and writing? The consensus is that these alternatives are time consuming, costly, of uncertain reliability, and difficult to aggregate for policy purposes (Haertel, in press). Present enthusiasm will surely dissipate unless advocates can show that the benefits outweigh the costs. The argument rests on two distinct purposes served by alternative assessment: (1) a valid connection to high-level literacy outcomes, and (2) the potential to strengthen district, state, and national indicators of literacy.

The first purpose is more directly linked to the educational process. Assessment is part of a tripartite system along with curriculum and instruction (Calfee & Hiebert, 1988, 1990). Alternative assessment methods that spring directly from instructional processes are more likely to mirror student learning. In this model, the teacher decides what to teach, how to teach, and whether students have achieved their objectives. Moreover, the teacher is responsible for explaining the system to parents and administrators; it is not enough to say, "I use the ABC reading system, the test says that Johnny is reading at the 3.5 grade level, and that's why I've assigned a particular book and other materials." Nor does it suffice to assert, "Trust me; I know what I'm doing."

Most educators agree that assessment of critical literacy—the higher-level capabilities involved in comprehending, composing, and communicating—is beyond the reach of group-administered paper-and-pencil tasks. These abilities emerge in the flow of complex activities performed by groups of students working under the teacher's guidance. The teacher is in a unique position to observe and document performance and understanding. Viewed in this manner, assessment is a daunting task, requiring both professional knowledge and wisdom.

The second purpose of alternative performance assessments is to bridge the chasm between policymakers and teachers. Research has shown that teachers' judgments about student achievement are generally both consistent and valid (Hoge & Coladarci, 1989); thus, they can be an excellent way to complement the information from standardized tests.

These two purposes are synergistic: as performance-based techniques become more rigorous, they attract greater attention from policymakers; as teachers realize that their assessments are taken seriously, they refine their methods.

Under what conditions can teacher assessments serve as indicators of student achievement? Three points keep reappearing in published articles: common meaning, common routines, and common scoring. Not surprisingly, this list comes from administrators, not teachers. Administrators need assurance that achievement data do not vary widely in meaning among teachers, that performance data are gathered in a standardized manner, and that the outcomes can be aggregated. Standardized tests meet these criteria quite well—as long as no one looks carefully at "real" meaning.

The three criteria are sensible, but they can undercut the purposes of alternative assessment methods unless care is taken to sustain the instructing function while arranging for the reporting role. Valencia's (1990) proposal combines the standardization needed by policymakers and the flexibility that teachers require. Portfolios would include three entries: *required* (everyone assesses the same thing in the same way), *semirequired* (teachers and students have a choice in developing certain entries), and *open-ended* (teachers and students select works that highlight specific accomplishments).

This design provides a helpful framework for reviewing state efforts to mount large-scale portfolio and performance assessment, while connecting teachers to the fundamental purpose of this type of assessment. We see encouraging signs in the collaboration between teachers and policymakers in developing new approaches. The evidence suggests that teachers are willing and able to take on this responsibility, given time and a guiding framework. Documen-

Hiebert & Calfee

tation of these activities is sparse, however, mostly in the form of news releases.

The Michigan and Illinois reading assessments described earlier both rely on required components. These systems use multiple choice formats, but they attempt to tap underlying reading processes in addition to surface-level skills. Maine has moved a step further by asking students to read ten authentic texts and answer open-ended questions (Maine Department of Education, 1987).

Michigan and Illinois built their assessment programs through collaboration between two previously isolated groups: curriculum specialists and measurement experts. In Michigan, the groups agreed on assessment goals before developing the test (Roeber & Dutcher, 1989; Wixson et al., 1987). The impetus for a change in assessment measures came from curriculum specialists after the Michigan Reading Association adopted an innovative reading framework in 1983.

A second example comes from the California writing assessment, where teacher involvement has ranged from planning the tests to supporting students in the classroom to evaluating and interpreting achievement. Teachers' involvement in the early stages of test development reflects an openness to collaboration found in several states (Moses, 1990). In the past, teachers might have been asked to score protocols following guidelines developed by others; in California they are asked to select topics, prepare instructions, and construct scoring rubrics. These three facets are at the core of the writing assessment (Huot, 1990).

Teachers have played an active role in setting goals for the Vermont project described earlier, as well as in creating techniques for collecting and evaluating data. Their plan, which incorporates all three facets in Valencia's design, demands a lot of the classroom teacher. As the program evolves, participants may need to remind themselves of the original purposes. At a statewide meeting in September 1990, many teachers expressed concern about the workload demands, lack of technical expertise, and methods of teacher evaluation (Rothman, 1990b). These comments suggest that engaging a small, active group of teachers in the design of a statewide assessment system does not guarantee approval from the entire teaching force.

A common vision is most likely to emerge (and remain) when the participants focus on concepts as well as routines. For instance, in a school district studied by Hagerty, Hiebert, and Owens (1989), teachers responded to the school board's request for information on students' growth in literature-based instruction. Teachers agreed to gather comparable data (literature logs, writing samples, miscue analyses, and student interviews about literacy strategies and attitudes) to allow aggregation. While the additional work was a burden, teachers believed that it was worthwhile because the measures provided better indicators of their instruction and summaries of the information were studied by the school board.

We have emphasized the importance of a clear purpose because we have found two recurring threats in the examples we have studied. First, in the absence of a well-articulated set of goals, alternative assessment techniques—even though solidly grounded in classroom practice—can become so routine and decontextualized that they lose the feeling of authenticity that validated them at the outset. If techniques take over, even the most innovative performance and portfolio practices can be distorted to serve mundane purposes. As Linn et al. (in press) observe, "We should not be satisfied, for example, if the introduction of a direct writing assessment led to great amounts of time being devoted to the preparation of brief compositions following a formula that works well in producing highly rated essays in a 20-minute time limit." The same observation could be applied if excessive amounts of time are spent on perfecting portfolio entries that are part of a prescribed assessment, while other valid activities that are not part of the portfolio assessment receive short shrift.

The second threat is that even if the methods remain true to the aims of authentic literacy assessment, the effort may fail to connect to policy levels that bring the information to public attention. The bureaucratic proclivity is to report simple data. In NAEP, for instance, a rich array of indicators are available to inform reading and writing performance (Mullis, Owens, & Phillips, 1990). Newspaper reports, however, tend to reduce rich data to a few snippets: scores are up or down since the previous assessment; minorities are still doing worse than mainstream students. The replacement of standardized tests by classroom portfolios is no guarantee that legislators, administrators, or practitioners will know how to employ the information effectively.

Using Multiple Indicators

Everyone knows that kicking the tires is no way to judge a used car. A serious evaluation entails looking at all the major systems, probably consulting an expert on technical matters. The same principle holds for educational assessments. A standardized test is one of many ways of evaluating students' abilities and progress. Just as kicking a tire *may* tell you something about a car, multiple choice scores may say something about achievement. The format has both advantages and limitations: content coverage is broad but thin; any student can complete a multiple choice test, but the task reveals little about reflective and productive capabilities; scoring is objective but provides no room for professional judgment.

The performance tests now being recommended for state adoption also have strengths and weaknesses. Many of these programs standardize the topic, the task, and the conditions of administration, which solves some problems but causes others. Some of the more readily identified problems with performance tests are that time may limit test coverage to one or two topics, students who have not been effectively taught to express themselves in writing or speech may be at a disadvantage, and subjective evaluation allows the possibility of bias.

Alternative assessments grounded in classroom practice are naturally inclined to rely on numerous sources of evidence; capable teachers seldom rely on a single test score. Little attention has been directed toward creating standards in this area, however. Valencia, McGinley, and Pearson (1990) have proposed three criteria for classroom-based assessment: *structure* (Is the assessment standardized or open-ended?), *intrusiveness* (Does the test occur regularly or is it special?), and *locus of control* (Is assessment determined by the student or by the teacher?). Variation in the facets will likely yield multiple perspectives.

As classroom assessments are taken more seriously for district and state accountability, they must not lose the features that set them apart from standardized tests. Calfee and Drum (1979) suggested three criteria for classroom assessments: *profile information* (the data show students' strengths and needs), *discriminability* (performance is all-or-none rather than normally distributed and criterion-referenced rather than norm-referenced), and *suitability* (feedback is available immediately; the test is "open" and can be repeated).

Finally, because performance assessments are more sensitive to instruction than standardized tests, they provide a unique view of instructional effectiveness. This feature, which is of particular importance in many state programs, is a virtue from some viewpoints but a shortcoming from others. Ideally, assessment is integrated with curriculum and instruction planning, guiding decisions about what is taught and how. The teacher then has many data sources for reaching summative judgments about student achievement, including final products, classroom observations, and students' explanations during a project. However, this ideal assumes that (1) all teachers share common concepts of curriculum and instruction, and (2) all teachers are competent at helping all students realize their potential in achieving mandated educational goals. Otherwise, performance tests are likely to reflect instructional opportunities more than student performance, but with the lens aimed at the student rather than at instruction.

The critical role of convergent evidence from a number of sources to support the validity of an assessment is the foundation for current test standards (Messick, 1989). Unfortunately, the dominant traditions in psychometric theory and practice are poorly suited to this idea. Performance and portfolio assessments provide a new opportunity to validate assessments by collecting data from multiple sources.

Performance assessment is an ideal vehicle for enhancing convergent validity for two reasons. The first is a practical matter: many teachers intuitively search for multiple indicators of student strengths and needs. The third grader who is struggling with writing mechanics but is adept in making oral presentations requires a different assessment approach than one who has the mechanics but lacks imagination. One student may thrive on flowery novels while

Hiebert & Calfee

another enjoys writing reports in science. Both read and write capably under some conditions and less well in other contexts.

The second reason for the promise of performance assessment is technical. Generalizability theory (Cronbach et al., 1972; Shavelson, Webb, & Rowley, 1989) provides a method for examining data from many sources for both internal consistency (reliability) and external relevance (validity). The method has been available for almost two decades, but educators rarely use it in assessment. The basic idea is simple: if a student's achievement profile looks similar over variations in task, topic, time, and other factors, the profile is trustworthy. This approach has potential as an integrated framework for handling reliability and validity. The need for improvement in present techniques is highlighted by Linn et al. (in press), who note that "reliability has been overemphasized at the expense of validity, and validity has been viewed too narrowly."

Student Diversity

However performance is assessed, appropriateness and fairness for individual students is a thorny issue. We assume that all students possess the potential to achieve high levels of intellectual and linguistic competence in the use of literacy (Calfee & Nelson-Barber, 1991). When a student performs poorly on a test, the first question is whether the results are a valid indicator of student achievement.

Large-scale standardized tests gather the same information under the same circumstances from all students. In a certain sense, tasks like the directed reading lesson, with its typical questioning of vocabulary and comprehension share the aim of eliciting similar information from all students. These tasks contrast with instruction that seeks to accommodate children with different interests, backgrounds, cultures, and languages.

Portfolio and performance assessments have a similar potential for individualization. At one extreme is a 15-minute writing test in which sixth graders pen a letter to the school board about a proposed school regulation. This task is no more likely than a multiple choice test to let all youngsters display their talents and limitations. At the other extreme, the exhibition concept (Sizer, 1990) permits teachers to collaborate with students in deciding on topic, format, and standards for evaluation. If a school regulation is the topic, a student might make the argument verbally, in writing, or through an art project.

Performance and portfolio assessments should have advantages over standardized formats for accommodating cultural and linguistic diversity. Assessment outcomes play a larger role in determining educational opportunities for culturally and linguistically diverse students than for mainstream groups (Miramontes & Commins, 1991). Thus, the first requirement for assessment innovations is not to harm diverse students. The possibilities for enhancing instructional decisions seem promising, although relatively little has been written on this topic.

Garcia and Pearson (1991) suggest that the keys to realizing the potential of alternative approaches for student equity are greater flexibility in assessment approaches and improvement in teachers' capacity to make informed professional judgments. Flexibility comes from coupling performance to the classroom situation, providing support and guidance, connecting students' backgrounds to the task demands, and allowing pupils to express themselves in the form most accessible to them for a particular purpose. These practices will foster high levels of performance instead of raising obstacles to students' success. The ideal is to eliminate hurdles that are not essential to the primary objective (Calfee & Venezky, 1969).

Obstructions in performance tests can be subtle. Heath (1980) found that standardized instructional routines undercut the performance of minority students. Basal discussions, for instance, proved mysterious to black rural children. Accustomed to genuine discourse exchanges, they were puzzled when teachers asked questions from the basal manual that they clearly knew the answers to. The teacher viewed students' failure to respond as evidence of poor achievement. From the children's perspective, however, the questions made no sense and did not merit a response. Similarly, Burke, Pflaum, and Knafle (1982) found that the efforts of students who spoke black dialect to make sense of text material were interpreted as poor reading. A recent NAEP writing assessment showed that Hispanic and African-American students lost ground to white students when additional time was allowed; the white students apparently used the extra time to improve their performance (NAEP, 1990). The issue is clearly complicated by other factors; recall the finding reported earlier in this chapter by Simmons (1990) showing the opposite pattern.

Assessing the achievement of students whose first language is not English is a particular challenge. Portfolios may be the best way of handling the complex array of linguistic and cultural differences, but fundamental issues remain to be addressed. For instance, if a student inserts Spanish expressions when writing or speaking in English, how should the insertions be evaluated? Professional writers often employ this device to good advantage. Reyes (1990) discovered that bilingual students showed normal learning progress in Spanish compositions—but only English writing samples counted in the district assessment. Thus, Spanish speaking students were at a disadvantage.

Which language is involved makes a difference. English resembles Spanish in form and structure; the correspondence between English and many other languages is more complex. The culture also matters. Performance-based methods may actually penalize youngsters whose culture discourages less than perfect public exhibitions. Group-administered multiple choice approaches disregard these issues in the name of objectivity. Performance-based methods provide the opportunity to address student diversity, but they are no guarantee of success.

Support for Teachers

Any major change in traditions or routines causes stress. Those who are asked to change may need assistance. For the past three decades, reading and writing assessments have been dominated by externally developed and mandated tests. The rise of alternative assessments has considerable potential for improving curriculum and instruction. But this promise will not be realized unless teachers receive institutional support to practice their craft in a fundamentally different manner.

To address this matter adequately would require an entire chapter in itself. We will insert only a couple of comments here. First, some observers have proposed that changes in assessment (and subsequently in instruction) will come as teachers gain greater power within the educational system (Cambourne & Turbill, 1990; Johnston, 1984, 1989). We believe that the issue needs to be addressed directly rather than incidentally.

Second, an effective approach might be for teachers in preservice programs to construct their own portfolios, including cumulative records of their experiences as well as documents of student achievement (Berliner, 1985). Investigations along these lines support the effectiveness of explicit professional development in alternative assessment. For instance, Richert (1990) found that portfolios coupled with peer discussion had significant impact on student teachers' development. Novice teachers who "captioned" their journals were especially aided in reflecting on their growth. This approach stands in stark contrast to the current emphasis on routinized activities, in which student teachers follow instructions with little understanding or purpose (Goodlad, 1990).

Conclusions

Recently, and for the first time in decades, a classroom teacher received a research award from a professional organization (Rothman, 1990a). Nancie Atwell won the Russell Award for Distinguished Research from the National Council of Teachers of English for her work, *In the Middle: Writing, Reading, and Learning with Adolescents* (1987). Throughout our chapter, a recurring theme has been the potential of alternative assessment methods to reestablish the classroom teacher as a professional whose role includes making informed judgments about student achievement. We think teachers are best positioned to make judgments in assessments designed to support effective instruction. In addition, the accountability needs of policymakers and the public will be best served when teachers' judgments complement standardized assessment information. At the heart of this proposition is a shift in the task of teaching from the execution of assembly-line routines toward the professional roles exemplified by Atwell.

The current interest in alternative assessment methods offers a window of opportunity to realize such visions. As Brown (1989) argues, these methods have the potential to capture students' reasoning and communication competence in authentic settings and to test the type of "thoughtful" literacy students need to thrive in the diverse, technological society of the twenty-first century. This opportunity brings both challenge and adversity.

On the one hand, the best that can be gained from authentic assessment will dramatically alter public discussions and decisions about schooling. The move beyond a skills-oriented concept of reading and writing will require professional judgment. Medical doctors rely on complex instruments to augment their craft, but they do not leave significant decisions to machines. Neither should teachers.

On the other hand, the present interest in alternative assessment springs as much from districts and states as from classrooms. Convinced that multiple choice methods have inadvertently promoted a recognition mentality about schooling, policymakers are seeking to drive curriculum and instruction toward a greater emphasis on higher-level thought and language. Although well intended, this effort faces perils from at least two sources. The first is the press for standardization. The need for design and structure in assessment is clear, but this need can subvert the portfolio concept when it leads to fixed topics, tasks, time, and conditions. The second danger arises when external authorities fail to support the professional development required for appropriate application of new ideas and methods. We have noted examples in which states and districts have called on teachers for advice and involvement. These activities typically have engaged a fairly small group of practitioners for small amounts of time on a limited set of issues. A more comprehensive and coherent effort is needed.

We think the potential in alternative assessment is most likely to be realized through a better balance of power between policy and practice. The fundamental issues at the core of authentic assessment play out in the classroom during the interplay between teacher and students, a marvelous blend of art and science and of intuition and research. To skeptics who ask whether we can really trust teachers to judge student achievement, the answer is that we must.

For the past three decades, parents who are curious about report cards have been the primary audience for teacher judgments. Alternative assessments open the way for teachers to replace standardized tests as the source of information on students' attainment of critical literacy goals. This shift will demand from the teaching profession a level of articulateness that blends the skills of applied social science with a passionate appreciation for the value of children. As we move toward this goal, we may well approach the time when today's standardized tests are viewed as "alternative assessments."

References

Afflerbach, P. (1990). The statewide assessment of reading. In P. Afflerbach (Ed.), *Issues in statewide reading assessments.* Washington, DC: American Research Institutes.

Allington, R.L. (1986). Policy constraints and effective compensatory reading instruction: A review. In J.V. Hoffman (Ed.), *Effective teaching of reading: Research and practice* (pp. 261-289). Newark, DE: International Reading Association.

Applebee, A.N., Langer, J.A., & Mullis, I.V.S. (1989). *America at the crossroads.* Princeton, NJ: Educational Testing Service/National Assessment of Educational Progress.

Aschbacher, P.R. (1990, June). *State activity and interest in performance-based assessment.* Paper presented at the annual meeting of the Educational Commission of the States, Colorado Department of Education, Boulder, CO.

Atwell, N. (1987). *In the middle: Writing, reading, and learning with adolescents.* Portsmouth, NH: Boynton/Cook.

Barrs, M., Ellis, S., Hester, H., & Thomas, A. (1988). *Primary language record.* Portsmouth, NH: Heinemann.

Berliner, D.B. (1985). Laboratory settings and the study of teacher education. *Journal of Teacher Education, 36,* 2-8.

Bird, T. (1989). The schoolteacher's portfolio: An essay on possibilities. In J. Millman & L. Darling-Hammond (Eds.), *Handbook of teacher evaluation: Elementary and secondary personnel* (2nd ed.). Newbury Park, CA: Sage.

Brandt, R. (Ed.). (1989). Special issue on redirecting assessment. *Educational Leadership, 46.*

Brewer, R. (1989, June). *State assessments of student performance: Vermont.* Paper presented at the annual meeting of the Education Commission of the States, Colorado Department of Education, Boulder, CO.

Brown, R. (1989). Testing and thoughtfulness. *Educational Leadership, 46,* 31-34.

Burke, S.M., Pflaum, S.W., & Knafle, J.D. (1982). The influence of black English on diagnosis of reading in learning disabled and normal readers. *Journal of Learning Disabilities, 15,* 19-22.

Burstall, C. (1989, June). *Integrated assessment in the United Kingdom.* Paper presented at the annual meeting of the Education Commission of the States, Colorado Department of Education, Boulder, CO.

Calfee, R.C. (Ed.). (1982). Special issue on assessment of formal school language: Reading, writing, and speaking. *Topics in Language Disorders, 2.*

Calfee, R.C. (1988). *Indicators of literacy.* Santa Monica, CA: Rand Corporation, Center for Policy Research in Education.

Calfee, R.C., & Drum, P. (1979). How the researcher can help the reading teacher with classroom assessment. In L.B. Resnick & P.A. Weaver (Eds.), *Theory and practice of early reading.* Hillsdale, NJ: Erlbaum.

Calfee, R.C., & Hiebert, E.H. (1988). The teacher's role in using assessment to improve learning. In C.V. Bunderson (Ed.), *Assessment in the service of learning.* Princeton, NJ: Educational Testing Service.

Calfee, R.C., & Hiebert, E.H. (1990). Classroom assessment of literacy. In R. Barr, M. Kamil, P. Mosenthal, & P.D. Pearson (Eds.), *Handbook of research on reading* (2nd ed.). White Plains, NY: Longman.

Calfee, R.C., & Nelson-Barber, S. (1991). Diversity and constancy in human thinking: Critical literacy as amplifier of intellect and experience. In E.H. Hiebert (Ed.), *Literacy for a diverse society: Perspectives, practices, and policies* (pp. 44-57). New York: Teachers College Press.

Calfee, R.C., & Venezky, R.L. (1969). Component skills in beginning reading. In K.S. Goodman & J.T. Fleming (Eds.), *Psycholinguistics and the teaching of reading.* Newark, DE: International Reading Association.

California Department of Education. (1987). *California English/language arts framework.* Sacramento, CA: author.

California Department of Education. (1990). *CAP elementary field test reading/writing test.* Sacramento, CA: CAP/author.

Cambourne, B., & Turbill, J. (1990). Assessment in whole-language classrooms: Theory into practice. *Elementary School Journal, 90,* 337-349.

Camp, R. (1990). Thinking together about portfolios. *The Quarterly of the National Writing Project & the Center for the Study of Writing, 12,* 8-14, 27.

Cannell, J.J. (1988). Nationally normed elementary achievement testing in America's public schools: How all 50 states are above the national average. *Educational Measurement: Issues and Practice, 7,* 5-9.

Carter, M.A., & Tierney, R.J. (1988). *Reading and writing growth: Using portfolios in assessment.* Paper presented at the annual meeting of the National Reading Conference, Tucson, AZ.

Claggett, F., Cooper, C., & Brenneman, B. (1989). *Writing achievement of California eighth graders: Year two (1987-1988 annual report).* Sacramento, CA: California Department of Education.

Clay, M. (1985). *Early detection of reading difficulties* (3rd ed.). Portsmouth, NH: Heinemann.

Cole, N.S. (1988). A realist's appraisal of the prospects for unifying instruction and assessment. In C.V. Bunderson (Ed.), *Assessment in the service of learning*. Princeton, NJ: Educational Testing Service.

Collins, A., Brown, J.S., & Newman, S.E. (1989). Cognitive apprenticeship: Teaching the craft of reading, writing, and mathematics. In L.B. Resnick (Ed.), *Knowing, learning, and instruction: Essays in honor of Robert Glaser* (pp. 453-494). Hillsdale, NJ: Erlbaum.

Cronbach, L.J., Gleser, G.C., Nanda, H., & Rajaratnam, N. (1972). *The dependability of behavioral measurements*. New York: Wiley.

Crooks, T.J. (1988). The impact of classroom evaluation practices on students. *Review of Educational Research, 58*, 438-481.

Dillon, D. (Ed.). (1990). Special issue on evaluation of language and learning. *Language Arts, 67*.

Dorr-Bremme, D.W., & Herman, J.L. (1986). *Assessing student achievement: A profile of classroom practices* (CSE Monograph #11). Los Angeles, CA: University of California at Los Angeles, Center for the Study of Evaluation.

Drum, P.A., Calfee, R.C., & Cook, L.K. (1980). The effects of surface structure variables on performance in reading comprehension. *Reading Research Quarterly, 16*, 486-514.

Edelsky, C., & Harman, S. (1988). One more critique of reading tests—with two differences. *English Education, 20*, 157-171.

Educational Testing Service. (1990). *Integrated reading performance record on the 1992 NAEP Reading Assessment*. Princeton, NJ: Author/National Assessment of Educational Progress.

Eresh, J.T. (1990, April). *Portfolio assessment as a means of self-directed learning.* Paper presented at the annual conference of the American Educational Research Association, Boston, MA.

Flood, J., & Lapp, D. (1989). Reporting reading progress: A comparison portfolio for parents. *The Reading Teacher, 42*(7), 508-514.

Foertsch, M., & Pearson, P.D. (1987, December). *Reading assessment in basal reading series and standardized tests.* Paper presented at the annual meeting of the National Reading Conference, St. Petersburg, FL.

Freedman, S.W. (1990). *Evaluating writing: Linking large-scale testing and classroom assessment.* Paper presented to the Council of State School Officers, Berkeley, CA.

Garcia, G.E., & Pearson, P.D. (1991). The role of assessment in a diverse society. In E.H. Hiebert (Ed.), *Literacy for a diverse society: Perspectives, practices, and policies* (pp. 253-278). New York: Teachers College Press.

Gil, D., Polin, R.M., Vinsonhaler, J.F., & Van Roekel, J. (1980). *The impact of training on diagnostic consistency* (Technical Report No. 67). East Lansing, MI: Institute for Research on Teaching.

Goodlad, J.I. (1990). *Teachers for our nation's schools.* San Francisco, CA: Jossey-Bass.

Goodman, K.S., Goodman, Y.M., & Hood, W.J. (1989). *The whole language evalua-tion book*. Portsmouth, NH: Heinemann.

Goodman, K.S., Shannon, P., Freeman, Y., & Murphy, S. (1988). *Report card on basal readers*. New York: Richard C. Owen.

Gray, W.S. (1920). The value of informal tests of reading achievement. *Journal of Educational Research, 14*, 103-111.

Greer, E.A., Pearson, P.D., & Meyer, L.A. (1990, December). *A multifaceted investi-gation of the validity of the reading portion of the Illinois Goal Assessment pro-gram*. Paper presented at the annual meeting of the National Reading Conference, Miami, FL.

Haertel, E. (in press). Performance measurement. In M. Alkin (Ed.), *Encyclopedia of educational research* (6th ed.). New York: Macmillan.

Hagerty, P., Hiebert, E.H., & Owens, M.K. (1989). Students' comprehension, writing, and perceptions in two approaches to literacy instruction. In S. McCormick & J. Zutell (Eds.), *Cognitive and social perspectives for literacy research and instruc-tion* (pp. 453-460). Chicago, IL: National Reading Conference.

Harris, L.A., & Lalik, R.M. (1987). Teachers' use of informal reading inventories: An example of school constraints. *The Reading Teacher, 40*, 624-630.

Heath, S.B. (1980). Questioning at home and at school: A comparative study. In G. Spindler (Ed.), *Doing the ethnography of schooling: Educational anthropology in action*. Orlando, FL: Holt, Rinehart & Winston.

Hiebert, E.H., Hutchinson, T.A., & Raines, P.A. (in press). Alternative assessments of literacy: Teachers' actions and parents' reactions. In S. McCormick & J. Zutell (Eds.), *Fortieth yearbook of the National Reading Conference*. Chicago, IL: Na-tional Reading Conference.

Hill, C., & Parry, K. (1988). *Reading assessment: Autonomous and pragmatic models of literacy* (Literacy Center Report 88-2). New York: Teachers College Press.

Hoge, R.D., & Coladarci, T. (1989). Teacher-based judgments of academic achieve-ment: A review of the literature. *Review of Educational Research, 3*, 297-313.

Howard, K. (1990). Making the writing portfolio real. *The Quarterly of the National Writing Project & the Center for the Study of Writing, 12*, 4-7, 27.

Huot, B. (1990). The literature on direct writing assessment: Major concerns and prevailing trends. *Review of Educational Research, 60*, 237-263.

Johnston, P.H. (1984). Assessment in reading. In P.D. Pearson (Ed.), *Handbook of reading research*. White Plains, NY: Longman.

Johnston, P.H. (1989). Constructive evaluation and the improvement of teaching and learning. *Teachers College Record, 90*, 509-528.

Johnston, P.H., Weiss, P.B., & Afflerbach, P. (1989). *Teachers' evaluation of teaching and learning in literacy and literature*. Albany, NY: Center for the Learning and Teaching of Literature.

Koretz, D. (1988). Arriving in Lake Wobegon: Are standardized tests exaggerating achievement and distorting instruction? *American Educator, 12*, 8-52.

Langer, J.A. (1987). The construction of meaning and the assessment of compre-hension: An analysis of reader performance on standardized test items. In R.O. Freedle & R.P. Duran (Eds.), *Cognitive and linguistic analyses of test perform-*

ance. Norwood, NJ: Ablex.

Lidz, C. (Ed.). (1987). *Dynamic assessment: An interactional approach to evaluating learning potential.* New York: Guilford.

Linn, R.L. (1990). Essentials of student assessment: From accountability to instructional aid. *Teachers College Record, 91,* 422-436.

Linn, R.L., Baker, E.L., & Dunbar, S.B. (in press). Complex, performance-based assessment: Expectations and validation criteria. *Educational Researcher.*

Linn, R.L., Graue, M.E., & Sanders, N.M. (1990). Comparing state and district test results to national norms: The validity of claims that "Everyone is above average." *Educational Measurement, 9,* 5-14.

Maine Department of Education. (1987). *Maine Educational Assessment.* Augusta, ME: Department of Educational & Cultural Services.

Massachusetts Department of Education (1987). *Reading and thinking: A new framework for comprehension.* Quincy, MA: Massachusetts Educational Assessment Program.

Mathews, J. (1990). From computer management to portfolio assessment. *The Reading Teacher, 43,* 420-421.

McLain, E. (1989). *Juneau integrated language arts portfolio for grade 1.* Juneau, AK: Juneau School District.

McNeil, L.M. (1988). Contradictions of control, part 2: Teachers, students, and curriculum. *Phi Delta Kappan, 70,* 433-438.

Mehrens, W.A., & Kaminski, J. (1988, April). *Using commercial test preparation materials for improving standardized test scores: Fruitful, fruitless, or fraudulent?* Paper presented at the annual meeting of the National Council on Measurement in Education, New Orleans, LA.

Messick, S. (1989). Validity. In R.L. Linn (Ed.), *Educational measurement* (3rd ed., pp. 13-103). New York: Macmillan.

Miramontes, O.B., & Commins, N.L. (1991). Redefining literacy and literacy contexts: Discovering a community of learners. In E.H. Hiebert (Ed.), *Literacy for a diverse society: Perspectives, practices, and policies* (pp. 75-89). New York: Teachers College Press.

Morrow, L.M., & Smith, J.K. (Eds.). (1990). *Assessment for instruction in early literacy.* Englewood Cliffs, NJ: Prentice Hall.

Moses, S. (1990, November). Assessors seek test that teaches. *The APA Monitor, 21*(11), 1, 37.

Mullis, I.V.S., Owens, E.H., & Phillips, G.W. (1990). *Accelerating academic achievement: A summary of findings from 20 years of NAEP.* Princeton, NJ: Educational Testing Service/National Assessment of Educational Progress.

Murphy, S., & Smith, M.A. (1990). Talking about portfolios. *The Quarterly of the National Writing Project & the Center for the Study of Writing, 12,* 1-3, 24-27.

National Assessment of Educational Progress. (1990). *Learning to write in our nation's schools.* Princeton, NJ: Educational Testing Service/Author.

Northwest Regional Educational Laboratory. (1990, July). *Portfolio bibliography.* Portland, OR: Author.

Pipho, C. (1985, May). Tracking the reforms, part 5: Testing—can it measure the success of the reform movement? *Education Week, 4*(35), 19.

Point/counterpoint: State by state comparisons on national assessments. (1989-1990, December/January). *Reading Today, 1,* 11-15.

Popham, W.J., Cruse, K.L., Rankin, S.C., Sandifer, P.D., & Williams, P.L. (1985). Measurement-driven instruction: It's on the road. *Phi Delta Kappan, 66,* 628-634.

Reading Consensus Planning Project for 1992 NAEP. (1990). *Reading framework: 1992 National Assessment of Educational Progress reading assessment.* Washington, DC: Council for Chief State School Officers.

Resnick, L.B., & Resnick, D.P. (1990). Tests as standards of achievement in schools. In J. Pfleiderer (Ed.), *The uses of standardized tests in American education.* Princeton, NJ: Educational Testing Service.

Reyes, M. de la Luz (1990, April). *Comparison of L1 and L2 pre- and postwriting samples of bilingual students.* Paper presented at the annual meeting of the American Educational Research Association, Boston, MA.

Richert, A.E. (1990). Teaching teachers to reflect: A consideration of program structure. *Journal of Curriculum Studies, 22,* 509-528.

Roeber, E., & Dutcher, P. (1989). Michigan's innovative assessment of reading. *Educational Leadership, 46,* 64-69.

Rothman, R. (1990a, December 12). Award heralds recognition of the role of teachers as researchers. *Education Week,* 1, 36.

Rothman, R. (1990b, October 10). Large "faculty meeting" ushers in pioneering assessment in Vermont. *Education Week,* 1, 18.

Ruddell, R.B. (1985). Knowledge and attitudes toward testing: Field educators and legislators. *The Reading Teacher, 38,* 538-543.

Salmon-Cox, L. (1981). Teachers and standardized achievement tests: What's really happening? *Phi Delta Kappan, 62,* 631-634.

Shavelson, R.J., Webb, N.M., & Rowley, G. (1989). *American Psychologist, 44,* 922-932.

Shepard, L. (1988, April). *Should instruction be measurement-driven?* Paper presented at the annual meeting of the American Educational Research Association, New Orleans, LA.

Shulman, L.S. (1988). A union of insufficiencies: Strategies for teacher assessment in a period of educational reform. *Educational Leadership, 45,* 36-41.

Simmons, J. (1990). Portfolios as large-scale assessment. *Language Arts, 67,* 262-268.

Sizer, T. (1990). Performances and exhibitions: The demonstration of mastery. *Horace, 6*(3), 1-12.

Spivey, N.N., & King, J.R. (1989). Readers as writers composing from sources. *Reading Research Quarterly, 24,* 7-26.

Stiggins, R.J. (1985). Improving assessment where it means the most: In the classroom. *Educational Leadership, 43,* 69-74.

Stiggins, R.J. (1987). Design and development of performance assessments. *Educa-*

tional Measurement, 6, 33-42.

Stiggins, R.J., Conklin, N.F., & Bridgeford, N.J. (1986). Classroom assessment: A key to effective education. *Educational Measurement, 5,* 5-17.

Valencia, S. (1990). A portfolio approach to classroom reading assessment: The whys, whats, and hows. *The Reading Teacher, 43,* 338-340.

Valencia, S., McGinley, W., & Pearson, P.D. (1990). Assessing reading and writing. In G. Duffy (Ed.), *Reading in the middle school* (2nd ed.). Newark, DE: International Reading Association.

Valencia, S., & Pearson, P.D. (1987). Reading assessment: Time for a change. *The Reading Teacher, 40,* 726-732.

Wiggins, G. (1989). Teaching to the (authentic) test. *Educational Leadership, 46,* 41-47.

Wixson, K.K., Peters, C.W., Weber, E.M., & Roeber, E.D. (1987). New directions in statewide reading assessment. *The Reading Teacher, 40,* 749-754.

Wolf, D.P. (1989). Portfolio assessment: Sampling student work. *Educational Leadership, 46,* 35-39.

Wolf, K. (in press). The schoolteacher's portfolio: Practical issues in design, implementation, and evaluation. *Phi Delta Kappan.*

CHAPTER 5

The Role of Decoding in Learning to Read

ISABEL L. BECK
CONNIE JUEL

The authors of this chapter emphasize the importance of attaining decoding skills early because this early ability accurately predicts later skill in reading comprehension. Failure to teach the code in a straightforward manner can leave many children without the ability to independently enter the world of quality literature. The authors outline prerequisite understandings about print that help make learning to decode easier. They move on to address the activities that appear to foster such learning. Stressing that phonics is not a single procedure, they note that teachers can use a variety of strategies to show the relationship between letters and sounds. Finally, the authors discuss the strengths and weaknesses of major strategies and offer practical suggestions for ameliorating problems associated with them.

As anyone knows who has both read to young children and watched them begin learning to read, there is a great difference in the sophistication of their abilities in the two arenas. As an illustration, consider a typical activity in a first grade classroom.

Twenty-six first graders are sitting on the floor around their teacher, Ms. Jackson. She opens a copy of McCloskey's (1941, 1969) *Make Way for Ducklings* and shows the children a double-page picture of two mallards flying over a pond. Jackson tells them that the birds are mallards, which are a kind of duck, and begins to read.

As the teacher reads, the children's attention, facial expressions, and giggles (for example, when a policeman stops traffic to let the mallards waddle across the road) suggest that they are enjoying the story. Their giggling also provides evidence that they understand the story. Even stronger evidence of their understanding is found in the discussion Jackson initiates. For example, one of the questions she asks is why the mallards didn't want to live next to foxes and turtles. The only information given in the story is that "[Mrs. Mallard] was not going to raise a family where there might be foxes or turtles." The reason is not explained, yet the children are able to infer that Mrs. Mallard doesn't want to live next door to foxes and turtles because they might harm the ducklings.

The discussion also provides evidence that the children have control over some sophisticated language structures. Consider such complicated syntax as "But the people on the boat threw peanuts into the water, so the Mallards followed them all round the pond and got another breakfast, better than the first." When the teacher asks several of the children what that sentence means, none has difficulty capturing the notion that the mallards liked the peanuts more than what they had gotten to eat on their own.

Most children entering school have fairly sophisticated knowledge about language and stories. The children described here had enough knowledge of syntax, vocabulary, story elements, and aspects of the world around them to comprehend and enjoy *Make Way for Ducklings*. But no story in any first grade preprimer can match the literary quality and level of language found in *Make Way for Ducklings*. Why? Because the children will be unable to read many words and therefore have no reliable way to translate the written text into their familiar spoken form of language. Until their word recognition skill catches up to their language skill, they are unable to independently read a story that matches the sophistication of their spoken vocabularies, concepts, and knowledge.

There has been much legitimate criticism of the reading materials used in early reading instruction. Although these materials need improvement, it is important to acknowledge that because children can recognize only a limited number of words, even the most creatively developed materials cannot compete with stories such as *Make Way for Ducklings*. Our goal as educators is to quickly provide children with the tools they need to read some of the marvelous stories gifted writers have created for them. The major tools we can give children are ones that allow them to decode printed words for themselves. To facilitate a discussion of the issues associated with helping children gain control of the code that links the printed word to the spoken word, let us first define some terms.

Defining Reading Terms

Various terms have been used to describe the way children come to recognize printed words. We begin with a discussion intended to sort out a set of easily confused terms: the code, decoding, word attack, word recognition, phonics, and sight words.

One dictionary definition of *code* is "a system of signals used to represent assigned meanings." Signals can be numbers (as in a military code), dots and dashes (Morse code), or letters (as in an alphabetic language like English). In themselves these signals are meaningless. They become meaning-bearing units only when an individual knows what meanings can be assigned to the signals. When an individual can apply meaning to signals, that person has learned to decode.

In written alphabetic languages such as English, the code involves a system of mappings, or correspondences, between letters and sounds. When an individual has learned those mappings, that person is said to have "broken the code." Now the individual can apply his or her knowledge of the mappings to figure out plausible pronunciations of printed words. Most of the time competent adult readers do not need to apply their knowledge of the mapping system consciously to recognize the words they encounter. If they do encounter a word they have never seen before, however, they are able to bring their knowledge of the code to bear in a deliberate and purposeful way.

A number of terms are used to describe the application of the code when reading. It may be useful to consider the terms in light of two extremes of attention a reader pays to the code. At one extreme readers apply their knowledge of the code immediately and without any apparent attention. The terms used to describe this immediate phenomenon are *word recognition, word identification,* and *sight word recognition.* At the other extreme readers consciously and deliberately apply their knowledge of the mapping system to produce a plausible pronunciation of a word they do not instantly recognize, such as the name of a character an English-speaking reader might encounter in a Russian novel. The term associated with this self-aware "figuring out" is *word attack.*

Individuals involved in either extreme are decoding in that they are using symbols to interpret a unit that bears meaning. Hence, word recognition, word identification, word attack, and sight word recognition are all terms applied to decoding, albeit to decoding with different levels of conscious attention.

Two terms that can be confused are sight word *vocabulary* (sometimes called sight word recognition) and sight word *method.* The former is a critical goal of all reading instruction—that children come to respond to most words at a glance, without conscious attention. This goal should not be confused with the instructional strategy called the sight word method (also known as the whole word or look-say approach), in which words are introduced to children as whole units without analysis of their subword parts. By repeated exposure to words, especially in meaningful contexts, it is expected that children will learn to read the words without any conscious attention to subword units. Hence, sight word recognition, or the development of a sight word vocabulary, is a goal of sight word instruction.

The issue of instructional strategies brings us to the terms *phonics* and *word attack.* Phonics embraces a variety of instructional strategies for bringing attention to parts of words. The parts can be syllables, phonograms (such as *an*), other letter strings (such as *ple*), or single letters. The goal of phonics is to provide students with the mappings between letters and sounds but, unlike the goal of the sight word method, phonics is not an end point. Rather, phonics merely provides a tool that enables students to "attack" the pronunciation of words that are not recognizable at a glance; hence the term word attack.

The Importance of Early Decoding Skill

Early attainment of decoding skill is important because this early skill accurately predicts later skill in reading comprehension. There is strong and persuasive evidence that children who get off to a slow start rarely become strong readers (Stanovich, 1986). Early learning of the code leads to wider reading habits both in and out of school (Juel, 1988). Wide reading provides opportunities to grow in vocabulary, concepts, and knowledge of how text is written. Children who do not learn to decode do not have this avenue for growth. This phenomenon, in which the "rich get richer" (i.e., the children who learn early to decode continue to improve in reading) and the "poor get poorer" (i.e., children who do not learn to decode early become increasingly distanced from the "rich" in reading ability), has been termed the Matthew effect (Stanovich).

The importance of early decoding skill can be illustrated through the findings of several studies. In a longitudinal study of 54 children from first through fourth grades, Juel (1988) found a .88 probability that a child in the bottom quartile on the Iowa Reading Comprehension subtest at the end of first grade will still be a poor reader at the end of fourth grade. Of 24 children who remained poor readers through four grades, only 2 had average decoding skills. By the end of fourth grade the poor decoders still had not achieved the level of decoding that the average/good readers had reached by the beginning of second grade. The poor decoders also had read considerably less than the average/good readers, both in and out of school. They had gained little vocabulary compared with the good decoders, and expressed a real dislike of both reading and the failure associated with reading in school.

Lesgold and Resnick (1982) found that a child's speed of word recognition in first grade was an excellent predictor of that child's reading comprehension in second grade. In a longitudinal study of children learning to read in Sweden, Lundberg (1984) found a .70 correlation between linguistic awareness of words and phonemes in first grade and reading achievement in sixth grade. Moreover, Lundberg found that of 46 children with low reading achievement in first grade, 40 were still poor readers in sixth grade.

Clay (1979) discusses results of a longitudinal study of children learning to read in New Zealand:

> There is an unbounded optimism among teachers that children who are late in starting will indeed catch up. Given time, something will happen! In particular, there is a belief that the intelligent child who fails to learn to read will catch up to his classmates once he has made a start. Do we have any evidence of accelerated progress in late starters? There may be isolated examples which support this hope, but correlations from a follow-up study of 100 children 2 and 3 years after school entry lead me to state rather dogmatically that where a child stood in relation to his age-mates at the end of his first year in school was roughly where one would expect to find him at 7:0 or 8:0 (p. 13).

What Helps Children Learn the Code

The studies reported above all point to the importance of arranging conditions so that children gain reading independence early. The task of learning to decode printed words is made easier when the child has certain prerequisite understandings about print. These include knowing that print is important because it carries a message, that printed words are composed of letters, and that letters correspond to the somewhat distinctive sounds heard in a spoken word. Often these prerequisites develop as a result of a child's having been read to (especially by an adult who has made occasional references to aspects of the print), having attended preschool and kindergarten programs, or having watched instructional television programs like *Sesame Street*. Let us look at these three prerequisites and why children sometimes have difficulty acquiring them.

Printed Words Carry Messages

First, young children need to know that some systematic relationship exists between printed symbols and spoken messages. They need to know that looking at the print itself is important to determine these messages. This idea is not as obvious as it may first appear. Storybooks contain colorful, enticing pictures designed to capture children's interest and attention. In comparison, the black marks at the bottom of the page are rather uninteresting. Likewise, print in the environment is often embedded in rich contexts that are more noticeable and "readable" than the print itself (e.g., for a child, the color and shape of a stop sign has more meaning than the letters forming the word *stop*).

Words Are Composed of Letters

Observations of children's first unguided attempts to use print show that they frequently find some distinctive feature of a word that acts as a cue to identify the word for them (Gates & Boeker, 1923; Gough & Hillinger, 1980). Often this distinctive feature will be tied to a picture or a page location (e.g., *police car* is the last string of letters on the page with a picture of a policeman). Or a child will remember distinctive features of a particular word (e.g., *mallard* is a long string of letters with two straight lines in the middle). Initial letters are frequently used as recall cues (for instance, *duck* starts with a *d*). The problem with this approach is that for each additional word it is harder to find a single, distinctive cue (*d* for *duck* will no longer suffice when *deer* is encountered). At this point, reading can become an increasingly frustrating activity unless a better cue system is developed.

Children often try to combine distinctive features of words (for instance, first letters) with context cues to figure out an unknown word. This hybrid approach is not particularly reliable, however. For example, consider the difficulty a young child would encounter in figuring out an unknown word in the sentence "Mrs. Mallard _____ her eight ducklings." What word fits in the blank? It could be almost any verb. What if the child looked at the first letter (which in this case is *l*), or looked at the first and last letters (*l* and *s*) and approximate length (five letters)? Even with these three feature cues, the word might be *loves, likes, loses,* or *leads,* to list a few. Learning to look at *all* the letters is important.

Letters Correspond to the Sounds in Spoken Words

Once children know that words are composed of letters, they need to be able to map, or translate, the printed letters into sounds. In order to do that, children first need to be able to "hear" the sounds in spoken words—that is, to hear the /at/ sound in *cat* and *fat,* for example, and perceive that the difference between the two words lies in the first sound. (In this chapter slashes // indicate a speech sound.) If children cannot perceive these sound segments, they will encounter difficulty when trying to sound out words, in both reading and writing. This understanding has been termed phonemic awareness.

Phonemic awareness is not a single insight or ability. Rather, there are various phonemic insights, such as being able to rhyme words as in the cat/fat example above, or knowing that *fat* has three distinctive, yet overlapping and abstract, sounds. This last insight is particularly difficult because phonemes often overlap in speech (e.g., we begin saying the /a/ sound in fat while still uttering the /f/).

Although it is not clear how children gain phonemic awareness, certain activities do appear to foster it. Home factors such as time spent on word play, nursery or Dr. Seuss rhymes, and general exposure to storybooks appear to contribute to phonemic awareness. In a 15-month longitudinal study of British children from age 3 years, 4 months, Maclean, Bryant, and Bradley (1987) found a strong relationship between children's early knowledge of nursery rhymes and the later development of phonemic awareness. In addition, phonemic awareness predicted early reading ability. Both relationships were found after controlling for the effects of IQ and socioeconomic status.

There is growing evidence that phonemic awareness can be taught to young children and that such teaching can occur in a playful, interactive way. Lundberg, Frost, and Petersen (1988) showed that preschool children can be trained to manipulate the phonological elements in words. Their 8-month training program involved a variety of games, nursery rhymes, and rhymed stories. A

Beck & Juel

typical game designed to foster syllable synthesis included a troll who told children what they would get as presents through the peculiar method of producing the words syllable by syllable. Each child had to synthesize the syllables in order to figure out what the troll was offering. Children who participated in the training showed considerable gains in some phonemic awareness skills—such as phoneme segmentation—compared with children who did not participate in the program. Positive effects of the preschool training were still evident in children's reading and spelling performance through second grade.

Clay (1979) found that many 6-year-olds who were not making adequate progress learning to read could not "hear" the sound sequences in words. She adapted a phonemic awareness training program developed by the Russian psychologist Elkonin (1973) to train these children. Clay found that the children could learn and apply the strategy of analyzing the sound sequence of words. This strategy improved both their reading and their writing.

Unfortunately, many children come to school without phonemic awareness, and some fail to gain it from their school experiences. Juel, Griffith, and Gough (1985) found that well into first grade the spelling errors of many children were not even in the domain of what has come to be known as invented spellings (such as using the sounds captured in letter names to spell *light* as *lt* or *rain* as *ran*). These researchers found that many children entered first grade with little phonemic awareness and had difficulty learning spelling-sound relationships. For example, these children's misspellings of *rain* used in a sentence included such things as *yes, wetn, wnishire, rur,* and drawings of raindrops. The course of learning the code for these children will be different and more difficult than for children who are able to hear the sounds in spoken words and who know that these sounds can be mapped to letters.

Instructional Approaches

Given that letters and sounds have systematic relationships in an alphabetic language such as English, it stands to reason that those responsible for teaching initial reading would consider telling beginners directly what those relationships are. Indeed, until about 60 years ago this is what most teachers in the United States did. The techniques used, however, left much to be desired.

Phonics: The Past

It is important to recognize that phonics is not a single procedure. Under the label phonics can be found a variety of instructional strategies for teaching the relationship between letters and sounds. It appears that the kind of phonics practiced in the first decades of this century was an elaborated "drill and more drill" method. Diederich (1973) describes the scene:

> Initial instruction in letter-sound relationships and pronunciation rules was done to death...children had to learn so much abstract material by rote before doing any significant amount of reading (p. 7).

To illustrate more concretely what Diederich was describing, picture the following: It is October 1921, and 40 first graders are seated at rows of desks. The teacher stands at the front of the class and points with a long wooden pointer to a wall chart that contains columns of letters and letter combinations. As she points to a column of short vowel and consonant *b* combinations, the class responds with the sound of each combination: /ab/, /eb/, /ib/, /ob/, /ub/. She goes to the next column and the class responds, /bab/, /beb/, /bib/, /bob/, /bub/. Then the teacher asks, "What's the rule?" The children respond in unison, "In a one-syllable word, in which there is a single vowel followed by a consonant...." So it went day after day, with "letter-sound relationships and pronunciation rules...done to death."

It is no wonder that educators as prominent as William S. Gray described this kind of phonics as "heartless drudgery" and urged that it be replaced with what initially was termed the look-say approach and subsequently called the sight word or whole word method. The relief from extended drill with letter sounds, their synthesis into often meaningless syllables, and the recitation of rules of pronunciation is evident in Diederich's (1973) own response to the look-say method:

When [this] writer began his graduate study of education in 1928...no less an authority than Walter Dearborn had to send his students to observe several classes that were learning to read by the new "look-say" method before they would believe that it was possible. When prospective teachers like the students of Walter Dearborn discovered what a relatively painless process the teaching of reading could be, using the...whole word approach, they were not disposed to demand evidence of superior results. It was enough to know that the new method worked about as well as the old and with far less agony (p. 7).

Look-Say

By the 1930s, the look-say method prevailed. The idea behind this approach was that children could learn to recognize words through repeated exposure without direct attention to subword parts. The existence of ideographic writing systems (like Chinese or Japanese Kanji, which is based on Chinese characters) shows that this type of visual learning can occur, but it is difficult. The characters are learned slowly. A child in Japan is expected to learn only 76 Kanji in first grade and 996 by the end of sixth grade. In contrast, many Japanese children enter school already reading Kana, which is based on phonetic segments. Most ideographic writing systems have been (or are in the process of being) replaced by alphabetic ones.

English is not an ideographic written language. To teach it as if it were ignores the systematic relationships between letters and the sounds that underlie them. Proponents of the look-say method have been quick to point out the imperfections of these relationships, which are most apparent in some high frequency words (e.g., *come, said*). It should not be overlooked, however, that the pronunciations of even these irregular words do not deviate widely from their spellings. We do not pronounce *come* as *umbrella*, or *said* as *frog*.

The look-say method continued virtually unchallenged until 1955, when Flesch, in his book *Why Johnny Can't Read*, vehemently attacked the approach and demanded a return to phonics. Although the general public and press reacted favorably to Flesch's book, it was rejected by reviewers in educational journals—chiefly because it took the form of a propagandistic argument that presented conclusions beyond what research evidence allowed. A decade later, Chall's (1967) *Learning to Read: The Great Debate* provided a reasoned presentation of the research with the conclusion that the evidence points to benefit from those programs that include early and systematic phonics. Subsequent researchers confirmed this advantage (e.g., Barr, 1972, 1974, 1975; DeLawter, 1970; Elder, 1971; Evans & Carr, 1983; Guthrie et al., 1976; Johnson & Baumann, 1984; Resnick, 1979; Williams, 1979.)

Phonics: The Present

Several years ago, the National Commission on Reading, comprising a range of representatives from the research community (and sponsored in part by the National Institute of Education), developed a report that synthesized and interpreted the existing body of research on reading. The report, entitled *Becoming a Nation of Readers* (Anderson et al., 1985), observes in its discussion of early reading that "most educators" view phonics instruction as "one of the essential ingredients." It goes on to note: "Thus, the issue is no longer...whether children should be taught phonics. The issues now are specific ones of just how it should be done" (pp. 36-37). Approaches to phonics instruction generally can be described by one of two terms—explicit phonics and implicit phonics, referring to the explicitness with which letter sounds (phonemes) are taught in a given approach.

In explicit phonics, children are directly told the sounds of individual letters (the letter *m* represents the /m/ in *man*). In implicit phonics, children are expected to induce the sounds that correspond to letters from accumulated auditory and visual exposure to words containing those letters (for instance, they would induce /m/ from hearing the teacher read *man, make,* and *mother* as she or he points to the words on the chalkboard). In terms of the effectiveness of one approach over the other, *Becoming a Nation of Readers* observes that "available research does not permit a decisive answer, although the trend of the data favors explicit phonics" (p. 42). Let us look more closely at both approaches, beginning with implicit phonics.

As noted above, in implicit phonics the sounds of individual letters are never pronounced in isolation. Instead, the child is expected to induce these sounds from reading words in stories and lists that contain similar spelling-sound patterns. Continuing with the *m* example, a child who encountered the new word *met* and who had seen and heard *man* and *make* would be instructed to think of other words that begin with the letter *m* in order to identify the sound at the beginning of the new word. In order to comply with the instructions, the child needs to be able to identify distinct sounds in spoken words to make a connection between the sound and the target letter. To be able to induce the sound of the letter *m* or the sound of the *et* phonogram, the child must be able to distinguish between the sound of the initial consonant and the rest of the word. This is a difficult task because in speech the sounds of individual letters actually overlap and blend as a word is pronounced. Thus, in actuality, the ability to extract the sound of a letter from a spoken word is more "in the mind" than "in the mouth."

A problem with implicit phonics is that many children fail to induce the sounds because they are unable to segment a word into distinctive sounds. It takes very sophisticated phonemic awareness to do so. Many children do not come to school with such awareness, yet implicit phonics requires this ability right from the start.

Explicit phonics requires less sophisticated phonemic awareness because the sounds associated with letters are directly provided. Explicit phonics, however, has its own potential problem: the sounds of some consonant letters cannot be said in isolation without adding a schwa, or /uh/ (e.g., the isolated sound of the letter *b* in *bat* is distorted to /buh/). Do we harm children by telling them these distortions? Not if instruction in how to blend letter sounds is provided. In reviewing the research associated with this question, Johnson and Baumann (1984) noted that "there is no substance to the long-held belief that pronouncing sounds in isolation is detrimental" (p. 592). Similarly, the commission that developed *Becoming a Nation of Readers* concluded that "isolating the sounds...and teaching children to blend the sounds of letters together to try to identify words are useful instructional strategies" (p. 42). Thus, the prevailing conclusion seems to be that isolating sounds offers an advantage when it is done in moderation and when it includes good blending instruction.

Explicit phonics is helpful because it provides children with the real relationships between letters and sounds, or at least approximations of them. But knowledge of letter-sound relationships is of little value unless the child can use that knowledge to figure out words. Whether children have learned the sounds of letters through implicit or explicit phonics, figuring out a new word still requires that the sounds of the letters be merged or blended.

We will return to the topic of blending in considering instructional issues. First we address another major issue associated with phonics—the relationship between what children learn in phonics and the stories they read.

Phonics and Reading Materials

We begin this section by recalling that among the serious problems Diederich (1973) pointed to about the way phonics was presented in the past was that "children had to learn so much abstract material [i.e., letter-sound relationships] by rote before doing any significant amount of reading" (p. 7). This "abstractness" problem can be eliminated by recognizing that adequate instruction gives students opportunities to apply what they are learning. Children need a lot of early experience reading meaningful material that includes many words that exemplify the sound-spelling patterns being introduced.

Current beginning reading programs tend to fall into two groups: (1) those in which there is a strong relationship between the sound-spelling patterns children are learning in their phonics lessons and the words in the stories they read, and (2) those in which this relationship is weak. To illustrate the differences, *Becoming a Nation of Readers* presented excerpts from two representative programs. Both excerpts came from material that would be read some time in or near November of first grade, when both programs would have introduced about 30 letter-sound relationships. A 26-word passage from the weak-relationship program contained 17 different words, out of which "only 3 (or 17 percent) could be decoded entirely on the basis of letter-sound relationships that [had] been introduced in the program's phonics lessons" (p. 45). In contrast, out of 18 different words in the passage from the strong-relationship program, 17 (or 94 percent) "could be decoded entirely on the basis of letter-sound relationships that students should know from the program's phonics lessons" (p. 46).

This gap in the percentage of decodable words results from the word selection process for the stories of each program. The first program selected high-frequency words that are likely to be in a young child's vocabulary. Word choice was not constrained by the letter-sound relationships or letter patterns introduced in the program's phonics lessons. In the second program, word choice was, to a large extent, constrained by the letter patterns introduced.

These two excerpts reflect the findings of Beck's (1981) analysis of eight beginning reading programs. The analysis included all the material students would read in the first third of each program. The percentage of decodable words in the four programs that based word selection on the letter-sound relationships introduced in their phonics lessons was 100 percent, 93 percent, 79 percent, and 69 percent, respectively. In contrast, the percentage of decodable words in the programs that selected their words from high-frequency lists was 0 percent for two programs, 3 percent for the third, and 13 percent for the fourth.

Problems arise when the relationship between what children learn in phonics and the stories they read is either too low or too high. When too few of the words are decodable it is questionable whether what is taught in phonics is of any use. On the other hand, when all but one or two of the words in a selection are constrained by the letter sounds introduced, it is virtually impossible to write interesting selections in natural sounding language. This is, in part, a result of the exclusion of such high-frequency but irregular words as *said, come, have,* and *you.* At its extreme, excluding such words and overemphasizing the last few letter sounds introduced results in sentences of the "Dan had a tan can" variety.

Is there an optimal relationship between the letter sounds children are learning in phonics and the words in their readers? Clearly, the answer is no. *Becoming a Nation of Readers* makes the point that establishing a rigid guideline is a poor idea: "What the field of reading does not need is another index that gets applied rigidly. What the field does need is an understanding of the concepts at work" (p. 47). The concept at work is that "a high proportion of the words in the earliest selections children read should conform to the phonics that they have already been taught." However, "requiring that, say, 90 percent of the words...conform to letter-sound relationships already introduced would destroy the flexibility needed to write interesting, meaningful stories" (p. 47).

The issues we have raised in the last two sections concern instructional strategies for teaching phonics and the relationship between what is learned in phonics and the selections children read. Having raised these issues in terms of existing instructional materials, let us turn to the teacher's role.

What Teachers Can Do

It is well established that basal reading programs are the most widely used resources for teaching reading in the elementary school. Although program implementation undoubtedly varies with individual teachers, there is strong evidence that the program teachers use heavily influences their classroom teaching (Diederich, 1973). Hence, we will frame our discussion of what teachers can do in relationship to the kinds of programs in use.

Since the most widely used reading programs employ implicit phonics, this seems to be the most prevalent approach. In implicit phonics, individual sounds are not produced in isolation. However, we would encourage teachers to make the individual sounds available. As teachers told Durkin (1984), who observed them producing sounds in isolation even though their manuals did not recommend it, "Children need to hear the sounds" (p. 740).

Although we recommend making individual sounds explicitly available, we caution against using them in isolation. Specifically, we recommend that teachers start with a word the children already know from oral language, extract the sound from that word, and then place it back into the word. For example, in preparation for learning the sound of the letter *d*, the teacher can draw students' attention to a word like *duck* from a recent story or use a line from a nursery rhyme, such as "diddle, diddle, dumpling." Then the teacher should explain that the first letter of these words, called a *d*, represents the /d/ sound.

This strategy not only overcomes the problem in implicit phonics of requiring children to extract a sound from a spoken word, but it also reduces a potential problem in explicit phonics—the difficulty of saying the sounds of some of the consonant letters in isolation. By starting with strong words, extracting the sound from those words, and placing the sound right back into words, teachers can avoid the pitfalls of explicit phonics approaches in which a string of isolated letter sounds is accumulated.

As noted earlier, an important issue associated with phonics is blending. *Becoming a Nation of Readers* makes two important points that can be applied to this topic. The first is that blending "is a difficult step for many children. Until a child gets over this hurdle, learning the sound of individual letters...will have diminished value" (p. 39). The second point is that when children attempt to figure out a word by blending sounds, it is not necessary for them to produce a perfect pronunciation. Rather, they need to be able to "come up with approximate pronunciations—candidates that have to be checked to see whether they match words known from spoken language" (p. 38).

We have two suggestions for promoting children's blending ability. In one the teacher models decoding of unknown words by slowly blending their component letter sounds. A model of blending involves stretching out each component sound until it merges with the next sound and then collapsing the sounds together so the word can be heard more clearly. For example, the teacher could select a new word that will be encountered in an upcoming selection, let's say *met*, write it on the board, and demonstrate how one might go about sounding it out. She or he would note that the first letter, the *m*, represents the /m/ sound, like at the beginning of *mittens*. Next the teacher would produce /m/ and add the short *e*, first elongating the sounds, /mmee/, then collapsing them, /me/. Then the teacher would add the /t/, at first giving a slightly exaggerated, then a more natural, pronunciation of *met*.

It is not difficult to involve the children in practicing this strategy. For example, the teacher can write a word on the board and tell the children to think of the sound of the first letter and keep saying it until he or she points to the next letter, and keep saying the sound of the two letters until they add on the sound of the last letter.

Resnick and Beck (1976) note that an important feature of blending instruction is merging different sounds successively—that is, /m/, /me/, /met/. Teachers should avoid using sequences in which the merging does not occur until each sound has been produced, such as /m/, /e/, /t/, /met/. Among the reasons that successive blending is preferable is that it avoids the need to keep a string of isolated sounds in memory.

Blending instruction does not have to be tedious. Teachers can choose from a variety of active and fun possibilities. For example, the teacher might give large cardboard letters to some children and start a word by telling the child who has the card that says /m/ to stand up. Then the child whose card makes /m/ say /me/ can go up and stand next to the /m/ child, followed by the /t/ bearer, who can complete the word *met*. The teacher might then ask the child who can make *met* say *bet* to go up and change places with the /m/ child.

This last example brings us to the second instructional strategy that promotes blending. Here children are involved with many opportunities to make words and to experiment with and observe the results of a letter change. A traditional implementation of this strategy involves a variety of letter substitution techniques. For example, the teacher places a phonogram such as *an* on a flannel board and then puts various consonants in front of the pattern, having the children read the resulting words (e.g., *can, man*). Or the teacher places the letters *s, a, t* on a flannel board and after the children read *sat*, she or he changes the vowel so the word reads *sit*, then changes it again to read *set*. This technique can be extended so that children use their own letter cards (which they can make or get from the teacher) to create words by changing letters in all positions—for instance, *sat* to *sit* to *hit* to *hot* to *hop* to *mop* to *map*. By deleting, adding, or substituting letters, more complex sequences, such as *black* to *back* to *tack* to *tick* to *trick*, can be developed.

Building words in this fashion externalizes the blending process. It makes the process readily accessible to children by making it very concrete. Children physically handle the letter cards, attach sounds to them, and manipulate the cards to produce new words.

Now let us turn to instructional issues associated with the relationship between what children are learning in phonics and the words in the stories they read and consider what the teacher can do if the relationship is either too low or too high. First, if the selections do not use words that allow the children to practice what has been taught in phonics, the teacher will need to write or find materials that do.

One teacher developed a way to write stories that incorporated the sound spelling patterns introduced in the program she was using. Essentially, she made "little books" by revising some of the stories in the basal. She started with a selection and inserted new words whose letter-sound relationships had already been taught. She found she was able to develop meaningful stories by adding and deleting various sentences, phrases, and words. Most often her revised stories were longer than the original ones. Sometimes they were elaborated versions of the original stories, but frequently the deletion and addition of words allowed her to vary the plots of these stories.

The teacher reported that she enjoyed revising the selections, but found it very time consuming. Since all teachers cannot be expected to have the time or knack for making such little books, published materials are needed. Some published children's stories (such as Dr. Seuss's *The Cat in the Hat, Hop on Pop, Fox in Socks,* and *There's a Wocket in My Pocket*) can be used. If a book contains too many unknown words, the teacher could use it in a shared reading situation in which she reads some of the story to the children and the children read the parts (perhaps from a "Big Book") that contain the words with learned sound spelling patterns. Other sources of material that may be useful are nursery rhymes ("How now brown cow") and tongue twisters ("How many cans can a canner can..."). In addition, teachers can give children opportunities to write their own tongue twisters.

If the program being followed is too constrained in using only phonics-related words (the "Dan had a tan can" variety), the teacher needs to incorporate into the selections some high-frequency words that have lots of utility for future readings. The teacher also should include words of interest to the children and words that have appeared in the children's writings. So we might get "Dan had a big can full of tan monsters." Or the teacher can leave blanks in a story where the children can fill in words: "Dan had a _____ can full of _____. A _____ man took the can." Basically the teacher leaves blanks where adverbs, adjectives, and prepositional phrases could go. The children might copy and illustrate these stories, collecting them into storybooks that can be taken home and read to others. The teacher also can use these types of text in chart stories or Big Books.

Children's writing can be used to foster phonic skill. For this strategy to work, children must have the prerequisite understandings discussed earlier in the section on phonemic awareness. Bissex (1980) gives an example of how a child who could analyze words into spoken sounds gained knowledge of the code through writing. Bissex's 5-year-old son, Paul, advanced by asking his mother questions concerning letter-sound relationships as he wrote. For example, Paul asked what made the "ch" sound in *teach*, to which his mother responded "c-h" (p. 12). Or this dialogue:

> Paul: What makes the "uh" sound?
> Mother: In what word?
> Paul: Mumps.
> Mother: u (p. 13).

To ask such questions, Paul had to have rather sophisticated phonemic awareness (for instance, he could segment the /uh/ sound in *mumps*). Likewise, teachers of young children may be able to foster such interaction as they respond to their young students' questions about how to write the sounds in certain words.

Just as teachers model blending to decode unknown words, they can model how to sound and blend sounds into written words. For example, "If I wanted to write the word *met* in a story, I'd first say the word to myself very slowly, /mmeett/. Then I'd think of the letter that makes the /m/ sound at the beginning of met and write it [writing the letter *m* on the board]. Then I'd think of what letter needs to be added to make it say /meee/ [adding the letter *e*]. Then I'd think of what letter needs to be added to make it say *met* [adding the letter *t*]." The teacher can encourage children to sound out and write the words in their stories in a similar manner.

As teachers can help children induce the code by repeatedly answering the question "What's this word?" they also can help them by answering "What letter stands for this sound in this word?" With either reading or writing, successful induction of the code will depend both on whether the child has the prerequisite understandings (i.e., phonemic awareness) and whether someone is around to answer these questions frequently. The fortunate child who has both of these conditions in place can learn the code even more quickly by being directly informed about the alphabetic code (e.g., through explicit phonics). The child who has little prerequisite knowledge about print and who lacks an informed partner in learning may need to *depend* on systematic and explicit phonics instruction. This child has fewer opportunities to induce the code through exposure to print and is thus more dependent on instruction to lay bare the alphabetic system.

The course of acquiring the code for a child like Paul, who at age 5 wrote above his workbench DO NAT DSTRB GNYS AT WRK (Bissex, 1980, p. 23), will be very different from that of the child who in the middle of first grade is spelling *rain* as *yes* or *wnishire*. Paul already had a good understanding of the alphabetic system and knew a fair amount about the code prior to first grade. He would have learned to read in first grade no matter what the instruction. Many children are not as fortunate as Paul. They depend almost exclusively on the instruction they receive in school to learn to read and write.

We have discussed the extreme importance of learning the code in first grade because early decoding reliably predicts reading comprehension in subsequent grades. Failure to teach the code in the most straightforward manner (e.g., through good, explicit phonics instruction coupled with reasonably constrained texts) would leave many children without the key to unlock the printed message. Children without this key cannot independently enter the world of quality literature; some may learn to dislike reading entirely. Each day that goes by without the child being able to read a book like *Make Way for Ducklings* is a day in which the knowledge and joy that can come from such reading are lost.

References

Anderson, R.C., Hiebert, E.H., Scott, J.A., & Wilkinson, I.A.G. (1985). *Becoming a nation of readers: The report of the Commission on Reading*. Washington, DC: National Institute of Education.

Barr, R. (1972). The influence of instructional conditions on word recognition errors. *Reading Research Quarterly, 7*, 509-529.

Barr, R. (1974). Influence of instruction on early reading. *Interchange, 5*(4), 13-21.

Barr, R. (1975). The effect of instruction on pupil reading strategies. *Reading Research Quarterly, 4*, 555-582.

Beck, I.L. (1981). Reading problems and instructional practices. In G.E. MacKinnon & T.G. Waller (Eds.), *Reading research: Advances in theory and practice* (vol. 2, pp. 53-95). New York: Academic.

Bissex, G.L. (1980). GNYS AT WRK: *A child learns to read and write*. Cambridge, MA: Harvard University Press.

Chall, J.S. (1967). *Learning to read: The great debate*. New York: McGraw-Hill.

Clay, M.M. (1979). *Reading: The patterning of complex behavior*. Portsmouth, NH: Heinemann.

DeLawter, J. (1970). *Oral reading errors of second grade children exposed to two different reading approaches*. Unpublished doctoral dissertation, Teachers College, Columbia University, New York.

Diederich, P.B. (1973). *Research 1960-1970 on methods and materials in reading* (TM Report 22). Princeton, NJ: Educational Testing Service.

Durkin, D. (1984). Is there a match between what elementary teachers do and what basal reader manuals recommend? *The Reading Teacher, 37*, 734-744.

Elder, R.D. (1971). Oral reading achievement of Scottish and American children. *Elementary School Journal, 71*, 216-230.

Elkonin, D.B. (1973). U.S.S.R. In J. Downing (Ed.), *Comparative reading* (pp. 551-579). New York: Macmillan.

Evans, M.A., & Carr, T.H. (1983). *Curricular emphasis and reading development: Focus on language or focus on script*. Symposium conducted at the biennial meeting of the Society for Research on Child Development, Detroit, MI.

Flesch, R. (1955). *Why Johnny can't read*. New York: Harper & Row.

Gates, A.I., & Boeker, E. (1923). A study of initial stages in reading by preschool children. *Teachers College Record, 24*, 469-488.

Gough, P.B., & Hillinger, M.L. (1980). Learning to read: An unnatural act. *Bulletin of the Orton Society, 30*, 179-196.

Guthrie, J.T., Samuels, S.J., Martuza, V., Seifert, M., Tyler, S.J., & Edwall, G.A. (1976). *A study of the locus and nature of reading problems in the elementary school*. Washington, DC: National Institute of Education.

Johnson, D.D., & Baumann, J.F. (1984). Word identification. In P.D. Pearson (Ed.), *Handbook of reading research* (pp. 583-608). White Plains, NY: Longman.

Juel, C. (1988). Learning to read and write: A longitudinal study of fifty-four children from first through fourth grade. *Journal of Educational Psychology, 80*, 437-447.

Juel, C., Griffith, P.L., & Gough, P.B. (1985). Reading and spelling strategies of first grade children. In J.A. Niles & R. Lalik (Eds.), *Issues in literacy: A research perspective* (pp. 306-309). Rochester, NY: National Reading Conference.

Lesgold, A.M., & Resnick, L.B. (1982). How reading disabilities develop: Perspectives from a longitudinal study. In J.P. Das, R. Mulcahy, & A.E. Wall (Eds.), *Theory and research in learning disability.* New York: Plenum.

Lundberg, I. (1984, August). Learning to read. *School Research Newsletter.* Sweden: National Board of Education.

Lundberg, I., Frost, J., & Petersen, O. (1988). Effects of an extensive program for stimulating phonological awareness in preschool children. *Reading Research Quarterly, 23,* 263-284.

Maclean, M., Bryant, P., & Bradley, L. (1987). Rhymes, nursery rhymes, and reading in early childhood. *Merrill-Palmer Quarterly, 33,* 255-281.

McCloskey, R. (1941/1969). *Make way for ducklings.* New York: Viking.

Resnick, L.B. (1979). Theories and prescriptions for early reading instruction. In. L.B. Resnick & P.A. Weaver (Eds.), *Theory and practice of early reading* (vol. 2, pp. 321-338). Hillsdale, NJ: Erlbaum.

Resnick, L., & Beck, I.L. (1976). Designing instruction in reading: Interaction of theory and practice. In J.T. Guthrie (Ed.), *Aspects of reading acquisition.* Baltimore, MD: Johns Hopkins University Press.

Stanovich, K.E. (1986). Matthew effects in reading: Some consequences of individual differences in the acquisition of literacy. *Reading Research Quarterly, 21,* 360-406.

Williams, J.P. (1984). Reading instruction today. *American Psychologist, 34,* 917-922.

CHAPTER 6

Reading Fluency: Techniques for Making Decoding Automatic

S. JAY SAMUELS
NANCY SCHERMER
DAVID REINKING

In this chapter the authors examine the role of fluency in reading. As you read the chapter, attempt to answer the following questions: Why is fluency important? If a student can recognize words with ease, will this be enough to guarantee good comprehension? What is meant by the term "automaticity," and how can it be measured in the classroom? Can metacognitive skills and strategies that facilitate comprehension be learned to the point where they are applied automatically? What can teachers do to develop automaticity in reading? How can the principles underlying fluency and automaticity be extended to include other aspects of literacy, such as writing and speaking?

As teachers are well aware, researchers and others have long disagreed about the best way to teach reading. More than three-quarters of a century ago, Huey (1908) described these ongoing controversies in his classic book, *The Psychology and Pedagogy of Reading*. He wrote, "The methods of learning to read that are in common use today may be classed as alphabetic, phonic, phonetic, word, sentence, and combination methods" (p. 265).

In Huey's day, the major disagreements were between those who advocated the spelling method—the dominant method at that time—and those who advocated the whole-word method. Huey stated, "Horace Mann had already advocated the word-method for years, and ridiculed the en-o, no; pee-you-tee, put; tee-aitch-ee, the, way of beginning reading, as it was taught in Webster's Spelling Book" (p. 259). By the time Huey's book was published, the whole-word method had replaced the spelling method as the dominant approach to instruction.

Becoming a Nation of Readers (Anderson et al., 1985) has taken a more recent look at these ongoing disagreements and, with the follow account, places one aspect of the disagreement into historical context:

> During the first third of this century, educators such as William S. Gray were responsible for turning American schools away from what they perceived to be the "heartless drudgery" of the traditional approach. In its place, Gray and others advocated the look-and-say approach. The thinking was that children would make more rapid progress in reading if they identified whole words at a glance, as adults seem to do.
>
> The look-say approach gradually came to dominate the teaching of beginning reading. Nonetheless, educators continued to debate the best way to introduce children to reading. Rudolph Flesch brought the debate forcibly to the public's attention in the mid-1950s with his book *Why Johnny Can't Read*, in which he mounted a scathing attack against the look-say method and advocated a return to phonics. More influential in professional circles, though, was Jeanne Chall's now-classic book a decade later, *Learning to Read: The Great Debate*. Chall concluded on the basis of evidence available at the time that programs that included phonics as one component were superior to those that did not (p. 36).

While we recognize that disputes about how to teach beginning reading continue, the purpose of this chapter is not to prolong "the great debate." Rather, it is to find common ground. Experts from diverse ends of the pedagogical spectrum recognize the importance of fluency, regardless of whether they favor a holistic, a decoding, or an eclectic approach to reading. For example, at one end of the instructional spectrum Goodman and Goodman (1979, p. 149) have stated that fluent reading "consists of optical, perceptual, syntactic, and semantic cycles, each melting into the next as readers try to get meaning as efficiently as possible using minimal time and energy," while at the other end of the spectrum Carnine and Silbert (1979, p. 32) have stated that fluency means reading smoothly, easily, and quickly.

Despite general agreement that fluency is an essential element of reading, we may be hard pressed to find any reference to it in many of the most widely used textbooks on reading instruction. The same is true of the teacher's guides to many of the most widely used basal readers. The anomalous situation we find ourselves in is that, despite general recognition of the importance of fluency, the topic is rarely discussed in instructional materials for teachers.

Thus, we seem to face a lack of information about how fluency is achieved, how it influences reading, and how it can be measured. The purpose of our chapter is to explain how to help students become fluent readers. To achieve this goal, we will discuss what it means to be fluent, why fluency is important, how to build fluency through techniques such as repeated reading, and how to determine whether a student is fluent.

Definitions of Fluency

How we use the term *fluency* in conversation provides a clue to its meaning. In conversation we may hear a distinction being made between novice and expert performance in reading or between beginning and fluent reading. When the term is used in this way, it implies that there is a qualitative difference between unskilled and skilled stages of reading. In recognition of this qualitative difference, teachers have associated beginning reading with the "learn-

Samuels, Schermer, & Reinking

ing to read" stage and fluent reading with the "reading to learn" stage.

This distinction suggests that until the student is fluent in reading, learning from text poses two formidable burdens: (1) the barrier posed by difficulty in identifying words, and (2) the comprehension problem of constructing a coherent representation of the information in the text. After fluency is reached, word identification is achieved with relative ease, and the primary burden is comprehension. Thus, educators seem to recognize that students cannot focus on the real goal of reading—to read for meaning—until they can read fluently.

In *Stages in Reading Development*, Chall (1983) refers to these broad stages of reading development. During the initial reading, or decoding, stage—which Chall believes takes place in grades 1 and 2—the student learns letter-sound correspondences, how to blend sounds to form words, and how to use context as an aid in word recognition. In other words, during the decoding stage, the student learns the rudiments of how to convert the printed symbols on the page into their appropriate sound equivalences. During the next stage, which Chall calls the "fluency stage," the student continues to work on decoding skills to the point where he or she becomes "unglued" from the print. By this Chall means that word recognition becomes easy and no longer serves as a barrier to acquiring meaning.

Leu and Kinzer (1987) also differentiate between beginning and fluent reading stages. They state that during the beginning reading stage one of the causes of difficulty is not knowing symbol-to-sound relationships. They define decoding as the process used to determine the oral equivalent or pronunciation of a written word. They note that decoding is important because most of the printed words encountered by beginning readers are already known to them in oral language. According to these authors, fluent reading is characterized by a lack of trouble with word identification or comprehension. A similar definition of fluent reading can be found in *A Dictionary of Reading and Related Terms* (Harris & Hodges, 1981). Here we find fluency defined as "freedom from word identification problems."

The definitions of fluency offered thus far have emphasized characteristics such as ease of word recognition, the ability to become "unglued" from print, and greater emphasis on comprehension. While these explanations help us understand what is meant by the term *fluency,* if our goal is to help students become fluent, a more theoretically based understanding is required.

Fortunately, automaticity theory can explain how reading fluency develops. It helps us understand the differences between early reading stages, when the student is "glued" to the print, and later stages, when the student can focus attention on meaning. In fact, the terms *fluency* and *automaticity* often are used interchangeably.

Automaticity Theory and Fluency

Automaticity theory, as described by LaBerge and Samuels (1974), can be used to explain the development of fluency using three components of the reading process: decoding, comprehension, and attention.

Decoding is an essential part of the reading process. By decoding we mean the process by which the letters of a printed word are converted to their spoken representation. For example, in decoding the letters c-a-t, the reader says "cat." Of course, a spoken representation does not necessarily mean that the word is spoken out loud since the reader can subvocalize and decode silently.

The idea of decoding has led linguists such as Fries (1965) to characterize the process of learning to read as a mapping task, where the student must learn the correspondence between printed symbols and their representations in spoken language. Fries states, "The process of learning to read in one's native language is the process of transfer from the auditory signs for language signals, which the child has already learned, to the new visual signs for the same signals" (p. 120). According to Fries, in the learning to read stage, the sequence of mental operations during reading goes from print to speech and then to meaning.

It is important to emphasize that decoding does not include understanding meaning. It is possible to decode words such as *merlon* without knowing their meaning. In the United States, for

Samuels, Schermer, & Reinking

example, many Hebrew school students learn the correspondences between Hebrew letters and their sounds without learning any vocabulary. These students can pronounce the Hebrew words and sentences (i.e., decode them), but they have no understanding of what they have read.

Comprehension, or the production of meaning from decoded words, is the second major component of the reading process. Producing meaning is viewed as a generative process in that the reader's understanding of the text results from combining information from the text with personal knowledge and experience. To the extent that the reader and the author have similar knowledge and experiences, they will share similar understanding. If reader and writer have different experiences, their interpretation may differ.

For example, in her introduction to *The Golden Notebook,* Lessing (1973) comments on the diverse interpretations readers had of her book:

> Naturally these incidents bring up again questions of what people see when they read a book, and why one person sees one pattern and nothing at all of another pattern, and how odd it is to have, as author, such a clear picture of a book that is seen so very differently by its readers (p. xxi).

The final component of automaticity theory is attention. Attention is an essential ingredient in all cognitive processing, whether the task involves reading, arithmetic, or typing a letter. However, the word *attention* can be confusing because it is a general term that includes overt, directly observable behaviors (e.g., when the teacher says "Johnny, pay attention") as well as covert aspects that are not directly observable (e.g., alertness, vigilance, selective attention).

For our present discussion, we are concerned only with selective attention. Selective attention is the ability to focus our mental energy and effort on certain aspects of the environment and to filter out other parts that we do not want to process. A number of examples of selective attention relate specifically to reading. For example, the student may wish to focus attention on a part of a word rather than on the entire word. And, since there are limits on how much information the human mind can process at one time, readers tend to focus attention on one line of printed words at a time, filtering out the lines above and below.

LaBerge and Brown (1986) compared the focusing of attention to a spotlight. Attention, like a beam of light, can be either broadly or tightly focused. The mind will analyze whatever part of the page falls within the attention spotlight. Similarly, if the attention spotlight is focused only on decoding and not on comprehension, the reader will decode the words but will not generate meaning.

Every machine requires energy to run, and the human mind is no exception. Mental energy and effort are needed for reading, doing arithmetic, or engaging in any other cognitive activity. Attention provides that energy. In his book *Attention and Effort,* Kahneman (1973) contends that attention is the driving force behind information processing. Neither learning nor comprehension will take place without attention.

Beginning Reading

Having discussed decoding, comprehension, and attention, we can now describe the beginning and fluent reading stages. Attention is required for decoding and comprehension, whether the student is a beginner or a fluent reader. We must keep in mind that the amount of attention or energy each person has available is limited, and decoding and comprehension both require attention. The ideal reading situation is one in which the demands of decoding and comprehension require less attention than the reader has available. Unfortunately, in beginning reading the combined attention demands of decoding and comprehension are greater than the reader's attention resources.

Unlike banking, in which individuals can spend more than they possess by borrowing, human information processing does not permit debt. If a task requires more effort or attentional energy than is available, either the task does not get done or a strategy must be devised to overcome the problem.

For the beginning reader, the problem of demand for attention exceeding supply can be overcome with a simple strategy: "divide

Samuels, Schermer, & Reinking

Figure 1
A Developmental Model of Beginning Reading

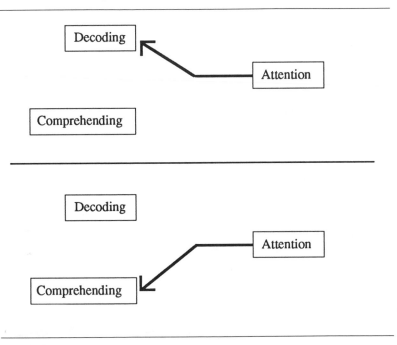

and conquer." Instead of combining the decoding and comprehension tasks, the beginning reader tackles these tasks individually. As seen in the upper part of Figure 1, first the reader focuses attention on decoding. Once that task is completed, the reader's attention switches to comprehension. By dividing the tasks and getting them done one at a time, the student avoids overtaxing attention resources and is able to move along one word at a time.

Although this beginning reading strategy allows the student to derive meaning from the text, it comes at high cost. The strategy places a heavy load on memory and attention, making beginning reading slow and difficult.

For beginning readers, the decoding task by itself is formidable; in fact, it is usually so great that the demands of decoding a word as a single unit may be too much (McCormick & Samuels, 1981; Samuels, LaBerge, & Bremer, 1978; Terry, Samuels, & LaBerge, 1976). If the task of recognizing a word as a unit is too difficult, students use a divide and conquer strategy to decode the word. The students break the word into parts and focus attention on one part at a time until they recognize the entire word.

One of the major factors determining the length of the visual unit used in decoding is the number of times the student has read a word (Samuels, Miller, & Eisenberg, 1979). When beginning readers first encounter a word, the visual unit is shorter than the whole word, often as small as a single letter. But with practice and repeated exposure to a particular word, the length of the visual unit increases. By the time the student becomes fluent in reading, the unit of recognition is the whole word. The advantage of recognizing a word as a whole unit is that words have meaning, and less memory is required for a meaningful word than for a meaningless letter.

Fluent Reading

As a result of extended practice in reading, an important change takes place: students learn how to decode the printed words using significantly less attention. Because they require so little attention for word recognition, they have enough left over for comprehension. Now they are able to focus attention simultaneously on decoding and comprehension. In fact, the hallmark of fluent reading is the ability to decode and comprehend at the same time. Figure 2 shows how in fluent reading the attention spotlight is broad, encompassing both decoding and comprehension. Fluent readers not only decode and comprehend text simultaneously, they also expend less effort in doing so.

In summary, beginning reading is characterized by the need to alternate attention between decoding and comprehension, a slow, laborious process that places a heavy demand on memory. The visual unit used by the beginner in word recognition is small, often as

Samuels, Schermer, & Reinking

Figure 2
A Developmental Model of Fluent Reading

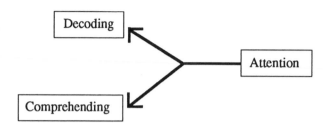

short as a single letter. With practice, the beginning reader becomes fluent. Because in fluent reading decoding requires significantly less attention and effort, decoding and comprehension can occur simultaneously. The visual unit in fluent reading is the whole word, making the process fast and seemingly effortless.

Automaticity

Automaticity is based on the principle that tasks become easier, requiring less attention, through practice. When less attention is required for a task and it seems to run on its own, we say the task is automatic. With regard to reading, it is decoding that becomes automatic through practice; comprehension always requires considerable attention, especially if the concepts are unfamiliar.

Since the beginner can do only one task at a time—either decode or comprehend—while the fluent reader can do both at once, a logical basis can be established for testing fluency. If a student can simultaneously decode and comprehend, then one of the tasks (decoding) is automatic. However, if the student is able to decode with reasonable accuracy but has difficulty with the meaning of a passage containing familiar concepts, we assume the student is not decoding automatically.

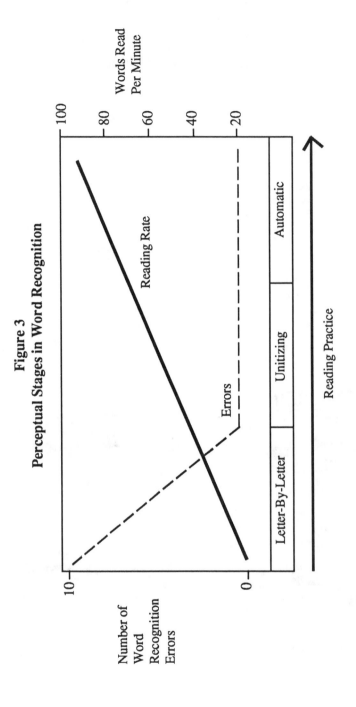

Figure 3
Perceptual Stages in Word Recognition

Samuels, Schermer, & Reinking

Automaticity in Oral and Silent Reading

While there is considerable overlap between oral and silent reading, the two processes have some major differences. The most important difference relates to the purpose of each type of reading. The primary purpose of oral reading is to communicate to an audience; in silent reading the audience factor is missing. In oral reading, because of the need to sound as if you are speaking normally, it is important to put expression in the voice. The need to sound normal also puts pressure on the reader to "keep up the pace," even if he or she does not understand the text. In silent reading, on the other hand, keeping up the pace is not important, and the reader is free to reread until the meaning is clear.

Despite these differences, the principles of the automaticity theory operate whether the reading is oral or silent. Thus, the classroom teacher can use oral reading to test for automaticity. (This testing procedure is explained later in the chapter.)

Perceptual Stages in Word Recognition

The first time a beginning reader encounters a new word, the strategies used to recognize it are different from when the student has read the word many times. Figure 3 depicts the perceptual changes that occur. This model describes what happens to accuracy of word recognition, speed of word recognition, and the length of the visual unit used in word recognition when a beginning reader reads and rereads a passage. Basically, with repeated practice, errors decrease and speed increases. At the same time, word recognition shifts from letter-by-letter processing to unitizing and finally to automatic processing.

Imagine that a first grader with some reading skill is learning to read a simple 100-word story. The student is given the opportunity to reread the story many times in order to develop fluency. Between each reading the student is given a chance to study a few of the words that were missed.

Each time the student reads the story, we record on a graph the number of word recognition errors (shown on the left vertical axis of Figure 3) and words read per minute (shown on the right vertical axis). The horizontal axis marked "reading practice" on the bottom of the figure indicates repeated reading practice from start to finish. This horizontal axis is divided into three sections, denoting progressive stages of word recognition: letter-by-letter, unitizing, and automatic. Research done at the University of Minnesota on automaticity and the unit of word recognition supports this model (Samuels & Kamil, 1984).

In looking at the figure, first note the number of word recognition errors. With repeated practice, the number decreases quickly. Next, note the words read in one minute, our measure of reading speed. Reading speed continues to increase after complete accuracy in recognition is achieved. In other words, with continued practice there is improvement beyond accuracy.

In the beginning stages of this exercise, word recognition is achieved using a letter-by-letter process. With practice, the length of the visual unit used in word recognition increases through a process called unitizing, which means simply that the units used are larger than a single letter. These larger units might include digraphs (such as *gh* in ghost or *sch* in school), syllables (such as *con* in continued), or affixes (such as *ing* in going). With practice, holistic processing takes place and the entire word can become the unit of recognition. The final stage is automaticity. At this point, recognition is fast and accurate, requiring little attention; the whole word is the unit of recognition.

Several pertinent implications for instruction can be derived from this model of word recognition. Many teachers seem to be satisfied when the number of word recognition errors approaches zero, but even at this stage there is still room for improvement. With continued practice the length of the visual unit increases, as does reading speed. The model indicates clearly that accuracy in recognition is not sufficient for fluent reading. As teachers of reading, our goal should be to move beyond accuracy to automaticity—and automaticity is achieved only with practice.

Developing Automaticity in Word Recognition

Repeated reading is an excellent technique for helping students achieve automaticity. Since the method was tested and described by Samuels (1979) and Chomsky (1978) more than a decade

Samuels, Schermer, & Reinking

ago, it has been shown to facilitate automatic decoding among average readers as well as among special populations. Furthermore, research has shown that repeated reading can lead to improved comprehension (Dowhower, 1987; Herman, 1985; Rasinski & Reinking, 1987).

While previous research on repeated reading has examined decoding and comprehension, what happens to eye movements as readers repeatedly read the same text is not well known. Knowledge about eye movement is important because this movement can reflect both cognitive processing and level of reading skill. For our purposes, we will look at three aspects of readers' eye movements: (1) the number of fixations—or stops—the eye makes while recognizing words, (2) the duration of the eye fixation, or the amount of time it takes the reader to identify and understand a segment of text before moving on, and (3) the number of times the eye regresses, or goes back to a previously encountered portion of text.

These three aspects differ depending on whether the reader recognizes the words in a passage automatically. If a reader is not automatic, there are many fixations per line, especially if the reader is processing letter by letter. Also, the duration of fixation is quite long, and regressions are numerous. When automaticity has been achieved on the passage, fixations are few, the duration of fixation is short, and there are few regressions.

In one study, the authors of this chapter observed the eye movements of college students who were asked to read coherent texts displayed in mirror image on a computer screen. Because of the reversed image, the students had as much difficulty decoding the words as a beginning reader typically would have with normal text. The college students were put in two experimental conditions. One group read the same text repeatedly, while the other group read a different text each time.

Although students in both groups improved in fluency, the eye movement patterns showed that those in the repeated reading condition made significantly greater progress. With the same amount of practice, the repeated reading group had fewer fixations per line, which indicates that they were taking in larger chunks of text with each fixation. In addition, the duration of fixation was shorter, indicating that the mental processing necessary to recognize the word was faster. Finally, this group made fewer regressions to previous sections of the text. When one combines the evidence from eye movements with the published research reports on repeated reading, the method stands out as a useful addition to the strategies used to promote reading fluency.

Several theories have been advanced to explain why repeated reading facilitates the development of fluency. According to Dowhower (1987):

> A rationale for the use of repeated reading can be found in whole language theory (Clay, 1985; Holdaway, 1979; Hoskisson, 1975a, 1975b). Support for repeated reading can also be found in theories based on information processing paradigms such as Samuels and LaBerge's (1983) automaticity theory and Perfetti and Lesgold's (1979) verbal efficiency theory, in which practice such as repeated reading is seen as increasing the speed of word recognition. Schreiber (1980, 1987) suggests a third rationale, that of prosodic cue development. He argues that repeated reading helps [beginning readers] learn to compensate for the lack of prosodic information in printed text...so that they read not word-by-word but in meaningful phrases (prosodic reading) (p. 390).

Using Repeated Reading in the Classroom

Repeated reading is easy to incorporate into the reading program. Bear in mind that although it is a useful technique for nonautomatic decoders, it is not recommended for students who are already reading fluently. The method is satisfying because it works, and students who have had histories of reading failure can experience the feeling of being able to read with expression and understanding.

In essence, the method consists of having the student reread a short passage of about 100 words until it can be read in one minute. When this goal has been reached, the student moves on to the next 100 words. Although the reading practice can be done silently, the testing for accuracy and speed is done orally. Accuracy of reading, while desirable, is not essential. What is essential is speed. There is a trade-off between these two factors: poor readers who are being

Samuels, Schermer, & Reinking

tested for both accuracy and speed often become so fearful of making a word recognition error that they lose speed. Since speed is the preferred indicator of automaticity, that is where the emphasis lies in repeated reading.

After the student reaches the criterion speed on the first 100 words, he or she moves on to the next portion of text. Some teachers have students segment a story into 100-word parts. Students practice each part until they reach the speed/accuracy criterion; then they proceed to the next segment. When they have completed all the parts, they can read the entire story fluently.

Teachers can use repeated reading in several ways. One way is to chart reading accuracy and speed. Students at all levels, even those who are mentally handicapped, can be taught to keep their own charts. Charting motivates students by allowing them to see progress with each reading.

Another technique involves having students work in pairs. One student reads orally while the other keeps a record of errors and time. The student who records also can ask comprehension questions. As in reciprocal teaching, the students can switch roles and take turns reading orally, recording, and asking comprehension questions (Brown, Palincsar, & Purcell, in press).

Taping can help students see the benefits of repeated reading. Students read into a tape recorder on their first reading of a passage and then again after they have practiced to the point where they believe they have mastered the passage. Students then can compare their performance on the two readings. They can listen for expression, count the number of word recognition errors, and compare the time it took them to read. Often the differences are so dramatic that the students are motivated to continue to improve.

Repeated reading has been used successfully with mentally handicapped children. Figure 4 shows the progress made with one such student in the original study used to test the method (Samuels, 1979). The student, who was classified as mentally retarded, repeatedly read short passages from a story. As the student progressed from one short selection to another over several days, many of the same words came up. Note that within each selection, as word recognition errors decreased, reading speed increased. Also note that

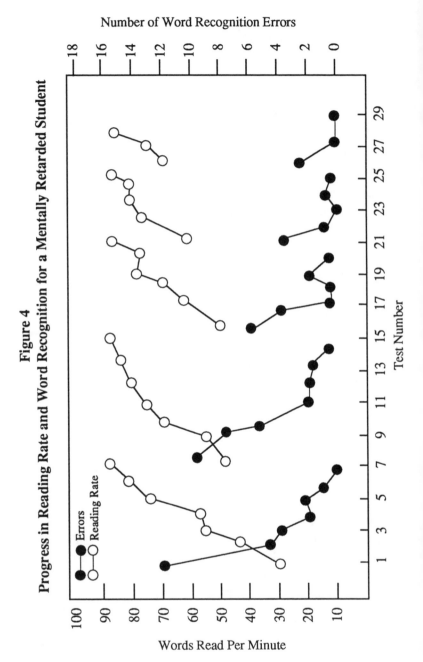

Figure 4
Progress in Reading Rate and Word Recognition for a Mentally Retarded Student

with each new selection, the beginning reading rate increased, the number of word recognition errors dropped, and fewer trials were required to reach the speed criterion of 90 words a minute.

Building Better Readers by Increasing Reading Time

Teachers can do three things to help students acquire reading fluency: (1) motivate students to read so they keep practicing long enough to become accurate and then automatic in decoding; (2) help students acquire useful decoding strategies through direct instruction; and (3) provide students with enough reading practice for them to become automatic. Remember that practice is the key to building automaticity. There is strong evidence that students who spend a lot of time reading become good readers (Allington, 1977; Stanovich, 1986).

In addition to repeated reading, a useful approach to building fluency is to encourage students to spend more time reading enjoyable stories. Ask your students how they can become good at a sport and they will tell you that skill comes from practice. Let them know that reading skill is acquired in exactly the same way. To provide such practice, we recommend that teachers devote about 30 minutes of each reading period to stories that children clearly enjoy. Thus, when the students are not involved with the teacher in direct instruction or relevant follow-up work, they can be reading new literature or previously read stories in their basal readers.

Considerable teacher guidance is necessary to get students to read appropriate material. They should be encouraged to read easy stories written at their independent reading level. They should also be encouraged to read at home; communication between teacher and parents about the need to read at home is useful. It is only by practicing with easy-to-read, real literature that students acquire automaticity.

Indicators of Automaticity

Teachers may wonder how they can determine whether the student is automatic or fluent in decoding. Fortunately, several easy-to-use indicators provide clues about students' degree of fluency. For one thing, teachers can ask students to read several passages out loud. If the students read the passages with expression, they are probably automatic.

When teachers ask their students to read with expression, they imply that all it takes is putting your mind to it. In truth, if one is not automatic, it is almost impossible to read with expression. When the college students in our study—who read regular print automatically—read the mirror image texts out loud for the first time, they sounded just like beginning readers. They read without expression and with great hesitancy. Thus, the ability to read orally with expression can be taken as one indicator of automaticity.

Another way to determine whether students are automatic is to instruct them to read a passage out loud and then tell you everything they can remember about it. It is almost impossible to remember everything read, but if students can recall some key elements of the passage, chances are they were decoding automatically. To perform the dual task of reading orally and comprehending the passage, students had to decode automatically.

Yet another way to determine whether students are decoding automatically is to compare their listening comprehension of a passage with their oral reading comprehension of a similar passage. If the students' recall is about equal for listening and oral reading conditions, chances are they are decoding automatically.

We encourage teachers to use a variety of methods to determine whether a student is automatic at decoding. By gathering information in a number of different ways, teachers can increase the reliability of their diagnosis.

Summary

Regardless of their position on how reading should be taught, educators agree that students need to become fluent or automatic in decoding to become skilled readers. After students have achieved accuracy in word recognition, additional practice enables them to become automatic.

Recent research indicates that while the amount of time it takes to achieve task accuracy varies greatly from student to student, the time required to become automatic is far less variable

Samuels, Schermer, & Reinking

(Naslund, 1987). This evidence suggests that once students reach accuracy, similar amounts of practice will produce automaticity in each. By exposing students to repeated reading and providing ample reading practice with easy material, teachers can help students become automatic decoders and thus good readers.

References

Allington, R. (1977). If they don't read much, how they ever gonna get good? *Journal of Reading, 21,* 57-61.

Anderson, R.C., Hiebert, E.H., Scott, J.A., & Wilkinson, I.A.G. (1985). *Becoming a nation of readers: The report of the Commission on Reading.* Washington, DC: National Institute of Education.

Brown, A., Palincsar, A., & Purcell, L. (in press). Instructing comprehension: Fostering activities in interactive learning situations. In H. Mandel, N. Stein, & T. Trabasso (Eds.), *Learning from texts.* Hillsdale, NJ: Erlbaum.

Carnine, D., & Silbert, J. (1979). *Direct instruction reading.* Westerville, OH: Merrill.

Chall, J. (1983). *Stages in reading development.* New York: McGraw-Hill.

Chomsky, C. (1978). When you still can't read in third grade: After decoding, what? In S.J. Samuels (Ed.), *What research has to say about reading instruction* (1st ed., pp. 13-30). Newark, DE: International Reading Association.

Clay, M.M. (1985). *The early detection of reading difficulties* (3rd ed.). Portsmouth, NH: Heinemann.

Dowhower, S.L. (1987). Effects of repeated reading on second grade transitional readers' fluency and comprehension. *Reading Research Quarterly, 22,* 389-406.

Fries, C.C. (1965). *Linguistics and reading.* Orlando, FL: Holt, Rinehart & Winston.

Goodman, K., & Goodman, Y. (1979). Learning to read is natural. In L. Resnick & P. Weaver (Eds.), *Theory and practice of early reading* (vol. 1, pp. 137-153). Hillsdale, NJ: Erlbaum.

Harris, T.L., & Hodges, R.E. (1981). *A dictionary of reading and related terms.* Newark, DE: International Reading Association.

Herman, P. (1985). The effect of repeated readings on reading rate, speech pauses, and word recognition accuracy. *Reading Research Quarterly, 20,* 553-564.

Holdaway, R. (1979). *Foundations of literacy.* Sydney, Australia: Ashton Scholastic.

Hoskisson, K. (1975a). Successive approximations and beginning reading. *Elementary School Journal, 75,* 442-451.

Hoskisson, K. (1975b). The many facets of assisted reading. *Elementary English, 52,* 312-315.

Huey, E. (1908). *The psychology and pedagogy of reading.* Cambridge, MA: MIT Press.

Kahneman, D. (1973). *Attention and effort.* Englewood Cliffs, NJ: Prentice Hall.

LaBerge, D., & Brown, V. (1986). Variations in the size of the visual field in which targets are presented: An attentional range effect. *Perception and Psychophysics, 40,* 188-200.

LaBerge, D., & Samuels, S.J. (1974). Toward a theory of automatic information processing in reading. *Cognitive Psychology, 6,* 293-323.

Lessing, D. (1973). *The golden notebook.* New York: Bantam.

Leu, D., & Kinzer, C. (1987). *Effective reading instruction in the elementary grades.* Westerville, OH: Merrill.

McCormick, C., & Samuels, S.J. (1981). Word recognition by second graders: The unit of perception and interrelationships among accuracy, latency, and comprehension. *Journal of Reading Behavior, 13,* 33-48.

Naslund, J. (1987). The effect of automaticity on individual variation and retention. Munich, Germany: Max Planck Institute for Psychological Research.

Perfetti, C.A., & Lesgold, A.M. (1979). Coding and comprehension in skilled reading and implications for reading instruction. In L.B. Resnick & P.A. Weaver (Eds.), *Theory and practice of early reading* (pp. 57-84). Hillsdale, NJ: Erlbaum.

Rasinski, T., & Reinking, D. (1987). Redefining the role of reading fluency. *Georgia Journal of Reading,* Fall/Winter, 21-27.

Samuels, S.J. (1979). The method of repeated readings. *The Reading Teacher, 32*(4), 403-408.

Samuels, S.J., & Kamil, M. (1984). Models of the reading process. In P.D. Pearson (Ed.), *Handbook of reading research* (pp. 185-224). White Plains, NY: Longman.

Samuels, S.J., & LaBerge, D. (1983). A critique of a theory of automaticity in reading. Looking back: A retrospective analysis of the LaBerge-Samuels reading model. In L. Gentile, M. Kamil, & J. Blanchard (Eds.), *Reading research revisited* (pp. 39-55). Westerville, OH: Merrill.

Samuels, S.J., LaBerge, D., & Bremer, C. (1978). Units of word recognition: Evidence for developmental changes. *Journal of Verbal Learning and Verbal Behavior, 17,* 715-720.

Samuels, S.J., Miller, N., & Eisenberg, P. (1979). Practice effects on the unit of word recogniton. *Journal of Educational Psychology, 71,* 514- 520.

Schreiber, P.A. (1980). On the acquisition of reading fluency. *Journal of Reading Behavior, 12,* 177-186.

Schreiber, P.A. (1987). Prosody and structure in children's syntactic processing. In R. Horowitz & S.J. Samuels (Eds.), *Comprehending oral and written language.* San Diego, CA: Academic.

Stanovich, K. (1986). Matthew effects in reading: Some consequences of individual differences in the acquisition of literacy. *Reading Research Quarterly, 21,* 360-407.

Terry, P., Samuels, S.J., & LaBerge, D. (1976). The effects of letter degradation and letter spacing on word recognition. *Journal of Verbal Learning and Verbal Behavior, 15,* 577-585.

7

Developing Expertise in Reading Comprehension

P. DAVID PEARSON
LAURA R. ROEHLER
JANICE A. DOLE
GERALD G. DUFFY

The authors begin this chapter by synthesizing the research about reading comprehension processes as a set of seven strategies that consistently surface as a part of the repertoire of successful readers. Then they turn to issues of instruction, and organize that work as a set of five principles of teaching comprehension that they call effective instructional actions. Finally, in an attempt to integrate the what and how of a comprehensive curriculum, they offer a set of "rules of thumb" about how to help students become active, self-directed readers.

Note: The research upon which this chapter was based was supported by the Office of Educational Research and Improvement under Cooperative Agreement No. G0087-C1001-90, the Center for the Study of Reading at the University of Illinois at Urbana-Champaign, and the Institute for Research on Teaching at Michigan State University. The publication does not necessarily reflect the views of the agency or institutions supporting the research. (For a related version of this chapter, see Dole et al., 1991.)

There was a time when some educators believed that reading comprehension had to be "caught rather than taught." Teaching phonics and word identification processes was possible and desirable, but after that native intelligence and experience determined the degree to which comprehension could take place (see Pearson & Johnson, 1978, for a discussion of this view). Research conducted over the past decade has persuaded most reading educators that reading comprehension can be taught, either by setting up learning conditions in the classroom that enhance growth in comprehension or by teaching strategies for coping with text directly and explicitly.

What Should be Taught?

Our Skills-Based Curriculum Tradition

Few would argue with the observation that the current comprehension curriculum is dominated by the teaching of specific skills. Even with the rise in popularity of whole language and literature-based reading programs, teachers in more than 90 percent of U.S. classrooms use basal reading programs. And even the most avant-garde of the 1990 editions of basals reveal the vestiges of a discrete skills commitment. The sheer inertia of tradition seems to account for these skill sequences in basals; the best predictors of the skills of the 1990s basals are the skills that were taught in the 1980s basals (and, most likely, tested in the commercially available tests of the 1980s).

Of course, educators did not always have a tradition to build on in establishing a scope and sequence of skills. The history of basals and comprehension skills reveals that at any given time from the 1930s through the 1980s, the comprehension curriculum has reflected the generally accepted view of comprehension as a process. Before the 1940s, reading often was divided into two categories: recreational and work-type (Smith, 1965/1986). Recreational reading was to promote enjoyment; work-type reading, to learn new information. Basal reading programs of this era reflected these distinctions. Under the general categories of recreational and work-type reading in basal programs were listed skills such as silent reading,

Pearson, Roehler, Dole, & Duffy

oral reading, comprehension, and skillful use of books, libraries, and other sources of information (Smith, 1965/1986).

During the 1940s a number of important sociocultural developments and a renewed interest in reading research led basal program developers to undertake extensive revisions, culminating eventually in the skills-based curriculum currently seen in basals (Smith, 1965/1986). During this period, Davis (1944) conducted his classic study to determine the unique components of reading comprehension. Davis's finding that a large number of presumably independent skills ultimately resolved themselves into three factors (a word meaning factor, a gist factor, and a reasoning factor) did not stop reading educators from expanding their schemes of essential comprehension skills. Other educators during this period (Crossen, 1940; Gans, 1940) and even later (Smith, 1963; Spache, 1965; Williams, 1959) attempted to determine which comprehension skills were essential.

It was also during this period that authors of basals first broke down the term *comprehension*. They began to discuss specific subcategories of comprehension processes—for instance, skills needed to use an expanded vocabulary; locate information; select, evaluate, and organize materials; retain information; and develop speed in comprehension. Basal programs often broke down each of these skills even further into more specific subskills.

With the publication of Russell et al.'s *Ginn Basic Readers* (1951), an important and lasting organizational device, vertical arrangement, arrived on the scene. Beginning in this period, basal programs were planned horizontally within grade levels and vertically across grade levels to ensure continuity in skill development throughout the elementary grades (Smith, 1965/1986). This construct brought with it the inauspicious beginning of the now omnipresent scope and sequence of skills as the backbone of a reading series.

The next three decades witnessed expansion and refinement of the various skills considered important to reading comprehension. Reading researchers continued to try to discover the "real" skills involved in reading comprehension (Davis, 1968; Schreiner, Hieronymus, & Forsyth, 1969), and to focus increasing attention on higher cognitive skills (Wolf et al., 1967). These concerns were reflected in attempts at building new basals.

Thus, history documents two forces at work, both of which affected the comprehension curriculum. First, basal reading programs were being reevaluated, refined, and expanded on the basis of current research and thinking about the reading process. Along with this basal evolution came the proliferation of skills into which comprehension was divided. These skills grew to become the comprehension curriculum.

We do not have to wait until the 1970s and 1980s to find critics of the discrete comprehension skills curriculum. In 1959 Sochor summarized the problem with researchers' understanding of critical reading skills in particular and reading in general. She also foreshadowed what was needed to understand the reading process and to change the comprehension curriculum.

> Much of the variability in what constitutes...reading is due to insufficient research evidence on the reading abilities themselves and on basic and related factors which might contribute. Research workers have been unable to clarify sufficiently the nature, independence, or difficulty levels of comprehension abilities in reading. Consequently, those concerned with reading abilities resort to logic for a definition of...reading (pp. 47-48).

Sochor's comments help explain the proliferation of reading comprehension skills in textbooks, journal articles, and basal reading programs over the past 40 years. Instruction has focused on the comprehension skills that were *believed* to be the most important.

Since 1975, however, researchers and educators have reached a new understanding about reading in general and the comprehension process in particular. This new understanding has led to a different view of comprehension and an accompanying shift in our views about how to teach it. Reading comprehension is no longer thought to be a series of discrete skills that can be added together to achieve comprehension ability. Instead, comprehension is viewed as a complex process involving interactions between readers and texts in various contexts and for various purposes (Lipson & Wixson, 1986).

A Schema Theory View of the Reading Process

The most popular example of this type of interactive view of

Pearson, Roehler, Dole, & Duffy

reading comprehension is derived from schema theory (Anderson & Pearson, 1984). It differs sharply from a skills-based focus. In this view, reading is seen as an active process of constructing meaning by connecting old knowledge with new information encountered in text. Readers build meaning by engaging in a series of recursive interactions. In each interaction readers generate a model that provides the best possible fit with the data perceived to be in the text. New text data provides an invitation to reconsider the adequacy of the model; new information either is made to conform to the existing model or prompts a revision of the model. Gradually, iteration by iteration, readers construct their own meaning. That meaning probably resembles the meaning the author had in mind in setting pen to paper, but no reader will develop the same model as the author; nor will any two readers develop exactly the same model. Each of us prints a unique personal stamp on every act of reading we undertake.

This interactive view of reading comprehension can be illustrated through profiles of readers with different levels of ability. For example, when readers of different degrees of expertise read the same passage, they interact with the text in different ways (Table 1).

The readers in Table 1, novice to expert, use many similar strategies to comprehend the given text. Emily, the expert adult reader, has a wealth of knowledge to bring to the text. She uses her knowledge to connect and render meaningful new information in the text and to develop a tentative model of what the text means. Her thinking reflects this continuous and recursive interaction between text information and existing knowledge, or between text and reader (Rosenblatt, 1978).

The two novice readers, Gary and Albert, also actively construct meaning. Like Emily, they make extensive use of their background knowledge to comprehend new textual information. Gary, the good fifth grade reader, also asks himself questions to help him monitor his reading—an effective strategy to make sense out of text. Even Albert, the average fourth grade reader, uses his knowledge to draw many important inferences from the text.

Several distinctions can be made between the expert and novice readers. First, Emily is better able to distinguish between important and unimportant information, although Gary does seem to sort out the important information in his summary. Second, Emily demon-

Table 1
An Example of How Readers with Different Levels of Ability Comprehend Text

Whole Text

Beryl Markham lived in Africa more than 50 years ago, when people were just beginning to fly airplanes. There were no airports or control towers. Planes had one engine and no radio or heat. Yet she flew her tiny plane to many faraway villages, carrying mail, supplies, and sometimes passengers.

What was this story about?

Sentence 1

Beryl Markham lived in Africa more than 50 years ago, when people were just beginning to fly airplanes.

Emily—Expert Adult Reader

Thoughts: Okay, this is about a woman (strange name—Beryl—could be a man I suppose); anyway, this person lived in Africa. Reminds me of Isak Dinesen—I wonder if they knew each other—she lived in Africa then too. Rest of sentence makes me think Beryl will fly a plane or be in one or something like that.

Comments: Reader is active—uses background knowledge in text. Develops hypotheses about the content of the upcoming text.

Gary—Good Fifth Grade Reader

Thoughts: What I'm thinking is that what would he be doing, and how we would react to planes because they are so new. And I would also be thinking why would someone live in Africa for 50 years. Until airplanes came out.

Comments: Reader is active—uses background knowledge to connect to new knowledge in the text. Asks questions rather than develops hypothesis, but is seeking more information from text.

Albert—Average Fourth Grade Reader

Thoughts: There are airplanes flying around...jungles.

Comments: Reader is less active than other two readers. Has difficulty developing hypothesis, asking questions. Responds literally to the text. Connects new knowledge to old—jungles—in a limited sense.

Pearson, Roehler, Dole, & Duffy

Sentence 2

There were no airports or control towers.

Emily—Expert Adult Reader

Thoughts: Of course, this makes sense! Not 50 years ago. I know that! But what about Beryl?

Comments: Reader is active again. New knowledge in text neither adds to nor deletes from hypotheses; reader is looking for new knowledge to confirm or invalidate hypotheses.

Gary—Good Fifth Grade Reader

Thoughts: I think it would be a little bit hard to fly a plane, because there is nobody to tell you where you should land, how actually and you wouldn't really be able if you fly a far distance. It would be hard to contact back from where you started in the first place so you would have to bring a compass.

Comments: Reader is again active—new knowledge in text is again related to old knowledge. Reader is drawing inferences about difficulty of flying.

Albert—Average Fourth Grade Reader

Thoughts: Bare fields. Looks like bare fields with airplanes landing on it.

Comments: Reader is developing visual representation of text. Draws inferences that contradict old information, but doesn't seem to be concerned.

Sentence 3

Planes had one engine and no radio or heat.

Emily—Expert Adult Reader

Thoughts: Right, I know that. What about Beryl?

Comments: Reader is impatient for new knowledge instead of additional knowledge she already knows.

Gary—Good Fifth Grade Reader

Thoughts: Well, since he had one engine I would think he wouldn't go very fast, no radio so if crash and um getting ready to crash definitely not going to be able to tell anybody. And if flying in the winter no heat then he will get froze.

Comments: Reader is again active, drawing inferences about speed of plane, getting help if needed, and freezing in winter. Also drawing text-based inferences.

Albert — Average Fourth Grade Reader

Thoughts: People wearing heavy coats and gloves — because they don't get any heat — 'cause they might get cold and it's cold up there.

Comments: Reader draws inferences from information in text, uses old knowledge to connect to new knowledge.

Sentence 4

Yet she flew her tiny plane to many faraway villages, carrying mail, supplies, and sometimes passengers.

Emily — Expert Adult Reader

Thoughts: Okay, now I get it. That's what I expected — she flew an airplane! Amazing that a woman would do that — very dangerous. I'd never have the courage to do that. And so long ago.

Comments: Reader confirms existing model or hypothesis with new knowledge from the text. Reader draws inferences, connects new knowledge to old, reacts and responds personally to ideas in the text.

Gary — Good Fifth Grade Reader

Thoughts: That's pretty nice, because you know a little while ago when there weren't many airplanes then that was the fastest way to travel, and I think it still is. I think it was pretty nice to take people, and mail especially. And supplies to other places.

Comments: Reader again active, but doesn't seem to connect this portion of text to earlier sentences. Comments sentence-related, but not hypothesis-related.

Albert — Average Fourth Grade Reader

Thoughts: Plane carrying mail and stuff, just a few passengers, not a whole bunch of them.

Comments: Reader simply recalls information in text. No inference drawn here — also no carryover from earlier information in the text.

Question

What was this story about?

Gary — Good Fifth Grade Reader

Thoughts: Tells about a person who owned an airplane, when people had just begun to fly airplanes that person around an airplane and

Comments: Notice how — despite local-level inferences drawn — reader develops overall understanding of the paragraph.

carrying mail supplies and passengers to villages and what the plane
had, didn't tell what kind of plane it
was, but told what the plane had
what the person who owned it did.

Albert—Average Fourth Grade Reader

Thoughts: They're different from
here because they don't got any airports and control towers and they
only got one engine—they might not
last longer in the air.

Comments: Notice the focus on a
few details from the selection.

---

strates an awareness of her comprehension of the text. She comments, "Okay, now I get it," indicating that she is monitoring her own
understanding. She also says, "That's what I expected," indicating
awareness that she has confirmed her hypothesis. So Emily uses effective strategies not only to comprehend the text but also to monitor
that comprehension. Gary shows some signs of monitoring (the self-
questions), but Albert does not overtly mention—and indeed may not
be aware of—his own understanding.

Toward a Model of a Thoughtful, Expert Reader

This schema theory based view of comprehension has been the
foundation of much of our recent work on the comprehension processes employed by expert readers, the factors that discriminate expert
from novice readers, and the methods teachers can use to foster or
improve comprehension ability. From this work, we have learned
much about what readers do when they read, what unsuccessful
readers fail to do, and what needs to be done to help novices work
toward expertise. We have learned, for example, that active, expert
readers:

- Search for connections between what they know and the new
  information they encounter in the texts they read.

- Monitor the adequacy of their models of text meaning.
- Take steps to repair faulty comprehension once they realize they have failed to understand something.
- Learn early on to distinguish important from less important ideas in texts they read.
- Are adept at synthesizing information within and across texts and reading experiences.
- Draw inferences during and after reading to achieve a full, integrated understanding of what they read.
- Sometimes consciously, and almost always unconsciously, ask questions of themselves, the authors they encounter, and the texts they read.

These are the characteristics of active, thoughtful, expert readers. It is our contention that these traits should drive our search for a comprehension curriculum that is based solidly on the research of the past 15 years. To develop truly thoughtful readers, we must ensure that they possess these characteristics.

Thoughtful readers use existing knowledge to make sense of texts. While reading, thoughtful readers use prior knowledge constantly to evaluate the adequacy of the model of meaning they have developed. This is true for readers of all ages or levels of sophistication. Recall from Table 1 how both Emily and Gary used their general world knowledge as they read and interpreted the passage about Markham. Emily recalled knowledge about what Africa was like 50 years ago, and Gary used his prior knowledge about airplanes to extend and elaborate on what he read about planes with one engine and no radio.

Thoughtful readers also use their existing knowledge when they have to demonstrate to others that they have understood what they have read. They use it to determine what's important in a text, to draw inferences (which rely almost completely on prior knowledge), or to generate questions about a text.

Research with adults and children and with experts and novices points to the same general conclusion. New information is

Pearson, Roehler, Dole, & Duffy

learned and remembered best when it is integrated with relevant prior knowledge, or existing schemata. Existing schemata form frameworks that serve as organizing structures for incorporating new information (Anderson, Spiro, & Anderson, 1978). And, as we shall later demonstrate, these findings hold whether the knowledge is accurate or inaccurate. Misconceptions are schemata too (in fact, often they are incredibly well-developed, resistant, and resilient schemata). In addition, studies have demonstrated that:

1. Students with greater prior knowledge comprehend and re- member more (Brown et al., 1977; Pearson, Hansen, & Gor- don, 1979).

2. Merely having prior knowledge is not enough to improve comprehension; the knowledge must be activated, implying a strong metacognitive dimension to its use (Bransford & Johnson, 1972; Dooling & Lachman, 1971).

3. Young readers and poor readers often do not activate their prior knowledge (Paris & Lindauer, 1976).

4. Good readers use their prior knowledge to determine the importance of information in the text (Afflerbach, 1986).

5. Good readers use their prior knowledge to draw inferences from and elaborate on text (Gordon & Pearson, 1983; Hansen, 1981; Hansen & Pearson, 1983).

What kinds of knowledge do good readers use to help them comprehend and remember what they've read? Resnick (1984) ar- gued that three kinds of prior knowledge come into play: (1) spe- cific knowledge about the topic of the text, (2) general world knowledge about social relationships and causal structures, and (3) knowledge about the text's organization.

A number of studies have been conducted over the past 10 years to demonstrate how prior knowledge facilitates comprehen- sion. In a series of studies reported by Bransford, Vye, and Stein (1984), good and poor fifth grade readers were asked to identify anomalous information in text and then to generate elaborations of text segments to help them improve their recall. Good readers were successful at identifying anomalous information and at creating helpful elaborations. Poor readers, on the other hand, could not identify anomalous information. Their responses suggested that they attended to surface rather than deep structure features of the text. For example, good readers could explain why the sentence "The strong man helped the woman lift the heavy piano" is easier to remember than "The strong man wrote a letter to his friend." Poor readers thought the second sentence was easier because it was shorter. Poor readers could, however, be taught to use their general world knowledge to identify anomalous information and to generate elaborations that helped them remember better. To do this, poor readers need to be taught that they already have ideas in their heads, and that they can use those ideas to help them understand what they read.

The past few years have witnessed a growing interest in misconception research. Several studies in reading (Alvermann, Smith, & Readence, 1985; Maria & MacGinitie, 1982) and in science education (Dole & Smith, 1987; Eaton, Anderson, & Smith, 1984; Roth, 1985) have demonstrated that students' inaccurate knowledge can often overwhelm information in the text or even instruction designed to overcome the misconceptions (Anderson & Smith, 1987). Anderson (1977) has argued that students are unlikely to change their existing ideas or schemata unless (1) they recognize that their current schemata no longer provide an adequate account of the data they gather in everyday experience, and (2) they can see a way out of their difficulty.

Students *can* overcome misconceptions. Roth (1985) was able to help students change their ideas by giving them specially prepared text that confronted their inappropriate schemata about photosynthesis, specifically pointing out why these views were inadequate. Dole and Smith (1987) developed another effective instructional intervention that helped students change their schemata. They asked students to identify their prior knowledge about scientific topics before reading about those topics. Students wrote down their ideas and later compared them with the ideas found in the science textbooks. Then they discussed whether their ideas were the same or different from scientists' ideas. This strategy proved effective in helping students change their inappropriate schemata and develop scientifically accurate schemata.

Pearson, Roehler, Dole, & Duffy

In summary, an impressive body of research points to the importance of prior knowledge in text comprehension. Research clearly indicates that good readers use prior knowledge to help make sense of text, while poor readers often do not. Poor readers can be taught to use, and even alter, their prior knowledge; when they learn to put such knowledge to use, their comprehension improves. Prior knowledge is so pervasive and so important that we can only wonder why it traditionally has received so little curricular attention as an area worthy of specific training.

Thoughtful readers monitor their comprehension throughout the reading process.   Monitoring is the primary mechanism readers use to accomplish sense making. Intuitively, we have always known that good readers are more careful in their reading than are poor readers. First, they are more aware of how well or how poorly the reading is going. Recall that Emily remarks, "Okay, now I get it," indicating her awareness that comprehension had clicked in. Second, good readers are better able to alter their reading strategies to compensate for a problem once they realize that one exists; in other words, they have a wider range of fix-up strategies.

Poor readers, by contrast, tend to be much less aware of problems when they do exist and less able to compensate even when they are aware. For example, in the Markham passage, Albert doesn't seem to be aware of his lack of overall understanding. Teachers' longstanding intuitions about good and poor readers' monitoring have been corroborated by numerous research studies completed over the past 15 years under the general rubric of metacognition (see Baker & Brown, 1984; Garner, 1987, this volume; Wagoner, 1983).

In a typical comprehension monitoring study, subjects are given text that contains something that doesn't make sense. This anomalous information can be inconsistent either with knowledge about the world (e.g., elephants can fly) or with information in another part of the text (e.g., one sentence states that John lived on Green Street and another says he lived on Brown Street). Furthermore, the anomalous information can come from domains of knowledge known to people of all ages (e.g., animals that fly or simple rules of gravity) or obscure domains of knowledge (e.g., the effect of heat on metal magnetism or the habits of light-emitting animals in the sea). The subject's task is to recognize and report the inconsistency. Using a wide range of tasks and texts, researchers have found that the ability to detect inconsistencies varies as a function of both age and ability (Garner, 1987). Interestingly, students seem to develop a nonverbal awareness of anomalies before they are able to report them. In at least three studies (Flavell et al., 1981; Harris et al., 1981; Patterson, Cosgrove, & O'Brien, 1980), even students who were unable to report certain anomalies spent more time reading the sections of the text containing them than they did on sections without anomalies.

Metacognitive ability does not seem to follow a purely developmental pattern (i.e., as you get older, you get more of it or better at it). Vosniadou, Pearson, and Rogers (1988) found that three different factors—mode of presentation, topic familiarity, and textual explicitness—had varying influences on the ability of students of different ages to detect inconsistencies. Third grade students were better able to detect inconsistencies when listening to a story than when reading it. When the topic was familiar, even first grade children were able to detect inconsistencies. When it was unfamiliar, first grade children were unlikely to detect the anomalous data even when it was explicitly contradicted in another part of the text. However, older children (third and fifth grade) reading about an unfamiliar topic had an easier time detecting inconsistencies when the anomaly contradicted a previous statement in the text.

Notice that the typical comprehension monitoring study imposes roadblocks to comprehension by using only prepared texts with anomalies embedded. This presents problems of ecological validity for all comprehension monitoring studies using this error detection paradigm; in real reading, blatant anomalies are rare (good writers, in fact, strive to avoid them). For most of us, what we read becomes anomalous only when we lack the knowledge necessary to understand a text or when we are victims of a gross misconception. Novice readers (and occasionally expert readers) encounter additional anomalies when they misread something and later become aware of an inconsistency between what they misread and what came before or after.

Pearson, Roehler, Dole, & Duffy

Fortunately, a few studies have addressed the comprehension monitoring phenomenon using normal texts. Revelle, Wellman, and Karabenick (1985) studied preschoolers' reactions to requests to undertake certain actions in a play environment. Even in young children, they found a wide variety of reactions (mostly requests for clarification or additional information) to experimenter requests that posed varying degrees of comprehension problems for the children. In addition, their behavior and the number and type of requests they made for clarification demonstrated that the children were able to discriminate between experimenter requests that posed problems and those that did not.

Palincsar and Brown's (1984) instructional study on reciprocal teaching (see the later sections on synthesizing and question-asking) required students to seek clarification of hard parts of the passages they read (taken from commonly used expository materials). Students were able to engage in discussions about what parts of the text were difficult for them, although of the four strategies used, this clarifying of difficult text was the hardest for the students to complete on their own. Also on the positive side, when lessons on comprehension monitoring have been included in larger metacognitive training programs (Duffy et al., 1987; Paris, Cross, & Lipson, 1984), elementary students have improved their ability to apply these strategies to their reading.

Despite concerns about the validity of the error detection tasks (Winograd & Johnston, 1982), there is reason to take the development of comprehension monitoring strategies seriously. First, the evidence indicates quite clearly that comprehension monitoring distinguishes the expert from the novice reader. Second, comprehension monitoring is amenable to instruction. Third, it matches our intuition about what good readers ought to be able to do. Fourth, it goes hand in glove with another (and possibly more important) characteristic of the strategic reader—regulating or repairing comprehension once a problem has been detected.

Thoughtful readers repair their comprehension once they realize it has gone awry. Comprehension repair has acquired a host of aliases, among them regulation strategy, repair strategy, and fix-up strategy. By any name, it is critical to expert reading. Good readers know what to do when they find that they no longer comprehend. They know what to do when comprehension fails. They anticipate problems and take action to solve them as soon as they arise.

Unfortunately, the evidence to support adaptation as a key characteristic of the strategic reader is not as plentiful as the evidence in favor of comprehension monitoring. In fact, Baker and Brown (1984) bemoaned the lack of progress on this dimension of metacognitive development (which they termed regulation). There are, however, some classic fix-up strategies that distinguish the expert from the novice reader (see Garner, 1987).

First, good readers tend to be more flexible in their allocation of study time. Masur, McIntyre, and Flavell (1973) found that when told to memorize a set of difficult drawings, older students adopted a much more efficient and adaptive strategy from one trial to the next than did younger students. The younger students tended to use the same approach each time, whereas the older students tended to focus on what they had missed in the previous trial. Working on a similar problem of managing resources, Owings et al. (1980) obtained similar results. When students were given an opportunity to study two stories that they knew were of different difficulty levels (they had previously rated the stories for difficulty themselves), the better students spent significantly more time on the difficult story than on the easier story. By contrast, the poorer students studied the two stories for approximately equal periods of time.

Second, expert readers are more likely than novices to look back at the text to resolve a problem. In their study on this phenomenon, Alessi, Anderson, and Goetz (1979) found that college students' knowledge deficits could be almost completely overcome with an induced look-back strategy. Garner and her colleagues (Garner, Macready, & Wagoner, 1984; Garner & Reis, 1981; Garner, Wagoner, & Smith, 1983) have investigated the look-back phenomenon extensively. The general conclusion to be drawn from their work is that there is a consistent positive relationship between reading comprehension and use of the look-back strategy (Garner, 1987).

Pearson, Roehler, Dole, & Duffy

Third, expert readers are more flexible and adaptable than novices in their use of strategies; they are far more likely to change strategies to meet different circumstances. Work by Raphael and her colleagues (Raphael & Pearson, 1985; Raphael, Winograd, & Pearson, 1980; Raphael & Wonnacott, 1985) has consistently demonstrated a positive relationship between students' overall comprehension and their ability to learn to adapt question-answering strategies to the demands imposed by the question and the context in which it is asked. For example, given a choice between answering a question by going right to the part of the text the question comes from, searching through the text to find a response that fits the question, and relying primarily on one's prior knowledge, good readers are better able to select the appropriate strategy than are poor readers (Raphael, Winograd, & Pearson, 1980). These researchers also found that regardless of what they say they are going to do to answer a question, poor readers tend to be unilateral in their actions, with many pursuing little more than a simple text-matching or answer-grabbing (Pearson & Johnson, 1978) approach.

In one sense, fix-up strategies are more pervasive than we might recognize at first glance. Almost any skill worth teaching is a plausible candidate for use as a regulatory or fix-up strategy when readers find themselves confronted by a comprehension problem. In other words, readers who find themselves in trouble when monitoring their reading comprehension can resort to a deliberate search for main ideas, cause-effect relationships, or sequences of key events. They can consciously try to summarize, draw inferences, or ask themselves questions to try to improve the situation. Furthermore, given the interactive and recursive nature of the reading process, it is likely that in any given regulatory attempt, readers will invoke two or more of these strategies simultaneously.

Thinking about traditional skills as fix-up strategies can be extremely productive. Usually, when reading is going well and we experience one after another click of comprehension, we are completely unaware of how we are processing the text. We are operating in an automatic processing mode. But when we realize that things are not going well, when we experience one of the "clunks" of comprehension, we shift from an automatic to a conscious control mode of processing. We may say to ourselves, "I've just read the last four pages and don't remember a thing; I'd better go back and look for some main ideas." This may be exactly where those specific skills and strategies that characterize our comprehension curricula are useful—as conscious strategies we call on when the going gets tough.

Thoughtful readers are able to determine what's important in the texts they read. Determining importance is a critical part of the comprehension process. Because of its central role, the ability to determine importance has attracted considerable attention and research interest (Afflerbach & Johnston, 1986; Baumann, 1986; Cunningham & Moore, 1986; Williams, 1986a, 1986b), most often under the rubric of main idea comprehension.

Williams (1986b) and Winograd and Bridge (1986) note that the instructional terminology for determining importance differs from one researcher to another and from one instructional program to another. In addition to the ubiquitous term "main idea," Williams reported the use of gist, topic, topic sentence, macrostructure, superstructure, summary, key word, thesis, theme, and interpretation. Regardless of the terminology used, it is clear that teachers spend considerable instructional time trying to help students determine what's important in a selection. We have consciously declined to use the term main idea, opting instead for the phrase "determining importance." Our rationale is that separating the wheat from the chaff in a text is what really counts. Finding the main idea is merely one way to determine what's important.

How do we differentiate what's important from what's unimportant? Williams (1986b), Tierney and Cunningham (1984), and Winograd and Bridge (1986) make a distinction between author-determined importance and reader-determined importance. For example, a study by Pichert and Anderson (1977) demonstrates reader-determined importance. They found that readers selectively determine what's important depending on the purpose set for reading. In their study, students who read an ambiguous passage about a house from the perspective of a home buyer found different parts of the passage to be important than did students who read the same selection from the perspective of a burglar.

Pearson, Roehler, Dole, & Duffy

Most, if not all, school-based reading requires readers to determine author-based (i.e., text-based) importance. Good-reader/poor-reader studies have found consistently that good readers are better able to judge author-based importance than are poor readers (Afflerbach, 1986; Englert & Hiebert, 1984; Johnston & Afflerbach, 1985; Winograd, 1984). Winograd and Bridge (1986) and Afflerbach (1986) argue that good readers use three different strategies. First, they use their general world knowledge and domain-specific knowledge to gain partial access to the meaning of the text. For example, notice in Table 1 how Emily immediately activates her knowledge about Isak Dinesen as she begins to read the Markham passage, then uses her knowledge about Africa to help her focus on the content. She also demonstrates her understanding of the author's intentions when she develops her hypothesis about the topic of the paragraph after reading the first sentence. Second, good readers use their knowledge of text structure to help them identify and organize information. Text structure knowledge includes attention to key words, phrases, graphics, summarizing statements, and other surface-level cues. Emily demonstrates her knowledge of text structure by hypothesizing what the paragraph will be about on the basis of surface cues in the first sentences. Third, adult proficient readers use their knowledge of author biases, intentions, and goals to help determine importance (Afflerbach, 1986).

Certainly a comprehension curriculum ought to include strategies for determining important information. What we have in mind goes well beyond what typically has been included in main idea instruction. We advocate a broader view of the strategy, as encompassed in our proposed new name, as well as explicit instruction in extracting important information from text.

Thoughtful readers synthesize information when they read. A logical extension of determining importance is the ability to synthesize information across larger units of text (or even between texts) to create summaries. While a good deal of research supports the usefulness of determining importance, probably even more work confirms the usefulness of summarizing as a comprehension and studying strategy. We know that while young children can synthesize the plot structure of simple narratives (such as folktales), they have much greater difficulty with more complex tasks, such as rating the importance of each section to the theme (Brown & Smiley, 1977; Brown, Smiley, & Lawton, 1978). With maturity, children become more adept at the complex tasks (Brown & Smiley, 1977; Pichert, 1979), apparently because they become more aware of how texts are organized and how to adapt their study strategies to maximize the time they spend on information they have not previously learned (Brown & Campione, 1979). It is interesting to note that in the studies conducted by Brown and her colleagues (Brown & Campione, 1979; Brown, Smiley, & Lawton, 1978), sophisticated college students, given several study trials to try to remember information in a text, actually shifted their emphasis downward each time, from text ideas that had been independently rated as high in importance to those rated moderate and finally to those rated low.

Perhaps the most crucial work in summarizing has been done following a tradition started by Brown and Day (1983) and Brown, Day, and Jones (1983). Extending the text analysis work of Kintsch and van Dijk (1978), they identified five operations critical to creating summaries:

1. Delete irrelevant information.
2. Delete redundant information.
3. Create a superordinate label for a list of things or actions (e.g., food for beef, carrots, pie, and salad).
4. Try to locate topic sentences for paragraphs and use them in your summary when appropriate.
5. Invent topic sentences when you are unable to locate them.

Noting that expert readers use these rules routinely, Brown and Day (1983) set out to determine their use by novices. They found that average ability fifth grade students could perform all the deletion rules accurately. On the other hand, they never used the invention rule. These findings indicate a strong tendency for developmental differences to appear more prominently as the rule increases in complexity.

An encouraging aspect of these summarization operations is that they appear to be amenable to instruction. For example, Day

(1980) was able to teach both regular and remedial community college students to apply the rules to improve the quality of their summaries. Subsequent studies by Cunningham (1982), Hare and Borchardt (1984), and Taylor and her colleagues (Taylor, 1982; Taylor & Beach, 1984; Taylor & Berkowitz, 1980) have evaluated similar summary training programs for high school and intermediate grade students. In all the studies, such training improved comprehension; in the Taylor and Beach study, the effects of summarization training extended to both reading comprehension and writing activities.

While Palincsar and Brown's (1984) highly successful reciprocal teaching program does not focus exclusively on summarizing, summarization is an important part of the program's training. In this program, students are taught to apply four strategies to any text they read: (1) summarize it, (2) ask a few questions that get at what is important in the text, (3) clarify any parts that were difficult to understand, and (4) predict what the author will talk about next. Although there is no way to determine the relative contribution each of these strategies makes to comprehension improvement, it is useful to know that summarization is a part of this highly successful technique.

Thoughtful readers constantly draw inferences during and after reading. Drawing inferences is a skill commonly found in many basal reading programs. Thinking that only older children are able to draw inferences, some programs postpone teaching this technique until later in the elementary grades. But such delays seem both unnecessary and harmful to students. If we look at our least expert reader from Table 1, Albert, we can see that he continually draws inferences as he reads, despite his lack of expertise in comprehending the overall meaning.

One of the most common findings of recent research on reading is that drawing inferences is an essential part of the ongoing comprehension process readers engage in (Anderson & Pearson, 1984). Despite the conventional wisdom that teachers should delay inferential activities until students have mastered literal comprehension, both basic and applied research in reading clearly support a strong emphasis on inferential activities from the outset of instruction.

Inference is the heart of the comprehension process. Schemata serve as organizing frameworks on which to fit pieces of information. Readers and listeners use these frameworks to fill in omitted details and to make extensive elaborations (Anderson, 1977; Anderson, Spiro, & Anderson, 1978; Bransford, Barclay, & Franks, 1972; Brown et al., 1977; Kail et al., 1977; Paris & Carter, 1973). For example, in the Kail et al. study, second and sixth graders read sentences such as: "Mary was playing in a game. She was hit by a bat." Although the game of baseball is never mentioned in these sentences, the students—even the second graders—had no difficulty drawing the inference that Mary was playing baseball. These studies demonstrate that children can draw inferences, although not that they will always do so automatically (Paris & Lindauer, 1976). They also suggest that even the simplest text requires readers to draw inferences.

Several instructional studies provide strong evidence that children can learn to improve their inferencing abilities as early as second grade. Two instructional activities of interest were used for these studies. In the Hansen (1981) and Hansen and Pearson (1983) studies, experimenters discussed how inferences are made. They helped students learn how to use their existing knowledge and the information in the text to help them answer questions. In addition, they gave students visual and kinesthetic reminders of how to use existing and text knowledge to draw inferences. In the studies by Raphael and her colleagues (Raphael & McKinney, 1983; Raphael & Pearson, 1985; Raphael & Wonnacott, 1985), the researchers asked students to identify and label the strategies they used to answer comprehension questions, especially inference questions. They showed students that sometimes they could answer questions just from their prior knowledge, and that other times they needed to use information in the text as well. All these strategies were effective in improving students' comprehension of text, as well as their ability to answer inferential questions.

Thoughtful readers ask questions. Teacher-generated questions have proliferated as a major comprehension activity in basal reading programs as well as in classrooms. But student-generated questions have not, although we have evidence that they should.

Pearson, Roehler, Dole, & Duffy

Why would student-generated questions be useful to readers? One theoretical explanation is that the process of generating questions, particularly higher-order questions, leads to deeper levels of text processing (Andre & Anderson, 1979; Craik & Lockhart, 1972), thereby improving comprehension and learning.

In a quest to help students learn how to assume control over their own learning, several studies have tried to teach students to generate their own questions. Results of these empirical studies have been uneven. Tierney and Cunningham (1984), for instance, reported mixed and inconclusive results. Nonetheless, two studies worth reporting are those conducted by Singer and Donlan in 1982 and Palincsar and Brown in 1984 (see also Brown & Palincsar, 1985; Brown, Palincsar, & Armbruster, 1984).

In the Singer and Donlan study, high school students were taught to generate story-specific questions from a set of general questions about story structure (e.g., "What action does the leading character initiate?"). Students who generated their own questions showed greater improvement in comprehension than did students who simply answered questions constructed by their teachers. Apparently, "active comprehension" of stories led to improved understanding of text.

Palincsar and Brown (1984) provide additional strong evidence for the effectiveness of student-generated questions. In a series of studies, they trained junior high students in four important learning strategies: summarizing, questioning, clarifying, and predicting. Careful modeling in the form of a teacher-student dyad was established to train students how to ask good questions. The researchers reported impressive effects for their instructional intervention program. Of course, their intervention came in a packaged program including all four learning strategies, not just questioning, but there is good reason to believe that students' comprehension of expository materials can be improved with instruction in asking questions.

A closer examination of these studies may answer the nagging question of why requiring students to generate questions is not always an effective technique. In the Singer and Donlan study and the Palincsar and Brown studies, students were trained carefully and given a set structure in which to work. Such training may be critical to the effectiveness of the questioning strategy. Support for this argument comes from a study by Andre and Anderson (1979). In their study, students who were trained in generating questions outperformed students who either generated questions on their own or merely reread the text. Students without training in generating questions performed no better than students who simply reread the material.

Searching for a Comprehension Curriculum

What a comprehension curriculum ought to look like is one of the most important questions in reading instruction. It is especially important for those of us who would like to debunk the specific skills myth and provide a more effective alternative.

We propose that the strategies identified in our review of the behavior of expert readers should form the basis of a comprehension curriculum for the 1990s. These strategies have been shown to be important for readers as they move along the continuum of expertise from novice to expert readers. In addition, we argue that the seven characteristics of the thoughtful reader we have identified and reviewed can be used to create our comprehension curriculum. These characteristics can be the goals that constitute the infrastructure of what we teach in the name of comprehension instruction.

One essential characteristic of our suggested curriculum distinguishes it from the comprehension skills curriculum in basal reading programs. A curriculum derived from the cognitively oriented research of the past decade would be better characterized as a range of flexible, adaptable strategies than as a scope and sequence of skills. Traditionally, basal reading programs have discussed and taught various reading comprehension skills, including identifying main ideas, sequencing, and recognizing cause and effect relationships. Within the more recent instructional research tradition, it is more common for researchers to discuss comprehension strategies. One reason for this preference is more political than substantive; researchers working within a cognitive framework may wish to avoid identification with the "reading as the assembly of a set of discrete skills" tradition. But there is a second and more important

Pearson, Roehler, Dole, & Duffy

reason for the use of the term strategies instead of skills. In the current reading curriculum, comprehension skills are characterized as isolated activities employed with small pieces of texts, usually on workbook pages. For example, finding the main idea of a paragraph is sometimes taught through the repeated practice of reading short paragraphs and choosing from four possible main idea statements. Or, if teachers give direct instruction in the skill, they often tell students simply that "the main idea is the most important idea" (Baumann, 1986; Hare & Bingham, 1986).

Those who use the term strategy, however, have in mind something more than repeated practice or simple directives. Strategies refer to conscious and flexible plans that readers apply and adapt to particular texts and tasks. For example, when teaching students to find the main idea of a paragraph, teachers might model how they use a flexible plan for figuring out what's central to the content of particular paragraphs. The implementation would vary from one paragraph to the next, but the plan would remain similar across paragraphs. This similarity would constitute the core of the lesson plan.

Skills and strategies, then, have several important differences. First, strategies emphasize conscious plans under the control of the reader, whereas skills are used without conscious planning. Expert readers like Emily make decisions about which strategy to use and when to use it. Second, strategies emphasize the reasoning process readers go through as they comprehend text, while skills seldom involve such self-awareness. Third, strategies emphasize the adaptable nature of the comprehension process; the strategies readers use change when reading different kinds of text or when reading for different purposes. Skills, on the other hand, connote an automatic, consistent, invariant behavior.

One final point deserves explicit mention before we turn from issues of curriculum to issues of instruction. In opting for a loosely coupled range of strategies rather than a tightly knit sequence of skills, we are asking teachers to completely rethink traditional notions of skill mastery and instruction. We really do expect *all* readers of *all* ages to engage in *all* of these strategies at some level of sophistication. We really are arguing that there are no first grade skills, third grade skills, sixth grade skills, and so on. Readers of all ages should engage in these strategies; with age and experience, they get better and are able to apply them to a wider range of texts, tasks, and situations. But these strategies are as important for the novice as they are for the expert. Granted, first graders may not ask sophisticated questions, but they can ask something, and what they ask is likely to be important to them.

What we have, then, is more of an emerging expertise model of strategy acquisition instead of a scope and sequence of skills. This distinction will become very important as we turn our attention to instruction and address the critical issue of how students develop these flexible strategies.

A Caveat

It is beyond our intention in this paper to lay out a total reading comprehension program for the elementary grades, and we do not claim that our suggestions could or should be used exclusively and inclusively for such purposes. While we argue that readers of all age levels can benefit from the particular strategies included here, we are not suggesting that the comprehension curriculum should consist only of these strategies. Several important issues remain unaddressed. For example, we have not discussed what young and novice readers need to understand about the relationship between oral and written language. It is difficult to envision the direct teaching of this relationship. Children come to understand the relationship in different ways and at different times. An understanding of how talk relates to print often arises from whole language activities and language experiences where young children see their words translated into symbols. We would never want to be construed as arguing that such activities are unnecessary if one chooses to follow our curricular guidelines.

Another worthwhile comprehension activity we have not discussed is the directed reading lesson. We know from research that comprehension can be improved through a series of well-developed and thoughtful lines of questions (Beck, Omanson, & McKeown, 1982; Hansen, 1981). In a comprehension curriculum, we would want to see questions and activities that ask children to respond to literature as reflections of their lives and experiences. These activities should be included in a total reading program that focuses not only on comprehension but also on reading as an aesthetic experience.

How Should Comprehension Be Taught?

Now that the question of what should be taught has been addressed, we turn to the question of how it should be taught. This half of the chapter is a search for instructional actions in teaching the comprehension curriculum. We must establish at the outset, however, that an important global characteristic of these instructional actions is their capacity to bring joy and excitement to literacy. Just as the shift in curricular focus from skills to strategies brings with it the capacity for making the reading curriculum more meaningful and compelling for students, the instructional focus should empower students to experience the gifts and rewards of literacy.

Earlier we noted how cognitive research has suggested changes in the comprehension curriculum. Similarly, instructional research has suggested changes in how to teach such a curriculum. Traditionally, reading teachers have relied on a practice model; that is, students are exposed repeatedly to certain tasks, primarily answering comprehension questions and completing skill exercises. In both cases, instructional materials—particularly basal reading textbooks—dominate because teachers look to materials both for what students will practice and for what teachers will discuss with students during practice.

Whether the focus is on primary grades (Duffy & McIntyre, 1982), middle grades (Durkin, 1979), high school (Palmer, 1982), or community college (Herrmann, 1985), teachers follow the dictates of commercial reading materials and emphasize completion of isolated skill tasks prescribed by those materials. Often, the teacher's role is primarily that of a technician who follows directions and prescriptions, rather than that of a decision maker who engages in substantive pedagogical maneuvering in response to students' needs (Duffy, 1982; Duffy, Roehler, & Putnam, 1987).

However, drill-and-practice instructional models are inadequate for our new comprehension curriculum. This is especially true in a technologically sophisticated society—a society that will increasingly value workers who can solve problems over those who can only follow prescribed routines. It is no longer good enough to have students answer questions and memorize isolated skill responses. Students must be self-regulated constructors of meaning from text; hence, more flexible, interactive, and problem-focused instructional actions are needed. What follows is a search for those actions.

History of Instructional Research

Until about 1970, instructional research was virtually unknown. Teaching was viewed as a craft, and teachers were "born, not made." However, research such as Coleman's (1979), which implied that teachers do not make a difference in student achievement, spurred researchers to examine teacher effects. The result was a body of work called process-product research.

Process-product research. Process-product research examines the instructional acts (processes) of teachers who produce high reading achievement scores (products) and compares them with the instructional acts of less effective teachers. Results are generally cataloged as "teacher effectiveness" research. Researchers such as Brophy (1979), Good (1983), Rosenshine (1979), and Rosenshine and Stevens (1984) used process-product research findings to list teacher behaviors associated with high achievement test scores. Many of these behaviors were validated in a frequently cited experimental study (Anderson, Evertson, & Brophy, 1979), in which the effectiveness of first grade reading teachers who were directed to use these techniques was compared with the effectiveness of first grade teachers who tended not to use them. The teachers who used the prescribed techniques produced significantly better achievement test results than teachers who did not. This study is one of many (see Brophy & Good, 1986) that are sometimes referred to as "direct instruction" research because the results indicated that effective teachers present curricular goals in direct and explicit ways.

Process-product research was significant because it established the simple but important fact that specific teacher actions

Pearson, Roehler, Dole, & Duffy

can result in improved student outcomes. However, this research was plagued by three serious weaknesses. First, the criterion for effectiveness was performance on achievement tests—which focus on skill-based tasks in basic reading and mathematics—rather than the acquisition of self-regulated comprehension strategies (or, for that matter, the problem-centered strategies in mathematics). Second, the research was based on the drill-and-practice model of instruction employed by many teachers; as such, it tended to produce results that suggested how best to employ a drill-and-practice model. It did not determine whether other instructional models might be even more effective. Third, suggestions for how best to employ drill-and-practice focused almost exclusively on teacher actions that increase students' time on academic tasks.

Ultimately, the major contribution of process-product research was to establish that techniques that increase students' attentiveness during instruction result in improved student achievement. Because getting and holding students' attention is associated with classroom management, process-product research is frequently disseminated to teachers in the form of classroom management instruction (Anderson, Evertson, & Emmer, 1980; Brophy & Putnam, 1979; Doyle, 1979).

To summarize, these early attempts at studying instruction were important for four reasons. First, they established the relationship of good classroom management to instructional effectiveness; it is now almost a given in supervision that good management is a prerequisite to any sort of instruction. Second, this research helped us learn to distinguish classroom management (i.e., getting students on task and keeping them there) from instruction (i.e., helping students build understandings). This distinction was significant because it ultimately led to instructional research that went well beyond getting students on task; in a sense, it permitted the discovery of many of the findings we discuss later. Third, process-product research established the fact that teachers do make a difference, particularly with academically at-risk students. Finally, this research demonstrated that the actions of effective teachers are not limited to mysterious, inherited capabilities; instead, they include many common-sense techniques that all teachers can use to improve their effectiveness.

A current view of instruction. As useful as the process-product findings of the 1970s were, they have little application to current comprehension instruction because students need to do more than practice answering questions and completing skill sheets. Several forces have caused reading educators to think differently about instruction; these forces, in turn, lead to alternatives to traditional drill-and-practice models of comprehension instruction.

One force behind this new view of instruction was the schema theory view of learning from text (Anderson & Pearson, 1984). Earlier in the chapter we noted the impact of this view on how students comprehend text. However, it also has an impact on our understanding of how students comprehend instruction. In the schema theory view, both learning from text and learning from instruction are active processes of constructing meaning in which old knowledge is connected in sensible ways with new knowledge encountered in text or in class. Readers build meaning by engaging in a series of recursive interactions with text. In instruction, learners build meaning by engaging in a series of recursive interactions with the teacher. Students make predictions about what the teacher will do or say; they build a tentative model of meaning. As they receive new information from the teacher's talk or actions, they either fit it into the existing model or revise the model so the information fits. Just as readers reconstruct an author's meaning during reading, so students gradually reconstruct a teacher's meaning during instruction.

A second force affecting views of instruction, which grows directly out of the schema theory perspective, is called the "cognitive mediational paradigm" (Winne & Marx, 1982). The cognitive mediational paradigm, like the schema theory view, characterizes students as active rather than passive. From this perspective, students are active interpreters of instructional cues provided by the teacher; they make sense of instruction by combining these cues with prior knowledge about both the curricular topic and ways to survive in the classroom. Shulman (1986) describes this view as follows:

> The learner does not respond to the instruction per se. The learner responds to the instruction as transformed, as actively

Pearson, Roehler, Dole, & Duffy

apprehended. Thus, to understand why learners respond (or fail to respond) as they do, ask not what they were taught, but what sense they rendered of what they were taught. The consequences of teaching can only be understood as a function of what that teaching stimulates the learner to do with the material (p. 17).

The cue students most often use to make sense of instruction is the academic work teachers provide (Doyle, 1983). Academic work is used broadly to mean the conceptual sum of the tasks the teacher assigns and the information the teacher provides about these tasks. For instance, suppose a teacher wants to provide main idea instruction to help students determine what is important in textbooks. To do so, suppose she or he assigns worksheets requiring students to repeatedly select the best title for short paragraphs. Suppose further that this teacher tells students their grade will be based not on how they use this main idea instruction in textbooks but on their accuracy and neatness in completing the worksheets. Although the teacher may intend for the worksheets to be a stepping stone to real application, students are likely to infer that the real purpose of learning about main ideas is to complete the worksheets. Further, they are likely to infer that identifying main ideas is something you do with paragraphs or worksheets, not with real text. This is because when students are confronted with school tasks, they mediate them. In other words, they negotiate meaning for them just as they negotiate meaning for text; they combine incoming information with what is already known, make inferences about what really is intended, and construct an interpretation that makes sense in terms of their prior experience.

One classic illustration of this mediational process was seen in a study of reading seatwork in a first grade class (Anderson et al., 1985). While the teachers all intended the assigned seatwork on letter sounds, dot-to-dot drawings, and so on to help students learn how to be better readers, students (particularly those of lower ability) concluded that the purpose of worksheets was to "get done." Given this type of academic work, students' prior knowledge about how things work in their classrooms and about letters and drawing caused them to construct a meaning for seatwork that did not reflect their teachers' intentions. Similarly, while teachers hope that skill activities will help students become better readers, students often mediate these activities to mean something quite different (Winne & Marx, 1982). Hence, instruction is heavily influenced by student interpretation of what goes on in the classroom.

A third force shaping current views of instruction focuses on the teacher's mediational role. Just as students are cognitively active in interpreting what the teacher says and does—and, on the basis of these cues, in deciding what is really important—effective teachers also are cognitively active. They interpret what students say and do during instruction and, on the basis of how well these interpretations match what they perceive the intended outcome to be, provide students with additional instructional information (Duffy & Roehler, 1987; Roehler & Duffy, 1987). When teachers engage in such activity, they are negotiating in an attempt to bring student understandings in line with intended curricular outcomes. For instance, if after modeling how to activate background knowledge before reading teachers notice that their students think they are to use only their prior knowledge (as opposed to combining their prior knowledge with text cues), they must spontaneously clarify and elaborate on the strategy so that students restructure their understandings and alter their inappropriate views. Teachers may, for example, provide more examples, models, analogies, and other aids to illustrate how to combine prior knowledge with text cues. This aspect of instruction has been referred to as "alternative representations" (Wilson, Shulman, & Richert, 1987), "responsive elaboration" (Duffy & Roehler, 1987), and "adaptive actions" (Roehler, Duffy, & Warren, 1988).

Present understandings of instruction are also influenced by research on metacognition and metacognitive awareness (Baker & Brown, 1984; Flavell, 1981; Garner, 1987, this volume). As mentioned earlier, this research suggests that expert readers of any age can become consciously aware of their own cognition. Moreover, as a result of this awareness, they can monitor and regulate their own comprehension. Students who are aware of how they make sense out of text can regulate sense making. Rather than simply answer-

Pearson, Roehler, Dole, & Duffy

ing comprehension questions or completing worksheets, students must be consciously aware of *how* they answer questions and *how* they employ strategies. This awareness empowers them to access and apply such cognitive processes when needed. For instance, Meloth (1987) concluded that metacognitive awareness of lesson content is a crucial mediating variable between instruction and student application of that instruction to outcome measures. As such, awareness is key to being in control of both comprehension and transfer of learning from one situation to another. This argument stems from the assumption that readers cannot repair problems with their understanding if they are not conscious of comprehension resources and how they work. Consequently, instruction should build students' awareness of what they know so they can consciously call on that knowledge when needed.

Finally, current views of instruction are influenced by the explicit instructional tradition (Duffy et al., 1986; Pearson, 1985). Because students build curricular understandings by combining information provided by the teacher with their prior knowledge, it is reasonable to expect that the more explicit the instructional cues, the more likely students are to infer teachers' intended curricular goals unambiguously. From another perspective, we can say that explicitness increases the likelihood that the inferences students draw in the process of cognitive mediation will match the teacher's intentions. Further, explicitness expedites student metacognitive awareness. When teachers are explicit, students demonstrate greater metacognitive awareness of lesson content (Duffy et al., 1987). Hence, rather than simply providing students with practice, teachers must share with students information they can use to construct understandings about how reading works, and *then* provide practice.

Summary. These five forces suggest that comprehension instruction is a more complex and fluid process of teacher-student interactions than suggested by drill-and-practice models where the teacher's role is essentially one of directing student attention to tasks. In the new view, the teacher plays a pivotal role in helping students gradually construct curricular understandings. Teachers cannot simply ask comprehension questions and supervise completion of accompanying workbook pages. Instead, their instructional actions must include sharing with students explicit information about how expert readers make sense of text and adjusting that information as instruction proceeds to accommodate students' emerging understandings and awareness.

Shulman (1986) describes this view of instruction as "transforming [one's] own comprehension of the subject matter, [one's] own skills of performance or desired attitude values, into pedagogical representations and actions." Shulman goes on to note that "There are ways of talking, showing, enacting, or otherwise representing the ideas so that the unknowing can come to know, those without understanding can comprehend and discern, the unskilled can become adept" (p. 7). What are these "pedagogical actions"? What should teachers do to help students take charge of the process of constructing meaning from text?

Searching for an Instructional Plan of Action

As opposed to older views of instruction in which teachers repeatedly exposed students to practice materials, in this new view the teacher is a mediator who negotiates development of student understandings through recursive, reciprocal interactions in which both teacher and students play active roles and in which curricular understandings are gradually developed over time. Elements of this perspective are seen in virtually all significant comprehension instruction research (e.g., Duffy et al., 1987; Palincsar & Brown, 1984; Paris & Jacobs, 1984; Pearson, 1985). When taken as a whole, the instruction reflected in such research can be described as four kinds of teacher actions: planning, providing motivational opportunities, sharing information, and nurturing student understanding.

Planning. Traditionally, teacher planning has been thought to be static; that is, pedagogical actions are planned in advance and then followed much like scripts. However, in our current view, planning is a much more fluid process. Because instruction is dynamic, it cannot be entirely planned in advance. It *begins* with a plan which states the teacher's intentions regarding the goal and the procedures to be followed. In that form, it *looks* static. However, as soon as implementation begins, the plan is modified. Students create unanticipated meanings that render the plan obsolete. This tension between teacher intentions and student meanings requires the teacher to modify the plan. This recursive process of reciprocal mediation by teacher and students continues until one of three outcomes results: the students achieve the goal, the teacher modifies the goal, or time runs out. Hence, while planning remains a crucial component of good instruction, it provides not a set script but a foundation from which teachers make adjustments in response to student mediation.

The selection of academic work to be pursued during any lesson or series of lessons is a critical part of planning instruction because academic work is the primary medium through which students make sense of instruction (Doyle, 1983). Academic work in reading provides students with experiences that become part of their prior knowledge about reading and thus part of what they use to make sense out of subsequent reading activities.

To make this point clear, let's compare two hypothetical teachers. Suppose the academic work in Mr. Williams's classroom emphasizes literature reading tasks, while the work in Ms. Smith's room down the hall emphasizes workbook tasks. Students in Mr. Williams's classroom will view subsequent reading encounters from the perspective that reading is what you do with literature and books; the meaning they construct for reading will reflect that perspective. Students in Ms. Smith's classroom, on the other had, will view subsequent reading encounters from the perspective that reading is something you do with workbooks; consequently, they will construct a very different meaning for reading.

At a more subtle level, academic work includes the environment defining the context for that work—what some have labeled the situational context. For instance, a lesson on drawing inferences taught in a classroom that emphasizes genuine communication purposes, such as writing letters to order books from catalogs, causes students to associate what they learn about reading with genuine communication. In contrast, the same inferencing lesson taught in a classroom that routinely emphasizes only school-related reading tasks, such as filling in worksheets, causes students to associate what they learn about reading with artificial school situations.

As such, academic work has a powerful influence on the views students develop about reading.

To illustrate the power of academic work, let's look at three different examples of comprehension instruction. Each is effective in developing a different kind of comprehension outcome. We are not presenting them as examples of good and poor instruction but rather as examples of how different kinds of academic work influence what students learn about comprehension.

One common kind of academic work in comprehension is answering teacher-generated questions about reading selections. Teachers can ask questions based on a systematic analysis of text (Beck, Omanson, & McKeown, 1982; Ogle, 1986). The academic work in this instance is answering comprehension questions about the content of the selection. If the curricular goal focuses on knowledge of a selection's content, this kind of academic work can be highly effective. For instance, the directed reading lesson, in which questions about a selection's content are asked before, during, and after reading to guide students to meaning, is a good technique if you want to focus on content. The academic work of answering questions about the content helps students conclude that knowing a selection's content is important.

The technique of reciprocal teaching offers a second kind of academic work in comprehension (Palincsar & Brown, 1984). With this technique, students and teachers take turns being the teacher and eliciting responses from peers. Participants ask questions in much the same way as described above. The difference here is that students do not simply respond to the teacher's questions; instead, they share equally in dialogues that focus on processing text meaning through predicting, questioning, summarizing, and clarifying. The academic work here is the dialogue about these activities. Students learn to engage in these activities as they process text meaning. The academic work helps students conclude that active processing of text meaning is something expert readers do.

A third kind of comprehension instruction focuses on direct explanation of the reasoning behind strategies to repair meaning blockages (Duffy et al., 1987). The teacher explicitly explains the reasoning expert readers employ when adjusting predictions to fit new text information, determining what is important in text, clarifying information, and so on. The focus is on developing conscious awareness of reasoning so students can regulate the use of such reasoning in future reading situations. This kind of academic work is effective when the curricular goal for students is to monitor how they construct meaning, how they activate appropriate strategies when they encounter blockages, and how they remove such blockages. It helps students conclude that expert readers reason in adaptive, flexible ways when they encounter blockages to meaning.

These three forms of comprehension instruction are all effective, but for different reasons. Because each engages students in different kinds of academic work, each encourages students to think differently about comprehension; consequently, each causes students to construct different understandings about what strategic readers do. Because all three outcomes are desirable, teachers will want to select one kind of academic work one time and other kinds at other times.

Providing motivational opportunities. The environment for reading instruction is optimum when students are enthusiastic about reading and have an I-can-do-it attitude. Teachers' ability to help students develop this enthusiasm depends on the presence of two factors: success and usefulness. All humans enjoy being successful and avoid doing things they can't do successfully. Motivated students are those whose encounters with reading are reasonably successful. Teachers can create lessons with which their students will achieve success if they (1) assess their students' understandings and then provide lesson content that is at the zone of proximal development (Vygotsky, 1978), (2) set reasonable expectations (Brophy & Good, 1986), and (3) help students develop self-regulated approaches to learning (Book et al., 1988; Sivan & Roehler, 1986).

Teachers can provide students with opportunities for success by giving them instruction and assessment measures that are within the zone of proximal development. This involves giving students information and asking them to act on that information at a level that allows them to complete the task with assistance but not without assistance. When students complete a difficult task with assistance, they experience feelings of success. Success with difficult tasks leads to enthusiasm and an I-can-do-it attitude.

A second way to provide success is to set reasonable expectations. Such expectations can create a motivating environment. Brophy (1986) has shown that reasonable expectations can be set when teachers support student efforts; assign appropriately difficult tasks; specify how learning is useful; and most important, model learning as rewarding, self-actualizing activity.

Finally, teachers can help students become successful by developing self-regulated approaches to reading. This can be accomplished when teachers provide instructional talk that signals to the students that they are responsible for monitoring and cannot rely on an external monitor such as the teacher. Sivan and Roehler (1986) found that the students of teachers who provided such talk in their lessons were more internally motivated and possessed better attitudes than the students of teachers who did not. Book et al. (1988) found that teacher statements about self-regulation related directly to student awareness of the need to be self-regulating. Therefore, teachers who want to help students become self-regulated and develop positive attitudes that lead to success can do so by adding statements to lesson discussions about students being in control of their own learning.

In summary, teachers who want to develop feelings of success in their students can do so by assisting students with difficult tasks, setting reasonable expectations, and supporting self-regulated learning.

Usefulness is the second factor that develops enthusiastic readers who possess I-can-do-it attitudes. Students' understanding of the usefulness of reading strategies can be greatly enhanced when teachers explicitly explain when and why strategies should be used (Brown et al., 1983; Duffy & Roehler, 1989; O'Sullivan & Pressley, 1984; Paris, Lipson, & Wixson, 1983). Several experiments have shown that if teachers include in their instructional tasks statements about when or why to use strategy knowledge, students are more likely to apply strategies following instruction (Borkowski, Levers, & Gruenfelder, 1976; Cavanaugh & Borkowski, 1979). Post hoc analysis of experimental data about teacher explanations suggests that stating why or when students should use strategies may contribute more to their success than stating either what is being learned or how to do it (Meloth & Roehler, 1987). Usefulness statements about when or why to use reading strategies are helpful additions to teachers' strategy lessons.

Sharing information.   Instruction is designed to help students build understandings—or schemata—for curricular goals. Experience is the fuel for schema development. This is true whether the schema in question is for a dog, a fancy restaurant, a comprehension strategy, or a teacher's mode of instruction. Furthermore, it is not experience, per se, that matters; experience simply provides helpful information. It is not enough just to see a collection of dogs. One must see an array of dogs in juxtaposition with an array of nondogs (for example, cats, wolves, horses, coyotes) or accompanied by some explanation of key features to look out for (fur, snout, bark, sloppy tongue). Similarly, for students to develop a schema for a strategy, they need to encounter lots of opportunities to use the strategy as well as some explanations of the activity's key features.

Two conditions govern our view of this interchange of information. The first relates to the kind of information teachers provide early in a lesson. When a lesson begins, students may lack an adequate schema for the curricular goal at hand, or worse, they may possess misconceptions about it. Thus we might provide instruction in how to monitor meaning-getting because students lack a schema for what one does to monitor or because they have a misconception about monitoring. In order to create or modify schemata about monitoring, we might provide helpful hints about how to monitor meaning; students then might use that information to create or modify their schemata about how to make sense of text.

The second condition governing information sharing is teacher modeling. Modeling, or physically demonstrating the performance of a task, is recommended frequently for a variety of instructional approaches (Good, 1983; Rosenshine, 1979). Modeling is what teachers do when they silently read their own library book during Uninterrupted Sustained Silent Reading (USSR) or when they show students how to complete a worksheet. However, the advent of the new comprehension curriculum encourages a more specific meaning for modeling in which teachers not only demonstrate physical aspects of reading but also, to one degree or another, explain the invisible mental reasoning involved in performing tasks.

The effectiveness of this kind of modeling depends on three factors. The first is the explicitness of demonstrations (Duffy et al., 1987; Pearson, 1985; Pearson & Dole, 1987). Demonstrations that provide explicit, unambiguous information are more effective than those that are vague or jumbled. The second factor is flexibility; demonstrations must communicate that cognitive processing is a matter of flexible adjustment to cues provided in the text or the situation rather than rigid adherence to rules or procedural steps. The third factor is specificity; to develop student control of the cognitive process, teachers must model the invisible mental processing involved. For instance, if the teacher merely asks questions without explaining the reasoning employed to answer the questions, students have difficulty assuming control of the comprehension process; the teacher's reasoning remains a mystery and the students' comprehension processes remain unsatisfactory (Bereiter, 1986; Duffy, Roehler, & Herrmann, 1988).

Nurturing student understandings.   Once teachers share information about how to comprehend, they must be prepared to nurture students' mediation of the strategy. Students do not passively receive instructional information; they interpret it. The extent to which students' interpretations reflect the intended curricular outcome will vary depending on their prior understandings about reading and the explicitness of the teacher's instruction. For instance, a teacher may have students complete a self-questioning activity with the intention that they will engage in deeper levels of thinking; however, students may interpret the activity as something to do only when the teacher is present to enforce compliance. While academic work and explicit information can minimize such discrepancies, *some* discrepancy almost always exists. Consequently, teachers must monitor students' evolving understandings as lessons progress and provide elaborated information, or feedback, to help students modify their understandings (Duffy & Roehler, 1987). To illustrate, if students misinterpret a self-questioning activity, the teacher can spontaneously create situations designed to help stu-

Pearson, Roehler, Dole, & Duffy

dents redefine their understanding. For instance, the teacher might have students work in pairs and gradually move toward working alone.

Helping students redefine their understandings as lessons progress is a subtle instructional enterprise. It requires that teachers use student responses as "windows into the mind," infer from these responses the quality of student understanding, and, on the basis of this assessment, spontaneously devise essential instruction—scaffolding, cueing, prompting, using analogies and metaphors, questioning, elaborating, remodeling—that provides students with elaborated information to use in restructuring understandings. Further, the explicitness of these spontaneous elaborations will vary depending on how close the student is to the desired outcome. That is, as students move from what Vygotsky (1978) calls "other-directed to self-directed stages," teachers socially mediate this progression by gradually diminishing the assistance provided. Early in the learning, teachers offer quite explicit and detailed help; gradually they diminish the amount of assistance as students begin to construct the curricular goals. Pearson (1985) has referred to this progression as the "gradual release of responsibility" on the part of the teacher as students gradually assume more control. This process of shifting from teacher control to student control is a subtle but crucial instructional action.

Helping students restructure their understandings is not limited to lesson-specific actions, however. Effective teachers engage in a similar progression across longer periods of time (Roehler & Duffy, 1987). For instance, teachers look for opportunities to help students build understandings about the global nature of strategic reading, the interrelationship among strategies, the adaptation of strategies, and the combining and recombining of strategies. These understandings are not lesson specific; that is, they do not focus on a strategy being taught on a given day. Instead, they cut across individual lessons and focus on holistic concepts of reading and language. With this focus, the gradual release of responsibility occurs over a long period of time rather than within a single lesson.

Summary.   Instruction can be characterized as a situation in which teachers attempt to make learning sensible and students attempt to make sense of learning. Both teachers and students negotiate instructional meaning. Teachers plan the understandings they want to create and select appropriate academic work to create instructional opportunities. They also provide motivation, share information, and nurture students' understandings in ways designed to help students construct intended curricular goals. Students interpret academic work and information in light of their prior knowledge about reading and of the rules governing life in a classroom. These important instructional actions help students interpret academic work accurately and move closer to the intended curricular goals.

What Does This All Mean for Classroom Instruction?

In a drill-and-practice model of instruction, practice in answering comprehension questions and in completing skill tasks drives instruction. The logic is that if students practice enough of those tasks, they will eventually develop the ability to read. A number of forces have brought this model into question. From a curriculum perspective, we now know that mastery of long lists of comprehension skills has very little to do with the development of expert reading ability. From an instructional perspective, we now know that students comprehend instructions by combining their prior knowledge with new information from the classroom to construct schemata for curricular goals.

If students are to learn how to be strategic readers, they must have instructional experiences that lead them to construct understandings that are consistent with what expert readers actually do. Creating such instructional experiences requires teachers to move well beyond managing assignments. Teachers must decide whether the academic work they assign promotes student thought about the intended outcome, provide information that will help students construct understandings about that outcome, and spontaneously elaborate on this information as students refine their understandings. Very little is fixed in this instructional milieu; teachers' instructional actions depend almost totally on what students know and how they respond to instructional experiences.

Teachers cannot simply follow the directions in instructional materials. They must assume regulatory control over materials

Pearson, Roehler, Dole, & Duffy

rather than be controlled by them, in much the same way teachers try to get students to take metacognitive control of their reading comprehension. Teachers have to regulate instruction by adapting prescriptions, suggestions, commercial materials, and recommended techniques to particular students and groups of students and by adjusting their plans for any given lesson to emerging student understandings.

Teacher metacognitive control of instruction is crucial for two reasons. First, infusing instruction with vitality and zest is a highly personal endeavor. Actually, it is both a personal and an interpersonal endeavor. Teachers and students create the electricity, the spontaneous spark that cannot be prescribed in advance by even the most thoughtful of authors or editors. Second, students construct instructional meanings throughout the flow of instruction. Hence it is impossible to prescribe in advance how instructional experiences should be structured or restructured. Teachers must be free to create these responses "responsively."

The bottom line is straightforward. Teachers begin the process with fairly well-planned intentions; they decide what to teach and what academic work to assign. Along the way they provide motivation, share key information, and respond in whatever ways are necessary to nurture student understandings. During this nurturing process, teachers must summon all their flexibility, adaptability, and problem-solving skills just to keep pace with the wondrous and varied understandings that students bring to and take from the instructional experience.

A Caveat

Just as we do not want our suggested comprehension curriculum to be used exclusively and inclusively, we do not want our search for instructional actions to be viewed as the final word. In fact, we have resisted the temptation to describe an "instructional model" for fear that such a label implies a static set of teaching procedures to be followed rigidly, when the truth is that effective instruction demands fluid and flexible teacher response to student understandings.

Further, other instructional issues remain to be addressed. While we argue that comprehension instruction should not be limited to random comprehension questions and the completion of skill sheets in a drill-and-practice mode, we are not saying that teachers should never ask questions, assign worksheets, or require practice. To the contrary, it is difficult to imagine instructional interactions that do not include questions. No matter how you disguise it, independent work is probably going to end up looking a lot like worksheets. Also, while we argue that teachers cannot rigidly follow prescriptions in instructional materials in a thoughtless way, we anticipate that instruction will involve the use of commercially published materials designed to ease teachers' burdens. In addition, while we emphasize *teacher* instructional actions, our emphasis on student mediation makes clear that instructional techniques focusing on *student* actions, such as cooperative learning (Slavin, 1980), are also important. And finally, while we talk about the actions of expert teachers, it is clear that expert teaching, like expert reading, develops on a novice-to-expert continuum. Just as students gradually develop reading strategies, so teachers gradually develop expertise in carrying out instructional actions.

Discussion of these issues has not been our purpose here. Instead, our purpose has been to identify those instructional actions documented to be effective in recent research, to organize them into a coherent framework, and to contrast them with existing practices. As more is learned about effective instruction, refinements and elaborations will be made on these principles. However, they represent a start that teachers can use to begin moving from a traditional drill-and-practice model of reading instruction to one that is more compatible with what we know about reading and learning as strategic cognitive processes.

Rules of Thumb

We close this essay on reading comprehension instruction with a set of rules of thumb about what to teach and how to teach it. There should be no surprises here; these guidelines are natural extensions of what we have discussed so far.

- *We need a few well-taught, well-learned strategies.* Currently, most reading curricula contain too many skills to teach. Pressured by so much to cover in so little time, teachers go quickly over everything, which leaves no time to teach anything very well. Everyone involved—teachers, students, parents—would benefit from a leaner, meaner comprehension curriculum composed of a handful of key strategies taught well and frequently applied to real texts.

- *Reading develops as a process of emerging expertise.* Reading is not best learned as a set of isolated skills, picked up one by one along an assembly line offered by the teacher and the reading program. Instead a single central goal—building meaning—carries through from one situation to the next. What changes over time is the students' level of expertise and the amount of conceptual and contextual support teachers need to provide. Teachers would be better off to regard their role as journeyman readers working with knowledgeable and purposeful apprentices rather than as purveyors of truth.

- *Good reading strategies are as adaptable as they are intentional.* Reading strategies begin as conscious plans that readers use to make sense of text. They are intentional; readers have in mind a few predetermined ideas about how to go about building meaning. But reading strategies are also adaptable; they can and should change quickly and easily depending on how readers size up the situation at hand. Good readers change what they do depending on their perceptions about the text, the task, the purpose, and the consequences of reading.

- *Good reading instruction is as adaptable as it is intentional.* Teachers begin instruction with some intentions, usually curricular goals—understandings about what reading is and how it works—that they want students to achieve. But they realize that they have to adapt their goals and their strategies on the basis of their students' and their own emerging and dynamic understanding of the instructional situation.

- *Good reading instruction depends on the creation of an environment that continually reinforces the usefulness and value of reading.* Good instruction includes an environment conducive to learning where the usefulness of reading is constantly seen. Students who daily interact with print, read what others have written, and write to others develop conceptual understandings about the value of reading. Reading is seen as a tool for gaining new knowledge and rethinking current knowledge.

- *Good reading instruction involves giving students opportunities to activate their background knowledge, discover new information, and construct new understandings.* For optimum learning to occur, students should think about what they already know about a topic, gather new information, and, through the mediation process, gradually come to understand the topic of the lesson. Students who do not receive help in learning the strategies used in these three areas usually have trouble with difficult reading material and, consequently, learn less.

- *Good reading instruction involves carefully building scaffolding that allows students to use a strategy before they fully understand it while they gradually gain control of it.* With analogies, explicit cues, redirecting, metaphors, elaborations, and modeling, teachers can create a form of assistance that allows students to complete the task before they cognitively understand how to do it and when to apply it. This form of assistance is highly productive as long as the scaffolding is gradually removed as students gain control of the task.

- *Good reading instruction involves helping students develop understandings about reading, both global conceptual understandings and more specific understandings about how, when, and where to use strategies.* Developing both types of understandings simultaneously is extremely difficult. The process is something like the creation of a tapestry, where specific patterns must be understood in order to understand and create the whole design. During the creating process, the specific patterns should be carefully attended to, but in the end it is the full tapestry that is enjoyed, understood, and used. The smaller patterns become a vehicle for making the whole tapestry accessible. While this duality is difficult to achieve in reading comprehension instruction, it is necessary if the appropriate understandings are to be developed.

Pearson, Roehler, Dole, & Duffy

- *Both reading comprehension and comprehension instruction are highly interactive and reciprocal.* The meanings students create for the texts they read are complex negotiations involving an unseen author, a teacher, and an interpretive community of peers with whom to share and revise meanings. The meanings students develop about their instructional situations involve similarly complex negotiations among self, teacher, peers, and the situation itself. Teachers and students provide one another with demonstrations of how to build, share, and revise models of meaning, both of the texts they read and the instruction they are trying to render sensible.

References

Afflerbach, P.P. (1986). The influence of prior knowledge on expert readers' importance assignment processes. In J.A. Niles and R.V. Lalik (Eds.), *Solving problems in literacy: Learners, teachers, and researchers* (pp. 30-40). Rochester, NY: National Reading Conference.

Afflerbach, P.P., & Johnston, P.H. (1986). What do expert readers do when the main idea is not explicit? In J.F. Baumann (Ed.), *Teaching main idea comprehension* (pp. 49-72). Newark, DE: International Reading Association.

Alessi, S.M., Anderson, T.H., & Goetz, E.T. (1979). An investigation of lookbacks during studying. *Discourse Processes, 2,* 197-212.

Alvermann, D.E., Smith, L.C., & Readence, J.E. (1985). Prior knowledge activation and the comprehension of compatible and incompatible text. *Reading Research Quarterly, 20,* 420-436.

Anderson, C.W., & Smith, E.L. (1987). Teaching science. In Z.V. Richardson-Koehler (Ed.), *Educator's handbook: A research perspective* (pp. 84-111). White Plains, NY: Longman.

Anderson, L., Brubaker, N.L., Alleman-Brooks, J., & Duffy, G. (1985). A qualitative study of seatwork in first-grade classrooms. *Elementary School Journal, 86*(2), 123-140.

Anderson, L., Evertson, C., & Brophy, J. (1979). An experimental study of effective teaching in first grade reading groups. *Elementary School Journal, 79*(4), 193-223.

Anderson, L., Evertson, C., & Emmer, E. (1980). Dimensions of classroom management derived from recent research. *Journal of Curriculum Studies, 12,* 343-356.

Anderson, R.C. (1977). The notion of schemata and the educational enterprise. In R.C. Anderson, R.J. Spiro, & W.E. Montague (Eds.), *Schooling and the acquisition of knowledge.* Hillsdale, NJ: Erlbaum.

Anderson, R.C., & Pearson, P.D. (1984). A schema-theoretic view of basic processes in reading. In P.D. Pearson (Ed.), *Handbook of reading research* (pp. 255-292). White Plains, NY: Longman.

Anderson, R.C., Spiro, R.J., & Anderson, M.C. (1978). Schemata as scaffolding for the representation of information in connected discourse. *American Educational Research Journal, 15,* 433-440.

Andre, M.E.D.A., & Anderson, T.H. (1979). The development and evaluation of a self-questioning study technique. *Reading Research Quarterly, 14,* 605-623.

Baker, L., & Brown, A.L. (1984). Metacognitive skills and reading. In P.D. Pearson (Ed.), *Handbook of reading research* (pp. 353-394). White Plains, NY: Longman.

Baumann, J.F. (1986). The direct instruction of main idea comprehension ability. In J.F. Baumann (Ed.), *Teaching main idea comprehension* (pp. 133-178). Newark, DE: International Reading Association.

Beck, I., Omanson, R., & McKeown, M. (1982). An instructional redesign of reading lessons: Effects on comprehension. *Reading Research Quarterly, 17*(4), 462-481.

Bereiter, C. (1986). The reading comprehension lesson: A commentary on Heap's ethnomethodological analysis. *Curriculum Inquiry, 16,* 65-72.

Book, C., Putnam, J., Meloth, M., & Sivan, E. (1988). *Teachers' concepts of reading, reading concepts communicated during instruction, and students' concepts of reading* (Research Series #190, Institute for Research on Teaching). East Lansing, MI: Michigan State University.

Borkowski, J.G., Levers, S.R., & Gruenfelder, T.M. (1976). Transfer of mediational strategies in children: The role of activity and awareness during strategy acquisition. *Child Development, 47,* 779-786.

Bransford, J.D., Barclay, J.R., & Franks, J.J. (1972). Sentence memory: A constructive versus an interactive approach. *Cognitive Psychology, 3,* 193-209.

Bransford, J.D., & Johnson, M.K. (1972). Contextual prerequisites for understanding: Some investigations of comprehension and recall. *Journal of Verbal Learning and Verbal Behavior, 11,* 717-726.

Bransford, J.D., Vye, N.J., & Stein, B.S. (1984). A comparison of successful and less successful learners: Can we enhance comprehension and mastery skills? In J. Flood (Ed.), *Understanding reading comprehension* (pp. 216-231). Newark, DE: International Reading Association.

Brophy, J. (1979). Teacher behavior and its effects. *Journal of Educational Psychology, 71,* 733-750.

Brophy, J. (1986). *Socializing student motivation to learn* (Research Series #169, Institute for Research on Teaching). East Lansing, MI: Michigan State University.

Brophy, J., & Good, T. (1986). Teacher behavior and student achievement. In M. Wittrock (Ed.), *Handbook of research on teaching* (3rd ed., pp. 328-375). New York: Macmillan.

Brophy, J., & Putnam, J. (1979). Classroom management in the elementary grades. In D. Duke (Ed.), *Classroom management.* Chicago, IL: University of Chicago Press.

Brown, A.L., Bransford, J.D., Ferrara, R.A., & Campione, J.C. (1983). Learning, remembering, and understanding. In J.H. Flavell & E.M. Markmans (Eds.), *Handbook of child psychology* (vol. 3, pp. 515-529). New York: Wiley.

Brown, A.L., & Campione, J.C. (1979). The effects of knowledge and experience on the formation of retrieval plans for studying from texts. In M.M. Gruneberg, P.E. Morris, & R.N. Sukes (Eds.), *Practical aspects of memory.* San Diego, CA: Academic.

Brown, A.L., & Day, J.D. (1983). Macrorules for summarizing texts: The development of expertise. *Journal of Verbal Learning and Verbal Behavior, 22,* 1-14.

Brown, A.L., Day, J.D., & Jones, R.S. (1983). The development of plans for summarizing texts. *Child Development, 54,* 968-979.

Brown, A.L., & Palincsar, A.S. (1985). *Reciprocal teaching of comprehension strategies: A natural history of one program to enhance learning* (Tech. Rep. No. 334). Urbana, IL: University of Illinois, Center for the Study of Reading.

Brown, A.L., Palincsar, A.S., & Armbruster, B.B. (1984). Instructing comprehension-fostering activities in interactive learning situations. In H. Mandl, N.L. Stein, & T. Trabasso (Eds.), *Learning and comprehension of text* (pp. 255-286). Hillsdale, NJ: Erlbaum.

Brown, A.L., & Smiley, S.S. (1977). Rating the importance of structural units of prose passages: A problem of metacognitive development. *Child Development, 48,* 1-8.

Brown, A.L., Smiley, S.S., Day, J.D., Townsend, M., & Lawton, S.C. (1977). Intrusion of a thematic idea in children's recall of prose. *Child Development, 48,* 1454-1466.

Brown, A.L., Smiley, S.S., & Lawton, S.C. (1978). The effects of experience on the selection of suitable retrieval cues for studying texts. *Child Development, 49,* 829-835.

Cavanaugh, J.C., & Borkowski, J.G. (1979). Metamemory-memory "connection": Effects of strategy training and maintenance. *Journal of General Psychology, 101,* 161-174.

Coleman, J. (1979). *Equality of educational opportunity.* Washington, DC: U.S. Government Printing Office.

Craik, F.I.M., & Lockhart, R.S. (1972). Levels of processing: A framework for memory research. *Journal of Verbal Learning and Verbal Behavior, 11,* 671-684.

Crossen, H.J. (1940). Effects of the attitudes of the reader upon critical reading ability. *Journal of Educational Research, 42,* 289-298.

Cunningham, J.W. (1982). Generating interactions between schemata and text. In J.A. Niles & L.A. Harris (Eds.), *New inquiries in reading research and instruction* (pp. 42-47). Rochester, NY: National Reading Conference.

Cunningham, J.W., & Moore, D.W. (1986). The confused world of main idea. In J.F. Baumann (Ed.), *Teaching main idea comprehension* (pp. 1-17). Newark, DE: International Reading Association.

Davis, F.B. (1944). Fundamental factors of comprehension in reading. *Psychometrika, 9,* 285-297.

Davis, F.B. (1968). Research in comprehension in reading. *Reading Research Quarterly, 3,* 499-545.

Day, J.D. (1980). *Teaching summarization skills: A comparison of training methods.* Unpublished doctoral dissertation, University of Illinois, Urbana-Champaign.

Dole, J., Duffy, G., Roehler, L., & Pearson, P.D. (1991). Moving from the old to the new: Research on reading comprehension instruction. *Review of Educational Research, 61,* 239-264.

Dole, J.A., & Smith, E.L. (1987, December). *When prior knowledge is wrong: Reading and learning from science text.* Paper presented at the National Reading Conference, St. Petersburg, FL.

Dooling, D.L., & Lachman, R. (1971). Effects of comprehension on retention of prose. *Journal of Experimental Psychology, 88,* 216-222.

Doyle, W. (1979). Making managerial decisions in classrooms. In D. Duke (Ed.), *Seventy-eighth yearbook of the National Society for the Study of Education,* (Part 2). Chicago, IL: University of Chicago Press.

Doyle, W. (1983). Academic work. *Review of Educational Research, 53*(2), 159-199.

Duffy, G. (1982). Fighting off the alligators: What research in real classrooms has to say about reading instruction. *Journal of Reading Behavior, 14*(4), 357-374.

Duffy, G., & McIntyre, L. (1982). A naturalistic study of instructional assistance in primary grade reading. *Elementary School Journal, 83*(1), 15-23.

Duffy, G., & Roehler, L.R. (1987). Improving reading instruction through the use of responsive elaboration. *The Reading Teacher, 40,* 514-520.

Duffy, G., & Roehler, L.R. (1989). Why strategy instruction is so difficult and what we need to do about it. In C. McCormick, G. Miller, & M. Pressley (Eds.), *Dialogues in literacy research.* Chicago, IL: National Reading Conference.

Duffy, G.G., Roehler, L.R., & Herrmann, B.A. (1988, April). Modeling mental processes helps poor readers become strategic readers. *The Reading Teacher, 41*(8), 762-767.

Duffy, G.G., Roehler, L.R., Meloth, M., & Vavrus, L. (1986). Conceptualizing instructional explanations. *Teaching and Teacher Education, 2*(3), 197-214.

Duffy, G.G., Roehler, L.R., & Putnam, J. (1987). Putting the teacher in control: Instructional decision making and basal textbooks. *Elementary School Journal, 87*(3), 357-366.

Duffy, G.G., Roehler, L.R., Sivan, E., Rackliffe, G., Book, C., Meloth, M.S., Vavrus, L.G., Wesselman, R., Putnam, J., & Bassiri, D. (1987). Effects of explaining the reasoning associated with using reading strategies. *Reading Research Quarterly, 22,* 347-368.

Durkin, D. (1979). What classroom observations reveal about reading comprehension. *Reading Research Quarterly, 14,* 481-533.

Eaton, J.F., Anderson, C.W., & Smith, E.L. (1984). Students' misconceptions interfere with science learning: Case studies of fifth-grade students. *Elementary School Journal, 84,* 365-379.

Englert, C.S., & Hiebert, E.H. (1984). Children's developing awareness of text structures in expository materials. *Journal of Educational Psychology, 71*(1), 65-74.

Flavell, J.H. (1981). Cognitive monitoring. In W.P. Dickson (Ed.), *Children's oral communication skills.* San Diego, CA: Academic.

Flavell, J.H., Speer, J.R., Green, F.L., & August, D.L. (1981). The development of comprehension monitoring and knowledge about communication. *Monographs of the Society for Research in Child Development, 46*(5).

Gans, R. (1940). *A study of critical reading comprehension in the intermediate grades* (Contributions to Education, No. 811). New York: Teachers College, Columbia University.

Garner, R. (1987). *Metacognition and reading comprehension.* Norwood, NJ: Ablex.

Garner, R., Macready, G.B., & Wagoner, S. (1984). Readers' acquisition of the components of the text-lookback strategy. *Journal of Educational Psychology, 76,* 300-309.

Garner, R., & Reis, R. (1981). Monitoring and resolving comprehension obstacles: An investigation of spontaneous text lookbacks among upper-grade good and poor comprehenders. *Reading Research Quarterly, 16,* 569-582.

Garner, R., Wagoner, S., & Smith, T. (1983). Externalizing question-answering strategies of good and poor comprehenders. *Reading Research Quarterly, 18,* 439-447.

Good, T. (1983). Research on classroom teaching. In L. Shulman & G. Sykes (Eds.), *Handbook of teaching and policy* (pp. 42-80). White Plains, NY: Longman.

Gordon, C.J., & Pearson, P.D. (1983). *The effects of instruction in metacomprehension and inferencing on children's comprehension abilities* (Tech. Rep. No. 277). Urbana, IL: University of Illinois, Center for the Study of Reading.

Hansen, J. (1981). The effects of inference training and practice on young children's reading comprehension. *Reading Research Quarterly, 16,* 391-417.

Hansen, J., & Pearson, P.D. (1983). An instructional study: Improving the inferential comprehension of good and poor fourth-grade readers. *Journal of Educational Psychology, 75,* 821-829.

Hare, V.C., & Bingham, A.B. (1986). Teaching students main idea comprehension: Alternatives to repeated exposures. In J.F. Baumann (Ed.), *Teaching main idea comprehension* (pp. 179-194). Newark, DE: International Reading Association.

Hare, V.C., & Borchardt, K.M. (1984). Direct instruction of summarization skills. *Reading Research Quarterly, 20,* 62-78.

Harris, P.L., Kruithof, A., Terwogt, M.M., & Visser, T. (1981). Children's detection and awareness of textual anomaly. *Journal of Experimental Child Psychology, 31,* 212-230.

Herrmann, B.A. (1985). Reading instruction: Dealing with classroom realities. *Community College Review, 13,* 28-34.

Johnston, P.H., & Afflerbach, P.P. (1985). The process of constructing main ideas from text. *Cognition and Instruction, 2,* 207-232.

Kail, R.V., Chi, M.T.H., Ingram, A.L., & Danner, F.W. (1977). Constructive aspects of children's reading comprehension. *Child Development, 48,* 684-688.

Kintsch, W., & van Dijk, T.A. (1978). Toward a model of text comprehension and production. *Psychological Review, 85,* 363-394.

Lipson, M.Y., & Wixson, K.K. (1986). Reading disability research: An interactionist perspective. *Review of Educational Research, 56*(1), 111-136.

Maria, K., & MacGinitie, W. (1982). Reading comprehension disabilities: Knowledge structures and nonaccommodating text processing strategies. *Annals of Dyslexia, 32*, 33-59.

Masur, E.F., McIntyre, C.W., & Flavell, J.H. (1973). Developmental changes in apportionment of study time among items in multiple free recall tasks. *Journal of Experimental Child Psychology, 15*, 237-246.

Meloth, M. (1987). *The improvement of metacognitive awareness and its contribution to reading performance of third grade low group readers who receive explicit reading instruction.* Unpublished doctoral dissertation, Michigan State University, East Lansing.

Meloth, M., & Roehler, L.R. (1987). *Dimensions of teacher explanation.* Paper presented at the annual conference of the American Educational Research Association, Washington, DC.

Ogle, D. (1986). K-W-L: A teaching model that develops active reading of expository text. *The Reading Teacher, 39*, 564-570.

O'Sullivan, J.T., & Pressley, M. (1984). Completeness of instruction and strategy transfer. *Journal of Experimental Child Psychology, 38*, 275-288.

Owings, R.A., Peterson, G.A., Bransford, J.D., Morris, C.D., & Stein, B.S. (1980). Spontaneous monitoring and regulation of learning: A comparison of successful and less successful fifth graders. *Journal of Educational Psychology, 72*, 250-256.

Palincsar, A.S., & Brown, A.L. (1984). Reciprocal teaching of comprehension-fostering and comprehension-monitoring activities. *Cognition and Instruction, 1*, 117-175.

Palmer, W. (1982). *Twelve English teachers: What observation reveals about reading instruction.* Paper presented at the National Reading Conference, Clearwater, FL.

Paris, S.G., & Carter, A.Y. (1973). Semantic and constructive aspects of sentence memory in children. *Developmental Psychology, 9*, 109-113.

Paris, S.G., Cross, D.R., & Lipson, M.Y. (1984). Informed strategies for learning: A program to improve children's reading awareness and comprehension. *Journal of Educational Psychology, 76*, 1239-1252.

Paris, S.G., & Jacobs, J. (1984). The benefits of informed instruction for children's reading awareness and comprehension skills. *Child Development, 55*, 2083-2093.

Paris, S.G., & Lindauer, B.K. (1976). The role of inference in children's comprehension and memory. *Cognitive Psychology, 8*, 217-227.

Paris, S.G., Lipson, M.Y., & Wixson, K.K. (1983). Becoming a strategic reader. *Contemporary Educational Psychology, 8*, 293-316.

Patterson, C.J., Cosgrove, J.M., & O'Brien, R.G. (1980). Nonverbal indicants of comprehension and noncomprehension in children. *Developmental Psychology, 16*, 38-48.

Pearson, P.D. (1985). Changing the face of reading comprehension instruction. *The Reading Teacher, 38*(8), 724-738.

Pearson, P.D., & Dole, J.A. (1987). Explicit comprehension instruction: A review of research and a new conceptualization of instruction. *Elementary School Journal, 88*(2), 151-165.

Pearson, P.D., Hansen, J., & Gordon, C. (1979). The effect of background on young children's comprehension of explicit and implicit information. *Journal of Reading Behavior, 11*, 201-210.

Pearson, P.D., & Johnson, D.D. (1978). *Teaching reading comprehension.* Orlando, FL: Holt, Rinehart & Winston.

Pichert, J.W. (1979). *Sensitivity to what is important in prose* (Tech. Rep. No. 149). Urbana, IL: University of Illinois, Center for the Study of Reading. (ED 179 946)

Pichert, J.W., & Anderson, R.C. (1977). Taking different perspectives on a story. *Journal of Educational Psychology, 69*, 309-315.

Raphael, T.E., & McKinney, J. (1983). An examination of fifth and eighth grade children's question answering behavior: An instructional study in metacognition. *Journal of Reading Behavior, 15*, 67-86.

Raphael, T.E., & Pearson, P.D. (1985). Increasing students' awareness of sources of information for answering questions. *American Educational Research Journal, 22*, 217-236.

Raphael, T.E., & Winograd, P., & Pearson, P.D. (1980). Strategies children use when answering questions. In M.L. Kamil & A.J. Moe (Eds.), *Perspectives on reading research and instruction.* Washington, DC: National Reading Conference.

Raphael, T.E., & Wonnacott, C.A. (1985). Heightening fourth-grade students' sensitivity to sources of information for answering questions. *Reading Research Quarterly, 20*, 282-296.

Resnick, L.B. (1984). Comprehending and learning: Implications for a cognitive theory of instruction. In H. Mandl, N.L. Stein, & T. Trabasso (Eds.), *Learning and comprehension of text* (pp. 431-443). Hillsdale, NJ: Erlbaum.

Revelle, G.L., Wellman, H.M., & Karabenick, J.D. (1985). Comprehension monitoring in preschool children. *Child Development, 56*, 654-663.

Roehler, L.R., & Duffy, G.G. (1987). *Characteristics of instructional responsiveness associated with effective teaching of reading strategies.* Paper presented at the National Reading Conference, St. Petersburg, FL.

Roehler, L.R., Duffy, G.G., & Warren, S. (1988). Adaptive explanatory actions associated with effective teaching of reading strategies. In J. Readance & S. Baldwin (Eds.), *Dialogues in literacy research* (pp. 339-346). Chicago, IL: National Reading Conference.

Rosenblatt, C.M. (1978). *The reader, the text, the poem: The transactional theory of the literary work.* Carbondale, IL: Southern Illinois University Press.

Rosenshine, B. (1979). Content, time, and direct instruction. In P. Peterson & H. Walberg (Eds.), *Research on teaching: Concepts, findings, and implications* (pp. 28-56). Berkeley, CA: McCutchan.

Rosenshine, B., & Stevens, R. (1984). Classroom instruction in reading. In P.D. Pearson (Ed.), *Handbook of reading research* (pp. 745-798). White Plains, NY: Longman.

Roth, K.J. (1985). *Conceptual change learning and student processing of science texts.* Paper presented at the American Educational Research Association, Chicago, IL.

Russell, D., et al. (1951). *Ginn Basic Readers.* Morristown, NJ: Silver Burdett & Ginn.

Schreiner, R.L., Hieronymus, A.N., & Forsyth, R. (1969). Differential measurement of reading abilities at the elementary school level. *Reading Research Quarterly, 5,* 84-99.

Shulman, L. (1986). Paradigms and research programs in the study of teaching: A contemporary perspective. In M.C. Wittrock (Ed.), *Handbook of research on teaching* (3rd ed., pp. 3-36). New York: Macmillan.

Singer, H., & Donlan, D. (1982). Active comprehension: Problem-solving schema with question generation for comprehension of complex short stories. *Reading Research Quarterly, 17,* 166-186.

Sivan, E., & Roehler, L.R. (1986). Motivational statements in explicit teacher explanations and their relationship to students' metacognition in reading. In J.A. Niles & R.V. Lalik (Eds.), *Solving problems in literacy: Learners, teachers, and researchers.* Rochester, NY: National Reading Conference.

Slavin, R.E. (1980). Effects of student teams and peer tutoring on academic achievement and time on task. *Journal of Experimental Education, 48,* 253-257.

Smith, N.B. (1963). *Reading instruction for today's children.* Englewood Cliffs, NJ: Prentice Hall.

Smith, N.B. (1965/1986). *American reading instruction.* Newark, DE: International Reading Association.

Sochor, E.E. (1959). The nature of critical reading. *Elementary English, 36,* 47-58.

Spache, G. (1965). *Reading in the elementary school.* Needham Heights, MA: Allyn & Bacon.

Taylor, B.M. (1982). Text structure and children's comprehension and memory for expository materials. *Journal of Educational Psychology, 15,* 401-405.

Taylor, B.M., & Beach, R.W. (1984). The effects of text structure instruction on middle-grade students' comprehension and production of expository text. *Reading Research Quarterly, 19*(2), 134-146.

Taylor, B.M., & Berkowitz, B.S. (1980). Facilitating children's comprehension of content material. In M.L. Kamil & A.J. Moe (Eds.), *Perspectives in reading research and instruction* (pp. 64-68). Clemson, SC: National Reading Conference.

Tierney, R.J., & Cunningham, J.W. (1984). Research on teaching reading comprehension. In P.D. Pearson (Ed.), *Handbook of reading research* (pp. 609-654). White Plains, NY: Longman.

Vosniadou, S., Pearson, P.D., & Rogers, T. (1988). What causes children's failures to detect inconsistencies in text? Representation versus comparison difficulties. *Journal of Educational Psychology, 80*(1), 27-39.

Vygotsky, L.S. (1978). *Mind in society: The development of higher psychological processes* (M. Cole, V. John-Steiner, S. Scribner, & E. Souberman, Eds. & Trans.). Cambridge, MA: Harvard University Press.

Wagoner, S.A. (1983). Comprehension monitoring: What it is and what we know about it. *Reading Research Quarterly, 18,* 328-346.

Williams, G. (1959). The provisions for critical reading in basic readers. *Elementary English, 36,* 323-331.

Williams, J.P. (1986a). Extracting important information from text. In J.A. Niles & R.V. Lalik (Eds.), *Solving problems in literacy: Learners, teachers, and researchers* (pp. 11-29). Rochester, NY: National Reading Conference.

Williams, J.P. (1986b). Research and instructional development on main idea skills. In J.F. Baumann (Ed.), *Teaching main idea comprehension* (pp. 73-95). Newark, DE: International Reading Association.

Wilson, S.M., Shulman, L.S., & Richert, A.E. (1987). 150 different ways of knowing: Representations of knowledge in teaching. In J. Calderhead (Ed.), *Exploring teachers' thinking* (pp. 104-124). London, UK: Cassell.

Winne, P.H., & Marx, R.W. (1982). Students' and teachers' views of thinking processes for classroom learning. *Elementary School Journal, 82,* 493-518.

Winograd, P.N. (1984). Strategic difficulties in summarizing texts. *Reading Research Quarterly, 19,* 404-425.

Winograd, P.N., & Bridge, C.A. (1986). The comprehension of important information in written prose. In J.F. Baumann (Ed.), *Teaching main idea comprehension* (pp. 18-48). Newark, DE: International Reading Association.

Winograd, P.N., & Johnston, P.H. (1982). Comprehension monitoring and the error detection paradigm. *Journal of Reading Behavior, 14,* 61-76.

Wolf, W., Huck, S., King, L., & Ellinger, B.D. (1967). *Critical reading ability in elementary school children* (Report of Project 5-1040). Washington, DC: Office of Education.

CHAPTER 8

Improving Reading Instruction in the Content Areas

STEPHEN SIMONSEN
HARRY SINGER

According to the authors of this chapter, content area teachers should supplement their lessons with developmental reading instruction, because students who receive this instruction show higher gains in general reading ability than students who do not. Citing the schema-interactive model of reading, the authors detail methods that content area teachers can use to provide clear goals that direct students' comprehension. These methods do not require special expertise for implementation, and do enhance the learning of the course content.

Like Sirens calling from a nearby shore, seductive alternatives to textbooks often tempt content area teachers away from assigning reading. Audio recordings, videos, lectures, experiments, and field trips can be entertaining and educational, thus permitting teachers to bypass texts that are sometimes perceived as poorly written and difficult (Stewart, 1989).

To what extent are content area teachers lured away from assigning reading? Ratekin and his colleagues (1985), observing math, science, social studies, and English teachers in eighth and eleventh grades, found that only the math instructors used textbooks for 50 percent or more of their instructional time. Out of all assignments given by these instructors, fewer than 1 percent required students to read outside class. Smith and Feathers (1983a, 1983b) surveyed students in three secondary social studies courses and found that even when reading was assigned, it was not a requirement for success in the course. Students reported doing an average of only 50 percent of the reading because they could get the information from other sources—primarily the teacher.

Despite the advantages of the alternatives to texts, neglecting reading may deprive students of their best avenue for learning. Chall (1983) posits that starting approximately in sixth grade, average and good readers learn faster and retain more information through reading than through listening. Maturing readers adjust their rates according to the demands of the text, review difficult passages, and exploit text organization devices—strategies not open to listeners. Neglecting reading also reduces the number of opportunities for content area teachers to teach comprehension, which correlates strongly with reading improvement (Chall, Jacobs, & Baldwin, 1990) and is essential for helping students cope with the literacy demands of the information age after leaving school (Crawley & Mountain, 1988; Dahlberg, 1990).

This chapter discusses guidelines and activities content area teachers can adopt to help their students learn from text, such as selecting comprehensible books, giving students information about a subject before they read, teaching vocabulary from the texts, and providing clear, understandable goals to guide students' reading. The first section describes the schema-interactive model of reading and discusses teacher activities as they relate to text characteristics, reader resources, and reader goals. The remaining sections expand on these categories and describe the actions teachers can take to improve learning from text. By the end of the chapter, the Sirens should be relegated to the role of text supplements rather than text surrogates.

The Schema-Interactive Model of Reading

The schema-interactive model of reading in the classroom assumes a close and interlocking set of relationships between teacher actions and the other factors that affect learning from text (Figure 1). It represents learning from text as a process in which readers mobilize their resources to interact with the text to create meaning. This meaning is created in accordance with the reader's goals and the guidance of the teacher (Singer, 1987).

The interaction of reader resources and text characteristics was demonstrated when physical education students and music education students read an ambiguous passage whose references to lying on a mat, running out of time, needing to break a lock, and making an escape could have been interpreted as describing either a jailbreak or a wrestling match. A majority of the physical education students interpreted the passage as a wrestling match, whereas the music education students, who presumably did not have specialized knowledge of either topic, were split between the interpretations. Later, few participants reported being aware of another interpretation. These patterns suggest that readers do not passively absorb information from text. Instead, they actively mobilize their own schemata (knowledge structures) to build meaning, with the text as a stimulus (Anderson, 1985).

Reader goals, which determine what is learned from text and which strategies are selected, often are established for students by tests (Singer, 1987). Indeed, knowing that their performance on tests determines their grades, students usually learn material that will be useful on tests and disregard teacher-assigned goals when the two diverge (McKeachie et al., 1986). Goals drive learning from text in other ways, as well. Students preparing for essay tests read

Figure 1
The Schema-Interactive Model of Reading

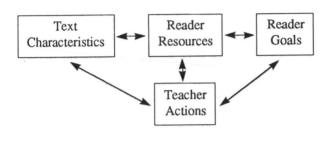

longer and learn more than do students preparing for multiple choice tests (d'Ydewalle, Swerts, & De Corte, 1983). In independent study, readers looking for facts often scan, but they read slowly when they need to draw inferences or piece together information from several passages (Raphael & Pearson, 1985).

Teacher actions affect all of the other components of learning from text. The teacher plays a role in choosing texts, helps students develop reader resources, and sets reader goals by selecting and administering tests (Yopp & Singer, 1985).

Text Characteristics

Readability of Reference Texts

Atlases, almanacs, and encyclopedias often are written in such difficult prose that secondary students find reading them frustrating. MacCormick and Pursel (1982) selected 100 passages from each of three encyclopedias—the *Academic American Encyclopedia, Encyclopedia Britannica,* and *World Book*—and used the Fry Readability Graph to estimate the grade level of each passage. The mean level for *World Book* was eleventh grade, with 44 passages estimated at the college level. The mean for both *Academic American Encyclopedia* and *Encyclopedia Britannica* was sixteenth grade; none of the passages in these series was below the ninth grade level. Thus, students who copy their research papers verbatim from reference texts may adopt that strategy because the texts are incomprehensible (Roe, Stoodt, & Burns, 1987).

Elaboration, Cohesive Ties, and Prereading Guides

Teachers should select texts whose readability matches students' reading levels. However, most readability formulas estimate grade levels only on the basis of sentence and word length, without taking into account three other important text characteristics: elaboration of information, the use of cohesive ties, and the presence of prereading guides. Texts with similar readability levels may be compared on these traits to help decide which to adopt (Vacca, Vacca, & Gove, 1987).

Elaboration.   Texts that are elaborative describe things, define terms, and explain the causes of events. Consider this sentence: *Minutes after every sunset, a reddish-gray band appears on the eastern horizon.* The sentence presents a fact that can be memorized, but it fails to explain the band or its significance. The following pair of sentences provide the same fact as well as some elaboration: *Minutes after every sunset, a reddish-gray band appears on the eastern horizon. This band is not smog, fog, or dust, but the earth's shadow, cast by our planet in the sun's light, projecting into outer space.* The second sentence makes the fact presented easier to comprehend and recall by (1) comparing the band to familiar objects, allowing the reader to tie in the new information with prior knowledge; (2) defining the band as the earth's shadow; and (3) explaining the relationships among the band, the earth, and the sun, allowing the reader to form a schema (Singer & Simonsen, 1989).

In their desire to reduce sentence length, shorten passages, and use basic vocabulary, publishers sometimes eliminate description, definition, and explanation. Ironically, these simplified texts are less comprehensible because the advantages of elaboration have been lost. Readers receive less data to use in building schemata and fewer prompts to tie in text information with their prior knowledge; therefore, they must rely more heavily on the rote memorization of facts whose significance is not clear (Bransford, 1985).

Simonsen & Singer

Cohesive ties.   Cohesive ties, including conjunctions, substitutions, and word repetitions, clarify relationships between ideas. Unfortunately, again to simplify text by reducing the lengths of sentences and passages, publishers sometimes give up clarity by eliminating cohesive ties (Clark, 1986). To illustrate, each of the two sentences that follow states a fact, but any relationship between the facts is ambiguous: *The Sioux and Cheyenne unilaterally stopped fighting after winning the Battle of the Little Big Horn. Their food supply ran out.*

Although in some cases cohesive ties increase average sentence length—and therefore raise estimated grade levels as calculated by readability formulas—they clarify the text and help readers create meaning by revealing the relationships between ideas. For example, joining the two simplified sentences above with the conjunction *because* creates one long sentence, but it establishes a causal relationship between the facts: that running out of food forced the Sioux and Cheyenne to quit.

Authors also use cohesive ties when, instead of using the same word in neighboring sentences, they replace one of the words with a synonym that contributes additional information. Like conjunctions, these substitutions clarify the relationships between ideas while sometimes lengthening sentences. In the following example, the information-rich phrase *these amateur radio operators'* is used instead of *their* to replace *hams* in the second sentence: *Hams often must wear very thick glasses. These amateur radio operators' exposure to powerful electromagnetic waves damages their corneas.* The substitution defines *hams* and suggests why they would be exposed to electromagnetic waves.

Word repetition, or use of the same noun in neighboring sentences, allows authors to clarify texts by avoiding ambiguous pronoun references. The elaborative sentences presented earlier on the earth's shadow provide a good example of cohesion created by word repetition. The word *band* is repeated in the second sentence, thus eliminating the potentially confusing pronoun *it.*

The number of cohesive ties does not decrease as texts grow more difficult through the grade levels. Irwin (1986a) determined that the number of "breaks" in social science texts increased significantly through the grade levels. (Breaks are adjoining main clauses that do not repeat an argument; an argument is a noun that is the subject or object of a verb, adjective, or adverb.) However, the same texts contained nearly identical numbers of cohesive ties.

Prereading guides. A prereading guide is information shared by the author to help the reader organize prior knowledge before reading a chapter or passage. When written as explicit questions or goals, prereading guides encourage active comprehension, which entails anticipating information and searching for answers rather than simply absorbing information passively from the text (Nolte & Singer, 1985). Britton et al. (1985) administered explicit prereading guides to one group of undergraduates, vague guides to another group, and none at all to a third group before assigning a five-page expository passage. The group receiving the explicit guides spent more time reading the passage and recalled significantly more information from it.

What are the differences between explicit and vague prereading guides? Explicit prereading guides name facts, processes, or generalizations to be learned; when possible, they also identify expected behavioral outcomes. Vague guides categorize information from the text but do not give cues about what to look for or identify expected behavioral outcomes (Santa, Havens, & Harrison, 1989). In Figure 2, the explicit prereading guide introduces a passage on comets, identifies facts and processes for the reader to look for, and specifies expected behavioral outcomes (draw a map, explain). The vague prereading guide provides only an abstract outline of the passage's content, and does not name expected behavioral outcomes.

Reader Resources

Prior Knowledge

Prior knowledge is a powerful resource that readers mobilize to comprehend text. The consensus of several studies, whose scope ranged from third grade to college, is that students with prior knowledge of the topic recall significantly more information from the text than do students with little or no prior knowledge (Hall, 1990; Holmes, 1983; Lipson, 1982; Marino, Gould, & Haas, 1985; Simonsen & Singer, 1985; Taft & Leslie, 1985).

Figure 2
Prereading Guides for a Passage on Comets

Explicit Prereading Guide

The next passage is on comets. Before you begin reading, look over the following questions. Try to find the answers as you read.

What are comets made of?

How big are they?

What is their shape?

What part of our solar system do they come from?

Draw a map, including the sun and the planets, that shows the shape and size of comets' orbits.

Explain why their tails always point away from the sun.

Vague Prereading Guide

The next passage will present the following information on comets.

Behavior
  tails
  orbits

Appearance
  in frozen state
  when heated by the sun

Composition

Location

Origin

Adapted from Santa, Havens, & Harrison, 1989.

An instructor can provide readers with prior knowledge before they read. Simonsen and Singer (1985) assigned remedial community college students to read a one-page passage on mainland China. The passage provided information on Far East geography by instructing students to identify and mark on a map pertinent countries, continents, and oceans. It also provided brief summaries of important events by year during the Mongol Dynasty (see Figure 3). After

Figure 3
Prior Knowledge Exercise on
the Mongol Dynasty

Shortly, you will be asked to read about the Mongol Dynasty of China. So that you will know the locations of the countries you will be reading about, please use the historical map of Europe and Asia on the next page to complete the following directions:

1. Trace China's borders and label the country with a *C*.
2. Draw a circle around Mongolia and label it with an *M*.
3. Draw a circle around Japan and label it with a *J*.
4. Label the Pacific Ocean with a *P*.
5. Draw a circle around India and label it with an *I*.
6. Draw a circle around Europe and label it with an *E*.

Take a minute to look at the map. Notice that Mongolia is to the north of most of China, and that China is much bigger. Also, notice how far Europe is from China.

Please take 10 minutes to study this overview of China's Mongol Dynasty.

1150 A.D.   The Mongols live inside Mongolia. They are tough people who live in small tribes. They wander constantly looking for grazing land. Frequently, Mongol tribes have to fight one another to the death over scarce grazing land.

1190 A.D.   Genghis Khan is a young, charismatic leader who organizes neighboring Mongol tribes into a large, powerful army, often by conquering them one at a time and killing their leaders.

1215 A.D.   By this time, Genghis Khan's armies have conquered half of China and much of eastern Europe. Already, the Mongol Empire is the largest empire in the history of the world.

1230 A.D.   Khan's armies conquer more of China. His armies are merciless. When they conquer a city, Khan orders all of the elderly killed. He also orders all boys and young men killed because they might fight against him in the future.

1271 A.D.   Genghis Khan's grandson, Kublai Khan, conquers the rest of China and declares himself Emperor of China. He plays host to Marco Polo for 20 years. Kublai Khan also passes laws naming Mongols as the premier race in China, Chinese as the lowest-class race, and all other races in the middle.

1294 A.D.   Kublai Khan dies. The Mongol government falls into civil war and collapses within 20 years.

Adapted from Simonsen & Singer, 1985.

working on this passage, the students read a 1,500-word text on Mongol military strategy and scored significantly higher on a comprehension test than did a group that did not work on the short passage before reading.

In short, a brief prepared passage can provide students with sufficient prior knowledge to improve their comprehension of a longer text, even if the passage and the text provide different information about the topic. Guidelines for writing such a passage follow:

1. Write brief passages. Franks and his colleagues (1982) found that unelaborative prereading passages worked as well as elaborative passages in improving recall for poor readers. And unelaborative prereading passages were *more* effective in improving recall for good readers.

2. Provide information that gives an overall picture, or schema, of the text, rather than just isolated facts. Schemata allow readers to organize stored information for easy retrieval (Anderson, 1985). In the prereading passage on Mongol China, the schemata were the sequence provided by the dates and the mental picture provided by the map.

3. Provide information that is likely to be novel.

An instructor also can activate prior knowledge that students already possess. Just before reading a 2,000-word passage from A. Rutgers Van der Loeff's *Oregon at Last*—a story about western pioneers—fourth graders were given 30 minutes to imagine themselves living in a historical setting of their choice and write to their grandparents about the experience. The next day, these students achieved significantly higher comprehension scores on a test of the story than did a group of students who had written about a contemporary experience before reading the text (Marino, Gould, & Haas, 1985).

Hall (1990) activated the prior knowledge of university students in a remedial class by assigning them to write one-page essays just before reading. The essays matched both the topics and the rhetorical modes of the texts. Students were instructed to write two reasons for and two reasons against the possibility of the existence of UFOs before reading a text weighing the same topic; three reasons why television is a good or bad influence on people before reading a text condemning television as an educational tool for criminals; and one paragraph condemning and another approving Ronald Reagan's policies before reading an editorial on the Reagan presidency. Although there was no evidence of improvement in overall reading comprehension or rate, students who wrote the essays recalled significantly more information from the texts than did control students.

Vocabulary

Throughout the grades, vocabulary is the single most reliable predictor of reading ability. Effective instruction in vocabulary can increase reading comprehension (Mulcahy-Ernt, 1990).

What is effective vocabulary instruction? Unfortunately, easy access to glossaries, dictionaries, and thesauruses can mold general vocabulary study into drill on definitions only, in spite of evidence that an equal amount of instruction in context more sharply increases students' reading comprehension and retention of the words (Barr, Sadow, & Blachowicz, 1990). Stahl (1983) taught both definitions and contexts of 30 words to fifth graders, who correctly matched more of these words to contexts on a posttest than did a group that learned definitions alone. McKeown and her colleagues (1983) instructed fourth graders in both the context and definitions of 104 words over 10 weeks. These students achieved significantly higher gains on the reading portion of the Iowa Test of Basic Skills than did another group that had learned definitions only.

Shown here are the methods used to teach context in these studies. Including both definition and context activities, students were exposed to each word at least 10 times.

1. Each word was introduced in two sentences that provided contexts as disparate as possible (McKeown et al., 1983). See Figure 4 for examples.

2. Students were assigned to write each word in an original sentence and to share and edit those sentences in groups of five students (Stahl, 1983).

3. Students completed half-finished sentences that contained the words from the lesson (Stahl; McKeown et al.).

4. Teachers provided handouts that gave definitions. Since students did not spend time finding words in dictionaries and copying definitions, they had more time to learn context (McKeown et al.).

Figure 4
Sentence Pairs to Provide Context for Vocabulary

Shoppers *boycotted* lettuce because of high prices.
College students organized a *boycott* of classes to protest trade with South Africa.

Crack cocaine is a *derivative* of coca powder, often with salt and flour added.
Gasoline and other *derivatives* of crude oil are responsible for over half of the smog in Los Angeles and New York.

Old family serials on television had *dominant* but kindly fathers who made all the important decisions for the family.
The United States is the world's *dominant* economic and military power.

Everyone in the cafeteria *grouses* about the terrible food, but they still eat it.
Ten students in the class *groused* about excessive homework.

Many people are afraid that gang warfare is a sign of *incipient* civil war in American cities.
In their *incipient* years, cars had top speeds of 10 miles an hour.

The tomcat yowled *insistently* all night until I fed him.
The *insistent* salesman finally sold me a vacuum cleaner.

She looked so sweet and *pristine* in her photograph until I learned that she was wearing gang colors.
The *pristine* forest was untouched by freeways, fast food restaurants, or smog.

Jerry *ventured* $15,000 in airline stock.
The fat man *ventured* into the woods without food for 20 days to try to lose weight.

My doctor *gazed* at my chest x-ray for ten minutes.
We *gazed* unbelievingly at the giant redwood all afternoon.

Figure 5
Hierarchical Array for Astronomy Vocabulary

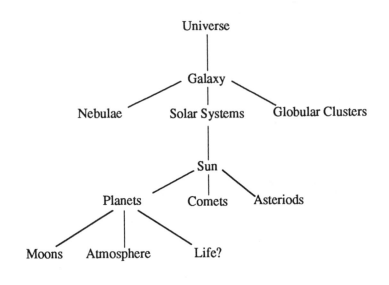

Technical vocabulary often exists in hierarchical relationships or semantic families that can be graphically displayed. Hierarchical vocabulary can be listed in arrays that branch from superordinate to subordinate words (Nagy, 1988). Figure 5 shows an example using vocabulary from a chapter in an astronomy book. These arrays aid recall by displaying context and the relationships between words (Mulcahy-Ernt, 1990).

Matrices can be used to display the traits of words in a semantic family (Figure 6). The words are listed to the left of the rows of a matrix, and traits common to the family (though not particular to each member of the family) are listed at the top of the columns. In each word's row, *yes* is written in the columns with traits that characterize the word. This display teaches relationships between the words and provides many exposures to the traits of the semantic family (Nagy, 1988).

Figure 6
Semantic Matrix for Vocabulary in Classical Music

	Large Orchestra?	Melodious?	Simultaneous Melodies?	Continuous Tempo?
Baroque		yes	yes	yes
Romantic		yes		
Classical	yes	yes		
Modern	yes			

Reader Goals

If learning is unsatisfactory despite comprehensible texts and adequate reader resources, the problem may be reader goals that are difficult, unchallenging, insufficient, or unclear. Goals determine what and how much is learned and what strategies readers employ. Without goals, readers do not know what is expected of them and have no purpose or plan for mobilizing their resources (Irwin, 1986b).

Matching Goals to the Learner

Realistic goal setting is important for maintaining motivation. When researchers mismatched objectives with readers' abilities, both good and poor readers learned less than when objectives and abilities were closely matched (Covington, 1985). Participants reported feeling bored and putting forth minimal effort when goals were too easy, and giving up entirely when frustrated by hard goals. Students whose goals matched their abilities showed the most gain in learning on posttests.

Moreover, the suitability of goals may have long term affective consequences. When a task is within grasp, students are more likely to perceive the link between effort and achievement and attribute success or failure to their own efforts. Such attribution promotes strong effort on other assignments. However, when goals are unreasonable and frustrating, students tend to attribute their failures to the task and their occasional successes to luck, rather than focus on the quality of their own efforts. This mindset discourages strong future efforts (Campione et al., 1984).

Clarity of Goals

Like explicit prereading guides, well-written goals presented before a reading assignment can improve learning. Hurst (1988) posits that instructors can use well-selected verbs to write objectives that require particular levels of thinking, and thus make expected behavioral outcomes clear. Six examples of goals made clear with carefully chosen verbs as listed here. Following Bloom's Taxonomy, the level of thinking demanded by the verb is given in parentheses.

- *List* the five crucial disadvantages suffered by the South in the American Civil War. (Knowledge)
- *Explain* in your own words the meaning of the Second Amendment to the U.S. Constitution. (Comprehension)
- *Diagram* a brain cell and its components. (Application)
- *Compare and contrast* the climates of southern California and Florida. (Analysis)
- *Judge* whether Romeo acted selfishly by committing suicide without first trying to see if Juliet could be revived. (Evaluation)
- *Produce* one general script that would explain the American, French, and Cuban revolutions. (Synthesis)

Table 1 provides a list of verbs, categorized by level of thinking, that can be used to write clear goals.

Summary

Content area teachers sometimes select Siren alternatives to textbooks to help their students learn. Ironically, these alternatives may reduce learning for average and good readers because readers

Table 1
Verbs for Writing Instructional Objectives

Level	Meaning	Verb
Knowledge	Remembering learned material	Define Recognize Match Memorize Repeat Select Name Label Recall List Record
Comprehension	Understanding the meaning of the information being learned	Translate Change Rearrange Explain Restate Summarize Discuss Describe Transform Express Review Locate
Application	Using learned materials in a new way	Distinguish Discriminate Compare Contrast Differentiate Diagram Describe Classify Categorize Subdivide
Evaluation	Judging the value of material for a given purpose	Judge Consider Evaluate Weigh Criticize Appraise Rate

Table 1 (continued)
Verbs for Writing Instructional Objectives

Level	Meaning	Verb
Synthesis	Combining previous experience with new material to form a whole structure	Design Plan Solve Produce

Adapted from Hurst (1988).

can use learning strategies (such as rereading and adjusting the rate of information intake) not available to listeners and observers. The alternatives also may reduce learning for poor readers because the teacher has fewer opportunities to teach comprehension strategies.

The schema-interactive model of reading posits three categories in which teachers can help their students learn from text: text characteristics, reader resources, and reader goals. Teachers can select comprehensible texts by checking estimated grade levels and examining passages for elaboration, cohesion, and prereading guides; they can develop reader resources by teaching or activating prior knowledge and teaching vocabulary through context; and they can set clear, reasonable goals to direct student activity. By helping students read and learn from text, content area teachers both improve learning in the course and prepare students to cope with the heavy reading loads demanded in the working world.

References

Anderson, R.C. (1985). Role of the reader's schema in comprehension, learning, and memory. In H. Singer & R. Ruddell (Eds.), *Theoretical models and processes of reading*. Newark, DE: International Reading Association.

Barr, R., Sadow, M., & Blachowicz, C. (1990). *Reading diagnosis for teachers*. White Plains, NY: Longman.

Bransford, J. (1985). Schema activation and schema acquisition: Comments on R.C. Anderson's remarks. In H. Singer & R. Ruddell (Eds.), *Theoretical models and processes of reading*. Newark, DE: International Reading Association.

Britton, B.K., Glynn, S.M., Muth, D.K., & Penfield, M.J. (1985). Instructional objectives in text: Managing the reader's attention. *Journal of Reading Behavior, 27*, 101-113.

Campione, J., Brown, A., Farrara, R.A., & Bryant, N. (1984). The zone of proximal development: Implications for individual differences and learning. In B. Rogoff & J. Wertsch (Eds.), *Children's learning in the zone of proximal development.* San Francisco, CA: Jossey-Bass.

Chall, J. (1983). *Stages of reading development.* New York: McGraw-Hill.

Chall, J., Jacobs, V.A., & Baldwin, L.E. (1990). *The reading crisis: Why poor children fail.* Cambridge, MA: Harvard University Press.

Clark, C. (1986). Assessing comprehensibility: The PHAN system. In J.W. Irwin (Ed.), *Understanding and teaching cohesion comprehension.* Newark, DE: International Reading Association.

Covington, M.V. (1985). Strategic thinking and the fear of failure. In J.W. Segal, S. Chipman, & R. Glaser (Eds.), *Thinking and learning skills, volume 1: Relating instruction to research.* Hillsdale, NJ: Erlbaum.

Crawley, S.T., & Mountain, L.H. (1988). *Strategies for guiding content reading.* Needham Heights, MA: Allyn & Bacon.

Dahlberg, L.A. (1990). Teaching for the information age. *Journal of Reading, 34,* 12-18.

d'Ydewalle, G., Swerts, A., & De Corte, E. (1983). Study time and test performance as a function of text expectations. *Contemporary Educational Psychology, 8,* 55-67.

Franks, J.J., Vye, N.J., Auble, P.M., Mezynski, K.J., Perfetto, G.A., Bransford, J.D., Stein, B.S., & Littlefield, J. (1982). Learning from explicit versus implicit text. *Journal of Experimental Psychology: General, 111,* 414-422.

Hall, C. (1990). Writing before reading: A role-playing model. *Journal of College Reading and Learning, 22,* 20-27.

Holmes, B.C. (1983). The effect of prior knowledge on the question answering of good and poor readers. *Journal of Reading Behavior, 15,* 1-18.

Hurst, W. (1988). *Instructional skills workshop kit.* Santa Rosa, CA: Santa Rosa Community College.

Irwin, J.W. (1986a). Cohesion factors in children's textbooks. In J.W. Irwin (Ed.), *Understanding and teaching cohesion comprehension.* Newark, DE: International Reading Association.

Irwin, J.W. (1986b). *Teaching reading comprehension processes.* Englewood Cliffs, NJ: Prentice Hall.

Lipson, M.Y. (1982). Learning new information from text: The role of prior knowledge and reading ability. *Journal of Reading Behavior, 14,* 243-261.

MacCormick, K., & Pursel, J.E. (1982). A comparison of the readability of the *Academic American Encyclopedia,* the *Encyclopedia Britannica,* and *World Book. Journal of Reading, 25,* 322-325.

Marino, J.L., Gould, S.M., & Haas, L.W. (1985). The effects of writing as a prereading activity on delayed recall of narrative text. *Elementary School Journal, 86,* 199-205.

McKeachie, W.J., Pintrich, P.R., Lin, Y.G., & Smith, D.A.F. (1986). *Teaching and learning in the college classroom: A review of the research literature.* Ann

Arbor, MI: National Center for Research to Improve Postsecondary Teaching and Learning.

McKeown, M.G., Beck, I.L., Omanson, R.C., & Perfetti, C.A. (1983). The effects of long-term vocabulary instruction on reading comprehension: A replication. *Journal of Reading Behavior, 15*, 3-18.

Mulcahy-Ernt, P. (1990). What's new in reading research? *Journal of College Reading and Learning, 22*, 37-48.

Nagy, W.E. (1988). *Teaching vocabulary to improve reading comprehension.* Urbana, IL: National Council of Teachers of English.

Nolte, R.Y., & Singer, H. (1985). Active comprehension: Teaching a process of reading comprehension and its effects on reading achievement. *The Reading Teacher, 39*, 24-31.

Raphael, T.E., & Pearson, P.D. (1985). Increasing students' awareness of information for answering questions. *American Educational Research Journal, 22*, 217-235.

Ratekin, N., Simpson, M., Alvermann, D.E., & Dishner, E.K. (1985). Why teachers resist content reading instruction. *Journal of Reading, 28*, 432-437.

Roe, B.D., Stoodt, B.D., & Burns, P.C. (1987). *Secondary school reading instruction: The content areas.* Boston, MA: Houghton Mifflin.

Santa, C., Havens, L., & Harrison, S. (1989). Teaching secondary science through reading, writing, studying, and problem solving. In D. Lapp, J. Flood, & N. Farnan (Eds.), *Content area reading and learning: Instructional strategies.* Englewood Cliff, NJ: Prentice Hall.

Simonsen, S., & Singer, H. (1985). *Metacognition: Use of standards as a function of content familiarity versus training.* Paper presented at the National Reading Conference, San Diego, CA.

Singer, H. (1987). *Instructor actions: The fourth component in the schema-interactive model.* Paper presented at the Annual Convention of the International Reading Association, Anaheim, CA.

Singer, H., & Simonsen, S. (1989). Comprehension and instruction in learning from a text. In D. Lapp, J. Flood, & N. Farnan (Eds.), *Content area reading and learning: Instructional strategies.* Englewood Cliffs, NJ: Prentice Hall.

Smith, F.R., & Feathers, K.M. (1983a). The role of reading in content area classrooms: Assumption vs. reality. *Journal of Reading, 26*, 262-267.

Smith, F.R., & Feathers, K.M. (1983b). Teacher and student perceptions of content area reading. *Journal of Reading, 26*, 348-354.

Stahl, S. (1983). Differential word knowledge and reading comprehension. *Journal of Reading Behavior, 15*, 33-50.

Stewart, R.A. (1989, December). *What color is my chalk? Literacy instruction in a secondary earth science classroom.* Paper presented at the National Reading Conference, Austin, TX.

Taft, M.L., & Leslie, L. (1985). The effects of prior knowledge and oral reading accuracy on miscues and reading comprehension. *Journal of Reading Behavior, 27*, 163-179.

Vacca, J.L., Vacca, R.T., & Gove, M. (1987). *Reading and learning to read.* Boston, MA: Little, Brown.

Yopp, H.K., & Singer, H. (1985). Toward an interactive reading instructional model: Explanation of activation of linguistic awareness and metalinguistic ability in learning to read. In H. Singer & R. Ruddell (Eds.), *Theoretical models and processes of reading.* Newark, DE: International Reading Association.

CHAPTER 9

Text Structure, Comprehension, and Recall

BARBARA M. TAYLOR

This chapter discusses why awareness of text structure is important in developing reading ability and why it should be a topic of concern to teachers—namely, because direct instruction in using text structure can enhance students' reading comprehension. Taylor concludes the chapter with a discussion of instructional strategies that have been successful in improving students' awareness and use of text structure, and therefore their reading comprehension and recall. The analysis includes strategies for use with both expository and narrative text.

Recent research on the reading process has demonstrated the importance of awareness of text structure in readers' comprehension and memory of material they have read. In this chapter I discuss what text structure comprises and why awareness of text structure is important. Next I address the difficulties students have in noticing and making use of text structure. Finally, I describe a number of instructional strategies focusing on expository and narrative text structure that have improved students' comprehension and recall of text.

What Is Text Structure and Why Is It Important?

Text structure is the organization of ideas in text. It includes the general organizational plan authors follow as they are writing. The organizational structure of a simple story consists of a situation that is introduced, developed, and resolved. The structure of a social studies text is reflected in headings that relate topics the author wishes to discuss.

Text structure also includes organizational patterns spanning several paragraphs that are selected by an author to make points or communicate information. Five types of organizational patterns are commonly found in students' textbooks: time order, listing, compare/contrast, cause/effect, and problem/solution (Englert & Hiebert, 1984; Horowitz, 1985; Meyer & Freedle, 1984).

Time order is represented by text patterns that have sequences, such as assembly instructions or a chronology of historical events. Listing involves a series of ideas that elaborate on an explicit or implicit generalization (e.g., Three things happened to improve working conditions during the Industrial Revolution. First...). Compare/contrast involves discussing similarities and differences among people, places, or events. A cause/effect text pattern consists of a description of events followed by a discussion of either what caused these events or what happened as a result of these events. With a problem/solution pattern, the author discusses a problem and suggests possible solutions.

Text structure also includes an author's interweaving of main points and supporting details. Numerous ideas with varying levels of importance will be found under a heading in a textbook. Less important (subordinate) ideas are included to support or elaborate on more important (superordinate) ideas.

Professional writers write (or at least revise) with text structure in mind. A story unfolds according to a general plan in the writer's head. Textbook writers have key points they wish to relate. Writers and editors strive for good organization, realizing that well-organized text will be easier for readers to understand than poorly organized text. In other words, structure is an essential aspect of text used by effective writers to communicate key ideas and by readers to understand the main points of a written text.

Skilled adult readers automatically discern the structure of text as they are reading and use this structure to facilitate their comprehension and recall of the material (van Dijk & Kintsch, 1983). For example, skilled adult readers typically organize their summaries of text in the same way the text was written, which suggests an awareness of structure. As they read, their awareness of text structure helps them understand the key points being made. When asked to recall what they have read, these readers tend to recall the most important ideas of the selection (Winograd & Bridge, 1986).

In contrast to adults, students tend not to be very skilled in using text structure to facilitate their comprehension and recall of text (McGee, 1982). Often, children do not organize their recall of expository text in the way the ideas were originally presented, which suggests an insensitivity to text structure (Taylor & Samuels, 1983). Many elementary and secondary students either do not understand or have considerable difficulty stating the important ideas of expository texts they have read, a skill that depends on sensitivity to text structure (Baumann, 1981; B.M. Taylor, 1980; K.K. Taylor, 1986; Winograd, 1984). Not surprisingly, poorer readers have more difficulty stating the important ideas in text than do better readers (Winograd & Bridge, 1986).

On the positive side, elementary and secondary students who are taught to identify the structure of expository and narrative text have been found to have better comprehension than students who have not received such instruction.

Instruction Focusing on Expository Text Structure

Many students, particularly those in the elementary grades, have difficulty reading for main ideas in their content area textbooks (B.M. Taylor, 1986; K.K. Taylor, 1986; Winograd, 1984). After reading several pages in a social studies text, for example, students often can recall very little about what they have read. The ideas they do remember may or may not be important; often they are details the students find interesting (Hidi & Anderson, 1986).

Instructional techniques that teach students to become aware of the structure of expository text, and to use this structure to focus on important information, have been found to be effective in improving students' reading comprehension. Such techniques include hierarchical summaries, maps, structural organizers, a modification of the SQ3R study procedure, and use of headings in textbook chapters. In addition to making use of text structure, these techniques involve generative learning in which students are required to respond, often in writing, to the material they are reading (Wittrock, 1986).

Hierarchical Summaries

Hierarchical summarizing has proved effective in teaching intermediate grade students to notice and use text structure to facilitate their understanding and recall of important ideas in textbook material (Taylor, 1982; Taylor & Beach, 1984; Taylor & Frye, 1987). With this technique, students are taught how to summarize in writing the most important ideas for a textbook section. Reading one section at a time (from one heading to the next), students identify the topic and write what they believe to be the most important idea, along with one or two other ideas about the topic (Figure 1). Students should write in their own words and should limit their summaries to two or three sentences so they focus on important information. After summarizing one section, students repeat the procedure with the next section. At the end of three to five pages, students review their summaries and recite the ideas they have written.

Figure 1
A Hierarchical Summary for Cities and Suburbs (fifth grade)

1. <u>American communities have changed a lot in the past 50 years.</u> People have moved from crowded cities to the suburbs.

2. <u>There are good things and bad things about cities.</u> There are a lot of things to do in cities. But cities have problems like too much traffic, dirt, and noise, and houses that need fixing.

3. <u>There are good things and bad things about suburbs.</u> People move to the suburbs to get away from crowded cities, but then suburbs become crowded too.

4. <u>Supercities are very large metropolitan areas.</u> The suburbs of one city meet the suburbs of another city. Boston, New York, and Washington, DC, are becoming supercities.

Studying in pairs has been found to be effective with this technique. One student can look at the summary of the student who is reciting and tell him or her if any important ideas have been omitted. It is important to point out to students that no two summaries will be exactly alike; in fact, they may vary considerably from one student to the next.

Taylor and Frye (1987) found that reciprocal teaching (Palincsar & Brown, 1984) is a successful approach to teaching intermediate grade students to write hierarchical summaries for textbook material. Working in groups of four, students move through their social studies text a paragraph at a time. For each paragraph, one student assumes the role of teacher. The "teacher" reads the paragraph to the group and asks an important question about the paragraph. Then he or she summarizes the paragraph on a sheet of paper. After working paragraph by paragraph for approximately three lessons, the groups spend another three or four lessons working section by section. Finally, students go through their textbooks on their own, writing summaries for each section.

Whether students begin in reciprocal teaching groups or on

their own, instruction in writing hierarchical summaries requires considerable modeling and guided practice. However, studies have shown that after 8 to 12 lessons, students who have learned the techniques have better recall of the important ideas in their content area textbooks than do students who have not learned the technique.

Maps

One limitation of the hierarchical summary procedure is that it depends on the use of headings in textbook material. Mapping (Berkowitz, 1986) is a similar technique that also has been found to work well with intermediate grade students, but that does not depend on textbook headings. Also, mapping requires less writing than the hierarchical summary procedure.

To make a map of informative text, students first read the entire selection (three to five pages), and then write the title or main subject in the middle of a sheet of paper. Next they list what they believe are the major topics of the selection clockwise around the title. Then the students skim the selection to pick out two to four important ideas about each topic. They write these ideas in phrase form under the topic (Figure 2).

Once the map is finished, students are instructed to study what they have read by reviewing the map. Again, studying maps in pairs has been found to work well. One student recites while the other listens and comments (students should state their ideas in complete sentences here instead of in phrases). Again, it is important to stress that students' maps will differ. Make sure that students have read through the text at least twice, focusing on the text structure and main ideas within this structure.

After six 1-hour sessions, fifth grade students who learned to make and study maps had better recall of material from social studies texts than did students who studied teacher-made maps, answered questions on the material, or simply reread the material.

Structural Organizers

Slater, Graves, and Piché (1985) have developed a technique that focuses on a number of top-level structures common in social

Figure 2
A Map for Cities and Suburbs (fifth grade)

---

1. **Changes** People move from cities to suburbs	2. **Cities** Lots of things to do. Problems: traffic, noise, dirt, run-down houses

Metropolitan Areas

4. **Supercities** Large cities start to grow together (like Boston, New York, Washington, DC)	3. **Suburbs** People move there to get away from city problems; suburbs become crowded

---

studies textbooks. Their structural organizers have been found to facilitate ninth grade students' ability to write summaries of what they have read.

With this technique, teachers give students written examples of four top-level structures (or organizational patterns) often found in social studies material. Then they have students read material containing each of these patterns. The top-level structures are claim/counterclaim, claim/support/conclusion, cause/effect, and problem/solution (Meyer, 1975). Before reading a social studies pas-

Figure 3
Problem/Solution Outline Grid for Working Conditions During the Industrial Revolution

Factory Workers During the Industrial Revolution

Problem:	Poor working conditions.
Support:	Low wages.
Support:	Long hours, even for children.
Support:	Unsafe factories and mines.
Solution:	People began to demand that something be done.
Solution:	Laws were passed.
Support:	To protect women and children.
Support:	To create safer working conditions.
Solution:	Labor unions were formed.
Support:	Demanded better pay and working conditions.

sage that follows one of these patterns, students are given a corresponding outline grid that contains key terms pointing out the top-level structure (e.g., *problem, support,* and *solution* for a problem/solution structure). As students read the passage, they are instructed to take notes by writing phrases in appropriate slots on the outline grid (Figure 3).

In the Slater, Graves, and Piché (1985) study, students who completed the outline grid as they read a passage from their social studies texts received better recall scores than did students in three other test conditions: (1) those who were instructed to read the material and take detailed notes, (2) those who were given a written example of the passage's particular top-level structure prior to reading, and (3) those who were instructed simply to read the material. Similar results were found in a related study involving fifth grade students (Armbruster, Anderson, & Ostertag, 1987).

A Modified SQ3R Study Strategy

Adams, Carnine, and Gersten (1982) developed an effective study strategy, centered around text structure, that facilitates fifth grade students' ability to answer short answer questions on passages from their social studies texts. The strategy is a modification of the SQ3R procedure developed by Robinson (1941).

Students first *preview* the text material by reading headings and subheadings. Then they return to the first subheading, read it, and *recite* it without looking. Next they *ask themselves questions*, based on the subheadings, about what might be important to learn in the section. Students then *read* the section to find answers to their questions and to locate other important information. Finally, they *reread* the subheadings and *recite* the important ideas in the section. These steps are repeated for the next section. At the end of the reading assignment, students rehearse by reading each subheading and reciting important ideas. Additional study is required if students are unable to recall information from particular sections.

Use of Headings

In a study similar to the one just discussed, Brooks and colleagues (1983) gave college students written instructions in how to use headings to help in studying 1,500-word textbook passages. They found that these students wrote better summaries of the material than did students who read the same material without using the headings. The instruction covered four areas: using headings to develop expectations about material in the passage, understanding why each heading is appropriate, memorizing the headings, and using headings as recall aids.

Summary

In general, effective techniques involving expository text require students to focus attention on the structure of the text, write or review important ideas from the material according to this structure, and study what they have read by reviewing their written notes.

In the first three procedures discussed above, students are asked to write and study some form of organized notes on textbook material. All three procedures highlight the organization of the material being read. In the last two procedures, students are asked to use headings as an aid in focusing on and reviewing important ideas in textbook material. Instead of writing down important ideas, students mentally review them.

Two valuable aspects of all of these techniques are that they focus students' attention on the organization of the material and they get students to do more with the material than simply read through it once. Periodically, students have to stop to reflect on the material and review the important information.

Instruction Focusing on Narrative Text Structure

By the time they enter school, most children have listened to many stories. In the elementary grades, they also will spend a fair amount of time reading and listening to stories. Through exposure to stories, students develop a knowledge of narrative structure—an understanding of the major parts of a story and the sequence of these parts, including setting, problem, goal, events, and resolution.

Many adults and children use their knowledge of narrative structure to understand and remember stories (Spiegel & Fitzgerald, 1986). Research indicates that students with better knowledge of story structure tend to be better readers (Fitzgerald, 1984).

Questioning strategies that focus on narrative structure are beneficial in terms of students' comprehension of stories. Presumably, these strategies focus attention on the central story elements, thus facilitating students' overall comprehension. These questioning strategies also may help some students improve their understanding of narrative structure. Discussion of several of these strategies follows.

Story Structure and Traditional Questions

In a study with kindergarten children, Morrow (1984) found that asking students story structure questions as well as traditional questions improved their overall ability to answer questions after listening to stories. The story structure questions dealt with setting (time, place, characters), theme (goal or problem facing the main character), plot (sequence of episodes that lead to the main character reaching his or her goal), and resolution (the way the main character reaches his or her goal, the story ending). Traditional questions included literal responses (recalling facts and details, cause and effect relationships, classifications), inferential responses (interpreting characters' feelings, relating story to children's experiences), and critical responses (problem solving).

Children listened to a total of eight stories. For the first three, the teacher posed story structure questions for the children to think about while listening: "Where do you think this story takes place? What trouble do you think Benjy [the main character] gets into? How do you think he gets out of trouble?" For the remainder of the stories, the teacher helped students generate their own questions to think about while listening. Postreading questions included both story structure and traditional questions. Prereading and postreading discussions lasted about 5 minutes each.

Overall, students involved in discussions of stories based on story structure questions and traditional questions together had better comprehension than did students involved in discussions based on story structure questions or traditional questions alone. Of course, any type of discussion was better than none.

Story Maps

After examining basal reader teacher manuals, Beck and colleagues (1979) concluded that the manuals gave teachers random story questions to ask. That is, the manuals did not present a cohesive line of questioning about major story elements that would facilitate students' comprehension.

In a study with second grade students, Beck, Omanson, and McKeown (1982) investigated the effects of story maps on teachers' questioning and students' comprehension of stories. Before assigning a story, teachers developed a story map—an outline of the important ideas in a story, including setting, problem, goal, events, and solution. Teachers then revised the directed reading lesson in the teacher manual by developing prereading, during reading, and postreading questions that focused on the story map (Figure 4). Students who received these revised lessons comprehended the story better than did students who received the directed reading lessons recommended in the teacher manual.

Self-Questioning

A self-questioning procedure developed by Singer and Donlon (1982) has been found to be successful with elementary (Nolte & Singer, 1985) and secondary students (Singer & Donlan). With this procedure, students ask themselves story-specific questions about the major elements of a story as they are reading. Story elements include the main character, goal, obstacles, outcome, and theme of the story.

The teacher shows students how to ask and answer questions about different story elements as they read. Students are to move from a general question (such as "Who is the leading character?") to a story-specific question (such as "Is *Little Red Riding Hood* more about the wolf or the little girl?").

Covering one story element per lesson, the teacher models for students how to convert a general question into a story-specific question for a particular story. Working together with familiar stories, the teacher and students generate story-specific questions about the element being considered. After all story elements have been covered, students work independently, asking themselves story-specific questions about the stories they read. (See Figure 5 for an example of general and story-specific questions for major story elements.)

Summary

In all three studies described above, teachers or students asked questions focusing on major story elements to facilitate their comprehension of stories. What seems to be valuable about such approaches is that students' attention is directed toward what is important in particular stories.

An advantage of the self-questioning procedure over the other two narrative questioning procedures is that students are not dependent on the teacher's questions; they learn to work independently.

Figure 4
Story Map and Related Questions for
Madge's Magic Show (second grade)

Madge's Magic Show by Mike Thaler

Story map	**Questions**
The Setting	
Characters: Madge, Jimmy	Who are the main characters in the
Place: Madge's house	story?
The Problem	
Jimmy isn't impressed with	What problem does Madge have
Madge's magic tricks.	with Jimmy?
The Goal	
For Jimmy to think Madge is a	What does Madge hope will hap-
good magician.	pen?
The Events	
Event 1	
Madge pulls a chicken in-	What are three things that happen
stead of a rabbit out of a hat.	when Madge tries to pull a rabbit
	out of a hat?
Event 2	
Madge pulls a fox instead of	
a rabbit out of a hat.	
Event 3	
Madge pulls a cow instead of	
a rabbit out of a hat.	
Event 4	
Madge pulls a rabbit out of a	
hat.	
The Solution	
Jimmy finally thinks Madge is	How does Jimmy react when Madge
a good magician.	pulls a rabbit out of a hat?

Conclusion

Over the past 10 years, a considerable amount of research has emerged on the role of text structure in reading. We have learned

Figure 5
General and Story-Specific Questions for *Little Red Riding Hood*

Story Element	Questions
Character	GQ: Who is the leading character?
	SQ: Is this story more about the wolf or Little Red Riding Hood?
Goal	GQ: What is the leading character trying to accomplish?
	SQ: What is Little Red Riding Hood trying to do in this story?
Obstacles	GQ: What obstacles does the leading character encounter?
	SQ: How does the wolf cause problems for Little Red Riding Hood?
Outcome	GQ: Does the leading character reach his or her goal?
	SQ: How is Little Red Riding Hood saved from the wolf and reunited with her grandmother?
Theme	GQ: What is the author saying to us about life in this story?
	SQ: What did I learn from Little Red Riding Hood's encounter with the wolf?

that awareness of text structure is very important to a reader of expository or narrative text.

Adults, who in most cases make use of text structure automatically, may wonder why teachers need to be concerned about students' awareness of text structure. Most students do learn to use text structure to some degree as they read. However, students also seem to benefit from some formal instruction in text structure to improve their comprehension and recall of expository and narrative text. This chapter presents a number of strategies focusing on text structure that have been found to be effective with elementary, secondary, and college students.

References

Adams, A., Carnine, D., & Gersten, R. (1982). Instructional strategies for studying content area texts in the intermediate grades. *Reading Research Quarterly, 18,* 27-55.

Armbruster, B.B., Anderson, T.H., & Ostertag, J. (1987). Does text structure/summarization instruction facilitate learning from expository text? *Reading Research Quarterly, 22,* 331-346.

Baumann, J.F. (1981). Effect of ideational prominence on children's reading comprehension of expository prose. *Journal of Reading Behavior, 13,* 49-56.

Beck, I.L., McKeown, M.G., McCaslen, E., & Burkes, A. (1979). *Instructional dimensions that may affect reading comprehension: Examples from two commercial reading programs.* Pittsburgh, PA: University of Pittsburgh, Learning Research and Development Center.

Beck, I.L., Omanson, R.C., & McKeown, M.G. (1982). An instructional redesign of reading lessons: Effects on comprehension. *Reading Research Quarterly, 17,* 462-481.

Berkowitz, S.J. (1986). Effects of instruction in text organization on sixth-grade students' memory for expository reading. *Reading Research Quarterly, 21,* 161-178.

Brooks, L.W., Dansereau, D.F., Spurlin, J.E., & Holley, C.D. (1983). Effects of headings on text processing. *Journal of Educational Psychology, 75*(2), 292-307.

Englert, C.S., & Hiebert, E. (1984). Children's developing awareness of text structure in expository materials. *Journal of Educational Psychology, 26,* 65-74.

Fitzgerald, J. (1984). The relationship between reading ability and expectations for story structures. *Discourse Processes, 7,* 21-41.

Hidi, S., & Anderson, V. (1986). Producing written summaries: Task demands, cognitive operations, and implications for instruction. *Review of Educational Research, 56*(4), 473-493.

Horowitz, R. (1985). Text patterns: Part 1. *Journal of Reading Research, 28,* 448-454.

McGee, L.M. (1982). Awareness of text structure: Effects on children's recall of expository text. *Reading Research Quarterly, 17,* 581-592.

Meyer, B.J.F. (1975). *The organization of prose and its effects on memory.* Amsterdam, Netherlands: North Holland.

Meyer, B.J.F., & Freedle, R.O. (1984). Effects of discourse type on recall. *American Educational Research Journal, 21,* 121-143.

Morrow, L.M. (1984). Reading stories to young children: Effects of story structure and traditional questioning strategies on comprehension. *Journal of Reading Behavior, 16,* 273-288.

Nolte, R.Y., & Singer, H. (1985). Active comprehension: Teaching a process of reading comprehension and its effects on reading achievement. *The Reading Teacher, 39,* 24-33.

Palincsar, A.S., & Brown, A.L. (1984). Reciprocal teaching of comprehension fostering and comprehension monitoring activities. *Cognition and Instruction, 1,* 117-175.

Robinson, F.P. (1941). *Diagnostic and remedial techniques for effective study.* New York: HarperCollins.

Singer, H., & Donlan, D. (1982). Active comprehension: A problem-solving schema with question generation for comprehension of complex short stories. *Reading Research Quarterly, 17,* 166-186.

Slater, W.H., Graves, M.F., & Piché, G.L. (1985). Effects of structural organizers on ninth-grade students' comprehension and recall of four patterns of expository text. *Reading Research Quarterly, 20,* 189-202.

Spiegel, D.L., & Fitzgerald, J. (1986). Improving comprehension through instruction about story parts. *The Reading Teacher, 39,* 676-682.

Taylor, B.M. (1980). Children's memory for expository text after reading. *Reading Research Quarterly, 15,* 399-411.

Taylor, B.M. (1982). Text structure and children's comprehension and memory for expository material. *Journal of Educational Psychology, 74,* 323-340.

Taylor, B.M. (1986). Teaching middle grade students to summarize content textbook material. In J.F. Baumann (Ed.), *Teaching main idea comprehension* (pp. 195-209). Newark, DE: International Reading Association.

Taylor, B.M., & Beach, R.W. (1984). The effects of text structure instruction on middle-grade students' comprehension and production of expository text. *Reading Research Quarterly, 19*(2), 134-146.

Taylor, B.M., & Frye, B. (1987). *Increasing time for pleasure reading and comprehension strategy instruction in the intermediate grades.* Unpublished manuscript, University of Minnesota, Minneapolis, MN.

Taylor, B.M., & Samuels, S.J. (1983). Children's use of text structure in the recall of expository material. *American Educational Research Journal, 20,* 517-528.

Taylor, K.K. (1986). Summary writing by young children. *Reading Research Quarterly, 21,* 193-208.

van Dijk, T.A., & Kintsch, W. (1983). *Strategies of discourse comprehension.* San Diego, CA: Academic.

Winograd, P.N. (1984). Strategic difficulties in summarizing texts. *Reading Research Quarterly, 19,* 404-425.

Winograd, P.N., & Bridge, C.A. (1986). The comprehension of important information in written prose. In J.F. Baumann (Ed.), *Teaching main idea comprehension.* Newark, DE: International Reading Association.

Wittrock, M.C. (1986). Students' thought processes. In M.C. Wittrock (Ed.), *Handbook of research on teaching* (3rd ed., pp. 297-314). New York: Macmillan.

CHAPTER 10

Metacognition and Self-Monitoring Strategies

RUTH GARNER

Over a decade ago, reading researchers began to study readers' knowledge and use of their own cognitive resources. Adopting a term from developmental psychologists, they called this line of research metacognition. The research literature has since expanded, and many implications for instructional practice have emerged. Among them are suggestions that teachers interview students about their understanding and remembering, show students how to monitor their comprehension, and give direct instruction in some broadly applicable comprehension strategies. This chapter addresses both metacognitive research related to reading and the implications for reading instruction that emerge from this research literature.

Metacognition is a label for a body of research and theory that examines thinking about thinking (Garner, 1987a). When I examine my test taking strengths and decide that I would prefer an essay exam to a multiple choice exam on the economic causes of the American Civil War, I am using metacognition. When I notice that I am turning the pages of a difficult text on natural selection but am actually thinking about dinner, my detection of mind-wandering is metacognitive. When I rehearse a just-heard telephone number so I can then make a call, I am engaging in metacognitive activity. Metacognitive activity is not exclusive to academic settings, but it always involves thinking. When I study, read, or solve problems, I engage in thinking, and I may act metacognitively.

The examples above come from different categories of metacognitive activity identified initially by Flavell (1981). The examination of personal test taking strengths is part of metacognitive knowledge; detection of profitless mind-wandering during reading is a metacognitive experience; and rehearsal of a telephone number is an example of strategy use. In this chapter, I take a close look at metacognitive activity in each of the three categories. Then I look briefly at important research conducted by psychologists and educators and discuss what teachers can do to assess and encourage metacognitive activity in students.

Metacognitive Knowledge

To be considered part of a metacognitive knowledge base, information must be about thinking, and it must be both relatively stable and usually statable. This information grows gradually with years of experience in thinking. From perceived patterns in experience, children and adults abstract, examine, and talk about person, task, and strategy factors in cognition.

An example of person information is knowing that one is more proficient at verbal tasks than at computation tasks—an intraindividual difference in performance. An example of task information is knowing that text written about a familiar topic generally is easier to understand than text written about an unfamiliar topic.

An example of strategy information is knowing how to reinspect text for material once read but no longer remembered as a means of answering questions about the content. In the case of metacognitive knowledge about strategies, it is important to note that *knowlege* is not *use*. A learner can know all the components of an effective strategy but still not use any of them in real-world situations where employing the routine would assist learning.

As Baker and Brown (1984) pointed out some time ago, one simple way of assessing what adults and children know about thinking is to ask them. In fact, researchers and teachers have been interviewing learners for years.

Interview research on thinking has yielded a number of interesting results related to reading:

- Older children understand the comparative ease of remembering information at gist, rather than verbatim, level, whereas younger children do not (Kreutzer, Leonard, & Flavell, 1975);
- Younger children are far more likely than older children to focus on decoding aspects of reading and to fail to understand the cognitive components of the process (Myers & Paris, 1978);
- Younger and less proficient readers are unlikely to differentiate between "study" reading and "fun" reading (Forrest & Waller, 1980); and
- Less skilled readers are not as aware as skilled readers are of the detrimental effects of poor reading practices such as allowing one's mind to wander or watching television while reading (Paris & Myers, 1981).

Schooling is an important part of the metacognitive knowledge bases uncovered in these interview studies. One reason young children know relatively little about stable characteristics of thinking may be that they have not experienced many of the deliberate learning situations that occur regularly in school. Thus, they have not had many opportunities to make thinking an object of study.

On the other hand, some school experiences may actually spread misinformation. If teachers and basal readers emphasize oral reading and decoding at the expense of silent reading and comprehension, children acquire mistaken notions about reading. Allington (1983) has noted that while teachers give skilled readers silent reading practice and instruction that emphasizes meaning, they often give less skilled readers instruction that emphasizes decoding, frequently interrupting the lesson to provide feedback on oral reading accuracy. One result of such instructional disparity is a lot of "down time" in instruction for less skilled readers; another is flawed metacognitive knowledge about reading among less skilled readers.

Teachers can assess readers' sense of the reading process and knowledge of a variety of reading and studying strategies by interviewing their students with questions originally generated for research purposes. For example:

1. Are any sentences in a paragraph more important than others?

2. Is it easier to retell a story if you tell it in your own words, or if you use the author's exact words?

3. Are reading to study and reading for fun the same?

4. What things does a person have to do to become a good reader?

5. What makes something difficult to read?

6. How do you answer a question in your textbook if you remember that you read about the topic, but you do not remember the answer?

7. How can you tell what an author thought was important in a passage?

8. How do you write a short summary of a long piece of text?

9. What do you do if you come to an unfamiliar word in something you're reading for homework?

10. How do you put something "in your own words"?

Researchers have discovered that research paradigms using verbal reports pose some problems. Teachers who interview students to find out what they know about reading and studying need to be aware of those problems when they interpret the verbal responses they get. The problems apply to a number of verbal tasks in the classroom, not exclusively to interviews.

One problem might be labeled *accessibility*. When we practice an activity a lot, eventually we no longer have to think about it; our behavior becomes automatic. Behaviors that are automatic for most adults include brushing one's teeth, folding sheets, pouring soda, and tying shoelaces. Because we perform the substeps unconsciously, we are not sufficiently aware of what we do to report our actions to an interested questioner. If a researcher or teacher asked what we did, we would infer what our actions might be, recall what someone prescribed for us to do, or provide an incomplete report of the as-yet-unautomated substeps. The problem is that our report would be incomplete or inaccurate or both, and the researcher or teacher would draw erroneous conclusions about our adeptness.

The best solution to the accessibility problem is to ask children and adults about their reading, studying, and problem-solving routines before they become completely automated. Complex, difficult, and novel tasks produce richer, more accurate introspective data about thinking.

A second problem is *memory failure*. This problem occurs when a learner is asked about cognitive activity that occurred previously. An adult reader might be quizzed about the relative efficiency of oral and silent reading when that person hasn't read aloud for years. Again, the account given by the adult is potentially incomplete, inaccurate, or both. The solution to this problem is fairly straightforward: inquire about mental activity shortly after it occurs. A teacher can give a class a short study period and immediately afterward ask what study strategies were used.

This example suggests the next problem, *inadvertent cuing*. A teacher might structure the class as suggested, but might pose the question about studying in a specific, direct manner (e.g., "Did any of you think to generate three or four questions, try to answer them, and then use your success or failure to dictate whether further study was needed?"). It would be difficult for savvy students—who spend a lot of school time trying to infer what the adult in charge of the classroom wants to hear—to say "no." A better approach would be for the teacher to ask an undirected question, such as "What specific activities did you use to study today?" Mimicry of instructors' statements about highly desirable strategies is still possible, but cuing to what those desirable strategies might be is diminished with this approach.

Perhaps the most important problem of all is that of *verbal facility*. Children (and adults) differ in language skills and in inclination to speak aloud. Some respondents to interviews say a lot; others say very little. These two groups may know an equal amount about their reading and studying, but researchers and teachers can track only differences in telling, not in knowing. One solution, particularly in work with young children, is to use pictures as stimuli. Yussen and Bird (1979) developed pairs of pictures depicting learners in situations that, from an adult perspective, represented either easy or difficult tasks. Children were asked to make decisions about the relative ease of the tasks. We can assume they examined what they knew about themselves, tasks, and strategies when they made those decisions.

Because of the problems associated with interview methods, some researchers have devised alternative means of assessing metacognitive knowledge in children and adults. Teachers are trying these methods as well.

One method that was informative in our work at Maryland used a tutoring paradigm (Garner, Macready, & Wagoner, 1984; Garner, Wagoner, & Smith, 1983). We asked students, acting as tutors (the actual subjects in our research studies) to help younger children read an expository text and answer detailed questions about the content. We were interested in whether the tutors would encourage their "students" to use text reinspection to locate information they had read but could not remember. We assumed the tutors would bring up the reinspection strategy if they knew about it. We matched tutors with students on the basis of race and sex and avoided pairing close friends; no adult assistance was available to the pairs.

In the Garner et al. (1984) study, the students were trained to feign strategy deficits. They were told not to answer the questions and not to reinspect text until the tutors prompted them to do so. In both studies, an investigator sat about 6 feet from the pairs. She audiotaped the session and took notes on tutoring behaviors.

Both studies found differences in strategy knowledge that corresponded to reading skill. Tutors who were skilled readers were more likely than less skilled readers to (1) encourage the use of lookbacks to text to solve the problem, (2) encourage reinspection only when the question cued text access (as opposed to access to a reader's knowledge base), and (3) encourage their "students" to scan the entire text using key words in the question to locate the relevant material. In other words, the skilled readers demonstrated knowledge of a text reinspection strategy.

Researchers have assessed metacognitive knowledge about reading for some time. Many teachers assess what their students know (and don't know) about the reading process in general and about important reading and study strategies in particular. This information can be useful for instructional planning (and for attempting to understand poor student performance on some academic tasks).

Metacognitive Experiences

A metacognitive experience occurs when a learner has an "aha" about cognition. Anderson (1980) describes metacognitive experiences in reading as "clicks" (awareness of cognitive success, usually of understanding and remembering) and "clunks" (awareness of cognitive failure, usually of information confusion or forgetting). The aha that something is wrong with the reading enterprise is as good as the aha that all is well. Only when readers detect problems can they adjust processing strategies, perhaps rereading a confusing portion of text, slowing down their pace, or consulting an external source for a key definition.

Obviously, readers' tolerance for feelings of failure to understand or remember is related to the importance of the reading or studying goal. Sometimes we are aware that we are not "getting it," but we do not care enough to expend extra energy to remedy the situation. Sometimes we are aware of cognitive confusion, but our metacognitive knowledge base is not rich enough to provide us with appropriate remedial strategies.

In still other instances, we are not aware of cognitive failure. Markman (1981) gives an example of such a situation. She describes a reading setting in which her mind begins to wander. As she becomes increasingly engrossed in her daydream, she understands less and less of what she is reading. She continues to turn pages, persisting in the pointless venture, because she is unaware that she is not understanding. This is poor comprehension monitoring, documented in research reviews as a pervasive phenomenon among young and less skilled readers (see Baker & Brown, 1984; Brown, Armbruster, & Baker, 1986; Wagoner, 1983).

How have researchers studied metacognitive experiences in reading? How do we know that young and less skilled readers are not adept comprehension monitors? Although some investigators have relied on retrospective accounts of monitoring or on corrections in oral reading, the dominant paradigm has been that of error detection.

The error-detection method involves "rigging" the material in such a manner that the text the readers are asked to read is incomplete or inconsistent. When readers who have been asked to edit, critique, or act on the text's content report that the text is flawed or spend more time reading rigged sections than unrigged sections, they have detected the error and are assumed to be good comprehension monitors with uncontrived materials as well.

Some texts used in these studies of comprehension monitoring in listening and reading situations present quite blatant inconsistencies. Markman's (1979) text about fish and light is such a text:

Fish must have light in order to see. There is absolutely no light at the bottom of the ocean. It is pitch black down there. When it is that dark the fish cannot see anything. They cannot even see colors. Some fish that live at the bottom of the ocean can see the color of their food; that is how they know what to eat.

When a number of children fail to detect such blatant inconsistencies in text, researchers speculate why. Some of the explanations offered are that children (1) forget material at the beginning of the text by the time they encounter the inconsistent material; (2)

draw "fix-up" inferences to make sense of a text (in the fish passage, children might infer that the author was talking about one ocean at the beginning of the text and a different one at the end); (3) refuse to admit comprehension failure to an adult (even in an editorial role); or (4) genuinely fail to monitor their comprehension.

Although it has been difficult for researchers to disentangle these explanations for poor detection performance, I encourage teachers to experiment with error-detection exercises in the classroom. At a fairly gross level, performance on these tasks is an index to comprehension monitoring proficiency.

Baker (1984) provides more diagnostic assistance for teachers who use these ideas in the classroom. Baker has distinguished three sorts of problems that might occur in text:

> *Lexical:* It is so hot there that most brugens would melt.
>
> *External Consistency:* They used sand from the trees to make many things.
>
> *Internal Consistency:* The temperature on Venus is much higher than boiling water. Venus is about the same size as Earth. But it is much too cold for us to live there.

Example 1 includes a nonword (*brugens*), example 2 is empirically false (sand does not come from trees), and example 3 is logically inconsistent (Venus cannot have a temperature that is both much higher than boiling water and too cold for us to live there).

Teachers with whom I have worked have used Baker's research procedure of embedding these errors in short expository texts and asking children to underline anything troublesome and to explain the nature of the problem. In general, Baker (1984) and the teachers have found that older and more skilled readers detect more problems than do younger and less skilled readers.

This is an important finding, but it is also useful to find out if some children rely exclusively on a single standard for comprehension. Less experienced readers tend to detect lexical anomalies in text but to ignore consistency problems, whether an inconsistency violates knowledge base (external consistency) or logic (internal consistency). If they discover reliance on a single standard, teachers can provide instruction about other standards for comprehensibility. They can teach students that text should make sense lexically, empirically, and logically.

Teachers should phase out work with contrived texts to work with uncontrived ones. Students can be instructed to make "pit-stops" at the end of every page of an important textbook assignment to assess whether they are understanding the content. If so, they should proceed (this is a "click," to use Anderson's term). If they are not understanding the material, they should take action to remedy the miscomprehension (this is a "clunk").

Taken together, examination of a metacognitive knowledge base and assessment of comprehension monitoring skill have generated much enthusiasm among researchers and teachers. However, the area of metacognitive research and theory that is currently making the greatest impact on educational practice is strategy use.

Strategy Use

Strategies are sequences of activities undertaken to reach goals efficiently. Teachers often teach strategies to students to help them improve their ability to process information efficiently and effectively. Some rudimentary strategies emerge among very young children without any explicit instruction.

For strategies to enhance learning, they must be employed flexibly. Readers who reread an entire text every time they don't readily remember the answer to a question are not flexibly employing the text reinspection strategy. Flexible application of the routine demands that a reader decide *when* the strategy is appropriate (when the question cues access to text rather than to a reader's knowledge base) and *where* to apply it (the relevant segment of text). As mentioned earlier, skilled readers use this strategy flexibly, while less skilled readers tend either to fail to reinspect any texts or to reread entire texts with little attention to question cues or to the most informative segments.

Strategies have cognitive, metacognitive, and affective components. The cognitive component is most obvious: we engage

Strategy X to make cognitive progress toward Goal Y. Examples in reading and studying are abundant. We read chapter headings in a science textbook before reading a chapter on endangered species to get an overall idea of the content we will be encountering; we categorize crops into fruits, vegetables, and grains for easy storage and retrieval of the information for a social studies quiz on products; we map differences between acids and bases, knowing that the graphic display of textbook information will help us prepare for an essay exam.

The metacognitive component of strategy use is extremely important. It is often a "clunk" that alerts us to the need for strategic action. Though we can experience clunks without explicitly asking ourselves "Do I understand this?" sometimes we experience them precisely *because* we pose that question. We make pit-stops at the end of a textbook page to ask ourselves about our comprehension. Perhaps we monitor our comprehension by trying to put the information we have just read into our own words (Garner, 1987b). If we are not satisfied that we have understood sufficiently, we re-read or engage some other appropriate strategy.

The affective component of strategy use is also important. Because engaging in strategies takes time and effort, students are unlikely to involve a routine unless they are interested in accomplishing a learning goal. As Paris, Lipson, and Wixson (1983) put it, students must have both skill and will to use strategies.

Recent research on strategies related to reading and studying has provided us with both bad news and good news. The bad news is that young children and less skilled readers usually fail to regulate their learning strategically. For instance, these children do not allocate study time wisely (Owings et al., 1980); they do not capitalize on the permanence of print to reinspect it appropriately (Garner et al., 1983, 1984); and they do not generate succinct summaries of just the important information found in text (Brown & Day, 1983; Winograd, 1984).

The good news is that academically fundamental strategies have been taught with good results to students who do not use them spontaneously. For a number of useful strategies, the three conventional tests of training have been met: immediate improvement of performance; durability of effects; and transfer of the instructed activity to new, related situations.

What are some examples of strategies that have been successfully taught? Hare and Borchardt (1984) taught low-income, minority high school students to apply summarization rules to reduce a long expository text to a succinct, polished summary. Garner et al. (1984) taught elementary and middle school students enrolled in a remedial reading clinic why, when, and where to use text reinspection to answer detailed questions about difficult expository text. Adams, Carnine, and Gersten (1982) taught fifth grade students a six-step studying routine. Hansen and Pearson (1983) taught less skilled fourth grade readers to draw inferences while they read and to answer "inferential" questions about the content after they were finished. In an ambitious project, Paris and his colleagues (Paris, Cross, & Lipson, 1984; Paris & Jacobs, 1984) provided 20 modules of direct strategy instruction and practice to third and fifth grade students over 4 months. Students were trained to hunt for reading treasure (establish purposes for reading), track down the main idea, weave ideas (draw inferences), engage in road repair (self-correction), and round up their ideas (write summaries) as part of the instruction.

As researchers provide consulting expertise to school districts, as they publish workable training programs, as school-based personnel generate curricula based on strategy research, some of these ideas are already working their way into classrooms. The strategy training plans are appealing to teachers both because there is evidence that they improve academic performance and because in many instances, they have been tested in the field, not in the laboratory.

All of this activity, reported in scholarly journals and observed in school buildings, is very exciting. It seems that researchers and teachers have adopted a metacognitive agenda, in particular a strategy agenda, for inquiry and instruction. I do have some concerns about current strategy work, however, particularly at the classroom level.

Attention to Affect

I worry about educators' use of the metaphor of a prescription pad or a bag of tricks for strategic repertoires. These metaphors imply that what teachers need to teach and what learners need to learn about strategies is mostly procedural: find out what's wrong (miscomprehension, forgetting, an overlong summary, an unknown word) and then match that with a "fix" from the pad or bag (consult an external source, reread, delete trivia and redundancy, use linguistic context).

Good strategy instruction undeniably has a strong procedural component, but there is more to it than that. It also involves attention to when and where the strategy is most appropriately used (the flexibility issue addressed earlier) and attention to monitoring successful use of the strategy. With the former, a learner achieves efficiency. With the latter, a learner achieves effectiveness in independent learning situations. Both certainly are instructional goals.

There is still more. Learners do not engage strategies—or persevere in using them at the first sign of hard work or frustration—if they do not believe themselves to be capable of completing the task at hand. If they have learned that they are unlikely to succeed at this type of academic activity or if they think success at such activities comes only with ability (in which they presume themselves to be deficient) rather than effort, then *not* pursuing an activity is an adaptive response. In a situation such as this, skill matters less than will. Learners' beliefs about their ability to perform a task is more potent than personal skill in determining their willingness to attack (and persevere at) that task.

When we teach strategies, we should stress that executing them takes time and effort—that learning is not always easy. I have done this at the college level by "thinking aloud" for instructional purposes (Garner, 1987a). I can model appropriate activities and also display the inevitability of some frustration while working through a complex task.

Strategies and Content Learning

Even before recent U.S.-wide surveys demonstrated that high school students are woefully unfamiliar with salient aspects of our culture (names of national documents, authors of major literary works, approximate dates of history-changing events), I started to worry that, in our zeal to teach the process of learning (especially strategies), we now were neglecting content. This dilemma stems from strange concepts of strategy instruction: strategies can be taught as the goal of learning rather than as a means for learning; strategies can be taught in the absence of content.

Certainly this is not true. One cannot teach categorizing or summarizing or any other "izing" without some information. The information best used in strategy instruction is the textbook material students are grappling with in their coursework. In this manner, students deal with the material more effectively and come to understand that the strategies they have learned work with their texts.

In some cases, students do not need to apply much strategic energy to a particular text or task because they have a lot of background knowledge about the topic at hand. Borkowski, Carr, and Pressley (1987) give the example of a soccer expert reading about the sport and not needing to apply much comprehension monitoring or many strategic remedies to enhance recall of information. Before they begin to read, experts know what will need to be recalled later. This is not true for the soccer novice, who needs to activate cognitive and metacognitive activities to enhance understanding and recall of information. The rich interaction between domain knowledge and strategy use needs to be examined systematically by researchers and acknowledged by teachers.

Avoiding the "Quick Fix" Syndrome

Strategies cannot be taught quickly. When teachers believe that part of their job is to teach optimal ways to reach learning goals, they also must understand that their job is to teach, to re-teach, to help students practice with instructional guidance, and then to entice students to practice independently. Just as processing capacities are taxed until extensive reading practice produces more efficient decoding skills and shifts cognitive resources from code-breaking to comprehension (Samuels, 1979), strategic processing capacities are taxed until practice produces more automatic subroutines so that a variety of strategies can be engaged simultaneously without overloading the system. Practice is the key.

Peterson and Swing (1983) describe classrooms as rushed environments where processing must be done in "real time." Given the nature of activity flow in most classrooms, students worry about being left behind, about being scolded for failing to complete work, and about having to complete in-school work as homework. They cannot be blamed for reverting to least-effort principles to get the job done (often ineffectively, but nonetheless done). This situation is not conducive to strategic activity. As mentioned earlier, strategies take time and effort. And because we usually make a conscious decision to use strategies, we also can decide not to use them—or to use less effective, but perhaps more rehearsed (and thus more rapidly executed), immature routines.

If students have insufficiently practiced and routinized a summarizing strategy, they are likely to copy some sentences and delete others rather than work at a reduced, coherent summary that integrates information from a number of key sentences. If students have insufficiently practiced and routinized a reinspection strategy, they are likely to respond to questions whose answers they remember and leave the others blank, rather than locate unrecalled information by reinspecting text.

For the students who do not develop strategic routines for reading and studying without formal instruction, teachers must structure tasks so that they are just difficult enough to demand strategic activity and just easy enough for students to assume they might be able to complete them with some effort. Another part of the instructional job is to provide explicit instruction in strategy use, emphasizing why a particular routine is used, how to use it, and how to know when it has been used well. Still another part of the instructional job is to provide practice opportunities for students to make the activities automatic, routine, and personal. The goal of all of this instructional effort is fairly obvious: efficient learning from text.

References

Adams, A., Carnine, D., & Gersten, R. (1982). Instructional strategies for studying content area texts in the intermediate grades. *Reading Research Quarterly, 18,* 27-55.

Allington, R.L. (1983). The reading instruction provided to readers of differing abilities. *Elementary School Journal, 83*, 548-559.

Anderson, T.H. (1980). Study strategies and adjunct aids. In R.J. Spiro, B.C. Bruce, & W.F. Brewer (Eds.), *Theoretical issues in reading comprehension* (pp. 483-502). Hillsdale, NJ: Erlbaum.

Baker, L. (1984). Spontaneous versus instructed use of multiple standards for evaluating comprehension: Effects of age, reading proficiency, and type of standard. *Journal of Experimental Child Psychology, 38*, 289-311.

Baker, L., & Brown, A.L. (1984). Metacognitive skills and reading. In P.D. Pearson (Ed.), *Handbook of reading research* (pp. 353-394). White Plains, NY: Longman.

Borkowski, J.G., Carr, M., & Pressley, M. (1987). "Spontaneous" strategy use: Perspectives from metacognitive theory. *Intelligence, 11*, 61-75.

Brown, A.L., Armbruster, B.B., & Baker, L. (1986). The role of metacognition in reading and studying. In J. Orasanu (Ed.), *Reading comprehension: From research to practice* (pp. 49-75). Hillsdale, NJ: Erlbaum.

Brown, A.L., & Day, J.D. (1983). Macrorules for summarizing texts: The development of expertise. *Journal of Verbal Learning and Verbal Behavior, 22*, 1-14.

Flavell, J.H. (1981). Cognitive monitoring. In W.P. Dickson (Ed.), *Children's oral communication skills* (pp. 35-60). San Diego, CA: Academic.

Forrest, D.L., & Waller, T.G. (1980, April). *What do children know about their reading and study skills?* Paper presented at the meeting of the American Educational Research Association, Boston, MA.

Garner, R. (1987a). *Metacognition and reading comprehension.* Norwood, NJ: Ablex.

Garner, R. (1987b). Strategies for reading and studying expository text. *Educational Psychologist, 22*, 299-312.

Garner, R., Hare, V.C., Alexander, P., Haynes, J., & Winograd, P. (1984a). Inducing use of a text lookback strategy among unsuccessful readers. *American Educational Research Journal, 21*, 789-798.

Garner, R., Macready, G.B., & Wagoner, S. (1984b). Readers' acquisition of the components of the text lookback strategy. *Journal of Educational Psychology, 76*, 300-309.

Garner, R., Wagoner, S., & Smith, T. (1983). Externalizing question-answering strategies of good and poor comprehenders. *Reading Research Quarterly, 18*, 439-447.

Hansen, J., & Pearson, P.D. (1983). An instructional study: Improving the inferential comprehension of good and poor fourth-grade readers. *Journal of Educational Psychology, 75*, 821-829.

Hare, V.C., & Borchardt, K.M. (1984). Direct instruction of summarization skills. *Reading Research Quarterly, 20*, 62-78.

Kreutzer, M.A., Leonard, C., & Flavell, J.H. (1975). An interview study of children's knowledge about memory. *Monographs of the Society for Research in Child Development, 40* (1).

Markman, E.M. (1979). Realizing that you don't understand: Elementary school children's awareness of inconsistencies. *Child Development, 50,* 643-655.

Markman, E.M. (1981). Comprehension monitoring. In W.P. Dickson (Ed.), *Children's oral communication skills* (pp. 61-84). San Diego, CA: Academic.

Myers, M., & Paris, S.G. (1978). Children's metacognitive knowledge about reading. *Journal of Educational Psychology, 70,* 680-690.

Owings, R.A., Petersen, G.A., Bransford, J.D., Morris, C.D., & Stein, B.S. (1980). Spontaneous monitoring and regulation of learning: A comparison of successful and less successful fifth graders. *Journal of Educational Psychology, 72,* 250-256.

Paris, S.G., Cross, D.R., & Lipson, M.Y. (1984). Informed strategies for learning: A program to improve children's reading awareness and comprehension. *Journal of Educational Psychology, 76,* 1239-1252.

Paris, S.G., & Jacobs, J.E. (1984). The benefits of informed instruction for children's reading awareness and comprehension skills. *Child Development, 55,* 2083-2093.

Paris, S.G., Lipson, M.Y., & Wixson, K.K. (1983). Becoming a strategic reader. *Contemporary Educational Psychology, 8,* 293-316.

Paris, S.G., & Myers, M. (1981). Comprehension monitoring, memory, and study strategies of good and poor readers. *Journal of Reading Behavior, 13,* 5-22.

Peterson, P.L., & Swing, S.R. (1983). Problems in classroom implementation of cognitive strategy instruction. In M. Pressley & J.R. Levin (Eds.), *Cognitive strategy research: Educational applications* (pp. 267-287). New York: Springer-Verlag.

Samuels, S.J. (1979). How the mind works when reading: Describing elephants no one has ever seen. In L.B. Resnick & P.A. Weaver (Eds.), *Theory and practice of early reading* (vol. 1, pp. 343-368). Hillsdale, NJ: Erlbaum.

Wagoner, S.A. (1983). Comprehension monitoring: What it is and what we know about it. *Reading Research Quarterly, 18,* 328-346.

Winograd, P.N. (1984). Strategic difficulties in summarizing texts. *Reading Research Quarterly, 19,* 404-425.

Yussen, S.R., & Bird, J.E. (1979). The development of metacognitive awareness in memory, communication, and attention. *Journal of Experimental Child Psychology, 28,* 300-313.

CHAPTER 11

Teaching the Disabled or Below–Average Reader

JEANNE S. CHALL
MARY E. CURTIS

This chapter identifies several major trends emerging from a review of what research has to say about teaching the disabled or below-average reader. With respect to the causes of reading failure, the authors describe how the focus of research has shifted away from the study of basic psychological processes and toward study of the reading process itself. As researchers have come to focus on the reading itself as the cause of reading problems rather than as just a symptom, concerns have been raised about the appropriateness of existing diagnostic methods and techniques. So too has research raised doubts about instructional techniques that target the reading skills of specific groups of children. Instead, Chall and Curtis say, current research supports teaching designed to improve specific areas of need in reading. Their chapter concludes with a discussion of some of the features that research suggests are critical for remediation to be successful.

The 1978 edition of this book contained a chapter entitled "A Decade of Research on Reading and Learning Disabilities." In it Chall described the many changes that had taken place in the theory and research on reading difficulties between the 1960s and the 1970s. With the passing of another decade, we would now like to take another look. To provide a context for our review, let's begin with a brief glance at the past, for if progress in helping the disabled reader has not always been swift, it has not been for want of change in direction or approach.

History

During the 1920s and 1930s, being reading disabled meant being in the lower end of the normal curve of reading achievement. Multiple factors, such as health, visual or auditory perception, or even the way one was taught to read, were considered likely causes (Gates, 1922; Gray, 1922; Monroe, 1932). During the next two decades, a single explanation—emotional maladjustment at home or in school—became increasingly popular. The kinds of professionals concerned with reading disabilities also changed. Formerly, reading specialists and educational psychologists had the most direct involvement in diagnosing, treating, and researching reading difficulties; now social workers, psychiatrists, pediatricians, and therapists began to play a central role (Robinson, 1946).

During the 1960s and 1970s, changes occurred again. Interest now grew in the neuropsychological factors that might impede success in learning to read—although the important role the brain plays in reading had been noted much earlier (Morgan, 1896; Orton, 1937). A new group of professionals, this time mainly from special education, entered the field of reading disability. These newcomers, who introduced the term "learning disabilities," began to have a significant impact on theory, research, and practice (Chall, 1978). With the passage in 1975 of the Education for All Handicapped Children Act in the United States, a definition of learning disability was incorporated into law. It included neurological problems as a possible cause, but it excluded sensory, motor, intellectual, or emotional handicaps, as well as lack of opportunity to learn (Public Law 94-142).

What is our current concept of reading disabilities? Has recent research changed our views about its causes? Appropriate diagnos-

Begins with <u>History</u>

— 1920s + 1930's being RD meant
being at lower end of
normal curve in rdg
achieve.

Multiple factors such as-
health
vis or aud percep.
way one was taught to rd.

Coordination?
crawling?

Observable
health

— 1940's + 50's
single explainaton -
emotional maladjustment
or home or school

— 1960's + 70's
interest in neuropsychological
factors

In 1975 PL 94-142
included neuropsych - included
sensory, motor, intellect emotional cultural

Volume of literature in field of
L.D. doubled since 1975.

Trends to teaching methods &
      instruction than
      on causes

Reading research focused on
      factors related to being
      disabled
   L.D. research more on
            diagnosis & teaching

tic procedures? Effective remedial techniques? These are the questions that concern us in this chapter. From the outset, however, we would like to point out some general trends.

The volume of journal literature in the field of learning disabilities has more than doubled since 1975 (Summers, 1986), and reading has become one of the most frequently discussed topics. The literature in the field of reading also has grown at a phenomenal rate during this period, according to the annual summaries of reading research produced by Weintraub and his associates (1970-1991). Interestingly, however, the proportion of the literature in reading concerned with the causes and treatment of reading disabilities has remained constant, and quite small (less than 10 percent). Thus, a trend noted by Chall (1978) for the first half of the 1970s continued through the 1980s: reading is becoming of greater concern to professionals in the field of learning disabilities than reading disability is for those in reading.

A second general trend involves the topics of the articles being published in each of these fields. Summers (1986) analyzed the ERIC descriptors used to index the articles published in learning disabilities journals. Among the 278 most frequently used descriptors, "teaching methods" was used almost four times as often as "etiology," and "educational diagnosis" turned up more than twice as often. In other words, research in learning disabilities seems to have focused more on instruction and testing than on causes. A different pattern seems to hold in the field of reading. Of approximately 500 studies published each year between 1970 and 1978, about 20 concerned "factors related to reading disability," while only about 13 concerned "corrective and remedial instruction." Of approximately 1,000 studies published each year between 1978 and the present, twice as many have addressed reading disability (about 60 studies a year) as instruction (about 30 a year).

To sum up, specialists in both reading and learning disabilities have published articles on reading disability during the past decade, although this emphasis seems to be greater among the latter than among the former. Furthermore, differences exist in what the specialists in each field are studying: reading research has focused more on factors related to being disabled, whereas learning disabilities research has concentrated more on issues related to diagnosis and teaching.

Now let us look at what this research has to say about specific aspects of reading disability: its causes, diagnosis, and remediation.

Causes of Reading Disability

In her 1978 review, Chall concluded that theory and research on the causes of reading disability were increasingly being influenced by the neurosciences. This influence arose in part because of the way in which U.S. state and federal laws defined reading disability; only those children whose reading difficulties could be attributed to neurological origins were eligible for assistance in special programs for the learning disabled. In addition, however, research during this time began identifying clear links between reading disability and the brain (Chall & Mirsky, 1978). Studies of early reading failure suggested the importance of neurological factors such as premature birth, perceptual-motor development, and sequencing of sounds (deHirsch, Jansky, & Langford, 1966; Jansky & deHirsch, 1972). Furthermore, a study of the brain of a dead young man who had suffered from severe reading disability since childhood revealed abnormalities in those areas dealing with language (Galuburda & Kemper, 1979). Findings like these brought researchers in education and the neurosciences closer together, increasing the likelihood of their collaboration (Chall & Peterson, 1986).

This collaboration has continued during the past decade, although much of the research has moved away from the search for general, single-factor explanations of reading disability (e.g., a "weak" left hemisphere) and toward more multifactor views. As Denckla stated in 1977:

> My contention is that we need more rather than fewer labels (backed up by reproducible observations, of course) so that we can communicate economically the particular syndrome description and treatment can be tested for each syndrome. (For example, the reader would be horrified if he were treated for "anemia" without specific knowledge of which anemia had been diagnosed; iron will not cure when vitamin B-12 is needed.) Thus we come full circle back to the need for diagno-

Causes of Reading Disability

research now moved away from search for a general, single factor to multifactor view

need for diagnosis by inclusion than exclusion alone

257

research looked for subgroup of RD children where performance on a variety of neuropsych, linguistic + rdg tasks were similar

Groups of RD children were distinguished by different kinds of language difficulties with the most severely disabled having difficulties w/ segmentation + sequencing + the less severely disabled having diff. w/ syntactic + semantic aspects of language.

Another trend in theory & research on Causation was a return to the study of the reading process itself rather than more basic psychological processes.

researchers found that instruction designed specifically to improve childs performance on basic processing tasks had little effect on the childs reading sis by inclusion, rather than exclusion alone.... At least let us all be meticulous in describing "about whom we are speaking" before drawing conclusions about treatment (p. 33).

This perceived need for "more rather than fewer labels" led to a search for subtypes of reading disability during the 1970s and early 1980s. On the assumption that more than one factor caused reading disability (as Gray, Gates, and Monroe had suggested in the 1920s and 1930s), researchers looked for subgroups of reading disabled (RD) children—groups in which the performance of children on a variety of neuropsychological, linguistic, and reading tasks was similar.

The work of Doehring and his associates (1981) is an example of this kind of approach. Groups of RD children were distinguished by different kinds of language difficulties, with the most severely disabled having difficulties with segmentation and sequencing and the less severely disabled having difficulty with the syntactic and semantic aspects of language. Other examples of subtype research include the work of Boder (1973); Mattis, French, and Rapin (1975); Pennington and Smith (1983); Pirozzolo, Dunn, and Zetusky (1983); and Satz and Morris (1981).

Results from the subtype approach were quite varied, depending on which tasks researchers looked at and the rigor with which they attempted to establish differences among their groups (as well as differences between the performance of disabled and nondisabled children). Further advances in subtype research may come as we better understand the ways in which reading, language, and neuropsychological deficits interact (Doehring, Backman, & Waters 1983). It also may be that greater precision in subtyping will require the use of tests that more closely resemble the kinds of reading tasks on which RD children experience difficulties.

Another trend in theory and research on causation during the past decade was a return to the study of the reading process itself rather than the more basic psychological processes presumed to underlie reading difficulties. For many, this move was a matter of research being informed by practice. Researchers found repeatedly that instruction designed specifically to improve children's performance on basic processing tasks had little effect on the children's reading (see Arter & Jenkins, 1979, and Chall, 1978, for discussions of this research). As a consequence, researchers began to reconsider which should be the basic factor and which the splinter skill (Chall, 1978). Reading once again became the focus of research. Brown and Campione (1986) describe this shift as follows:

> Attempts to diagnose specific and enduring cognitive deficits in the learner differ from attempts to analyze performance in the basic academic disciplines. If researchers are armed with a detailed description of the knowledge and cognitive processes required for a particular academic task, it is possible for them to identify the specific components that a child is having difficulty mastering. The dominant aim thus changes from implicating a "diseased entity" (e.g., memory) in the child to focusing on a domain-specific task component that needs extra attention (p. 1059).

Efforts to identify the kinds of reading knowledge and processes that RD children have difficulty with took various directions. The earliest and most prevalent approach involved contrasting the performances of disabled and nondisabled readers on a number of reading-related language tasks, such as word naming (Denckla & Rudel, 1976; Rudel, Denckla, & Broman, 1981; Wolf, 1986); word segmentation and sound blending (Blachman, 1984; Liberman, 1983; Mann & Liberman, 1984); memory for digits, letters, and words (Ackerman & Dykman, 1982; Bauer, 1982; Torgesen & Greenstein, 1982); and sentence repetition and completion (Willows & Ryan, 1986).

Contrastive research of this kind has been valuable for at least two reasons. First, it has compelled us to reconsider the bases for some widely held beliefs about the causes of reading disability. For instance, what formerly had been viewed as primarily perceptual or attentional problems in RD children now have been reinterpreted as essentially linguistic in nature (Bauer, 1982; Kagan, 1983; Liberman, 1987; Vellutino & Scanlon, 1982). Second, contrastive research has provided us with a wealth of new pieces to the puzzle of reading disabilities. Studies have found below-average readers to have difficulties in processing linguistic information at several levels (phonological, syntactic, and semantic), and difficulty at all of

Efforts to identify the kinds of
reading knowledge + processes
the RD children have diff. w/
took various directions
  Contrastive Research =
        Contrasting what b.a.
      readers + non-disabled
      do on a reading task
      found that b.a. rders
      have difficulty in processing
      linguistic information
      at several levels.

        This approach cannot
      distinguish the consequences
      from the causes of being RD
      also lacks developmental
      perspective

    other approaches:
Model of <u>Skilled Reading</u> = processes,
        Strategies + knowledge used
          to understand text

skilled readers: skip very few wds
+ because they are so good at
word I.D., it requires less
attention + since the amt of
attention is limited the less
time spent of ID, more
available for understanding
what was read.

RD - not accurate at word ID to
decrease their dependance on
context + at the cost of their
attention.

these levels has been linked theoretically to reading failure (Adams, 1980; Liberman & Shankweiler, 1985; Vellutino, 1979, 1983).

Issues of cause and effect have been a stumbling block for the contrastive approach, however. Because contrastive research is correlational in design, by its very nature it cannot distinguish the consequences from the causes of being reading disabled (see Harris & Sipay, 1985, and Stanovich, 1986, for complete discussions of this problem). In addition, much contrastive research has lacked a developmental perspective, making it difficult to identify which aspects of reading difficulty are most critical at different points in reading development.

Thus, other approaches have been necessary for understanding the kinds of reading knowledge and processes that can cause difficulties for RD children. One of these approaches begins with a model of skilled reading. Over the past decade, we have made much progress in understanding the processes, strategies, and knowledge that skilled readers use in understanding texts (Just & Carpenter, 1987; Perfetti & Curtis, 1986; Samuels & Kamil, 1984). As a result, researchers have begun to question some previously held assumptions. For instance, we know now that when skilled readers read, they skip very few words in a text (Just & Carpenter; McConkie, 1984), relying much more on their proficiency in identifying words than on their ability to guess the words from context. The reason for this seems to be twofold: (1) skilled readers are so good at identifying words that it requires less attention to read them than it does to guess; and (2) the amount of attention available to readers is limited, so the less we spend on word identification, the more we have available for understanding what we have read (LaBerge & Samuels, 1974; Samuels, 1985).

The story seems to be a different one for many less able readers, however. Some of them are just not accurate enough at identifying words to be able to decrease their dependence on context. Others can be accurate, but only at the cost of most of their attention. As a consequence, these readers do not have enough attention left over to understand the meaning of what they have read (Perfetti, 1985), and some of them may opt to guess at the words . instead (Stanovich, 1980).

good word I.D. / comprehension

At present, the proportion of RD children whose difficulty stems primarily from inaccurate or inefficient word identification remains unclear. It is apparent that inaccurate and inefficient word identification can lead to other problems later (Stanovich, 1986), problems such as inadequate knowledge about the meanings of words (Chall & Snow, 1988). As a result, overall improvement in the reading abilities of RD children may require instructional focus not only on the origin of the problem (e.g., word identification) but also on other areas that may have failed to develop (e.g., knowledge of word meanings), or developed differently (e.g., strategies for comprehending), as a consequence of the problem.

A third research approach for studying the causes of reading disability is based on development. Past research has looked at the link between success in learning to read and mental age (Gates, 1937; Morphett & Washburne, 1931), neurological development (Denckla, 1977), and overall level of maturity (Ames, 1968). Hence, interest in developmental issues is not new. What *is* new is researchers' concern with children's levels of reading development in addition to more general factors such as their chronological and mental ages (Curtis, 1980; Frith, 1986; Lesgold & Curtis, 1981; Stanovich, 1986).

Chall (1979, 1983) has proposed a six-stage theory of reading development that encompasses moving from a global approach to reading to focusing on decoding and fluency to using reading as a means for gaining new information and perspectives. Each of her stages is defined in terms of the reading processes and knowledge it requires, as well as the cognitive and linguistic demands placed on the reader. In a recent study of the reading, writing, and language development of children from low-income families, Chall and her associates used the model to explain how students with a strong start in reading through grade 3 could experience a deceleration beginning in grade 4 and increasing with time (Chall, Jacobs, & Baldwin, 1990). Thus, Chall's theory provides us with a criterion-based framework for viewing reading development and the development of reading difficulties. The framework helps us understand what children can and cannot do, and what they need to be able to do in order to make progress (Chall & Curtis, 1987, 1990).

Chall & Curtis

Inaccurate + ineffective wd I D
can lead to other probs such as
inadequate knowledge about the
meaning of words

So

improvement needs instructional
focus on the identified
problem as well as other areas
which are not developed

Chall = 6 stage theory of rdg
develop that involves moving
from a global approach to
focusing on decoding +
fluency to using rdg as a
means for gaining new info
+ perspectives

Each stage is defined
in terms of the rdg process +
knowledge it requires as well as
the cognitive + linguistic demands
placed on rder.

Genetic
Lines

also ely & reading difficulties
& the way children are taught to
read.

When children experience reading
failure in early grades,
early intervention w/ intensive
1-1 help works best.

The past decade also witnessed renewed interest in the relationship between reading difficulties and the way children are taught to read. Evidence from New Zealand (Clay, 1985), as well as from the United States (Pinnell, 1989), indicates that some children who are totally immersed in reading and writing fail to learn either skill. The reasons for such failure have been much discussed. Some argue that these children have not had enough experience with literacy in their homes to get what they should from a curriculum rich in opportunities to use language (Pinnell, 1989). Others suggest that such a curriculum does not contain all of the elements necessary for meeting the needs of at-risk children (Adams, 1990; Chall, 1967, 1983). Whatever the reason, when children experience reading failure in the early grades, early intervention with intensive one-to-one help works best (Slavin & Madden, 1989).

What have we learned from the past decade's research on the causes of reading disability? Whereas from the late 1960s to the late 1970s neuropsychology was the dominant influence, this latest period has marked the return of reading researchers and educational psychologists. Two trends are apparent in the research: a shift from general, single-factor explanations of the causes of reading disability to more specific, multifactor views; and a move away from focusing on basic psychological processes and toward looking at the reading process and the ways in which reading ability develops.

Diagnosis of Reading Disability

During the past decade, diagnosis has been an area of interest in both reading and learning disabilities literature. (See, for example, special issues of *Topics in Learning and Learning Disabilities*, 2(4), and *The Reading Teacher*, 40(8).) In both fields, interest has focused on issues related to validity and reliability.

According to Gartner and Lipsky (1987), the number of students classified as learning disabled (LD) increased 119 percent between 1976-1977 and 1984-1985, ranging anywhere from 30 percent to 67 percent of the special education students in a given state. Of even more significance, these authors say, is the number of studies that have failed to find differences between children classified as LD and those classified as normal learners (Coles, 1978, 1987; Davis & Shepard, 1983; Shepard, Smith, & Vojir, 1983).

Reliability in diagnosing reading difficulties has also been questioned recently, largely due to a set of studies conducted by a group of researchers at Michigan State University (Vinsonhaler et al., 1983; Weinshank & Vinsonhaler, 1983). Specialists in reading and learning disabilities, along with classroom teachers, were asked to diagnose the reading difficulties presented in several simulated cases. The researchers then analyzed the diagnoses to determine agreement. The results were the same across all of the studies, regardless of who produced the diagnosis. The most frequently mentioned categories were potential for reading, sight words, word analysis, oral reading, attitude, comprehension, visual discrimination, and auditory acuity (Vinsonhaler et al., p. 159). Apart from these categories, however, little agreement was found among the majority of statements made about any given case. This finding led the researchers to conclude that the process of diagnosing reading difficulties is unreliable, and that "diagnoses as presently conducted should not be continued" (Vinsonhaler et al., p. 161).

Thus, there is a deep dissatisfaction with the accuracy of diagnosing reading and learning disabilities. It seems, however, that different factors underlie this trend in each of the two fields. With regard to learning disabilities, definition appears to be the crux of the problem (Kirk & Kirk, 1983). As focus has shifted away from identifying and treating underlying process deficits and toward identifying and correcting the academic tasks that present difficulty, being learning disabled has come to mean being in the lower end of the normal curve of academic achievement. As a consequence, as many as half of the children classified as LD no longer seem to meet the criteria established by law (Shepard, Smith, & Vojir, 1983).

With regard to reading disability, agreement seems to continue on the basic concept that a gap exists between achievement in reading and the potential to achieve. Researchers have disagreed over the ways in which that gap should be further described, as well as over the kinds of assessment instruments and techniques that are most appropriate for arriving at such descriptions.

For instance, Vinsonhaler and his associates (1983) used 162 categories to classify the statements that clinicians made in their diagnoses. With such a large number of categories, the researchers were able to analyze closely what each clinician said. But such a large number of categories also could be why so little agreement was found. Indeed, since the same categories tended to be mentioned frequently across all of the studies, it may be that agreement does exist in the areas of greatest importance for diagnosing reading difficulties, at least from the perspective of the practitioner.

Concerns about the kinds of information used for diagnosis also are prevalent. Grade-equivalent scores from standardized tests have been much discussed, with emphasis on their limitations (Baumann & Stevenson, 1982; Berk, 1981) and on recommendations that they no longer be used (International Reading Association, 1982). Standardized reading tests in general have come under similar fire (Johnston, 1987; Valencia & Pearson, 1987). Harris and Sipay (1985), among others, have suggested that:

> A well-constructed, well-administered, and well-interpreted informal reading inventory based on the reading series used locally is apt to indicate a child's instructional reading level more accurately than a standardized norm-referenced test (pp. 171-172).

Despite these objections, however, little research has looked at the relationship between the results of reading inventories and those of standardized tests. What research there is suggests that the relationship does differ, depending on the particular instruments used (Smith & Beck, 1980). A more important point, perhaps, is that teachers continue to find the results of standardized tests useful for diagnosis and instructional planning (Stetz & Beck, 1981), despite some researchers' claims that these tests do not help.

On the basis of our own clinical experiences and research, we must concur with teachers. We have found that grade-equivalent scores from standardized tests do have value (Chall & Curtis, 1987), particularly when a teacher draws on results from a number of tests, constructing a profile that summarizes a student's strengths and needs in the various components assessed (e.g., word recognition, spelling, word analysis, oral reading, word meaning, comprehension). Moreover, we have found that such scores are useful in estimating the appropriate level of difficulty for instructional materials, as well as in assessing students' progress. As described elsewhere in more detail (Chall & Curtis, 1990), teachers can use the results from testing to design a remedial plan for students—a plan that includes the components of reading to be focused on, activities and materials to be used, and the difficulty levels of those materials. Although we agree that it is important to recognize that results from standardized tests (and grade-equivalent scores in particular) can be misinterpreted, our experience is that teachers who are knowledgeable about tests find reading tests and grade-equivalent scores to be valuable diagnostic tools.

Related to this focus on kinds of assessment techniques is a recent emphasis in research on "dynamic" diagnostic techniques (Feuerstein, 1979). Brown and Campione (1986) have described this emphasis as a change from "a diagnosis that is regarded, at least implicitly, as static and permanent (e.g., the child has a memory problem) to one that is dynamic and transient" (p. 1059). They add:

> Traditional standardized tests yield static measures of current levels of competence, making little attempt to directly assess the processes that have led to those levels.... Dynamic assessment methods go beyond this state of affairs by providing a mini-learning environment in which the child's current status and potential for learning are evaluated (p. 1065).

In reading, dynamic assessment is the notion that underlies such techniques as trial lessons (Roswell & Natchez, 1989), diagnostic use of sample lessons (Harris & Sipay, 1985), and intervention assessment (Paratore & Indrisano, 1987). Roswell and Natchez discuss the relationship between standardized tests and trial lessons:

> When formal testing has been completed and the tests analyzed, a fairly clear picture of the student's achievement patterns should emerge. To facilitate evaluation we have devised trial sessions in order to determine which methods are most suitable. Essential as it is to administer these standardized tests, the teacher or examiner still does not know, at their con-

student has little understanding
of what is actually wrong
with his/her Rdg. + remains
apprehensive about the difficulty

Reliability + Validity have
been concerns

__Reliable__ tests will yield consistent
results if administered
many times

__Valid tests__ actually measure +
predict what they are
intended to measure
ie strong + weak deciding
skills

clusion, which methods and materials to recommend for remedial instruction. Also, the student has little understanding of what is actually wrong with his or her reading and in all probability remains apprehensive about the difficulty.... Therefore, trial procedures are recommended as an integral part of the diagnostic examination to guide the teacher to the most effective approaches and to demonstrate to the pupil the methods most suited to his or her learning (p. 68).

Trial lessons, say these researchers, have the following characteristics:

In contrast to the controlled standardized test situation, trial procedures are conducted in an informal, spontaneous atmosphere. The teacher tells the student that there are several methods and many kinds of reading matter especially designed to teach those who have similar difficulties....

The teacher observes whether the pupil is slow or quick to grasp salient points; whether he or she needs a great deal of repetition, support, and encouragement; how well the child recalls what has been read; how much effort he or she puts forth; and so on. However, the whole session is a collaborative one. The teacher explains which techniques seem suitable and helps the pupil understand his or her problem. The more insight a pupil gains, the more likely it is that he or she will summon the necessary strength to improve. Trial procedures contribute to such insight in a way that the regular test situation cannot. They may be used with pupils at all levels, from beginning reading through high school (pp. 68-69).

Thus, although the use of dynamic assessment in diagnosing reading difficulties is not new (Harris & Roswell, 1953), what does seem to be changing is the size and sophistication of the empirical base that supports such an approach (Brown & Campione, 1986).

During the past decade, validity and reliability have been the prevailing concerns of researchers studying the diagnosis of reading disability. As interest has returned to reading as the cause rather than a symptom of the problem, researchers have expressed doubts about the appropriateness of existing methods and techniques for identifying reading difficulties. As yet, however, research has not provided teachers with a more valid or reliable alternative.

Remediation of Reading Difficulties

Remedial instruction has been a major emphasis in the learning disabilities literature during the past decade. As Chall (1978) noted, by the mid-1970s disillusionment had begun to set in among clinicians and researchers regarding the effectiveness of treating basic psychological processes. During the 1980s, researchers' efforts focused more on examining prevailing teaching practices and their underlying assumptions.

Lewis (1983) described several "popularized misconceptions of learning disabilities" (p. 231), including the need to select instructional approaches on the basis of a student's preferred learning modality and the effectiveness of remediating deficit psychological processes. After reviewing the accumulated research calling these practices into question, Lewis was led to ask:

> Why are these misconceptions so impervious to change, given the weight of the empirical evidence? The fabled gap between research and practice is one explanation. Another is the intrinsic appeal of some of these notions; it makes sense that instructional procedures should take into account the strengths and weaknesses of the learner.
>
> An alternative explanation has to do with professional identity. If the major role of the learning disability specialist is the teaching of reading and other academic skills, what differentiates this educator from a reading teacher or a regular classroom teacher? (pp. 232-233).

In the remainder of her article, Lewis described current understandings of learning disabilities and made several recommendations for teaching reading to LD students, including providing direct training in skills and emphasizing decoding in beginning reading.

Hicks (1986) focused her examination of teaching methods more specifically on those recommended for dyslexic children. Included in her review were visual and perceptual training, special methods such as the Orton-Gillingham and Fernald approaches and their modifications, and modality/preference techniques. Among the concerns she raised about these methods were the lack of research to support their use and their foundation in single-factor views of the causes of reading disability.

Remediation of Rdg difficulties

i.e. direct training in
skills, emphasizing
decoding in begining reading
visual + preceptual training
modality - preference
techniques.

Much of the research evaluating
new methods of remediation
has moved away from
techniques designed to
improve the rdg of
specific groups of Children
toward techniques designed
to improve specific areas
of read in reading.

The area of "reading styles" (Carbo, 1983) is another topic of recent concern, particularly since little evidence seems to support matching reading styles and reading methods (Stahl, 1988).

Much of the research evaluating new methods of remediation has moved away from techniques designed to improve the reading of specific groups of children and toward techniques designed to improve specific areas of need in reading. Many studies have demonstrated success in teaching a wide variety of reading components. A partial list includes phonological awareness (Lundberg, Frost, & Petersen, 1988), phonemic blending and analysis (Blachman, 1987), fluency in word identification (Reitsma, 1988), fluency in oral reading of connected text (Dowhower, 1987), knowledge of word meanings (Beck, McKeown, & Omanson, 1987), sentence processing (Straw & Schreiner, 1982), main idea comprehension (Baumann, 1984), question-answering (Raphael, 1984), comprehension monitoring (Palincsar & Brown, 1984), and inferencing (Dewitz, Carr, & Patberg, 1987).

The above studies serve to suggest some of the features that appear to be essential for successful remediation. First, in all of the studies, instruction targeted a specific kind of knowledge, ability, or skill that relates directly to the task of reading. Second, the children who received the instruction had evidenced a clear need for it, either because they had reached a point in their reading development where that knowledge, skill, or ability was required, or because they had failed to progress because that element was missing. Hence, the studies all serve to underscore the importance of prediction and early detection (deHirsch, Jansky, & Langford, 1966; Slavin & Madden, 1989). Third, direct or explicit instruction was provided in all of the studies. Teachers guided their students throughout the process and provided them with feedback about their performance along the way. Thus, these studies all incorporated three features that research on effective teaching has shown to be important (Brophy, 1988; Stallings, 1985; Stevens & Rosenshine, 1981): instruction was focused, appropriate, and direct.

Less apparent in these studies, but no less important to their success, was the difficulty levels of the instructional materials used. Chall (1987) recently reviewed research on the school and teacher factors that have been found to improve reading achievement. In her review, she found that one factor identified by almost all of the studies was instruction at a challenging level—on or above students' current level of functioning.

The importance of offering an appropriate level of challenge is consistent with Betts's (1946) definition of an "instructional level" of reading. According to Betts, the instructional level is the highest level at which a student can read with supervision and support from the teacher. The instructional level is always higher than a student's "independent level" (the level at which he or she can read without help) and lower than the "frustration level" (the level at which the task is too difficult, even with the teacher's help). The significance of difficulty level also is compatible with Vygotsky's (1978) theory of development, in which he proposes that children learn best by receiving support and assistance from experts on tasks that would be too difficult for them to accomplish at first on their own.

Still another factor identified by Chall (1987), and an important part of studies in which remediation has been successful, is time spent reading. In general, the more time students spend on activities that are academically relevant and appropriate (in terms of difficulty), the more they achieve (Rosenshine, 1978). However, studies in which remediation has been successful also suggest that children must be provided with opportunities to transfer what they have been taught to "real" reading tasks. Hence, even though word meanings may be the primary focus of remediation, in order for the remediation to work (i.e., lead to an improvement in reading), children must spend time applying their new knowledge in reading situations beyond the vocabulary lesson itself. Ysseldyke and Algozzine (1983) made this point when they stated that:

> Reading diagnosis should begin with an examination of the extent to which adequate time is allocated to reading instruction and the student is actively engaged in reading.... Only when it can be shown that the student is actively engaged for a sufficient time in appropriate instruction should educators worry about diagnosing the learner (p. 68).

Chall & Curtis

Implications for the Teacher

In many ways, the past ten years of research on reading disability has served only to underscore the conclusion that Chall came to in 1978: Teachers are key to recognizing that reading problems exist and central to carrying out their treatment. In other ways, however, research has provided some further direction about how this critical role is best played. Thus, in concluding our review of the past decade's research on reading disability, we end with what we view as some of its major lessons:

- *Reading difficulties can arise from inefficiency as well as inaccuracy in identifying words.* A number of studies point to the impact that inefficient/dysfluent word identification can have on students' reading development. Hence, in diagnosis and remediation, we need to consider not only whether students are accurate but also whether they are efficient, and what this may be costing them.

- *Remedial instruction needs to be geared toward a student's level of reading development.* The cognitive, linguistic, and print demands placed on a reader differ at different stages of reading development. To be effective, remediation must be guided by students' current level of reading development and the level to which they need to go. For example, in the early stages of reading, heavier emphasis should be placed on decoding than on comprehension. Research has not found emphasis on other aspects of the learner, such as preferred modality or learning style, to be effective.

- *Diagnostic testing in reading should consist of finding out what children know and need to learn, as well as what kinds of methods and materials—and which difficulty levels—will most help them.* A reading difficulty may be caused by multiple factors that do not always seem to be related, in a straightforward way, to instructional solutions. Therefore, when remediation is the goal, testing should focus on identifying students' strengths and needs in reading and the methods and materials from which they will learn. Teachers can base these decisions on the results of standardized, individualized, and diagnostic tests, the level of the basal reader in use, informal tests, and results from trial lessons.

- *Instruction should be explicit and direct.* Disabled readers particularly require direction, guidance, and confirmation from their teachers. Independent tasks usually are not as effective; nor are indirect methods in which the teacher waits for knowledge, skills, or abilities to emerge.

- *Effective remediation requires teachers to challenge students in a supportive way.* The difficulty of materials and tasks needs to be beyond the level at which the student is already capable of independent functioning. With support and feedback from teachers, remediation becomes a collaborative process, ensuring students' interest and progress.

- *Frequent and timely assessment is essential.* Assessment enables both teachers and students to see progress and provides students with a concrete demonstration of what is expected. Assessment also permits teachers to see when and how methods and materials need to change.

References

Ackerman, P.T., & Dykman, R.A. (1982). Attention and effortful information-processing deficits in children with learning and attention disorders. *Topics in Learning and Learning Disabilities, 2,* 12-22.

Adams, M.J. (1980). Failure to comprehend and levels of processing in reading. In R.J. Spiro, B.C. Bruce, & W.F. Brewer (Eds.), *Theoretical issues in reading comprehension* (pp. 11-32). Hillsdale, NJ: Erlbaum.

Adams, M.J. (1990). *Beginning to read: Thinking and learning about print.* Cambridge, MA: MIT Press.

Ames, L.B. (1968). Learning disabilities: The developmental point of view. In H.R. Myklebust (Ed.), *Progress in learning disabilities* (vol. 1, pp. 39-74). New York: Grune & Stratton.

Arter, J.A., & Jenkins, J.R. (1979). Differential diagnosis—prescriptive teaching: A critical appraisal. *Review of Educational Research, 49,* 517-555.

Bauer, R.H. (1982). Information processing as a way of understanding and diagnosing learning disabilities. *Topics in Learning and Learning Disabilities, 2,* 33-45.

Baumann, J.F. (1984). The effectiveness of a direct instruction paradigm for teaching main idea comprehension. *Reading Research Quarterly, 20,* 93-115.

Baumann, J.F., & Stevenson, J.A. (1982). Understanding standardized reading achievement test scores. *The Reading Teacher, 35,* 648-654.

Beck, I.L., McKeown, M.G., & Omanson, R.C. (1987). The effects and uses of diverse vocabulary instructional techniques. In M.G. McKeown & M.E. Curtis (Eds.), *The nature of vocabulary acquisition* (pp. 147-163). Hillsdale, NJ: Erlbaum.

Berk, R.A. (1981). What's wrong with using grade-equivalent scores to identify LD children. *Academic Therapy, 17,* 133-140.

Betts, E.A. (1946). *Foundations of reading instruction.* New York: American Book.

Blachman, B. (1984). The relationship of rapid naming ability and language analysis skills to kindergarten and first grade reading achievement. *Journal of Educational Psychology, 76,* 610-622.

Blachman, B. (1987). An alternative classroom reading program for learning disabled and other low-achieving children. In R.F. Bowler (Ed.), *Intimacy with language: A forgotten basic in teacher education* (pp. 1-9). Baltimore, MD: Orton Dyslexia Society.

Boder, E. (1973). Developmental dyslexia: A diagnostic approach based on three atypical reading-spelling patterns. *Developmental Medicine and Child Neurology, 15,* 663-687.

Brophy, J. (1988). Research linking teacher behavior to student achievement: Potential implications for instruction of Chapter 1 students. *Educational Psychologist, 23,* 235-286.

Brown, A.L., & Campione, J.C. (1986). Psychological theory and the study of learning disabilities. *American Psychologist, 14,* 1059-1068.

Carbo, M. (1983). Research in reading and learning style. *Exceptional Children, 49,* 486-494.

Chall, J.S. (1967). *Learning to read: The great debate.* New York: McGraw-Hill. (Updated in 1983.)

Chall, J.S. (1978). A decade of research on reading and learning disabilities. In S.J. Samuels (Ed.), *What research has to say about reading instruction* (pp. 31-42). Newark, DE: International Reading Association.

Chall, J.S. (1979). The great debate: Ten years later, with a modest proposal for reading stages. In L.B. Resnick & P.A. Weaver (Eds.), *Theory and practice of early reading* (vol. 1, pp. 29-55). Hillsdale, NJ: Erlbaum.

Chall, J.S. (1983). *Stages of reading development.* New York: McGraw-Hill.

Chall, J.S. (1987). The importance of instruction in reading methods for all teachers. In R.F. Bowler (Ed.), *Intimacy with language: A forgotten basic in teacher education* (pp. 15-23). Baltimore, MD: Orton Dyslexia Society.

Chall, J.S., & Curtis, M.E. (1987). What clinical diagnosis tells us about children's reading. *The Reading Teacher, 40,* 784-788.

Chall, J.S., & Curtis, M.E. (1990). Diagnostic achievement testing in reading. In C.R. Reynolds & R.K. Kamphaus (Eds.), *Handbook of psychological and educational assessment of children.* New York: Guilford.

Chall, J.S., Jacobs, V.A., & Baldwin, L.E. (1990). *The reading crisis: Why poor children fall behind.* Cambridge, MA: Harvard University Press.

Chall, J.S., & Mirsky, A.F. (Eds.). (1978). *Education and the brain.* Chicago, IL: National Society for the Study of Education.

Chall, J.S., & Peterson, R.W. (1986). The influence of neuroscience upon educational practice. In S.L. Friedman, K.A. Klivington, & R.W. Peterson (Eds.), *The brain, cognition, and instruction* (pp. 287-318). San Diego, CA: Academic.

Chall, J.S., & Snow, C. (1988). School influences on the reading development of low-income children. *Harvard Education Letter, 4*(1), 1-4.

Clay, M.M. (1985). *The early detection of reading difficulties.* Portsmouth, NH: Heinemann.

Coles, G.S. (1978). The learning-disabilities test battery: Empirical and social issues. *Harvard Educational Review, 48,* 313-340.

Coles, G.S. (1987). *The learning mystique: A critical look at learning disabilities.* New York: Pantheon.

Curtis, M.E. (1980). Development of components of reading skill. *Journal of Educational Psychology, 72,* 656-669.

Davis, W.A., & Shepard, L.A. (1983). Specialists' use of test and clinical judgment in the diagnosis of learning disabilities. *Learning Disabilities Quarterly, 19,* 128-138.

deHirsch, K., Jansky, J.J., & Langford, W.S. (1966). *Predicting reading failure.* New York: HarperCollins.

Denckla, M.B. (1977). The neurological basis of reading disability. In F.G. Roswell & G. Natchez (Eds.), *Reading disability: A human approach to learning* (3rd ed., pp. 25-47). New York: Basic Books.

Denckla, M.B., & Rudel, R.G. (1976). Rapid "automatized" naming (RAN): Dyslexia differentiated from other learning disabilities. *Neuropsychologia, 14,* 471-479.

Dewitz, P., Carr, E.M., & Patberg, J.P. (1987). Effects of inference training on comprehension and comprehension monitoring. *Reading Research Quarterly, 22,* 99-119.

Doehring, D.G., Backman, J., & Waters, G. (1983). Theoretical models of reading disabilities, past, present, and future. *Topics in Learning and Learning Disabilities, 3,* 84-94.

Doehring, D.G., Trites, R.L., Patel, P.G., & Fiedorowicz, C.A.M. (1981). *Reading disabilities: The interaction of reading, language, and neuropsychological deficits.* San Diego, CA: Academic.

Dowhower, S.L. (1987). Effects of repeated reading on second-grade transitional readers' fluency and comprehension. *Reading Research Quarterly, 22,* 389-406.

Feuerstein, R. (1979). *The dynamic assessment of retarded performers: The learning potential assessment device, theory, instruments, and techniques.* Baltimore, MD: University Park Press.

Frith, U. (1986). A developmental framework for developmental dyslexia. *Annals of Dyslexia, 36,* 69-81.

Galuburda, A.M., & Kemper, L. (1979). Cytoarchitectonic abnormalities in developmental dyslexia: A case study. *Annals of Neurology, 6,* 94-100.

Gartner, A., & Lipsky, D.K. (1987). Beyond special education: Toward a quality system for all students. *Harvard Educational Review, 57,* 367-395.

Gates, A.I. (1922). *Psychology of reading and spelling with special reference to disability* (Contributions to Education No. 129). New York: Bureau of Publications, Teachers College, Columbia University.

Gates, A.I. (1937). The necessary mental age for beginning reading. *Elementary School Journal, 37*, 497-508.

Gray, W.S. (1922). *Remedial cases in reading: Their diagnosis and treatment* (Supplementary Educational Monograph No. 22). Chicago, IL: University of Chicago Press.

Harris, A.J., & Sipay, E.R. (1985). *How to increase reading ability* (8th ed.). White Plains, NY: Longman.

Harris, R.J., & Roswell, F.G. (1953). Clinical diagnosis of reading disability. *Journal of Psychology, 63*, 323-340.

Hicks, C. (1986). Remediating specific reading disabilities: A review of approaches. *Journal of Research in Reading, 9*, 39-55.

International Reading Association. (1982). Resolution: Misuse of grade equivalents. *The Reading Teacher, 35*, 464.

Jansky, J., & deHirsch, K. (1972). *Preventing reading failure.* New York: HarperCollins.

Johnston, P. (1987). Teachers as evaluation experts. *The Reading Teacher, 40*, 744-748.

Just, M.A., & Carpenter, P.A. (1987). *The psychology of reading and language comprehension.* Needham Heights, MA: Allyn & Bacon.

Kagan, J. (1983). Retrieval difficulty in reading disability. *Topics in Learning and Learning Disabilities, 3*, 75-83.

Kirk, S.A., & Kirk, W. (1983). On defining learning disabilities. *Journal of Learning Disabilities, 16*, 20-21.

LaBerge, D., & Samuels, S.J. (1974). Toward a theory of automatic information processing in reading. *Cognitive Psychology, 6*, 293-323.

Lesgold, A.M., & Curtis, M.E. (1981). Learning to read words efficiently. In C.A. Perfetti & A.M. Lesgold (Eds.), *Interactive processes in reading* (pp. 329-360). Hillsdale, NJ: Erlbaum.

Lewis, R.B. (1983). Learning disabilities and reading: Instructional recommendations from current research. *Exceptional Children, 50*, 230-240.

Liberman, I.Y. (1983). A language-oriented view of reading and its disabilities. In H. Myklebust (Ed.), *Progress in learning disabilities* (vol. 5, pp. 81-101). New York: Grune & Stratton.

Liberman, I.Y. (1987). Language and literacy: The obligation of the schools of education. In R.F. Bowler (Ed.), *Intimacy with language: A forgotten basic in teacher education* (pp. 1-9). Baltimore, MD: Orton Dyslexia Society.

Liberman, I.Y., & Shankweiler, D. (1985). Phonology and the problems of learning to read and write. *Remedial and Special Education, 6*, 8-17.

Lundberg, I., Frost, J., & Petersen, O. (1988). Effects of an extensive program for stimulating phonological awareness in preschool children. *Reading Research*

Quarterly, 23, 263-284.

Mann, V.A., & Liberman, I.Y. (1984). Phonological awareness and verbal short-term memory: Can they presage early reading problems? *Journal of Learning Disabilities, 17*, 592-599.

Mattis, S., French, J.H., & Rapin, I. (1975). Dyslexia in children and young adults: Three independent neuropsychological syndromes. *Developmental Medicine and Child Neurology, 17*, 150-163.

McConkie, G.W. (1984). The reader's perceptual process. In G.G. Duffy, L.R. Roehler, & J. Mason (Eds.), *Comprehension instruction* (pp. 10-25). White Plains, NY: Longman.

Monroe, M. (1932). *Children who cannot read.* Chicago, IL: University of Chicago Press.

Morgan, W.P. (1896). A case of congenital word blindness. *British Medical Journal, 2*, 1543-1544.

Morphett, M.J., & Washburne, C. (1931). When should children begin to read? *Elementary School Journal, 31*, 496-503.

Orton, S.T. (1937). *Reading, writing, and speech problems in children.* London: Chapman & Hall.

Palincsar, A.S., & Brown, A.L. (1984). Reciprocal teaching of comprehension-fostering and comprehension-monitoring activities. *Cognition and Instruction, 1*, 117-175.

Paratore, J.R., & Indrisano, R. (1987). Intervention assessment of reading comprehension. *The Reading Teacher, 40*, 778-783.

Pennington, B.F., & Smith, S.D. (1983). Genetic influences on learning disabilities and speech and language disorders. *Child Development, 54*, 369-387.

Perfetti, C.A. (1985). *Reading ability.* New York: Oxford University Press.

Perfetti, C.A., & Curtis, M.E. (1986). Reading. In R.F. Dillon & R.J. Sternberg (Eds.), *Psychology and curriculum design* (pp. 13-57). San Diego, CA: Academic.

Pinnell, G.S. (1989). Reading Recovery: Helping at-risk children learn to read. *Elementary School Journal, 90*, 161-183.

Pirozzolo, F.J., Dunn, K., & Zetusky, W. (1983). Physiological approaches to subtypes of developmental reading disability. *Topics on Learning and Learning Disabilities, 3*, 40-47.

Raphael, T.E. (1984). Teaching learners about sources of information for answering comprehension questions. *Journal of Reading Behavior, 27*, 303-311.

Reitsma, P. (1988). Reading practice for beginners: Effects of guided reading, reading-while-listening, and independent reading with computer-based feedback. *Reading Research Quarterly, 23*, 219-235.

Robinson, H.M. (1946). *Why pupils fail in reading.* Chicago, IL: University of Chicago Press.

Rosenshine, B. (1978). Academic engaged time, content covered, and direct instruction. *Journal of Education, 160*, 38-66.

Roswell, F.G., & Natchez, G. (1989). *Reading disability: A human approach to evaluation and treatment of reading and writing difficulties* (4th ed.). New York: Basic Books.

Rudel, R., Denckla, M.B., & Broman, M. (1981). The effect of varying stimulus content on word-finding ability: Dyslexia further differentiated from other learning disabilities. *Brain and Language, 13*, 130-144.

Samuels, S.J. (1985). Word recognition. In H. Singer & R.B. Ruddell (Eds.), *Theoretical models and processes of reading* (3rd ed., pp. 256-275). Newark, DE: International Reading Association.

Samuels, S.J., & Kamil, M.L. (1984). Models of the reading process. In P.D. Pearson (Ed.), *Handbook of reading research* (pp. 185-224). White Plains, NY: Longman.

Satz, P., & Morris, R. (1981). Learning disability subtypes: A review. In F. Pirozzolo & M. Wittrock (Eds.), *Neuropsychological and cognitive processes in reading* (pp. 109-141). San Diego, CA: Academic.

Shepard, L.A., Smith, L.A., & Vojir, C.P. (1983). Characteristics of pupils identified as learning disabled. *Journal of Special Education, 16*, 73-85.

Slavin, R.E., & Madden, N.A. (1989). What works for students at risk: A research synthesis. *Educational Leadership, 64*, 4-13.

Smith, W.E., & Beck, M.D. (1980). Determining instructional level with the 1978 Metropolitan Achievement Tests. *The Reading Teacher, 34*, 313-319.

Stahl, S.A. (1988). Is there evidence to support matching reading styles and initial reading methods? A reply to Carbo. *Phi Delta Kappan, 70*, 317-322.

Stallings, J. (1985). Effective elementary school classroom practices. In R. Kyle (Ed.), *Reaching for excellence: An effective schools sourcebook*. Washington, DC: National Institute of Education.

Stanovich, K.E. (1980). Toward an interactive-compensatory model of individual differences in the development of reading fluency. *Reading Research Quarterly, 16*, 32-71.

Stanovich, K.E. (1986). Matthew effects in reading: Some consequences of individual differences in the acquisition of literacy. *Reading Research Quarterly, 21*, 360-407.

Stetz, F.P., & Beck, M.D. (1981). Attitudes toward standardized tests: Students, teachers, and measurement specialists. *Measurement in Education, 12*, 1-11.

Stevens, R., & Rosenshine, B. (1981). Advances in research on teaching. *Exceptional Education Quarterly, 2*, 1-9.

Straw, S.B., & Schreiner, R. (1982). The effect of sentence manipulation on subsequent measures of reading and listening comprehension. *Reading Research Quarterly, 17*, 339-352.

Summers, E.G. (1986). The information flood in learning disabilities.: A bibliometric analysis of the journal literature. *Remedial and Special Education, 7*, 49-60.

Torgesen, J., & Greenstein, J.J. (1982). Why do some learning disabled children have problems remembering? Does it make a difference? *Topics in Learning and Learning Disabilities, 2*, 54-67.

Valencia, S., & Pearson, P.D. (1987). Reading assessment: Time for a change. *The Reading Teacher, 40*, 726-732.

Vellutino, F.R. (1979). *Dyslexia: Theory and research*. Cambridge, MA: MIT Press.

Vellutino, F.R. (1983). Childhood dyslexia: A language disorder. In H.R. Myklebust (Ed.), *Progress in learning disabilities* (vol. 5, pp. 135-173). New York: Grune &

Stratton.

Vellutino, F.R., & Scanlon, D.M. (1982). Verbal processing in poor and normal readers. In C. Brainerd & M. Pressley (Eds.), *Verbal processing in children* (pp. 189-264). New York: Springer-Verlag.

Vinsonhaler, J.F., Weinshank, A.B., Wagner, C.C., & Polin, R.M. (1983). Diagnosing children with educational problems: Characteristics of reading and learning disabilities specialists, and classroom teachers. *Reading Research Quarterly, 18*, 134-164.

Vygotsky, L. (1978). *Mind in society: The development of higher psychological processes*. M. Cole, V. John-Steiner, S. Scribner, & E. Souberman, Eds. Cambridge, MA: Harvard University Press.

Weinshank, A.B., & Vinsonhaler, J.F. (1983). On diagnostic reliability in reading: What's wrong and what can be done? *Topics in Learning and Learning Disabilities, 2*, 43-52.

Weintraub, S., et al. (1970-1991). *Annual summary of investigations relating to reading*. Newark, DE: International Reading Association.

Willows, D.M., & Ryan, E.B. (1986). The development of grammatical sensitivity and its relationship to early reading achievement. *Reading Research Quarterly, 21*, 253-266.

Wolf, M. (1986). Rapid alternating stimulus (RAS) naming in the developmental dyslexias: A developmental, process-differentiated account of rate deficits. *Brain and Language, 27*, 360-379.

Ysseldyke, J.E., & Algozzine, B. (1983). Where to begin diagnosing reading problems. *Topics in Learning and Learning Disabilities, 2*, 60-69.

CHAPTER 12

Reading and the ESL Student

JOANNE R. NURSS
RUTH A. HOUGH

How do teachers promote literacy among students whose first language is not English? Is oral language fluency required before introducing reading and writing? Should the students acquire literacy in their first language before learning to read and write English? Nurss and Hough address these questions within a whole language, communicative competence framework. They present classroom instructional methods based on current research in English as a second language and bilingual education.

The past decade has seen a dramatic increase in the number of elementary and secondary school students in the United States whose first language is not English. It is estimated that by the year 2000, the number of U.S. children and young adults (ages 5-17 years) who come from non-English-language homes will reach 3.4 million. Spanish is the first language of most of these students in Texas, California, and New York (Oxford-Carpenter et al., 1984). In other areas, the diversity of first languages in a given school makes it impractical to provide bilingual programs or teachers. Therefore, more and more regular classroom teachers find themselves teaching students whose native tongue is not English. Many of these students receive instruction in English as a second language (ESL) for a few hours each week from a specialized teacher. However, the majority of their schooling takes place in the regular classroom.

Increasingly, then, regular classroom teachers must develop language and literacy instructional strategies appropriate for these students (NCTE/TESOL Liaison Committee, 1989). This chapter reviews current research and writing on second language and literacy acquisition and makes instructional suggestions for regular classroom teachers. Literacy acquisition is viewed from the perspective of communication competence; that is, functional oral and written language within the social/cultural context of the school and community.

Recent observations of language and literacy learning in both first and second languages demonstrate the interrelatedness of the language processes of speaking, listening, reading, and writing. These studies suggest that language development is a strongly interactive process, integrating individual learners' cognitive and linguistic abilities with the need to communicate meaningfully with others in the social environment (Hudelson, 1984; Tough, 1985; Ventriglia, 1982; Wells, 1986; Wong-Fillmore, 1979).

Communication of meaning appears to be the common feature underlying these language processes. Savignon (1983) has defined communicative competence as "functional language proficiency; the expression, interpretation, and negotiation of meaning involving interaction between two or more persons...or between one person and a written or oral text" (p. 303). This definition implies

Nurss & Hough

development of skill in at least four aspects of language that are important to classroom functioning: grammatical competence, sociolinguistic competence, discourse competence, and strategic competence.

Grammatical competence is the narrowest of the areas, indicating mastery of the linguistic systems—the ability to recognize and manipulate the phonological, morphological, syntactic, and semantic features of language in order to understand and produce words and sentences. *Sociolinguistic competence* suggests mastery of the pragmatics of language, the ability to use language appropriate to particular social contexts. *Discourse competence* refers to the ability to understand longer pieces of oral or written text, including the meanings of expressed and implied connections between individual sentences. *Strategic competence* refers to the coping or survival strategies fluent language users rely on to compensate for limiting factors that otherwise might lead to communication failure. Native speakers of English come to school having developed skills in each of these areas of oral English; students learning English as a second language are likely to need support and opportunities to develop these competencies within the classroom.

Sociocultural Context for Literacy

Oral and written language are acquired and used within the environment in which the student lives and functions. Limited English proficient (LEP) students come to school with a different set of language and literacy experiences than do monolingual English-speaking students. The roles of spoken and written first and second languages in the home, community, and school must be considered in providing literacy instruction for all students.

Using Fishman's work as a basis, Wallace (1988) presents a framework within which literacy functions at home and school by asking, "*Who* reads *what* in *which language* to *whom*?" Initially, students observe the adults in their environment using literacy in certain ways—for example, reading signs, the newspaper, letters, or labels. Some may be reading to themselves, some to other persons; some may be reading in English, some in their native language, and some in both languages. From these experiences, the LEP student acquires two important concepts: first, that reading in the real world is for a purpose and fulfills a specific function; and second, that reading may be done in several languages. Wallace states that literacy instruction in school often violates the first of these concepts by using materials that have no function or content. She concludes that all reading instruction, especially for beginning LEP readers, "must be *about* something...must have a content" (p. 13). Classrooms that model and provide opportunities for functional reading and writing will include several types of literacy materials: regulatory (rules or instructions), representational (labels or information), personal (opinions or feelings), and imaginative (make-believe or humorous).

Of course, the amount of reading students observe—as well as the languages used in reading—varies with the specific family/community context. Are the parents and adults in the community literate in their native language? In English? Do they use materials written in the first language the same way they use those written in English? For example, native-language materials might be used for religious purposes and English materials for daily living purposes.

Schieffelin and Cochran-Smith (1984) report a study of the home literacy environment of a Chinese-speaking Vietnamese family and its impact on the literacy development of a 9-year-old boy. The family spoke Cantonese, Mandarin, Vietnamese, and some English (the English was spoken primarily by the father and older children); most reading and writing (e.g., of newspapers and correspondence) was done in Chinese. The parents did not read stories to the children, share books, or buy books—characteristics typical of "literate " American families. However, the children did live in a "very literate environment" (p. 19). They were exposed to functional literacy as a part of daily living, saw their parents reading newspapers and novels for information and pleasure, and observed reading and writing used for extensive correspondence. They entered school with the advantages of sociolinguistic competence and functional concepts of literacy, even though their English linguistic proficiency was limited.

In some instances students' concepts of literacy may differ from those expected by the school. In a study of three cultures within one community (and one language–English), Heath (1983) describes the different functions of language within each culture. In only one of the three did the use of language and literacy match that of the school. Thus, the sociocultural home/community context of many LEP students may foster different concepts of literacy than those expected by the teacher. If these students are to acquire literacy in English, teachers must be sensitive to possible differences and be prepared to adjust instruction accordingly.

Oral Language Competence: The Base for Literacy

Teachers also may need to adapt literacy instruction to accommodate the lower level of oral language competence the LEP student brings to the classroom. Hudelson (1984) suggests that LEP students, like preschool first language learners, begin to acquire literacy when they are exposed to a rich oral and print language environment before they are fully competent in oral English. Both children and adults need some level of oral proficiency in English as a prerequisite for effective literacy instruction, although the exact level required is unclear (Alderson & Urquhart, 1984; Devine, 1988). Most of the reading materials used in U.S. classrooms are developed on the assumption that learners bring with them a rich base of oral language on which literacy skills can be built. Texts for students and lesson plans for teachers are organized with the expectation that oral language will serve as a link between printed texts and the real-life objects and experiences they represent. Initial written vocabulary is chosen assuming that the reader has already developed relevant concepts and attached oral labels and descriptions to these objects, events, and relationships through direct, concrete experiences.

Oral language competence is needed to actively participate in literacy instruction because most of the directions, explanations, and interactions that make up instruction in elementary and secondary classrooms are oral. Experience with oral language skills also acquaints the language learner with the various functions that language can serve in the classroom and the community (Tough, 1985). These oral language functions are similar to the written language functions encountered in developing literacy (Wallace, 1988).

Studies of students from different ethnic and language backgrounds acquiring English as a second language offer insights about important teacher, learner, and classroom organization variables that affect the development of oral language competence (Chaudron, 1988; Ellis, 1985; Gomez, 1987; Kleifgen, 1985; Ventriglia, 1982; Wong-Fillmore, 1979). The most striking finding from all these studies is that successful second-language learners devise ways to work on the "big things" first, saving the details for later. In language, the big things that support communication are the strategic capability of keeping your audience interested even if you make mistakes, the discourse competence of getting your main idea across, and the sociolinguistic ability of choosing the right message and format to fit your communication partners.

Teacher Factors

To develop these levels of oral competence, the LEP student must have opportunities to hear what Krashen (1982) has labeled "comprehensible input." Comprehensible input is language with an understandable message that is interesting and relevant to the LEP learner, offered in sufficient quantity to allow access to the language, and sequenced for meaning rather than by grammatical forms. Exposure to language with these characteristics allows learners to tap their existing networks of skills and concepts (Cummins, 1988; Ventriglia, 1982).

In a review of classroom observation studies at the elementary, secondary, and adult levels, Chaudron (1988) concluded that teachers use a number of common techniques to adapt their language for LEP students. These adaptations include slower rate of speech, more frequent and longer pauses, exaggerated and simplified pronunciation, more basic vocabulary, a lower degree of subordination, more declaratives and statements rather than questions, and more repetition (p. 85). With kindergarten LEP students, Gomez (1987) found several additional teacher characteristics of importance to the development of oral language: provision of a comfortable, non-correcting atmosphere, with an emphasis on many language-oriented materials and language-productive activities; support for friendships between LEP children and native speakers; and commitment to use every resource available to encourage the learning and everyday use of English. And Kleifgen (1985), reporting on observations in a kindergarten classroom, noted that the teacher used more action directives and clarifications with LEP students than with native speakers.

During a summer program with a group of mixed LEP and monolingual (English-speaking) elementary students, teachers adapted their instruction to include repeated use of key vocabulary and concepts, often in slightly different sentence constructions and functional contexts. In addition, the teachers used somewhat exaggerated pauses and changes in intonation and volume to focus children's attention on key vocabulary terms. Often these extralinguistic cues were paired with gestures, bodily motions, facial expressions, or use of sensory aids that further clarified meanings (Enright, 1986).

Learner Factors

A number of researchers have investigated the learner's use of linguistic, social, and cognitive strategies in acquiring English as a second language. Once a week during a year-long longitudinal study, Wong-Fillmore (1979) observed five Spanish-speaking children, ages 5 to 7, interact with an English-speaking friend in a playroom stocked with school materials and toys. From these observations, Wong-Fillmore concluded that the children used a number of common cognitive and social strategies to solve problems presented by learning English as a second language. Individual differences occurred in the ease and rate of development and the way in which common cognitive and social factors interacted. The children appeared to consider their main task as establishing social relationships with their English-speaking peers, not as learning English per se. The most successful learners had a strong desire to be part of the social group and were willing to take risks by being playful and experimental in using whatever language they had to maintain communication. Use of the social strategies of joining a group, attempting to participate, and counting on friends for helpful feedback set up opportunities for attacking the difficult cognitive problems that learning a second language presented: comprehending what was said, gaining entry into the language, figuring out how the pieces of language fit together, developing fluency, and figuring out the correct structural details for native-sounding speech.

Ventriglia (1982) found similar patterns of cognitive and social strategy use in 450 conversations collected during play and classroom activities with children whose native languages included Japanese, Italian, Spanish, Chinese, Portuguese, and Haitian. Common cognitive strategies included bridging new vocabulary labels to known concepts, using unanalyzed chunks of language for early language interactions, and creating new combinations from known words and chunks. Social strategies that supported these meaning-getting cognitive strategies included listening to ongoing activities before trying to participate, imitating words and phrases heard in similar situations, socializing and role playing, and using visual and gestural cues to draw inferences about meanings of unknown language forms.

In her year-long study of the language development of three Cambodian kindergarten children, Gomez (1987) found that children used short-term "tactics" to gain immediate ends in the classroom rather than longer range strategies to learn English. These tactics appeared to serve two social purposes: (1) gaining access to input (e.g., listening to others as they converse, initiating interaction, acting responsive); and (2) gaining opportunities to practice output (e.g., taking conversational turns, asking questions). In addition, children used a number of cognitive strategies to link input and output—for instance, they used the senses to enhance concepts, looked for recurring patterns in the input heard, and compared their own verbalizations to those of others.

Other researchers have used teacher interviews and observations to identify learner strategies used by LEP students in secondary classrooms (O'Malley et al., 1985a, 1985b). The strategies used by these older learners can be grouped into three major categories: metacognitive, including regulation of mental processes such as planning and monitoring language use; cognitive, including mental

Nurss & Hough

operations such as analysis and transformation; and socioaffective, including social interactions such as cooperation and questioning.

In combination, these studies of teacher and learner behaviors have important implications for organizing classrooms to maximize the development of oral language among LEP students as a base for reading and writing. Opportunities for interacting with both teachers and English-speaking age peers are needed since the focus of these two groups is different. Teachers focus primarily on the content to be taught and the language requisite to learning and classroom management. On the other hand, peers focus on the socially appropriate ways of using language for communication, both in school and out (Ellis, 1985; Wong-Fillmore, 1985).

Classroom Organization

In a summary of the central assumptions of the communicative language teaching model, Enright and McCloskey (1985b) conclude that the elementary classroom can be organized to provide comprehensible input and to foster teacher and peer interaction. The features of such a classroom include organizing for (1) *collaboration*, planning small group activities in which students discuss and work together to solve problems; (2) *purpose*, providing activities with short term goals that have meaning to students; (3) *student interest*, using topics for study that reflect what students want to know; (4) *previous experience*, integrating students' prior knowledge and learning patterns into ongoing instruction; (5) *holism*, teaching skills in meaningful integrated curriculum units; (6) *support*, planning a range of formal and informal opportunities to use language and get constructive feedback; and (7) *variety*, providing a range of familiar and novel experiences to utilize and expand on students' previous experience.

Tough (1985) reported the work of 1,350 teachers from school systems across England who developed and tried out language techniques designed for LEP students. These activities were organized to introduce English used for the range of purposes that Tough's earlier longitudinal studies had identified as important for optimum cognitive and linguistic development and early academic success (Tough, 1976). Examples of basic patterns to integrate the

LEP speaker into ongoing classroom interactions include conversational dialogues to identify and locate objects, people, and events, as well as statements of possession and needs. More advanced activities include open-ended questions that invite LEP students to develop and practice new language forms, to direct and anticipate actions, and to make judgments about classroom activities.

Summary and Instructional Implications

Studies of LEP students suggest that a number of personal and environmental factors affect the development of oral language as a base for literacy instruction. Teachers can support children's primary goal of communicating meaning by creating a classroom environment in which English is used for a variety of authentic purposes. These natural language interactions can meet the individual needs of LEP students for modeling, practice, and feedback about appropriate language content and form. Teachers also can use a variety of adaptations to make their language input to LEP students comprehensible, allowing them to link the new language to concrete or familiar concepts and experiences.

Grouping patterns in the classroom can be used to expose LEP students to a range of language situations, including social interactions with peers as well as informational exchanges with the teacher. LEP students working with various sized groups and combinations of students will have the chance to use a full range of cognitive and social strategies to facilitate language learning.

The Reading Process

In the whole language/literature approach to literacy instruction, the acquisition of oral and written language is seen as a reciprocal, integrated process of constructing meaning rather than as a hierarchical, sequential set of skills. Most recent studies of reading among LEP students take an interactive view of the reading process (Barnitz, 1985; Coady, 1979; Grove, 1981; Hudelson, 1981; McLaughlin, 1987). This model assumes that the reader engages simultaneously in top-down and bottom-up processing of the text. That is, the reader coordinates perceptual decoding of visual aspects of the text with cognitive processing of meaning based on relevant past experience.

This view differs from the traditional notion that the LEP reader's primary task is to extract information accurately from text. Instead, the interactive model suggests that the reading process is a dialogue between the reader and the text; reading activates a range of reader knowledge that can be used to understand the text and that may be refined or extended by text information (Grabe, 1988). Whether the perceptual or the cognitive aspects of the task dominate depends on a number of factors, including the reader's perceived model of reading, linguistic and reading proficiency, and familiarity with the text's content. This means that teachers can help their LEP students improve in fluency and understanding by matching the reader with the appropriate reading material.

Word Recognition

McLaughlin (1987) identifies three important tasks that the LEP student must master to become fluent in word recognition: the rules governing sound-symbol correspondence in English; the ability to use these rules to learn words and decode them in a progressively automated way; and the complex set of skills that allows for rapid processing of incoming material and the comprehension of meaning. Development in these tasks occurs simultaneously rather than sequentially.

LEP students often find recoding letters to the sounds they represent the least difficult of these reading tasks. However, some do have difficulty establishing letter-sound correspondences in English. For instance, some students may hear no difference between sounds represented by different letters in English; they can be expected to misread and misinterpret words that contain these sounds (Hatch, 1979). Another potential problem is posed by irregularities in English spelling patterns in which one sound is represented by a number of different letters or letter combinations, or in which several different sounds are represented by one letter. LEP students whose first language has a close phoneme-grapheme fit will have trouble if they attempt to use their first language expectations to decode irregular English words (Barnitz, 1985). Other students may have difficulty applying their first language knowledge if their prior experience is with a non-Roman writing system in which characters represent syllables or concepts rather than sounds, or in which the characters flow in a different direction than the English conventions of left to right and top to bottom (Barnitz; Bruder & Henderson, 1986).

More serious problems with word recognition may occur when the student needs to decode words, phrases, and sentences in an increasingly automatic way to facilitate comprehension. Several authors cite the emphasis that many LEP students place on correctly decoding print to sound as a primary problem in achieving fluent reading (Devine, 1984; Hatch, 1979; Rigg, 1977). One study comparing the eye movements of monolingual and LEP college students showed longer eye fixations for LEP students, indicating that they were taking longer to sample perceptual data to confirm or deny predictions and make new ones to process the next piece of text. The increased processing time did not result in better comprehension, however, which suggests that LEP students were less able to use syntactic cues for accurate predictions than were monolinguals who were more familiar with typical English sentence patterns (Hatch).

Other studies suggest that LEP students are likely to use nonselective word-by-word visual processing strategies that result in misinterpretation of word groups, clause groups, and pronoun reference. For example, they may give equal attention to content and grammatical function words or ignore graphic cues such as commas, periods, and capitals that signal stress and intonation information (Hatch, 1979; McLaughlin, 1987). Poor LEP readers often have difficulty imposing a meaningful grammatical structure on the visual images they process from text, as indicated by the types of miscues they make. LEP students are much more likely than monolingual English speakers to suffer grammatical as well as lexical miscues, or to substitute words with graphic similarity rather than semantic similarity to the target word (Ammon, 1987; Grove, 1981; Hudelson, 1981; McLaughlin).

Textbooks for LEP students have recommended methods for teaching word recognition that reflect the same diversity as those

Nurss & Hough

recommended for native speakers, depending on the author's philosophy and beliefs about the reading process. Thus, a range of methods has been suggested, including phonics, syllabary, linguistic, whole word, language experience, and eclectic strategies (Barnitz, 1985; Hatch, 1979).

Clear evidence that any one method is superior to the others is lacking, although several traditional methods have been criticized. Phonics methods require well-developed auditory and visual discrimination skills specific to the sounds and print styles of English, and have been criticized for teaching students to rely too heavily on word-level decoding at the expense of meaning. The linguistic method—very popular in ESL materials of the 1960s and '70s—relies on analysis of common visual patterns in English. The major disadvantage of this method is the lack of focus on meaningful language that can be immediately useful in communicating with others. The whole word method allows students to learn words that are personally meaningful, but it makes heavy demands on memory if it is the only strategy a reader uses. The use of language experience materials in the context of a whole language curriculum is most widely advocated now as an effective way to develop communicative competence in students with a range of previous language and content area experiences. The major disadvantages of this approach appear to be the amount of time, expertise, and energy required to teach using this personalized method without packaged materials.

Two studies do suggest that with LEP students the whole language approach to literacy may be more effective than traditional approaches. In a study of Mexican-American migrant children in the fifth grade, Hayes, Bahruth, and Kessler (1985) describe a class in which several whole language features were substituted for skill instruction that was not succeeding (the children were not progressing academically and had very low self-concepts). Time for teachers to read stories to children was substituted for the daily oral reading period, and journal writing was added to the curriculum. Teachers read and responded to journal entries daily. At the end of the school year, the students averaged three years' growth in reading proficiency as measured by Individual Reading Inventories. Further, both their self-concepts and their oral fluency in English improved. Franklin (1984) reports on the failure of two traditional reading instruction methods—a basal reader sight approach and a phonics basal approach—in two first grade bilingual Hispanic classes. The lack of success of these methods led Franklin to recommend that second language students be exposed to a literacy program based on psycholinguistic principles, stressing the immediate use of whole texts rather than emphasizing skills and smaller bits of language.

Vocabulary

Vocabulary instruction for LEP students may be planned for several purposes, including both the need to learn English words for familiar objects, events, and concepts and the need to learn terms for concepts primarily associated with the new culture. Studies of vocabulary development in first and second languages suggest that the most effective methods for developing new meanings are those in which students actively use the selected words in an individually significant context (Johnson & Pearson, 1984; Nattinger, 1988; Ventriglia, 1982). Thus, vocabulary and concept development should occur together in oral and written contexts such as semantic mapping and other experience-based activities within the ongoing classroom curriculum.

Memory and understanding of vocabulary can be improved through the use of several techniques. Allowing students to participate in overt physical actions that illustrate the new terminology helps them make the direct link between comprehensible input and appropriate output (Asher, 1969). Presenting new terms with a concrete referent and in conceptual groupings with other related words encourages the learner to "bridge" new vocabulary to an existing network of meanings developed in the first language (Ventriglia, 1982). Identifying cues in the text that can help in guessing the meaning of unknown words from context gives learners a strategy they can use to avoid memorizing isolated words and to tap into their existing linguistic and experiential competence (Nattinger, 1988).

Although preteaching the vocabulary in reading materials can have a positive effect on comprehension, these types of lessons require a great deal of instructional time and effort. Thus, additional strategies must be used to help LEP students build the vocabulary needed for academic success (Nagy & Anderson, 1984; Nattinger, 1988). Several authors have suggested that the most effective way to build vocabulary is to read widely in materials that will support reasonable guesses for unknown words from context (Elley & Mangubhai, 1983; Hudelson, 1985; Nagy, Herman, & Anderson, 1985).

One technique recommended for mediating the meanings of words and phrases for beginning LEP readers is the oral reading of picture books that match language with illustrations and repeat language patterns. Teachers can help students learn unfamiliar vocabulary by pointing to the matching objects or events while reading the text. They can reinforce meanings by rereading the books using the same combination of words and gestures (Moustafa, 1980). Stories whose oral language and story schemata have been well established in this way also can be used as meaningful initial reading material.

Comprehension

Schema theory, which emphasizes the critical role in reading played by the mental structures of background knowledge, has had an important impact on ESL reading instruction. Application of schema theory suggests that success in reading depends on whether the student can activate appropriate schemata, or knowledge structures already stored in memory, to interpret a piece of written text (Carrell & Eisterhold, 1983). Three types of schemata used to organize previously acquired background information can be useful in understanding and interpreting written text: linguistic, based on prior language development; content, based on prior knowledge of the content area of the text; and formal, based on knowledge of the rhetorical structure of the narrative or expository selection (Carrell, 1987). The need to make connections between the features of a particular text and the schemata readers are likely to have developed through their previous personal and literacy experiences is an important implication of schema theory for effective instruction.

A common criticism of traditional ESL reading programs, which focus on decoding accuracy with immediate correction of errors, has been that these instructional practices encourage readers to process text word by word in a laborious fashion, ignoring the usefulness of the larger context for tapping their prior linguistic knowledge (Rigg, 1977). In a study of 20 adults in a community ESL program, Devine (1984) found that students who took advantage of their already developed linguistic skills and applied them to text by perceiving reading as a meaning-centered process read better than did students who perceived reading as a word- or sound-centered process.

Another way to improve performance is to modify classroom instructional procedures to be more consistent with students' previous language experiences. Alterations in small group reading lessons were successful in the Kamehameha Early Education Project (KEEP) with low-achieving children from native Hawaiian families (Au et al., 1986; Au & Jordan, 1981; Tharp, 1982). The modified lessons combined an emphasis on comprehension through a hierarchy of question types with an interaction style that resembled the storytelling familiar to children from their home culture. This instruction supported mutual participation of teacher and children in conarrating stories from the basal series. In addition, the teacher prepared the children to begin reading the text by eliciting and discussing any personal experiences that could, in combination with information from the text, help them make sense of the stories.

For efficient comprehension, readers must be able to relate text material to their own knowledge (Carrell, 1987; Carrell & Eisterhold, 1983). Studies of both young and adult readers have shown that comprehension improves when the reading material contains culturally familiar content (Rigg, 1986; Steffenson, Joagdev, & Anderson, 1979). In one study, American and Indian university students read two letters, one about the rituals observed in an American wedding and the other about important features of a wedding in India. Students in both groups were more successful in comprehending the passage that matched their cultural experience: they read faster, remembered more facts, and made fewer distortions and incorrect insertions. Texts with familiar content allow

Nurss & Hough

readers to make accurate predictions as they read, freeing them to read faster and with less dependence on visual cues. Such texts tend to activate entire networks of relevant concepts developed from the reader's own experience. Thus, readers of familiar material comprehend text content in the larger context of their own related experience rather than as isolated facts stated in the text. They are then more likely to recall and understand implicit as well as explicit information.

Comprehension can be improved by building background knowledge or helping readers activate relevant background experience before they read (Hudson, 1982; Johnson, 1982). Johnson had university ESL students read a story about Halloween to compare the effect on comprehension of vocabulary instruction versus direct experience that applied to understanding a text. She found that direct experiences were more effective than vocabulary practice, leading to improved general recall and sentence recognition and more accurate recall of the cohesive ties and relationships between ideas in the text. Hudson compared the effects of a vocabulary prereading activity with those of an activity that more explicitly drew on students' background knowledge, requiring them to discuss a set of cue pictures and then predict the content of the passage that followed. In general, beginning and intermediate LEP readers showed improved comprehension with the experience-based prereading activity.

Comprehension also improves when the text's narrative structure is consistent and thus predictable, rather than inconsistent, shifting unexpectedly from one style to another (Rigg, 1986). Using strategies developed for first language readers, Carrell (1985) has had some success in training LEP readers to be aware of the different types of organization possible in expository text.

Another important factor in teaching reading to LEP students is consideration of the comprehension strategies used to process written text. A study of third and fifth grade bilingual and monolingual English-speaking students revealed that the two groups used different numbers and types of comprehension strategies (Padron, Knight, & Waxman, 1986). Bilingual students used fewer strategies to understand text, leading the authors to suggest that the focus these students placed on decoding the text interfered with efficient comprehension. When they did use comprehension strategies, the bilingual students relied most heavily on reading to answer questions the teacher was likely to ask. In contrast, the monolingual English-speaking students relied least on their perception of the teacher's expectations; instead, they most often used the strategy of concentrating (thinking about the story, keeping it in mind, remembering it). Native English speakers also used several other strategies more often than did bilingual students, including noting or searching for relevant details and forming self-generated questions or comments about the story.

Summary and Instructional Implications

If reading is an interactive process in which the reader's primary goal is to obtain meaning, reading instruction for LEP students must focus on strategies for creating meaning from and with the text. Students who interact with the text are more likely to read fluently than are those who focus on decoding the text. Reading instruction also needs to relate the students' cognitive and cultural schemata (background knowledge and experience) to the text and to develop reading vocabulary as a part of the students' sociolinguistic context. In such an instructional approach, the teacher will develop word recognition as a verification technique, not as an end in itself.

Specific literacy skills that teachers need to help LEP students include:

- competence in the use of the literacy environment,
- linguistic and decoding competence,
- sociolinguistic competence,
- discourse competence, and
- competence in negotiating meaning between the reader and text (Savignon, 1983).

The next section presents specific instructional methods and approaches designed to develop these literacy/language competencies in LEP students.

Literacy Instruction

Researchers and practitioners recommend several meaning-centered instructional strategies for use with students for whom English is a second language (Sutton, 1989). The research basis and specific techniques of each are discussed in the following sections.

Story Reading with Fiction and Nonfiction

Students whose native language is not English frequently must acquire oral fluency along with literacy in the new language. To comprehend material written in English, these students have to acquire new cultural concepts, information, and an understanding of literary style. One way teachers can help students begin this process is to hold regular, frequent story reading sessions with both fiction and nonfiction books (Hough, Nurss, & Enright, 1986; Kitagawa, 1989; Krashen, 1985).

On the basis of research on story reading with monolingual students, we recommend reading stories daily to LEP students in small groups (five to seven people) to allow interaction both within the group and between the group and the teacher. As stories are read, the teacher must highlight certain aspects of the text so the students will recognize salient linguistic and cognitive information. Students must be actively involved in the story reading for it to help them acquire language and literacy skill. Strategies recommended for involving students in story reading include giving the students verbal and nonverbal cues to focus their attention on the salient clues to meaning, asking questions that engage the students cognitively and affectively, using books with predictable patterns to encourage completion and repetition of the story, selecting books with illustrations closely tied to the text to clarify meanings, allowing opportunities for rereading books, and engaging in follow-up activities related to the theme or content of the book.

Effective materials for oral reading with LEP students include predictable books that allow instant interaction between the student and text, as well as rhythmic pieces such as chants, songs, and poems (Feeley, 1983; Heald-Taylor, 1986). By displaying the text as it is read, teachers can make the aural/oral experience an oral/written language experience as well.

Shared Reading and Taped Books

In recent years, the use of large-sized (or "big") books that allow shared reading between the teacher and a small group of students and the use of taped stories in conjunction with books have been widely recommended for introducing monolingual students to reading. Researchers also recommend these techniques for second language literacy development.

In a study of Spanish-English bilingual students in fifth through seventh grades, silent reading with an audiotaped version of the story was compared with silent reading alone (Strauss & Knafle, 1984). Using the audiotape along with silent reading significantly improved students' literal and interpretive comprehension of the stories. In addition, the students exhibited improved attitudes toward reading and requested books with tapes for supplementary/recreational reading.

In shared reading the teacher reads a story aloud from a big book while the students echo read sentence by sentence. Later the students read the story orally, with the more fluent students assuming the role of teacher. This procedure, along with sustained silent reading (a time when everyone in the classroom including the teacher reads for pleasure), is encouraged for developing ESL literacy (Hamayan & Pfleger, 1987). This strategy is especially useful for introducing students from nonliterate backgrounds to literacy in a natural, enjoyable manner.

Bridging and Webbing

ESL students generally have different cultural backgrounds than most monolingual English-speaking students. The sociocultural context in which they live may have little connection to the sociocultural context of the school and the texts they are expected to read and comprehend. One of the essential tasks of the literacy teacher is to bridge or connect the student's home sociocultural context to that of the school in order to maximize text comprehension. One means of so doing is the experience-text relationship (ETR) method developed by Au (1979) for use with children of Hawaiian ancestry. The teacher first discusses students' experiences that relate in some way to the story to be read; then the class reads short segments of text; and finally, the teacher draws relationships between the text and the students' experiences. As students get older and become familiar with ETR, they are encouraged to use the method on their own as they read new material. The discussion of the experience as it relates to the students' own cultural context allows the teacher to relate familiar vocabulary and concepts to new vocabulary and concepts used in the English text.

Semantic webbing is another way to link existing concepts or experiences to one another and to new concepts. This technique involves drawing maps or diagrams showing the semantic aspects of a word or phrase. For example, the word *house* may be separated into types of houses, materials houses are made of, parts of a house, family uses of a house, animal houses, and ways of making a house into a home. Barnitz (1985) recommends this technique for helping ESL students build vocabulary. It is also a way to link these students' culture and language to their new culture by fully developing the semantic aspects of a new term rather than simply giving a dictionary definition or translation. Using brainstorming as a technique for developing the web allows students to participate and creates links between their past cultural and linguistic experiences and the new concept (Enright & McCloskey, 1988).

Language Experience Approach

With the language experience approach (LEA) to reading, the student—either individually or as a part of a small group—dictates a story about an actual, personal experience. Beginning with an oral discussion of the experience in which key words are recorded, the teacher transcribes the story as the student dictates it. The story then is read aloud by the teacher with gradual participation by the student. Eventually the student reads the story alone. The story then may be published (for example, in a class book or a class newspaper), shared with others, or taped. The language experience approach to literacy creates automatic links between the students' past experiences, oral language, writing, and reading (Hall, 1981).

LEA frequently is recommended as an introduction to reading for nonnative speakers of English since it incorporates personally relevant content (Hudelson, 1984; Rigg, 1981). However, LEA depends, in part, on students' oral fluency since the students must express their ideas, experiences, and feelings orally for the teacher to record the story. One way to alleviate this problem is to combine LEA with oral language modeling and concrete referents to meaning such as large study prints or models. The teacher asks specific questions to elicit responses that later can be dictated as part of chart stories. In this discussion the teacher can model and reinforce acceptable responses, offering enough repetition to allow the students to internalize them. The transition to reading can be made by introducing word cards for the key content words included in the discussion and asking students to dictate sentences about them. In studies combining LEA with this type of oral input, fourth and sixth grade LEP students were successful in building oral, reading, and spelling vocabularies. Most students were able to transfer sight words and word analysis skills used in these lessons to other reading material. In addition, this combined approach was successful in introducing reading in content areas, such as story problems in mathematics (Moustafa, 1987; Moustafa & Penrose, 1985).

Use of the students' own dictated language also reduces a problem common among LEP readers: relying almost exclusively on decoding of visual cues at the expense of comprehension. Since students' own language will include familiar vocabulary and concepts, using the language experience approach for initial literacy instruction reduces the need to process much of the perceptual data. The meaningfulness of these early encounters with print may be important in shaping whether students define reading as getting meaning or simply pronouncing words, which Rigg (1977) identifies as a critical difference between successful and unsuccessful LEP readers.

In their research guidelines for developing a second-language literacy program, Hamayan and Pfleger (1987) include principles intrinsic to LEA and incorporate comprehensible oral input into the process:

- Students acquire language most quickly when the language they encounter is made comprehensible.
- Instruction is most effective within a meaningful, natural context.

- Children learn by doing.
- Students show most progress with their new language if they are confident about using it.
- Literacy development in a second language follows the same principles as literacy development in the first language.
- Individual differences must be taken into account in the instructional approach used with LEP students (pp. 6-9).

Based on these principles, Hamayan and Pfleger developed a curriculum guideline—Preparing Refugees for Elementary Programs (PREP)—that depends heavily on the language experience approach to literacy. For students with almost no oral English, language experience is used to develop key vocabulary and to dictate pattern stories. As English is acquired, story dictation and, eventually, story revision are emphasized (Dixon & Nessel, 1983; Rigg, 1981). Reading-related activities in the language experience lesson include conversation, role-playing, listening to stories, editing, and responding to literature (Dixon & Nessel). Because it involves total communication, LEA is an ideal whole language approach for LEP students; because it is based on the students' own personal/cultural experiences, LEA provides an automatic bridge between the students' cultural knowledge and the written text. Further, LEA is a flexible method easily adapted to students' individual differences and needs.

Writing into Reading: Dialogue Journals

Moving from dictated stories in the language experience approach to having students write their own ideas may be accomplished with dialogue journals. In this approach, the students write in their journals daily, and the teacher responds to their entries in writing. Journal writing provides (1) regular opportunities for students to write, with an emphasis on communication rather than mechanics; (2) interactive student-teacher-student responses and modeling; and (3) individualized instruction. This technique has proved effective in increasing the reading proficiency and writing productivity of Spanish-speaking ESL students in the fifth grade (Hayes, Bahruth, & Kessler, 1985).

Computers provide another means of developing literacy through written expression. Zurn (1987) reports on the success of the IBM Writing to Read computer-generated writing program with both monolingual and LEP kindergarten children. Similarly, the IBM Principles of Adult Literacy System (PALS) writing program has been used successfully with secondary and adult LEP students (Martin, 1983). The kindergarten children in Zurn's study were more fluent when writing on the computer than by hand, presumably because the computer freed them from the chore of penmanship. The adults in the PALS program felt positive about the experience of computer writing and emphasized the opportunity to learn keyboarding skills as a part of the literacy program.

Central to a process approach to writing (by hand or by computer) is the student-teacher conference used to plan the writing, to read and discuss various drafts, and to read and edit the final product (Hamayan & Pfleger, 1987; Heald-Taylor, 1986). This technique combines oral expression, writing, and reading into an integrated literacy approach that is especially beneficial for second-language students (Enright & McCloskey, 1988).

Thematic Units for Integrating Literacy Instruction

Inherent in the whole language approach is the integration of oral and written language with the content of the discourse. The use of thematic units of instruction allows this integration by providing real content for literacy instruction. Themes may be drawn from topics of relevance and interest to the students or from social science or science content in the school curriculum. Themes that are culturally inclusive help students relate their background and experiences to the literacy materials while introducing them to their new culture and the social context of the school.

Central to each unit are the integration of real experiences (concrete, here-and-now activities needed for oral language acquisition); the use of speaking, listening, reading, and writing; the introduction of a variety of materials and activities, including literature, art, music, movement, drama, and cooking; and the integration of content areas (mathematics, science, social studies). A complete description of this instructional approach and examples of units developed for use with LEP students are given in Enright (1983), Enright and McCloskey (1984, 1985a, 1988), and McCloskey and Nations (1987).

Enright and McCloskey (1988) describe the process of developing an integrated curriculum as follows:

1. Select a theme based on student interest and input as well as teacher interest and observation (pp. 44-46).

2. Brainstorm and create webs around the theme drawing ideas from content areas, literature resources, student ideas, and peer teacher ideas (pp. 46-48).

3. Develop activities and objectives taking into account individual student needs, practicality and feasibility, the social environment of the classroom, instructional criteria (collaboration, purpose, student interest, previous experience, support, variety, and integration), test results, required curriculum, and teacher observations and evaluation (pp. 21-29, 48-59).

4. Sequence activities using the teaching cycle—motivation, introduction, experience, and incorporation (pp. 59-63).

5. Implement the unit with revisions as necessary (pp. 63-67).

Once the unit is planned, it is important to explicitly tell each student the oral and written language objectives in each activity. Engaging in this process of planning leads to an integrated instructional unit based on the principles of whole language theory and provides a rich language/literacy environment individualized for both LEP and monolingual students.

Content Area Instruction

Reading at middle and secondary school levels depends heavily on the student's ability to comprehend content area material. Teachers often comment that students for whom English is not a native language make good progress in their ESL classes but have difficulty with the literacy demands of their content area classes.

Reading comprehension research suggests that some of the problem may be that these students do not have the cognitive or cultural schemata for understanding content area texts because of differences in background knowledge, concept development, or vocabulary.

Most ESL students need specific instruction in comprehension of content materials (Dubin, 1986; Flatley & Rutland, 1986). Suggested classroom approaches include instruction in study techniques (for example, SQ3R—study, question, read, recite, review); explicit help in using graphic symbols (illustrations, maps, charts, graphs, abstracts, examples, summaries); and instruction in prereading/postreading strategies (e.g., oral discussion, open-ended questions, story maps). Specific skills such as reading to locate information, reading to remember and reproduce, notetaking, outlining, paraphrasing, and critiquing also need to be taught explicitly. Combined with increased familiarity with the style of writing in a particular field and specific instruction in the vocabulary and concepts of the area, this type of instruction should help the second language learner read content material successfully.

Use of think-aloud strategies with college-level native and nonnative speakers of English (Block, 1986) revealed that students with lower grades in content courses did not use an integration strategy. They relied on personal information to understand the text, used a reflexive (personal) rather than an extensive (textual) mode of responding, and failed to relate information within the text in an integrated fashion. This study suggests that LEP students would benefit from instruction in comprehension strategies leading toward a less personal style of comprehending content area material. Other suggestions include reading literature from the student's own culture translated into English (Marckwardt, 1978); reading texts from the new culture to become familiar with its style and content (Edelsky, Draper, & Smith, 1983); and providing instruction in previewing, skimming, adjusting reading rate, recognizing the author's purpose, making inferences, and separating fact from opinion (Jensen, 1986). Specific instruction in these reading strategies should assist LEP readers in comprehending content area material and in bridging the gap between ESL instruction and academic achievement.

Nurss & Hough

Assessment of Literacy

Currently, U.S. schools rely heavily on norm- and criterion-referenced standardized tests. LEP students probably will be unfamiliar with the skills needed to perform successfully on these tests, which usually use a multiple choice format with a separate answer sheet—a format rarely used in other countries. Most standardized language tests used to place LEP students in language classes—for example, the Language Assessment Battery (LAB), Language Assessment Scale (LAS), and the Test of English as a Foreign Language (TOEFL)—use this unfamiliar format. Tests of language dominance used in bilingual programs to determine the students' dominant language for beginning literacy instruction also use the multiple choice format. ESL instruction, then, needs to include test-taking skills—test format, marking systems, test vocabulary, whether to guess, and how to take timed tests. Interpretation of LEP students' scores on standardized tests needs to take into consideration possible unfamiliarity with the test format.

Another test format widely used with ESL students is the cloze procedure, in which every fifth to seventh word of a passage is omitted. The student's ability to replace the deleted words indicates the degree of comprehension of the passage (Cohen, 1969; Oller & Perkins, 1978). This format requires the reader to check to see if the choice makes semantic, syntactic, and graphophonic sense in the context of the sentence and paragraph. LEP students often need instruction in how to use the cloze procedure.

Evaluating the language and literacy skills of LEP students involves looking at the context within which the language is used to determine whether the student is communicating competently. Has the student grasped the important points of the material read? Has the purpose for reading been met? Does the student's written effort communicate the ideas being expressed? Can the student cope with the oral language and literacy demands of the instructional setting?

Evaluating the student's progress in attaining communication competence in English (including grammatical, sociolinguistic, discourse, and strategic oral and written language competence) requires integrated assessment techniques. Observation of students' language behavior in context, assessment of their concepts of print, analysis of their oral reading miscues, review of their responses on cloze and think-aloud tasks, use of checklists to assess oral communication tasks such as role playing, discourse analysis of interactive language, and holistic scoring of written compositions are procedures recommended for both first and second language assessment (Allerson & Grabe, 1986; Clay, 1989; Cohen, 1969; Cooper & O'Dell, 1977; Heald-Taylor, 1986; Oller & Perkins, 1978; Rigg, 1986).

Literacy in the Native Language First?

The question of native language literacy and the timing of instruction in native and nonnative languages arises frequently. In some instances the question is moot. If a public school has few students who speak a given language or no teachers who are fluent in that language, instruction in the student's native language is impossible. In some cases, older students may have attained native language literacy before coming to this country. In other instances, native language schooling may have been either absent or extremely limited. In that case, older as well as younger students may be learning to read for the first time in English. When young students enter school fluent in one language but without reading ability, the question of whether to teach them to read first in the native language and then in English is a real one. A related concern is whether teaching literacy in two languages reduces the student's level of literacy or causes cognitive confusion.

Immersion programs for young English-speaking students in French Canada begin with immersion in spoken French, followed by French literacy instruction. Only after initial literacy in French is attained (usually by grade 2) is literacy instruction in English introduced. Teachers in these programs are bilingual; eventually, they stress fluency in both languages (Cummins, 1988).

In a demonstration program in San Diego, both native Spanish- and English-speaking children received predominantly Spanish instruction in preschool through grade 3. A limited amount of English instruction (increasing by grade from 20 to 60 minutes a day) was included. After third grade, instruction was half in Spanish and half in English. In findings parallel to the Canadian studies, the students in this program were slightly behind those in the English program in the early grades. However, by grade 6 they were "performing above grade norms in both English and Spanish" (Cummins, 1988, p. 151). Cummins suggests that these programs tap into a common underlying language proficiency, allowing literacy instruction in one language to be used in the acquisition of literacy in both languages.

In a study of third and fourth graders (Reyes, 1987), students were asked to recall everything about a passage just read and then to answer comprehension questions about it. Three groups of students were studied: Spanish speakers taught to read first in Spanish, then English; Spanish speakers taught to read first in English (or transitioned from Spanish to English in first grade); and monolingual English speakers (some of Hispanic background) taught to read in English. The results indicated no detrimental effect on reading comprehension from learning to read in two languages. Reyes interprets the findings to support a bilingual reading program, suggesting that a maximum of a year to catch up is required with no negative cognitive effects.

Evidence from older LEP students who already have developed reading proficiency, as well as from students receiving first language literacy instruction in bilingual programs, supports the concept of a common underlying language proficiency (Cummins, 1988; Cummins & Swain, 1986). Thus, cognitive and academic skills learned in the first language are likely to transfer to learning in the second language. Older LEP students who have greater first language proficiency are likely to develop the cognitively demanding tasks of reading in a second language more rapidly than are younger students or those without reading experience.

Weinstein (1984) reports on a study of Hmong literacy at a refugee camp in Thailand. Four groups of students were present: those with no education and no Hmong literacy, those with no education but some Hmong literacy, those with some education (in Lao) and no Hmong literacy, and those with both education and Hmong literacy. Progress in acquiring English fluency and literacy was greatest for the students who had some literacy in any language (Hmong, Lao, or Thai). This included the students who could read some Hmong but who had never been to school. Weinstein concludes that the significance of these findings is that "those who are literate in their native language get more access to comprehensible input than those who are not and/or receive more opportunity for negotiation of listener-speaker interaction in natural communication" (p. 474). Nonliterates are of necessity more context-dependent for interpreting meaning and find it more difficult to decontextualize meaning, a process essential for acquiring literacy.

For students who do not read in their first language and whose environment has contained a limited amount of print, teachers must provide a social context for literacy in order to help students develop an understanding of the functions of literacy as well as the concept of print (Clay, 1989; Wallace, 1988). Many students will have had little or no previous schooling, and therefore will have limited background knowledge to use in comprehending written texts. Methods such as the language experience approach will be most effective with these students. Reading stories to LEP students in their native language has been used to help students make the transition from limited exposure to print to an understanding of the role of books and print in functional literacy (Walters & Gunderson, 1985). The use of parent volunteers for this daily reading program in the classroom provides the students with role models for reading.

These studies suggest that if literacy instruction in both languages is possible, it will not be detrimental and may be beneficial to students' ultimate literacy attainment. For both younger and older students, the underlying language proficiency and understanding of the reading process (metalinguistic and metacognitive knowledge) attained in learning to read in one language can be applied to learning to read in a second language. Literacy in any language helps students to decontextualize meaning and to use comprehensible oral and written language input in the process of acquiring literacy. Students who do not read in their native language, however, need opportunities to acquire an understanding of the sociocultural functions of literacy.

Summary and Conclusion

Literacy in English as a second language is acquired in much the same way it is acquired as a first language, that is, through meaningful encounters with functional print, stories, books, and personal writing. The figure that follows summarizes the research implications for literacy instruction for LEP students. These students need opportunities to hear stories read in English, to look at and attempt to read interesting fiction and nonfiction books, to see reading and writing functioning in their school and home environment, and to have opportunities to apply their growing understanding of print through reading and writing of actual texts. An integrated reading-writing-oral language program built around in-

Figure
Teaching Reading to ESL Students

1. Provide a classroom environment that allows meaningful oral language interaction with teachers and English-speaking peers; use concrete materials and experiences to make the oral input comprehensible.

2. Provide a meaningful written language environment that demonstrates the functional uses of print and links students' home and community print environments to the school's print environment.

3. Provide a model of reading for meaning rather than for decoding. Use culturally familiar material and integrate new vocabulary and concepts into students' existing knowledge by using prereading and postreading discussions and open-ended questions.

4. Provide a literacy program that incorporates interactive story reading, shared reading and taped books, the language experience approach, the use of writing through dialogue journals, and thematic units for integrated literacy instruction.

5. Provide instruction in how to comprehend content materials and to acquire study and test taking skills.

6. Provide native literacy instruction where feasible, recognizing the common language proficiency underlying reading and writing in both native and second languages.

7. Provide students who do not read in their native language with additional opportunities to understand the links between oral and written language, the functions of literacy, and the concept of print.

teresting content (themes) will be beneficial to LEP students of any age or literacy level. This same type of program also will be beneficial to monolingual students, allowing the classroom teacher to integrate LEP students into ongoing class activities.

References

Alderson, J.C., & Urquhart, A.H. (Eds.). (1984). *Reading in a foreign language*. White Plains, NY: Longman.

Allerson, S., & Grabe, W. (1986). Reading assessment. In F. Dubin, D.E. Eskey, & W. Grabe (Eds.), *Teaching second language reading for academic purposes* (pp. 161-181). Reading, MA: Addison-Wesley.

Ammon, M.S. (1987). Patterns of performance among bilingual children who score low in reading. In S.R. Goldman & H.T. Trueba (Eds.), *Becoming literate in English as a second language* (pp. 71-105). Norwood, NJ: Ablex.

Asher, J. (1969). The total physical response to second language learning. *Modern Language Journal, 53*, 3-17.

Au, K.H. (1979). Using the experience-text relationship method with minority children. *The Reading Teacher, 32*, 677-679.

Au, K.H., Crowell, D., Jordan, C., Sloat, C., Speidel, G., Klein, T., & Tharp, R.G. (1986). Development and implementation of the KEEP Reading Program. In J. Orasanu (Ed.), *Reading comprehension: From research to practice* (pp. 235-252). Hillsdale, NJ: Erlbaum.

Au, K.H., & Jordan, C. (1981). Teaching reading to Hawaiian children: Finding a culturally appropriate solution. In H.T. Trueba, G.P. Guthrie, & K.H. Au (Eds.), *Culture and the bilingual classroom* (pp. 140-152). New York: Newbury House.

Barnitz, J.G. (1985). *Reading development of nonnative speakers of English*. Orlando, FL: Harcourt Brace Jovanovich.

Block, E. (1986). The comprehension strategies of second language readers. *TESOL Quarterly, 20*, 463-494.

Bruder, M.N., & Henderson, R.T. (1986). *Beginning reading in English as a second language*. Washington, DC: Center for Applied Linguistics.

Carrell, P.L. (1985). Facilitating ESL reading by teaching text structure. *TESOL Quarterly, 19*, 727-752.

Carrell, P.L. (1987). Content and formal schemata in ESL reading. *TESOL Quarterly, 21*, 461-481.

Carrell, P.L., & Eisterhold, J.C. (1983). Schema theory and ESL reading pedagogy. *TESOL Quarterly, 17*, 553-572.

Chaudron, C. (1988). *Second language classrooms*. New York: Cambridge University Press.

Clay, M. (1989). Concepts about print in English and other languages. *The Reading Teacher, 42*, 268-276.

Coady, J. (1979). A psycholinguistic model of the ESL reader. In R. Mackay, B. Barkman, & R.R. Jordan (Eds.), *Reading in a second language: Hypotheses, organization, and practice* (pp. 5-12). New York: Newbury House.

Cohen, A.D. (1969). *Testing language ability in the classroom.* New York: Newbury House.

Cooper, C.R., & O'Dell, L. (Eds.). (1977). *Evaluating writing: Describing, measuring, judging.* Urbana, IL: National Council of Teachers of English.

Cummins, J. (1988). Second language acquisition within bilingual education programs. In L.M. Beebe (Ed.), *Issues in second language acquisition: Multiple perspectives* (pp. 143-166). New York: Newbury House.

Cummins, J., & Swain, M. (1986). *Bilingualism in education: Aspects of theory, research, and practice.* White Plains, NY: Longman.

Devine, J. (1984). ESL readers' internalized models of the reading process. In J. Handscombe, R.A. Orem, & B.P. Taylor (Es.), *On TESOL '83: The question of control* (pp. 95-108). Alexandria, VA: Teachers of English to Speakers of Other Languages.

Devine, J. (1988). The relationship between general language competence and second language reading proficiency: Implications for teaching. In P.L. Carrell, J. Devine, & D.E. Eskey (Eds.), *Interactive approaches to second language reading* (pp. 260-277). New York: Cambridge University Press.

Dixon, C., & Nessel, D. (1983). *The language experience approach to reading (and writing): Language experience approach for English as a second language.* Hayward, CA: Alemany.

Dubin, F. (1986). Dealing with texts. In F. Dubin, D.E. Eskey, & W. Grabe (Eds.), *Teaching second language reading for academic purposes* (pp. 127-160). Reading, MA: Addison-Wesley.

Edelsky, C., Draper, K., & Smith, K. (1983). Hookin' 'em in at the start of school in a "whole language" classroom. *Anthropology and Education Quarterly, 14,* 257-281.

Elley, W.B., & Mangubhai, F. (1983). The impact of reading on second language learning. *Reading Research Quarterly, 19,* 53-67.

Ellis, R. (1985). Teacher-pupil interaction in second language development. In S.M. Gass & C.G. Madden (Eds.), *Input in second language acquisition* (pp. 69-85). New York: Newbury House.

Enright, D.S. (Ed.). (1983). *From pancakes to puppets to poison ivy: The Garden Hills International Summer School curriculum guide* (vol. 1, Bilingual Education Bibliographic Abstracts, #BE 01 3320). Rosslyn, VA: National Clearinghouse for Bilingual Education.

Enright, D.S. (1986). "Use everything you have to teach English": Providing useful input to young language learners. In P. Rigg & D.S. Enright (Eds.), *Children and ESL: Integrating perspectives* (pp. 115-162). Alexandria, VA: Teachers of English to Speakers of Other Languages.

Enright, D.S., & McCloskey, M.L. (Eds.). (1984). *From balloons to bubbles to banana bread: The Garden Hills International Summer School curriculum guide* (vol. 2,

Bilingual Education Bibliographic Abstracts, #BE 01 3882). Rosslyn, VA: National Clearinghouse for Bilingual Education.

Enright, D.S., & McCloskey, M.L. (Eds.). (1985a). *From rainbows to rhythms to runaway cookies: The Garden Hills International Summer School curriculum guide* (vol. 3, Bilingual Education Bibliographic Abstracts, #BE 01 6223). Rosslyn, VA: National Clearinghouse for Bilingual Education.

Enright, D.S., & McCloskey, M.L. (1985b). Yes, talking!: Organizing the classroom to promote second language acquisition. *TESOL Quarterly, 19*, 431-453.

Enright, D.S., & McCloskey, M.L. (1988). *Integrating English: Developing English language and literacy in the multicultural classroom.* Reading, MA: Addison-Wesley.

Feeley, J.T. (1983). Help for the reading teacher: Dealing with the limited English proficient (LEP) child in the elementary classroom. *The Reading Teacher, 36*, 650-655.

Flatley, J.K., & Rutland, A.D. (1986). Using wordless picture books to teach linguistically/culturally different students. *The Reading Teacher, 40*, 276-281.

Franklin, E.A. (1984). *A naturalistic study of literacy in bilingual classrooms.* Crookston, MN: University of Minnesota-Crookston. (ED 258 179)

Gomez, B. (1987). *"Friends gotta talk": An ethnographic study of behavior patterns exhibited by young children in the process of acquiring English as a second language.* Unpublished doctoral dissertation, Georgia State University, Atlanta, GA. *Dissertation Abstracts International, 48*, 1651-A. (University Microfilm No. 87-22114.)

Grabe, W. (1988). Reassessing the term "interactive." In P.L. Carrell, J. Devine, & D.E. Eskey (Eds.), *Interactive approaches to second language reading* (pp. 56-70). New York: Cambridge University Press.

Grove, M.P. (1981). Psycholinguistic theories and ESL reading. In C.W. Twyford, W. Diehl, & K. Feathers (Eds.), *Reading English as a second language: Moving from theory* (pp. 3-20). Bloomington, IN: Indiana University.

Hall, M. (1981). *Teaching reading as a language experience* (3rd ed.). Westerville, OH: Merrill.

Hamayan, E., & Pfleger, M. (1987). *Developing literacy in English as a second language: Guidelines for teachers of young children from nonliterate backgrounds.* Washington, DC: Center for Applied Linguistics.

Hatch, E. (1979). Reading a second language. In M. Celce-Murcia & L. McIntosh (Eds.), *Teaching English as a second or foreign language* (pp. 129-144). New York: Newbury House.

Hayes, C.W., Bahruth, R., & Kessler, C. (1985). *To read you must write: Children and language acquisition.* San Antonio, TX: University of Texas-San Antonio. (ED 257 313)

Heald-Taylor, G. (1986). *Whole language strategies for ESL primary students.* Toronto, Ontario: Ontario Institute for Studies in Education.

Heath, S.B. (1983). *Ways with words: Language, life, and work in communities and classrooms.* New York: Cambridge University Press.

Hough, R.A., Nurss, J.R., & Enright, D.S. (1986). Story reading with limited English speaking children in the regular classroom. *The Reading Teacher, 39,* 510-514.

Hudelson, S. (1981). *Learning to read in different languages.* Washington, DC: Center for Applied Linguistics.

Hudelson, S. (1984). Kan yu ret an rayt en Ingles: Children become literate in English as a second language. *TESOL Quarterly, 18,* 221-238.

Hudelson, S. (1985). Beginning reading and the bilingual child. *Dimensions, 13,* 19-22.

Hudson, T. (1982). The effects of induced schemata on the "short circuit" in L_2 reading: Nondecoding factors in L_2 reading performance. *Language Learning, 32,* 1-31.

Jensen, L. (1986). Advanced reading skills in a comprehensive course. In F. Dubin, D.E. Eskey, & W. Grabe (Eds.), *Teaching second language reading for academic purposes* (pp. 103-124). Reading, MA: Addison-Wesley.

Johnson, D.D., & Pearson, P.D. (1984). *Teaching reading vocabulary* (2nd ed.). Orlando, FL: Holt, Rinehart & Winston.

Johnson, P. (1982). Effects on reading comprehension of building background knowledge. *TESOL Quarterly, 16,* 503-516.

Kitagawa, M.M. (1989). Letting ourselves be taught. In D.M. Johnson & D.H. Roen (Eds.), *Richness in writing: Empowering ESL students* (pp. 70-83). White Plains, NY: Longman.

Kleifgen, J.A. (1985). Skilled variation in a kindergarten teacher's use of foreigner talk. In S.M. Gass & C.G. Madden (Eds.), *Input in second language acquisition* (pp. 59-68). New York: Newbury House.

Krashen, S.D. (1982). *Principles and practice in second language acquisition.* Elmsford, NY: Pergamon.

Krashen, S.D. (1985). *Inquiries & insights: Second language teaching, immersion & bilingual education, literacy.* Hayward, CA: Alemany.

Marckwardt, A.H. (1978). *The place of literature in the teaching of English as a second or foreign language.* Honolulu, HI: University of Hawaii.

Martin, J.H. (1983). *A report of a field test of the Principle of Alphabet Learning System: A program for adolescents and adults below fifth grade competence.* Stuart, FL: JHM.

McCloskey, M.L., & Nations, M.J. (1987). *English everywhere: An integrated English as a second language curriculum guide.* Atlanta, GA: Educo.

McLaughlin, B. (1987). Reading in a second language: Studies with adult and child learners. In S.R. Goldman & H.T. Trueba (Eds.), *Becoming literate in English as a second language* (pp. 57-70). Norwood, NJ: Ablex.

Moustafa, M. (1980). Picture books for oral language development for non-English speaking children: A bibliography. *The Reading Teacher, 33,* 914-919.

Moustafa, M. (1987). Comprehensible input plus the language experience approach: A longterm perspective. *The Reading Teacher, 41,* 276-286.

Moustafa, M., & Penrose, J. (1985). Comprehensible input plus the language experience approach: Reading instruction for limited English speaking students. *The

Reading Teacher, 38, 640-647.

Nagy, W.E., & Anderson, R.C. (1984). How many words are there in printed English? *Reading Research Quarterly, 19,* 304-330.

Nagy, W.E., Herman, P.A., & Anderson, R.C. (1985). Learning words in context. *Reading Research Quarterly, 20,* 233-253.

Nattinger, J. (1988). Some current trends in vocabulary teaching. In R. Carter & M. McCarthy, *Vocabulary and language teaching* (pp. 62-82). White Plains, NY: Longman.

NCTE/TESOL Liaison Committee, 1988. (1989). A short bibliography for mainstream teachers with ESL students. *Language Arts, 66,* 466-467.

Oller, J.W., & Perkins, K. (Eds.). (1978). *Language in education: Testing the tests.* New York: Newbury House.

O'Malley, J.M., Chamot, A.U., Stewner-Manzanares, G., Kupper, L., & Russo, R.P. (1985a). Learning strategies used by beginning and intermediate ESL students. *Language Learning, 35,* 21-46.

O'Malley, J.M., Chamot, A.U., Stewner-Manzanares, G., Kupper, L., & Russo, R.P. (1985b). Learning strategy applications with students of English as a second language. *TESOL Quarterly, 19,* 557-584.

Oxford-Carpenter, R., Pol, L., Lopez, D., Stupp, P., Gendell, M., & Peng, S. (1984). *Demographic projections of non-English-language-background and limited-English-proficient persons in the United States to the year 2000 by state, age, and language group.* Rosslyn, VA: National Clearinghouse for Bilingual Education.

Padron, Y.N., Knight, S.L., & Waxman, H.C. (1986). Analyzing bilingual and monolingual students' perceptions of their reading strategies. *The Reading Teacher, 39,* 430-433.

Reyes, M. de la Luz. (1987). Comprehension of content area passages: A study of Spanish/English readers in third and fourth grade. In S.R. Goldman & H.T. Trueba (Eds.), *Becoming literate in English as a second language* (pp. 107-126). Norwood, NJ: Ablex.

Rigg, P. (1977). Getting the message, decoding the message. *The Reading Teacher, 30,* 745-749.

Rigg, P. (1981). Beginning to read in English the language experience approach way. In C.W. Twyford, W. Diehl, & K. Feathers (Eds.), *Reading English as a second language: Moving from theory* (pp. 81-90). Bloomington, IN: Indiana University.

Rigg, P. (1986). Reading in ESL: Learning from kids. In P. Rigg & D.S. Enright (Eds.), *Children and ESL: Integrating perspectives* (pp. 57-91). Alexandria, VA: Teachers of English to Speakers of Other Languages.

Savignon, S.J. (1983). *Communicative competence: Theory and classroom practice.* Reading, MA: Addison-Wesley.

Schieffelin, B.B., & Cochran-Smith, M. (1984). Learning to read culturally: Literacy before schooling. In H. Goelman, A.A. Oberg, & F. Smith (Eds.), *Awakening to literacy* (pp. 3-23). Portsmouth, NH: Heinemann.

Steffensen, M.S., Joag-dev, C., & Anderson, R.C. (1979). A cross-cultural perspective on reading comprehension. *Reading Research Quarterly, 15,* 10-29.

Strauss, W., & Knafle, J.D. (1984). *Reading comprehension in bilingual students with the aid of taped stories.* Chicago, IL: University of Illinois at Chicago. (ED 249 798)

Sutton, C. (1989). Helping the nonnative English speaker with English. *The Reading Teacher, 42,* 684-688.

Tharp, R.G. (1982). The effective instruction of comprehension: Results and description of the Kamehameha Early Education Program. *Reading Research Quarterly, 17,* 503-527.

Tough, J. (1976). *The development of meaning: A study of children's use of language.* New York: Wiley.

Tough, J. (1985). *Talk two: Children using English as a second language in primary schools.* London, UK: Onyx Press.

Ventriglia, L. (1982). *Conversations of Miguel and Maria.* Reading, MA: Addison-Wesley.

Wallace, C. (1988). *Learning to read in a multicultural society: The social context of second language literacy.* Englewood Cliffs, NJ: Prentice Hall.

Walters, K., & Gunderson, L. (1985). Effects of parent volunteers reading first language (L1) books to ESL students. *The Reading Teacher, 39,* 66-69.

Weinstein, G. (1984). Literacy and second language acquisition: Issues and perspectives. *TESOL Quarterly, 18,* 471-484.

Wells, G. (1986). *The meaning makers.* Portsmouth, NH: Heinemann.

Wong-Fillmore, L. (1979). Individual differences in second language acquisition. In C.J. Fillmore, D. Kempler, & W.S. Wang (Eds.), *Individual differences in language ability and language behavior* (pp. 203-228). San Diego, CA: Academic.

Wong-Fillmore, L. (1985). When does teacher talk work as input? In S.M. Gass & C.G. Madden (Eds.), *Input in second language acquisition* (pp. 17-50). New York: Newbury House.

Zurn, M.R. (1987). *A comparison of kindergarteners' handwritten and word processor generated writing.* Unpublished doctoral dissertation, Georgia State University, Atlanta, GA. *Dissertation Abstracts International, 49,* 427-A. (University Microfilm No. 88-08112.)

CHAPTER 13

Teaching Adults to Read

THOMAS G. STICHT
BARBARA A. McDONALD

The field of adult literacy encompasses diverse philoso-phies regarding the objectives and methods of instruction. This chapter focuses on what teachers who adhere to any philoso-phy can accomplish if they look at reading as a visual process, or part of the use of graphics technology. Several features set the graphics medium apart from speech, including permanence, spati-ality, and light. Literate people make use of these features to per-form a number of cognitive and communication tasks. For instance, the permanence of graphics displays allows people to store knowl-edge outside the head and makes it necessary for others to learn reading to retrieve the stored information. And the medium's use of space and light makes possible a wide variety of graphic designs that foster the communication of information. In this chapter, Sticht and McDonald describe the use of the graphics technology framework in developing work-related reading programs for midlevel literate adults.

Note: Preparation of this chapter was supported in part by a grant from the John D. MacArthur Foundation to Applied Behavioral & Cognitive Sciences. The opinions are solely those of the authors.

Like reading instruction for children, adult reading instruction engenders many controversies. In both fields the same debates rage about the whole language approach versus the word recognition, decoding, or phonics approach (McCormick, 1988). Debates about the purpose of teaching adults to read—generally framed in the larger context of teaching literacy—also abound. Some argue that literacy should be for empowerment, giving voice, or stimulating critical awareness and eschew "technical" reading instruction—that is, instruction aimed at teaching reading simply as a cognitive task (Street, 1984).

Although the many issues involved in these debates are important, our literature review has found no evidence to argue convincingly that students learn better, go farther in their education, or become more successful citizens when they attend programs that favor one or another point of view. Indeed, there is often considerable ambiguity about what the words being used to describe a point of view actually mean to different people (Ellsworth, 1989).

Given that no single view has been proved most effective, we've decided to step aside from the controversy and take a look at an approach that instructors in any type of program can use. Specifically, we have opted to present an analysis of what learners might learn and what teachers might teach if reading is viewed in its role as a visual means of conveying information. As such, reading can be considered one aspect of using graphics technology to develop tools to communicate, develop knowledge, and accomplish tasks (Bruner, 1968).

The advantage of this approach is that it presents a body of technical knowledge that may be learned within the context of any of the various ideologies or instructional belief systems held by teachers of adults. For instance, whatever instructional methods or broad goals a program espouses, learners who wish to attain or improve in literacy must learn to recognize, interpret, and produce graphics symbols and devices such as forms, maps, and textbooks.

An Orientation to Adult Reading Learners

Adults who are learning to read enter into the instructional setting with some history of learning. They have the capacity to learn and to solve problems in real world settings. They also have a knowledge base that includes the lexicon and syntax of the language, as well as the pragmatics of language use. Their lexical/semantic knowledge may be limited compared with that of their more literate peers, but most such learners will have been through at least several years of formal education.

In addition, most adult reading learners in a literate society possess some knowledge of the functional uses of written language and of graphics devices such as books, newspapers, and bus schedules. They simply need to develop this understanding in greater breadth and depth. Greater *breadth* means being able to perform more tasks in various domains of knowledge using graphics technology and symbolic systems. Greater *depth* means being able to perform specific literacy tasks more efficiently and with greater skill.

Finally, adult basic education students, like other adults, have many beliefs and attitudes about teaching, learning, opportunities, and success and failure. They have a general philosophy of what life is about and how it should be lived. Most have sought out reading instruction to change some aspect of their lives: to become better parents by learning to read to their children, to serve as better role models, to improve their chances in life and their self-esteem by getting a high school equivalency certificate, to improve their prospects at work, to administer to their spiritual needs by reading religious materials, or to improve their access to entertainment and personal enjoyment through reading.

This combination of language knowledge, experience with print and other graphics devices, and knowledge of the world means that adult reading students bring a good deal of sophistication to the learning situation. Most such students in industrialized nations know how to use tools for accomplishing various tasks in a technological society. Thus, they possess prior knowledge that can be used to construct an understanding of reading (and writing) as the use of graphics technology for communicating, developing knowledge, and accomplishing tasks. This point of view provides the content for reading instruction discussed later.

Literacy and Graphics Technology

In anthropological terms, technology is the body of knowledge a civilization uses to fashion implements, extract or collect materials, or practice various arts and skills (Morris, 1976, p. 1321). From this point of view, literacy may be thought of as technology for producing and comprehending graphics displays that serve as tools for accomplishing various cognitive and communication activities (Goody, 1977; Harris, 1986). In writing, a person "extracts" knowledge from the brain and "collects" (stores) it in graphics displays. Then, by practicing the skill of reading, the person extracts collected knowledge from the graphics display and reconstructs it in the brain.

By considering literacy an ability to work with graphics technology, instructors can help adult learners understand how the fundamental characteristics of graphics displays affect both the way print works and the demands placed on them as reading learners.

Characteristics of Graphics Technology

The major characteristics of graphics technology that relate to literacy are permanence, spatiality, and the use of light. These characteristics determine the types of products that may be produced by those in command of the technology, as well as the information processing demands these products require.

Permanence. Graphics information displays, such as this page of print, are more or less permanent. Therefore, they can be used to collect information, including an extended body of knowledge. The information can be stored over time, retrieved, and transported across space.

In reading instruction, the relative permanence of the graphics display permits the teaching of "reading-to-do" and "reading-to-learn" processes (Sticht, 1979). In reading to do, the quality of permanence permits the reader to consult the material repeatedly while performing a task. For instance, when filling out a parts form, an automotive supply clerk can look up the part number, hold it in working memory just long enough to complete that part of the form, and then forget it. Because the parts catalog serves as a graphic memory device for storing information, the part number can be looked up again when needed. There is no need for the clerk to memorize the information.

In reading to learn, much of what is taught as study skills or learning strategies reflects the same property of permanence. This property allows people to study printed material at length and read it repeatedly to extract information and relate that information to prior knowledge. Strategies that give suggestions for information processing before reading, during reading, and after reading (such as the variants of Robinson's [1946] SQ3R, or Survey, Question, Read, Recite, and Review) were invented because the permanence of graphics displays permits the storage of knowledge and drives the need for new learners to acquire that knowledge by reading.

The ability to store information over time and transport it over space makes it possible to remove information from its original setting or context. Thus, it is necessary to learn ways of making graphics displays that can be used out of context, as well as ways of comprehending such decontextualized displays. Much of what is taught about conventional writing devices such as topic sentences, greetings, narratives, and exposition comes from this decontextualization and the resulting need for "recontextualizing" modes of expression that help readers process the information displays efficiently.

Spatiality.   Unlike speech, graphic information displays can be arrayed in space. Signs can be placed on doors, over buildings, and alongside highways; words can be laid out on a printed page to re-create a temporal flow of speech; applications and other forms can be developed with slots containing labels (name, address, etc.); and myriad other graphics tools can be developed to accomplish various information transmission and processing tasks (e.g., labels, lists, bus schedules, flow charts, tables, schematics, transparencies).

In mathematics, spatial layout is especially important in the concept of place value. In reading, students may be taught to read graphs or figures, or to analyze text materials using graphics devices such as semantic maps, outlines, or tree structures that depend for their effectiveness on the arrangement of graphics displays in space.

Spatiality is especially important in the use of graphics displays for analysis and synthesis. Each of the three types of analysis identified by Upton (1973) has a primary graphics device that relies on spatiality. For classification, in which objects or events are analyzed by features and then sorted into categories, the matrix is the primary graphics device. In a matrix, information is sorted into various cells, or graphics "pigeonholes," to fit the categories indicated by the column and row headings. The white space of an empty cell serves as an information processing aid and reminds one to look for information that might fit in the cell (Schwartz, 1971).

For structural analysis, in which the relative location of objects or their parts is important, pictures, schematics, block diagrams, tree structures, or similar devices are the primary tools of analysis. Other devices may also be used; for instance, tables of contents and indexes display the relationships among the parts (chapters) and contents (indexed terms) of a text to the total book.

For process or procedural analysis, in which the sequencing of events over time is the object of analysis, the flow chart is the primary graphics device. The steps required to accomplish a task are arrayed spatially; symbols such as arrows allow the steps to be read sequentially and guide the reader's task performance.

With each of these tools, the products of analysis are synthesized into a new graphics display in which the spatial arrangement permits or facilitates information processing. The success of such displays reflects their use of visual perception. For instance, items grouped closely tend to be perceived as belonging together and as being distinct from other items. Thus, grouping information on a page is a useful method for uniting perceptual and semantic "chunking" to aid in overcoming memory limitations and to organize information for learning. The use of mind maps or other forms of semantic networks is a good example (Dansereau, 1978).

Light.   The third major feature of graphics technology that relates to literacy is the use of light. The marks made to produce graphics symbols such as written or printed words, numbers, flow charts, arrows, and matrix cells are built by structuring the light that leaves the surface of the medium in a way that allows the eye to detect the structure of the display.

Brightness and color are the properties of light used most often in graphics technology. Brightness provides the contrast that makes writing possible. That is, the black of the line of writing (or type) contrasts with the white background. Brightness also provides contrast that can be used in conjunction with permanence and spatiality to aid information processing. For instance, the use of white space in arranging information spatially on a page can facilitate semantic chunking for learning.

In addition to aiding memory and facilitating learning through semantic chunking and organizing devices, the properties of light are used extensively to aid attention during information processing. Boldfaced print, for instance, may be used to call attention to certain information. Color can similarly guide information processing, as when a red line is used in an electronics diagram to trace a particular circuit in an array of circuits printed in black.

These principles can be applied to learning strategies in a variety of ways. For instance, prereading activities in which students survey boldfaced, italic, or segregated (as by white space) words or phrases can activate prior knowledge about what is to be read. This strategy increases comprehension and makes learning more effective. In addition, study techniques such as highlighting or underlining use light and color to focus attention and reduce the amount of information that must be processed during rereading (itself a learning strategy made possible by the permanence feature of graphics technology).

As with all technology, graphics technology is used to develop tools for amplifying and extending human capabilities (Bruner, 1968). However, unlike hammers, sewing machines, automobiles, and other technological devices that extend human strength, dexterity, or locomotion, graphics displays gain their power from extending human cognition and the ability to manipulate information in symbolic form. In particular, the merging of graphics technology with spoken language (another form of technology for communicating with symbols) produces the power behind, and the awe and appreciation of, literacy.

Graphic Representation of Spoken Language

A breakthrough achievement in graphics technology was the development of the alphabet, a relatively simple system in which a few graphic marks represent enough aspects of the oral language to permit a reader to reconstruct a language-based message from the graphics display (Harris, 1986). This is important because it permits written language to combine the power of oral language (representing and communicating knowledge) with the power of graphics technology (the use of permanence, spatiality, and light) to develop new knowledge and tools for thinking and problem solving.

For adults with little or no reading ability, instruction generally centers on decoding or reconstructing a spoken message from the graphics display, or "code" (so called because it serves as an alternative representation of speech). In a simple substitution code one element in a message, such as the sequence 1,2,3, is substituted by another set of symbols, such as a,b,c. In decoding, *a* is converted to *1*, *b* to *2*, and *c* to *3*. Although such a simple, one-to-one correspondence of speech and graphics symbols does not hold over the full range of the English language, the correspondence is close enough to make the technology work.

In reading instruction involving decoding—sometimes called the principle of the alphabet (Liberman, Shankweiler, & Liberman, 1989)—learners are taught to substitute a speech sound for a graphic alphabet symbol (phonics). With writing, they are taught to make alphabet characters that can, in turn, represent speech sounds.

Of course, the success of this phonics approach depends on the learner's ability to detect the different sounds in speech and then associate the graphics symbol to the spoken sound. Because some learners have difficulty with both these activities, educators have developed instructional methods that first aim to ensure that the student can discriminate between different sounds of speech and then use mnemonic systems to help the student learn the essentially arbitrary associations between graphics symbols and spoken sounds.

The Auditory Discrimination in Depth (ADD) program (Lindamood & Lindamood, 1975) uses a number of graphics aids to teach students to discriminate speech sounds. For instance, big pictures of lips and tongues depict the position of the mouth (e.g., lips together versus apart) and manner of articulation (voiced, unvoiced) used with different speech sounds. This approach teaches how speech is made, provides conceptual awareness of the segments of speech, and offers a mnemonic system for learning the arbitrary sight-sound correspondences involved in reading.

Volunteer tutoring programs often teach decoding using some form of mnemonics to learn sight-sound associations. However, they do not routinely teach conceptual awareness of speech segmentation first, as in the ADD program. This may or may not pose a problem depending on how aware the learner is of the sounds of speech. It is a factor that should be considered when teaching adults (or children, for that matter) the associations used in reading decoding (Golinkoff, 1978).

The importance of mnemonics and phonemic awareness becomes clear when it is understood that when we teach phonics or similar techniques we are teaching decoding *knowledge*—an organized body of facts about the alphabet and speech—not decoding *skills*. We know that methods such as mnemonics, systematic organization to aid recall, and explanations that lead to understanding can help students learn facts. If teachers think in terms of skills, they can forget to use what they know about teaching knowledge. By keeping this distinction in mind, they can more successfully and expeditiously teach the knowledge students need to develop the skills used in reading.

Writing and Reading

It is particularly advantageous to teach reading by introducing learners to writing. This is a useful way to further clarify that the alphabet is a graphical representation of spoken language. In writing, ideas are first expressed, or encoded, in (mentally) spoken form and then recoded into written form. Teaching this idea emphasizes the importance of meaning in reading by helping learners understand that just as writing *starts* with meaning, in reading the point is to *end up* with meaning.

Sticht & McDonald

The importance of meaning in both writing and reading can be introduced by first having students represent their thoughts in a nonlanguage-based graphics technology—pictures. For instance, a learner may be asked to draw a picture illustrating the sentence "The car stopped at the crosswalk." This activity teaches that (1) meanings and thoughts—or, more generally, knowledge—come first, and (2) knowledge can be represented using graphics technology. This understanding can be extended to explain that written language, like drawing, may represent knowledge expressed in the spoken language.

Thinking of writing and reading together as the use of graphics technology for communicating knowledge brings up the issue of whether reading is best thought of as a "bottom-up" or a "top-down" process (McCormick, 1988). In writing, the goal is to construct and communicate knowledge. That entails first having knowledge that can be conveyed in writing and then formulating a plan for communicating that knowledge. Thus, the writing process proceeds from the top down (i.e., from the knowledge to the method employed to communicate it). But just as one cannot comprehend spoken language without attending to what is being said, one cannot comprehend written language without first looking at the graphics display. Therefore, reading is a bottom-up process.

It is important to make sure that adult new readers understand that the goal of reading is to construct meaning, as some whole language approaches stress (McCormick, 1988). Explicit instruction in the importance of meaning may be necessary because learners sometimes devote so much attention to decoding the words that they neglect to work on understanding the message.

Knowledge, Cognition, and Reading

Just as oral language is used to represent knowledge in the acoustic medium, the alphabetic writing system is used to represent knowledge in the graphics medium. In both cases, knowledge is both the beginning and the end product of communication.

Because knowledge can be represented in different modes—for instance, in drawings, speech, written language, and dance—it is useful to think of a person's knowledge base as being operated on by different sets of procedural rules (themselves a part of the knowledge base) to represent ideas or thoughts. Figure 1 presents a simplified model of the human cognitive system that encompasses this view. The system has a long term memory in which the knowledge base is stored and a short term, or working, memory that is actively involved in processing information.

When a person listens to speech, the cognitive system picks up information simultaneously from the acoustic medium and from the internal knowledge base and merges the two to comprehend the message. Similarly, in reading, the person picks up information from an external store of knowledge (e.g., a book, sign, list, or table) and merges it with knowledge picked up simultaneously from the internal knowledge base.

Figure 1
Simple Model of the Human Cognitive System

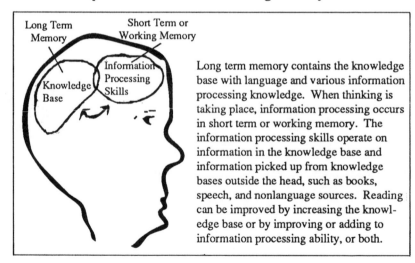

Long term memory contains the knowledge base with language and various information processing knowledge. When thinking is taking place, information processing occurs in short term or working memory. The information processing skills operate on information in the knowledge base and information picked up from knowledge bases outside the head, such as books, speech, and nonlanguage sources. Reading can be improved by increasing the knowledge base or by improving or adding to information processing ability, or both.

Sticht & McDonald

From this model, it is clear that the success of reading for comprehension rests on three factors:

- The possession (and accessibility) of content knowledge relevant to what is being read;
- The possession of task-relevant procedural knowledge, including (1) planning or goal-setting (metacognitive) knowledge, (2) knowledge of strategies for learning from text, (3) oral language representation knowledge (e.g., grammar, lexicon, and communication techniques, such as questioning for clarification), and (4) written language representation knowledge, including various communication conventions such as topic sentences and supporting details;
- An external information display that can be accessed, scanned (read), and transferred into working memory for use in performing some task (reading to do) or into long term memory for use in acquiring knowledge (reading to learn).

Organizing these components and processes of the human cognitive system into a program to help adults expand their knowledge of and skill in using graphics technology for reading is a formidable task. How one should proceed depends largely on the needs of the adults being served. For instance, adults with the absolute minimum knowledge of the alphabet, writing, and phonics require instruction in the alphabetic principle and its use in reading. These adults need extensive practice in decoding before they can read with skill.

Although not always, usually adults who possess little knowledge of or skill in reading also have low oral language ability, especially in lexicon. These adults require extensive knowledge development in a wide array of domains if they are to become broadly literate.

Some 5 to 10 percent of U.S. adults over the age of 15 (10 million or more) read at or below the level of children in the fourth grade (Sticht, 1986). However, the largest percentage of adults who enter reading programs (40 to 50 percent), are midlevel literates, with reading abilities at the fifth through ninth grade levels (Sticht & Hickey, 1987).

Reading programs must be carefully tailored to the needs of these midlevel literates and to the contexts in which they wish to function. These learners tend to leave literacy programs after relatively few (25-100) hours of instruction without developing either the broad knowledge necessary to be more generally literate or greater depth of knowledge in a specialized area. (In fact, most programs do not even make this distinction between breadth and depth in learning, and hence do not systematically address these different dimensions of literacy.)

Following is an example of a reading program for midlevel literates designed within the conceptual framework discussed earlier. In this approach, it is assumed that the learner's knowledge base needs to be expanded with regard to both knowledge of a particular content domain and knowledge and skill in using graphics technology for reading and learning in that domain.

Integrated Vocational and Reading Instruction

In a study to develop a program that integrated electronics and basic skills instruction, researchers surveyed several training schools to determine the nature of their basic skills programs (Sticht et al., 1987). Many of these programs received funds from the U.S. Job Training Partnership Act (JTPA), which required them to gauge whether learners' reading skills were developed enough to enter into a given job training program. Commonly, if reading skills were deemed too low, the learner was referred to the basic skills program. But because these learners frequently could not see the relevance of the basic skills education to the job training they needed, most did not enroll; those who did soon dropped out.

To a large degree, the typical basic skills program did not take into account the learners' functional context. This resulted in a mismatch between what the learners had in mind (job training so they could function in a workplace context) and what they were offered (basic skills instruction so they could function in an academic or other context).

A Workforce Literacy Approach

To provide a match between what learners want and what they are offered, these programs need to teach basic skills (i.e., reading) within the context of the vocational field. In this approach, reading instruction is aimed at helping people enter or advance in the workforce by providing access to needed vocational and technical training. Learners in such a setting are more likely to succeed because vocationally related reading instruction brings the basic skills program in line with the vocational training they came for in the first place. Thus, they are motivated to enroll in and continue with the course.

By learning reading with work-related texts, learners develop a body of knowledge that later will improve their ability to read and comprehend material in vocational education or technical training programs. They also learn strategies for using graphics tools (books, matrices, diagrams, flow charts) for performing reading-to-do and reading-to-learn tasks.

It should be noted that in this work*force* literacy approach to teaching adults to read, the goal is for learners to gain the reading ability needed to enter the vocational education or technical training that, in turn, is needed to get a job in a particular area. In a work*place* literacy approach to teaching adults to read, programs target the reading demands of a particular business with the aim of upgrading current employees. Because such demands can be identified with some precision, courses in a workplace program generally focus on developing *depth* of knowledge in a field; in contrast, a workforce literacy approach focuses more on *breadth* of knowledge within a vocational domain.

In earlier research, Sticht (1975) developed a set of workforce reading programs for the U.S. Army. Army personnel who read below the sixth grade level received six weeks of reading instruction to prepare them for technical training in areas like cooking, communications, medical corpswork, clerical and administrative work, and automotive mechanics. In the reading programs, students learned how to process information to perform reading-to-do and reading-to-learn tasks by reading materials pertinent to their respective career fields. For example, those who were going to become cooks developed both vocational knowledge and information processing skills by reading cooks' training materials.

This work indicates that it is feasible to integrate vocational and reading instruction. These programs produced as much gain in general literacy as did programs geared solely toward general literacy; at the same time, they produced much greater gain in vocational reading ability. Thus, they developed both breadth and depth of reading, with the most gain in depth within a vocational domain (Sticht et al., 1987).

A Functional Context Adult Reading Series

The work done by the U.S. military in developing a functional context approach to reading instruction has been adapted for civilian use. The principle of integrating reading and content instruction by employing a variety of appropriate, interactive reading strategies can be implemented in a variety of settings and with a variety of materials. Using an integrated approach will allow the use of original source materials, as well as specifically designed instructional materials. The discussion that follows is just one example of how the functional context approach can be used with adults.

The military work has been transferred to a civilian context in a textbook series produced by Glencoe/McGraw-Hill. This program is designed to develop reading (and mathematics) abilities within six vocational content areas (see Figure 2). These six areas share a common set of information processing skills when it comes to reading to do and reading to learn. However, each requires a different knowledge base. The need to develop both is consistent with the model of the human cognitive system in which information processing skills (in working memory) operate on the knowledge base (in long term memory) during the reading process.

The design of the textbook series takes this dual need into account. Each vocational content area has three books, one covering knowledge base and two covering information processing skills. Each knowledge base (KB) book is designed to present a coherent body of knowledge about a particular vocational field and to facilitate learning in that field.

Figure 2
A Functional Context Approach

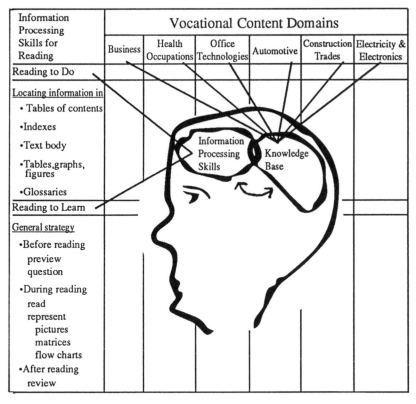

Information Processing Skills for Reading	Vocational Content Domains					
	Business	Health Occupations	Office Technologies	Automotive	Construction Trades	Electricity & Electronics
Reading to Do						
Locating information in						
• Tables of contents						
•Indexes						
•Text body						
•Tables,graphs, figures						
•Glossaries						
Reading to Learn						
General strategy						
•Before reading preview question						
•During reading read represent pictures matrices flow charts						
•After reading review						

Each vocational area's KB book begins with a two-page spread of photographs depicting people at work in a variety of positions within the field. For instance, the office technology KB text opens with pictures of a receptionist, mailroom personnel, people using wordprocessors, and so forth. Pictures like these are called memory icons because in Bruner's (1968) theory of cognitive development, children are said to progress from sensorimotor learning in an enactive mode, through a perceptual or iconic mode of learning, to a linguistic or symbolic mode of learning. The KB books follow this developmental sequence; learning begins in the iconic mode (with the photographs), which provides a perceptual basis for developing a schema for the positions and technical areas discussed in the text (the symbolic mode).

The KB books begin by asking the reader to study the pictures at the front. Then the text takes the reader from one photograph to the next, introducing the people working in each and having the workers explain what they do in their jobs. This introduction uses storylike dialogues and narrative text structures. Later, the text turns to expository structures. By moving from iconic-perceptual to story-narrative and then to expository text structures, the books follow a developmental sequence that allows the reader to construct an organized, accessible knowledge base.

Each KB text is designed to be used interactively with two information processing skills (IPS) texts, one for reading and one for mathematics. (Again, this arrangement follows the model of the human cognitive system in which information processing skills work on a knowledge base; in this case, the IPS Reading text is an external representation of internal information processing.) In use, the learner reads the IPS Reading text and is asked to perform a number of reading-to-do and reading-to-learn tasks (summarized in Figure 2). To perform these tasks, the reader must consult the KB book. For instance, the IPS book may ask readers to locate information in the corresponding KB book using the table of contents. The KB books' tables of contents are designed to be complex enough to help midlevel literates develop the ability to read the tables of contents of materials in vocational and technical training courses.

The reading-to-learn section teaches students a study strategy similar to Robinson's (1946) SQ3R. In this case, though, the "survey" part of the exercise is called "preview" to make it clear that it is a prereading activity. The strategy encompasses prereading, during reading, and after reading tasks to facilitate comprehension and learning. It is used extensively to allow students to master the strategy. This approach is, of course, made possible by the permanence feature of graphics technology; also, it illustrates the interactive

Sticht & McDonald

nature of reading, since the KB book contains a store of information that must be studied to be learned by drawing on prior knowledge.

As part of the set of during and after reading activities, the learner is asked to go to the KB book and extract information to construct a table listing different pieces of equipment, their functions, their advantages and disadvantages, and other data. This task develops complex information searching and synthesizing skills in what Upton (1973) calls the classification mode of analysis. Other exercises ask students to read the IPS text, locate information in the KB text, and draw pictures, thereby exercising Upton's structural analysis skills. Still other exercises require the reader to find procedural text in the KB book and develop a flow chart from it, thus using Upton's process or procedural form of analysis.

The interactive nature of the IPS and KB books means that the books had to be designed together to be usable together. The IPS volumes were not developed later as add-on workbooks, a procedure that would have precluded activities such as casting text information into tables, pictures, or flow charts. For these activities, the KB book had to have just the right material for the IPS book to teach the reader how to construct these different representations of knowledge.

This interactive system deliberately elicits the type of complex information processing identified in the National Assessment of Educational Progress (NAEP) study of literacy among America's young adults (Kirsch & Jungeblut, 1986). The study concluded that "while the overwhelming majority of young adults adequately perform tasks at the lower levels on each of the three scales (prose, document, quantitative), sizable numbers appear unable to do well on tasks of moderate complexity" (p. 4). The report goes on to state that "in many instances, literacy tasks require individuals to apply complex information processing skills and strategies. Some tasks require the reader to identify needed information, locate that information in a given source, remember it, combine it with additional information, and enter it onto a form or separate document" (p. 65).

Many reading materials consist solely of workbooks that require students to read a small segment of prose (or a simple table, form, or other graphics device) and then answer one or more ques-

Figure 3
Test Scores of Students in a Navy versus a General Literacy Course

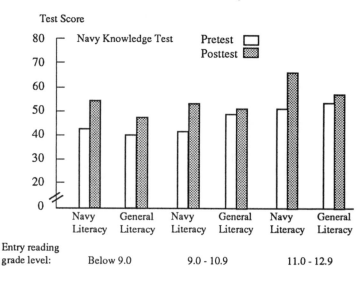

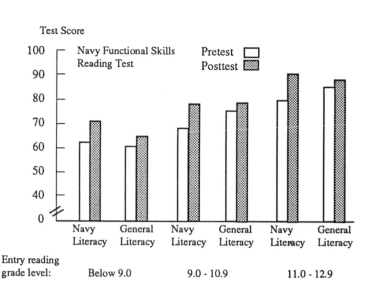

tions about the material. In contrast, the KB and IPS texts develop information processing skills more like those needed for the real world tasks identified in the NAEP assessment.

An Evaluation Study

In a small-scale study using the functional context approach with U.S. Navy personnel, sailors took part in a 45-hour remedial reading program. One group used a Navy KB book and an IPS text that taught reading-to-do and reading-to-learn skills (Sticht et al., 1986). A second group studied reading using high school oriented materials and workbooks. After the course, researchers compared the two groups' performance on tests of Navy knowledge and Navy-related reading (reading to do and reading to learn) as well as on a general reading test.

The results were similar to those for the large-scale Army program that integrated vocational and reading instruction. On the general reading test, students in the general reading course improved by about 8 months, while students in the Navy-related course improved by about 4 months. However, on tests that measured students' knowledge of and ability to read about the Navy, those in the Navy-related course typically improved more than twice as much as those in the general reading course (see Figure 3).

These and the earlier military studies indicate that the functional context approach can be profitably used in programs that teach adults to read. General information processing skills (reading, studying) can be developed while learning specific content materials. Reading skills, at least for midlevel literates, do not have to be raised before the learners can begin to read and learn the vocational (or other) material in which they are interested. Both content knowledge and reading skills contribute to students' ability to learn more about their field of interest. Teaching the two together keeps learners motivated and helps them achieve their goals.

References

Bruner, J.S. (1968). *Processes of cognitive growth: Infancy*. Worcester, MA: Clark University Press.

Dansereau, D. (1978). The development of a learning strategies curriculum. In H.F. O'Neil, Jr. (Ed.), *Learning strategies*. San Diego, CA: Academic.

Ellsworth, E. (1989). Why doesn't this feel empowering? Working through the repressive myths of critical pedagogy. *Harvard Educational Review, 59,* 297-324.

Golinkoff, R.M. (1978). Phonemic awareness skills and reading achievement. In F.B. Murray & J.J. Pikulski (Eds.), *The acquisition of reading: Cognitive, linguistic, and perceptual prerequisites.* Baltimore, MD: University Park Press.

Goody, J. (1977). *The domestication of the savage mind.* New York: Cambridge University Press.

Harris, R. (1986). *The origin of writing.* London: Duckworth.

Kirsch, I., & Jungeblut, A. (1986). *Literacy: Profiles of America's young adults.* Princeton, NJ: Educational Testing Service.

Liberman, I., Shankweiler, D., & Liberman, A. (1989). The alphabetic principle and learning to read. In D. Shankweiler & I. Liberman (Eds.), *Phonology and reading disability: Solving the reading puzzle.* Ann Arbor, MI: University of Michigan Press.

Lindamood, C.H., & Lindamood, P.C. (1975). *The A.D.D. program: Auditory discrimination in depth.* Hingham, MA: Teaching Resources.

McCormick, W.M. (1988). *Theories of reading in dialogue: An interdisciplinary study.* Landham, MD: University Press of America.

Morris, W. (Ed.). (1976). *The American Heritage dictionary of the English language.* Boston, MA: Houghton Mifflin.

Robinson, F.P. (1946). *Effective study.* New York: HarperCollins.

Schwartz, S.H. (1971). Modes of representation and problem solving: Well evolved is half solved. *Journal of Experimental Psychology, 2,* 347-350.

Sticht, T.G. (1975). *A program of Army functional job reading training: Development, implementation, and delivery systems* (Final Report, HumRo-FR-WD(CA)-75-7). Alexandria, VA: Human Resources Research Organization.

Sticht, T.G. (1979). Developing literacy and learning strategies in organizational settings. In H. O'Neil, Jr. & C. Spielberger (Eds.), *Cognitive and affective learning strategies.* San Diego, CA: Academic.

Sticht, T.G. (1986). Foreword. In I. Kirsch & A. Jungeblut, *Literacy: Profiles of America's young adults.* Princeton, NJ: Educational Testing Service.

Sticht, T.G., Armijo, L., Koffman, N., Roberson, K., Weitzman, R., Chang, F., & Moracco, J. (1986). *Teachers, books, computers, and peers: Integrated communications technologies for adult literacy development.* Monterey, CA: U.S. Naval Postgraduate School.

Sticht, T.G., Armstrong, W.B., Hickey, D.T., & Caylor, J.S. (1987). *Cast-off youth: Policy and training methods from the military experience.* New York: Praeger.

Sticht, T.G., & Hickey, D.T. (1987). Technical training for "mid-level" literate adults. In C. Klevens (Ed.), *Materials and methods in adult and continuing education: International illiteracy.* Los Angeles, CA: Klevens Publications.

Street, B.V. (1984). *Literacy in theory and practice.* New York: Cambridge University Press.

Upton, A. (1973). *Design for thinking: A first book in semantics.* Palo Alto, CA: Pacific Books.

Author Index

Note: "Mc" is alphabetized as "Mac." An "f" following a page number indicates that the reference may be found in a figure; an "n," that it may be found in a note; a "t," that it may be found in a table.

Ackerman, P.T., 258, 270
Adams, A., 228, 234, 247, 250
Adams, M.J., 259, 261, 270
Afflerbach, P., 72, 80, 94, 97, 155, 162, 163, 191, 195
Alderson, J.C., 281, 308
Alessi, S.M., 160, 191
Alexander, P., 251
Alford, J.A., Jr., 9,15
Algozzine, B., 268, 276
Alkin, M., 97
Alleman-Brooks, J., 191
Allen, J., 21, 22, 42
Allerson, S., 304, 308
Allington, R.L., 80, 94, 141, 143, 239, 251
Alvermann, D.E., 156, 191, 218
Ames, L.B., 260, 270
Ammon, M.S., 288, 308
Anderson, C.W., 156, 191, 194
Anderson, K.F., 19, 37
Anderson, L., 172, 173, 175, 191
Anderson, M.C., 155, 166, 192
Anderson, R.C., 9, 10, 15, 60, 68, 112, 122, 125, 143, 149, 155, 156, 162, 165, 166, 174, 191, 192, 197, 202, 209, 216, 291, 292, 312, 313
Anderson, T.H., 160, 167, 168, 191, 192, 227, 234, 242, 251
Anderson, V., 223, 234
Andre, M.E.D.A., 167, 168, 192
Applebee, A.N., 71, 94
Armbruster, B.B., 167, 193, 227, 234, 243, 251
Armijo, L., 334
Arter, J.A., 258, 270
Aschbacher, P.R., 77, 94
Asheim, L., 30, 37
Asher, J., 290, 308

Atwell, N., 59, 68, 92, 94
Au, K.H., 292, 296, 308
Auble, P.M., 217
August, D.L., 195

Backman, J., 257, 272
Baghban, M., 35, 38
Bahruth, R., 289, 299, 310
Baker, D.P., 30, 37
Baker, E.L., 71, 82, 98
Baker, L., 157, 160, 176, 192, 238, 243, 244, 251
Baldwin, L.E., 20, 217, 260, 271
Baldwin, S., 197
Ball, D.L., 61, 68
Barclay, J.R., 166, 192
Barkman, B., 309
Barnitz, J.G., 286, 287, 288, 289, 297, 308
Barr, R., 95, 112, 122, 210, 216
Barrs, M., 77, 94
Bassiri, D., 194
Bate, M., 27, 38
Bauer, R.H., 258, 270
Baumann, J.F., 112, 113, 122, 162, 169, 191, 192, 193, 195, 199, 222, 234, 235, 263, 267, 270
Beach, R.W., 165, 198, 223, 235
Becher, R.M., 21, 24, 26, 38
Beck, I.L., 115, 118, 122, 123, 170, 180, 192, 218, 230, 234, 267, 271
Beck, M.D., 263, 275
Beebe, L.M., 309
Bentley, L., 49, 52, 68
Bereiter, C., 184, 192
Berger, E.H., 26, 38
Berk, R.A., 263, 271
Berkowitz, B.S., 165, 198
Berkowitz, S.J., 225, 234
Berliner, D.B., 92, 94
Betts, E.A., 268, 271
Bingham, A.B., 169, 195
Bird, J.E., 241, 252

Bird, L.B., 64, 68
Bird, T., 82
Bissex, G.L., 19, 38, 53, 68, 120, 121, 122
Blachman, B., 258, 267, 271
Blachowicz, C., 210, 216
Blanchard, J., 16, 144
Block, E., 302, 308
Bloome, D., 23, 38
Boder, E., 257, 271
Boeker, E., 107, 122
Book, C., 181, 192, 194
Borchardt, K.M., 165, 195, 247, 251
Borg, W.R., 3, 4, 15
Borkowski, J.G., 182, 192, 193, 249, 251
Bowler, R.F., 271, 273
Bradley, L., 108, 123
Brainerd, C., 276
Brandt, R., 79, 94
Bransford, J.D., 155, 166, 192, 196, 204, 216, 217, 252
Branston, P., 31, 36, 38
Brantlinger, E., 25, 38
Breivogel, W.F., 26, 27, 40
Bremer, C., 132, 144
Brenneman, B., 72, 95
Brewer, R., 72, 77, 94
Brewer, W.F., 251, 270
Bridge, C.A., 162, 163, 199, 222, 235
Bridgeford, N.J., 73, 75, 100
Britton, B.K., 206, 216
Britton, J., 51, 68
Broman, M., 258, 275
Bronfenbrenner, U., 28, 38
Brooks, L.W., 228, 234
Brophy, J., 172, 173, 181, 191, 192, 267, 271
Brown, A.L., 139, 143, 155, 157, 159, 160, 164, 165, 166, 167, 176, 178, 180, 182, 192, 193, 196, 217, 224, 235, 238, 243, 246, 251, 258, 264, 265, 267, 271, 274

Brown, J.S., 80, 96
Brown, R., 71, 93, 95
Brown, V., 143
Brubaker, N.L., 191
Bruce, B.C., 251, 270
Bruder, M.N., 288, 308
Bruner, J.S., 315, 320, 329, 333
Bryant, N., 217
Bryant, P., 108, 123
Bullock, R., 53, 68
Bunderson, C.V., 95
Burchell, B., 26, 45
Burke, C.L., 18, 19, 22, 41
Burke, S.M., 90, 95
Burkes, A., 234
Burns, P.C., 204, 218
Burris, N.A., 19, 44
Burstall, C., 77, 95
Butler, S.R., 30, 38

Calderhead, J., 199
Calfee, R.C., 73, 76, 79, 83, 87, 89, 90, 95, 96
California Department of Education, 75, 78, 95
Cambourne, B., 92, 95
Camp, R., 81, 95
Campione, J.C., 164, 192, 193, 214, 217, 258, 264, 265, 271
Cannell, J.J., 71, 95
Carbo, M., 267, 271
Cardenas, R., 39
Carnine, D., 126, 143, 228, 234, 247, 250
Carpenter, P.A., 259, 273
Carr, E.M., 267, 272
Carr, M., 249, 251
Carr, T.H., 112, 122
Carrell, P.L., 291, 292, 293, 308, 309, 310
Carter, A.Y., 166, 196
Carter, M.A., 81, 95
Carter, R., 312
Carver, R.P., 9, 15
Castellan, D., 15
Cavanaugh, J.C., 182, 193
Celce-Murcia, M., 310
Chall, J.S., 6, 15, 112, 122, 127, 143, 201, 217, 254, 255, 256, 258, 260, 261, 263, 264, 266, 267, 268, 269, 271

Chamot, A.U., 312
Chang, F., 334
Chaudron, C., 282, 308
Chi, M.T.H., 195
Children First, 31, 38
Chipman, S., 217
Chomsky, C., 19, 38, 136, 143
Claggett, F., 72, 95
Clark, C., 205, 217
Clark, M.M., 18, 24, 38
Clay, M.M., 18, 19, 20, 22, 38, 80, 96, 106, 109, 122, 138, 143, 261, 272, 304, 306, 308
Cleve, S., 27, 38
Cloward, R., 25, 38
Coady, J., 286, 309
Cochran, M., 34, 38
Cochran-Smith, M., 18, 22, 43, 280, 312
Cohen, A.D., 303, 304, 309
Cole, M., 69, 198, 276
Cole, N.S., 76, 96
Coleman, J., 18, 39, 172, 193
Coles, G.S., 262, 272
Collins, A., 80, 96
Comer, J.P., 34, 39
Commins, N.L., 90, 98
Conklin, N.F., 73, 75, 100
Cook, L.K., 73, 96
Cooknell, T., 30, 39
Cooper, C., 72, 95
Cooper, C.R., 304, 309
Cosgrove, J.M., 158, 196
Coskey, M., 9, 15
Covington, M.V., 213, 217
Craik, F.I.M., 167, 193
Crawley, S.T., 201, 217
Criscuolo, N.P., 33, 39
Cronbach, L.J., 89, 96
Crooks, T.J., 73, 96
Cross, D.R., 159, 196, 247, 252
Crossen, H.J., 147, 193
Crowell, D., 308
Cruse, K.L., 99
Cuban, L., 57, 68
Cuckle, P., 24, 27, 39, 40
Cummins, J., 282, 304, 305, 309
Cunningham, J.W., 20, 44, 162, 165, 167, 193, 198
Curtis, M.E., 259, 260, 263, 264, 271, 272, 273, 274

Dahlberg, L.A., 201, 217
Danner, F.W., 195
Dansereau, D.F., 234, 319, 333
Darling-Hammond, L., 94
Darlington, R., 28, 41
Das, J.P., 123
Dauber, S.L., 28, 36, 39
Davidson, J.L., 10, 15
Davis, F.B., 8, 15, 147, 193
Davis, M.M., 262, 272
Day, J.D., 164-165, 193-194, 246, 251
Dean, C., 34, 38
De Corte, E., 203, 217
Deford, D., 19, 39
deHirsch, K., 256, 267, 272, 273
DeLawter, J., 112, 122
Denckla, M.B., 256, 258, 260, 272, 275
Devine, J., 281, 288, 292, 309, 310
Dewey, J., 49, 52, 68
Dewitz, P., 267, 272
Dickson, W.P., 41, 194, 251, 252
Diederich, P.B., 110, 114, 116, 122
Diehl, W., 31, 312
Dillon, D., 79, 96
Dillon, R.F., 274
Dishner, E.K., 218
Dixon, C., 299, 309
Doake, D.B., 20, 39
Doehring, D.G., 257, 272
Dole, J.A., 156, 184, 194, 197
Donhower, S.L., 137, 138, 143, 267, 272
Donlan, D., 167, 198, 231, 235
Dooling, D.L., 155, 194
Dornio, S., 16
Dorr-Bremme, D.W., 73, 96
Dorsey-Gaines, C., 19, 22, 44
Douglas, M.P., 41
Dowd, F.A., 34, 39
Downing, J., 20, 24, 39, 122
Doyle, W., 173, 175, 179, 194
Draper, K., 302, 309
Drum, P.A., 73, 76, 85, 87, 95, 96

Dublin, F., 302, 308, 309, 311
Dudley-Marling, C., 20, 39
Duffy, G.G., 61, 68, 100, 159, 171, 176, 177, 178, 180, 182, 184, 185, 191, 194, 274
Duke, D., 192, 194
Dunbar, S.B., 71, 82, 89, 98
Duncan, L.J., 31, 39
Dunn, K., 257, 274
Duran, R.P., 97
Durkin, D., 18, 24, 39, 116, 122, 171, 194
Dutcher, P., 74, 85, 99
d'Ydewalle, G., 203, 217
Dykman, R.A., 258, 270
Dyson, A.H., 19, 39

Eaton, J.F., 156, 194
Edelsky, C., 79, 96, 302, 309
Educational Testing Service, 76, 96
Edwall, G.A., 122
Eisenberg, P., 132, 144
Eisterhold, J.C., 291, 292, 308
Elder, R.D., 112, 122
Elkonin, D.B., 109, 122
Elley, W.B., 291, 309
Ellinger, B.D., 199
Ellis, R., 282, 285, 309
Ellis, S., 77, 94
Ellsworth, E., 315, 334
Emmer, E., 173, 191
Englert, C.S., 163, 194, 221, 234
Enright, D.S., 283, 285, 295, 297, 300, 301, 309, 310, 311, 312
Epstein, J.L., 26, 27, 28, 36, 39
Eresh, J.T., 78, 96
Eskey, D.E., 308, 309, 310, 311
Evans, M.A., 112, 122
Evertson, C., 172, 173, 191

Fantini, M.D., 26, 39
Farnan, N., 218
Fay, L.C., 34, 44
Feathers, K., 310, 312
Feeley, J.T., 295, 310

Feitelson, D., 20, 40
Ferrara, R.A., 192, 217
Ferreiro, E., 51, 63, 68
Feuerstein, R., 264, 272
Fiedorowicz, C.A.M., 272
Fillmore, C.J., 313
Fitzgerald, J., 229, 234, 235
Flatley, J.K., 302, 310
Flavell, J.H., 158, 160, 176, 192, 194, 195, 196, 237, 238, 251
Fleming, J.T., 95
Flesch, R., 111, 122
Flood, J., 21, 40, 79, 96, 218
Foertsch, M., 73, 96
Forrest, D.L., 238, 251
Forsyth, R., 147, 198
Franklin, E.A., 290, 310
Franks, J.J., 166, 192, 209, 217
Fredericks, A.D., 18, 20, 21, 30, 36, 43
Freedle, R.O., 97, 221, 234
Freedman, S.W., 73, 77, 82, 96
Freeman, Y., 50, 68, 97
French, J.H., 257, 274
Friedman, S.L., 272
Fries, C.C., 128, 143
Frith, U., 260, 272
Frost, J., 108, 123, 267, 273
Frye, B., 23, 224, 235

Galinsky, E., 27, 40
Gallagher, J.J., 41
Gans, R., 147, 195
Garcia, G.E., 90, 96
Garner, R., 157, 158, 160, 176, 195, 237, 241, 246, 247, 248, 251
Gartner, A., 261, 272
Gass, S.M., 309, 311, 313
Gates, A.I., 107, 122, 254, 257, 260, 273
Gentile, L., 16, 144
Gersten, R., 228, 234, 247, 250
Gibbs, C., 20, 21, 40
Gil, D., 79, 96
Glaser, R., 10, 11, 217
Glazer, S.M., 22, 35, 40
Gleser, G.C., 96
Glynn, S.M., 216

Glynn, T., 38
Goelman, H., 42, 44, 68, 312
Goetz, E.T., 160, 191
Goldenberg, C.N., 25, 40
Goldman, S.R., 308, 311, 312
Goldstein, Z., 20, 40
Golinkoff, R.M., 322, 334
Gomez, B., 282, 284, 310
Good, T., 172, 181, 183, 192, 195
Goodlad, J.I., 26, 40, 92, 96
Goodman, K.S., 49, 50, 51, 54, 56, 60, 62, 67n, 68, 75, 79, 95, 97, 126, 143
Goodman, Y.M., 47, 51, 54, 56, 60, 64, 68, 69, 79, 97, 126, 143
Goody, J., 317, 334
Gordon, C.J., 155, 195, 197
Gordon, I.J., 26, 27, 40
Gough, P.B., 107, 109, 122, 123
Gould, S.M., 206, 209, 217
Gove, M., 204, 219
Grabe, W., 287, 304, 308, 309, 310, 311
Graue, M.E., 71, 98
Graves, D., 51, 69
Graves, M.F., 225, 227, 235
Gray, W.S., 57, 69, 79, 97, 254, 257, 273
Green, F.L., 195
Greenstein, J.J., 258, 275
Greenwood, G.E., 26, 27, 40
Greer, E.A., 74, 97
Griffith, P.L., 109, 123
Griffiths, A., 29, 30, 36, 40
Grinnell, P.C., 35, 40
Grove, M.P., 286, 288, 310
Gruenfelder, T.M., 182, 192
Gruneberg, M.M., 193
Gunderson, L., 34, 45, 306, 313
Guthrie, G.P., 308
Guthrie, J.T., 13, 16, 112, 122, 123

Haas, L.W., 206, 209, 217
Haertel, E., 83, 97
Hagerty, P., 86, 97
Haley-James, S., 19, 40
Hall, C., 206, 209, 217
Hall, M., 297, 310

Hall, N., 21, 40
Halliday, M.A.K., 50, 51, 58, 69
Hamayan, E., 296, 298, 300, 310
Hamilton, D., 29, 30, 36, 40
Handscombe, J., 309
Hannon, P.W., 24, 27, 39, 40
Hansen, H.S., 24, 40
Hansen, J., 155, 166, 170, 195, 197, 247, 251
Hare, V.C., 165, 169, 195, 247, 251
Harman, S., 79, 96
Harris, A.J., 259, 263, 273
Harris, L.A., 79, 97, 193
Harris, P.L., 158, 195
Harris, R., 317, 321, 334
Haris, R.J., 265, 273
Harris, T.L., 127, 143
Harrison, S., 206, 207f, 218
Harste, J.C., 18, 19, 22, 41
Hatch, E., 287, 288, 289, 310
Haussler, M., 69
Havens, L., 206, 207f, 218
Hayes, C.W., 289, 299, 310
Haynes, J., 251
Haynes, N.M., 34, 39
Heald-Taylor, G., 295, 300, 304, 310
Heath, S.B., 20, 22, 23, 41, 90, 97, 281, 310
Henderson, R.T., 288, 308
Herman, J.L., 73, 96
Herman, P.A., 137, 143, 291, 312
Herndon, M.A., 9, 16
Herrmann, B.A., 171, 184, 194, 195
Hertz, K.V., 32, 41
Hess, R.D., 25, 41
Hester, H., 77, 94
Hewison, J., 24, 28, 41
Hickey, D.T., 326, 334
Hickman, C.W., 26, 27, 40
Hicks, C., 266, 273
Hidi, S., 223, 234
Hiebert, E.H., 15, 60, 68, 80, 83, 86, 95, 97, 98, 122, 143, 163, 194, 221, 234
Hieronymus, A.N., 147, 198
Hill, C., 73, 97
Hillinger, M.L., 107, 122

Hodges, R.E., 127, 143
Hoffman, J.V., 68, 94
Holdaway, D., 20, 41
Holdaway, R., 138, 143
Holley, C.D., 234
Holley-Wilcox, P., 9, 15
Holloway, S., 41
Holmes, B.C., 206, 217
Hood, W.J., 56, 68, 79, 97
Horowitz, R., 144, 221, 234
Hoskisson, K., 138, 143
Hough, R.A., 295, 311
Howard, K., 81, 97
Huck, S., 199
Hudelson, S., 278, 281, 286, 288, 291, 297, 311
Hudson, T., 293, 311
Huey, E., 125, 143
Huot, B., 85, 97
Hurst, W., 214, 216t, 217
Hutchison, T.A., 80, 97
Hutson, B.A., 38
Hymes, J.I., 26, 41

Indrisano, R., 264, 274
Ingram, A.L., 195
International Reading Association, 263, 273
Irwin, J.W., 205, 213, 217

Jacobs, J.E., 178, 196, 247, 252
Jacobs, V.A., 201, 217, 260, 271
Jacoby, S., 18, 41
Jansky, J.J., 256, 267, 272, 273
Jenkins, J.R., 258, 270
Jensen, L., 302, 311
Joag-dev, C., 292, 313
Johnson, D.D., 112, 113, 122, 146, 161, 197, 290, 311
Johnson, D.M., 311
Johnson, M.K., 155, 192
Johnson, P., 293, 311
John-Steiner, V., 69, 198, 276
Johnston, P.H., 71, 80, 92, 97, 159, 162, 163, 191, 195, 199, 263, 273
Jones, J., 25, 38
Jones, J.R., 20, 21, 41

Jones, R.S., 164, 193
Jordan, C., 308
Jordan, R.R., 309
Jowett, S., 27, 38
Juel, C., 105, 109, 122, 123
Jungeblut, A., 331, 334
Just, M.A., 259, 273

Kagan, J., 258, 273
Kahneman, D., 130, 143
Kail, R.V., 166, 195
Kamil, M.L., 8, 9, 13, 15, 16, 95, 136, 144, 197, 198, 259, 275
Kaminski, J., 71, 74, 98
Kamphaus, R.K., 271
Kanowitz, B.H., 13, 16
Karabenick, J.D., 159, 197
Karim, Y., 26, 41
Karnes, M.B., 28, 41
Kavanagh, J.F., 15
Kemp, M., 30, 41
Kemper, L., 256, 272
Kempler, D., 313
Kessler, C., 289, 299, 310
Kilpatrick, W.H., 52, 69
King, J.R., 78, 99
King, L., 199
Kintsch, W., 222, 235
Kinzer, C., 127, 144
Kirk, S.A., 262, 273
Kirk, W., 262, 273
Kirsch, I., 331, 334
Kitagawa, M.M., 295, 311
Kleifgen, J.A., 282, 283, 311
Klein, T., 308
Klevens, C., 334
Klivington, K.A., 272
Knafle, J.D., 296, 313
Knight, S.L., 293, 312
Koffman, N., 334
Koretz, D., 71, 97
Krashen, S.D., 282, 295, 311
Kreutzer, M.A., 238, 251
Kruithof, A., 195
Kupper, L., 312
Kyle, R., 275

LaBerge, D., 9, 16, 128, 132, 138, 143, 144, 259, 273
Lachman, R., 155, 194
Lalik, R.M., 79, 97
Lalik, R.V., 123, 191, 198, 199

Laminack, L.L., 18, 41
Langer, J.A., 71, 73, 94, 97
Langford, W.S., 256, 267, 272
Lapp, D., 79, 96, 218
Larrick, N., 18, 41
Lautenschlager, J., 32, 41
Lawton, S.C., 164, 193
Lazar, I., 28, 41
Leonard, C., 238, 251
Lesgold, A.M., 106, 123, 138, 144, 260, 273
Leslie, L., 206, 219
Lessing, D., 129, 144
Leu, D., 127, 144
Levers, S.R., 182, 192
Levin, J.R., 252
Lewis, R.B., 266, 273
Liberman, A., 321, 334
Liberman, I., 321, 334
Liberman, I.Y., 258, 259, 273, 274
Lidz, C., 80, 98
Lin, Y.G., 217
Lindamood, C.H., 321, 334
Lindamood, P.C., 321, 334
Lindauer, B.K., 155, 166, 196
Linn, R.L., 71, 73, 82, 86, 89, 98
Lipsky, D.K., 261, 272
Lipson, M.Y., 148, 159, 182, 195, 196, 206, 217, 246, 247, 252
Littlefield, J., 217
Lockhart, R.S., 167, 193
Logan, L.M., 22, 42
Logan, V.G., 22, 42
Loveday, E., 22, 28, 30, 42
Lundberg, I., 106, 108, 123, 267, 273

McAfee, O.D., 26, 42
MacCarry, B., 30, 42
McCarthy, M., 312
McCaslen, E., 234
McCloskey, M.L., 285, 297, 300, 301, 310, 311
McCloskey, R., 102, 123
McConkie, G.W., 259, 274
McCormick, C., 132, 144, 194
MacCormick, K., 203, 217
McCormick, S., 97

McCormick, W.M., 315, 323, 334
McGee, L.M., 222, 234
MacGinitie, W., 156, 196
McGinley, W., 87, 100
McIntosh, L., 310
McIntyre, C.W., 160, 196
McIntyre, L., 171, 194
Mackay, R., 309
McKeachie, W.J., 202, 217
McKeown, M.G., 170, 180, 192, 210, 211, 218, 230, 234, 267, 271
McKinney, J., 166, 197
MacKinnon, G.E., 13, 16, 122
McLain, E., 78, 98
McLaughlin, B., 286, 287, 288, 311
Maclean, M., 108, 123
McNeil, L.M., 74, 98
Macready, G.B., 160, 195, 241, 251
Madden, C.G., 309, 311, 313
Madden, N.A., 261, 267, 275
Maine Department of Education, 75, 85, 98
Malmquist, E., 19, 42
Mandel, H., 143
Mandl, H., 193, 197
Mangubhai, F., 291, 309
Mann, V.A., 258, 274
Marckwardt, A.H., 302, 311
Maria, K., 156, 196
Marino, J.L., 206, 209, 217
Markman, E.M., 192, 243, 252
Marrion, L.V., 19, 43
Marsh, M., 31, 44
Martin, J.H., 300, 311
Martuza, V., 122
Marx, R.W., 174, 176, 199
Mason, J., 274
Mason, J.M., 21, 42
Massachusetts Department of Education, 75, 98
Masur, E.F., 160, 196
Mathews, J., 78, 98
Matthews, V.H., 30, 37
Mattingly, I.G., 15
Mattis, S., 257, 274
Mavrogenes, N.A., 22, 42
Mayfield, M.I., 27, 42

Mehrens, W.A., 71, 74, 98
Meloth, M., 177, 183, 192, 194, 196
Messick, S., 88, 98
Meyer, B.J.F., 221, 226, 234
Meyer, L.A., 74, 97
Mezynski, K.J., 217
Miller, G., 194
Miller, N., 132, 144
Millman, J., 94
Milz, V., 54, 69
Miramontes, O.B., 90, 98
Mirsky, A.F., 256, 271
Moe, A.J., 197, 198
Moffett, J., 21, 42
Monroe, M., 254, 257, 274
Montague, W.E., 191
Moore, D.W., 162, 193
Moracco, J., 334
Morgan, W.P., 254, 274
Morphett, M.J., 260, 274
Morris, C.D., 196, 252
Morris, P.E., 193
Morris, R., 257, 275
Morris, W., 317, 334
Morrow, L.M., 20, 35, 44, 71, 98, 229, 234
Mortimore, J., 26, 45
Mosenthal, P., 95
Moses, S., 72, 85, 98
Mosteller, F., 18, 42
Mountain, L.H., 201, 217
Moustafa, M., 298, 311
Moynihan, O.P., 18, 42
Mulcahy, R., 123
Mulcahy-Ernt, P., 210, 212, 218
Mullis, I.V.S., 71, 86, 94, 98
Mundell, P., 30, 42
Murphy, S., 50, 68, 81, 97, 98
Murray, F.B., 334
Muth, D.K., 216
Myers, M., 238, 252
Myklebust, H.R., 270, 273, 275

NAEP. *See* National Assessment of Educational Progress
NAEYC. *See* National Association for the Education of Young Children

Nagy, W.E., 212, 218, 291, 312
Nanda, H., 96
Natchez, G., 264, 272, 274
Nathan, R.G., 19, 44
National Assessment of Educational Progress (NAEP), 72, 91, 98
National Association for the Education of Young Children (NAEYC), 61, 69
National Society for the Study of Education, 26, 42
Nations, M.J., 301, 311
Nattinger, J., 290, 291, 312
Nedler, S.E., 26, 42
Nelson-Barber, S., 89, 95
Nessel, D., 299, 309
Newman, J., 49, 69
Newman, S.E., 80, 96
Newson, E., 27, 42
Newson, J., 27, 42
Niles, J.A., 123, 191, 193, 198, 199
Niles, O., 68
Ninio, A., 22, 42
Nolte, R.Y., 206, 218, 231, 234
Northwest Regional Educational Laboratory (NWREL), 78, 98
Nurss, J.R., 295, 311
NWREL. See Northwest Regional Educational Laboratory

Oberg, A.A., 42, 44, 68, 312
O'Brien, R.G., 158, 196
O'Dell, L., 304, 309
Office of Educational Research and Improvement, 26, 42
Ogle, D., 180, 196
Oller, J.W., 303, 304, 312
Ollila, L.O., 19, 43
Olmstead, P.P., 27, 42
Olson, D., 20, 42
O'Malley, J.M., 284, 312
Omanson, R., 170, 180, 192, 218, 230, 234, 267, 271
O'Neil, H., Jr., 334

Orasanu, J., 251, 308
Orem, R.A., 309
Orton, S.T., 254, 274
Ostertag, J., 227, 234
O'Sullivan, J.T., 182, 196
Otto, W., 6, 16
Owens, E.H., 86, 98
Owens, M.K., 86, 97
Owings, R.A., 160, 196, 246, 252

Padron, Y.N., 293, 312
Palincsar, A.S., 139, 143, 159, 165, 167, 178, 180, 193, 196, 224, 235, 267, 274
Palmer, W., 171, 196
Paratore, J.R., 264, 274
Paris, S.G., 155, 159, 166, 178, 182, 196, 238, 246, 247, 252
Parry, K., 73, 97
Passow, A.H., 38
Patberg, J.P., 267, 272
Patel, P.G., 272
Patterson, C.J., 158, 196
Pearson, P.D., 16, 36, 43, 44, 73, 74, 87, 90, 95, 96, 97, 100, 122, 146, 148, 155, 158, 161, 166, 174, 177, 178, 184, 185, 191, 192, 195, 196, 197, 198, 203, 218, 247, 251, 263, 275, 290, 311
Penfield, M.J., 216
Pennington, B.F., 257, 274
Penrose, J., 298, 311
Perfetti, C.A., 138, 144, 218, 259, 273, 274
Perfetto, G.A., 217
Perkins, K., 303, 304, 312
Peters, C.W., 100
Petersen, G.E., 252
Peterson, G.A., 196
Peterson, O., 108, 123, 267, 273
Peterson, P.L., 250, 252
Peterson, R.W., 256, 272
Petty, W., 22, 42
Pflaum, S.W., 90, 95
Pflaum-Conner, S., 13, 16
Pfleger, M., 296, 298, 300, 310

Pfleiderer, J., 99
Phillips, G.W., 86, 98
Piché, G.L., 225, 227, 235
Pichert, J.W., 162, 164, 197
Pikulski, J.J., 334
Pinnell, G.S., 261, 274
Pintrich, P.R., 217
Pipho, C., 76, 99
Pirozzolo, F.J., 257, 274, 275
Pisoni, D., 15
Platt, J.S., 30, 43
Point/Counterpoint, 76, 99
Polin, R.M., 96, 262, 276
Popham, W.J., 74, 99
Potts, G., 15
Poy, C.A., 30, 42
Pressley, M., 182, 194, 196, 249, 251, 252, 276
Price, G.E., 41
Probst, A.M., 30, 43
Provis, M., 31, 36, 38
Purcell, L., 139, 143
Pursel, J.E., 203, 217
Purves, A., 68
Putnam, J., 61, 68, 171, 173, 192, 194

Rackliffe, G., 194
Raim, J., 32, 43
Raines, P.A., 80, 97
Rajaratnam, N., 96
Rankin, S.C., 99
Raphael, T.E., 161, 166, 197, 203, 218, 267, 274
Rapin, I., 257, 274
Rashotte, C.A., 7, 16
Rasinski, T., 18, 20, 21, 30, 43, 137, 144
Ratekin, N., 201, 218
Read, C., 54, 69
Readence, J.E., 156, 191, 197
Reid, J., 20, 43
Reinking, D., 137, 144
Reis, R., 160, 195
Reitsma, P., 267, 274
Resnick, D.P., 76, 99
Resnick, L.B., 13, 16, 76, 95, 96, 99, 106, 112, 118, 123, 143, 144, 155, 197, 252, 271
Revelle, G.L., 159, 197
Reyes, M. de la Luz, 91, 99, 305, 312

Reynolds, C.R., 271
Rice, J., 56-57, 69
Rich, D., 30, 34, 43
Rich, S., 48, 69
Richardson-Koehler, Z.V., 191
Richert, A.E., 92, 99, 176, 199
Rigg, P., 288, 292, 293, 297, 298, 299, 304, 309, 312
Roberson, K., 334
Roberts, K., 25, 43
Robinson, F.P., 228, 235, 318, 330, 334
Robinson, H.M., 254, 274
Roe, B.D., 204, 218
Roeber, E.D., 74, 85, 99, 100
Roehler, L.R., 61, 68, 171, 176, 182, 183, 184, 185, 194, 196, 198, 274
Roen, D.H., 311
Rogers, T., 158, 198
Rogoff, B., 217
Roop, K., 34, 45
Rosenblatt, C.M., 149, 197
Rosenshine, B., 172, 183, 197, 267, 268, 274, 275
Roser, N.L., 35, 43
Roswell, F.G., 264, 265, 272, 273, 274
Roth, K.J., 156, 198
Rothman, R., 77, 85, 92, 99
Rowley, G., 89, 99
Ruddell, R.B., 8, 9, 16, 73, 99, 216, 219, 275
Rudel, R.G., 258, 272, 275
Rumelhart, D.E., 9, 16
Russell, D., 147, 198
Russo, R.P., 312
Rutland, A.D., 302, 310
Ryan, E.B., 258, 276

Sadow, M., 210, 216
Salmon-Cox, L., 73, 99
Salzer, R., 22, 42
Samuels, S.J., 9, 16, 26, 36, 43, 122, 128, 132, 136, 138, 139, 143, 144, 222, 235, 249, 252, 259, 271, 273, 275
Sanders, N.M., 71, 98
Sandifer, P.D., 99
Sansone, R.M., 21, 43

Santa, C., 206, 207f, 218
Sartain, H.W., 26, 41, 43
Satz, P., 257, 275
Savignon, S.J., 278, 294, 312
Scanlon, D.M., 258, 276
Schieffelin, B.B., 18, 22, 43, 280, 312
Schofield, W.N., 28, 45
Schreiber, P.A., 138, 144
Schreiner, R.L., 147, 198, 267, 275
Schwartz, S.H., 319, 334
Scott, J.A., 9, 60, 68, 122, 143
Scribner, S., 69, 198, 276
Seashore, C., 69
Segal, J.W., 217
Seginer, R., 24, 43
Seifert, M., 122
Shankweiler, D., 259, 273, 321, 334
Shannon, P., 50, 60, 67n, 68, 69, 97
Shavelson, R.J., 89, 99
Shepard, L., 71, 74, 99
Shepard, L.A., 262, 272, 275
Shook, S.E., 19, 43
Shuck, J., 30, 43
Shulman, L., 174, 178, 195, 198
Shulman, L.S., 81, 99, 176, 199
Silbert, J., 126, 143
Silvern, L.R., 24, 35, 43
Silvern, S.B., 24, 35, 43
Simmons, J., 78, 91, 99
Simmons, K., 22, 28, 30, 42
Simonsen, S., 204, 206, 207, 208f, 218
Simpson, M., 218
Singer, H., 8, 9, 16, 167, 198, 202, 203, 204, 206, 207, 208f, 216, 218, 219, 231, 234, 235, 275
Sipay, E.R., 259, 263, 273
Sivan, E., 181, 182, 192, 194, 198
Sizer, T., 75, 90, 99
Slater, W.H., 225, 227, 235
Slaughter, D.T., 28, 43
Slavin, R.E., 261, 267, 275
Sloat, C., 308
Smiley, S.S., 164, 193

Smith, C.B., 18, 20, 34, 35, 44
Smith, D.A.F., 217
Smith, E.L., 156, 191, 194
Smith, F., 21, 42, 44, 63, 68, 69, 312
Smith, F.R., 201, 218
Smith, H., 31, 44
Smith, J.K., 71, 98
Smith, K., 302, 309
Smith, L.A., 262, 275
Smith, L.C., 156, 191
Smith, M.A., 81, 98
Smith, N.B., 146, 147, 198
Smith, S.D., 257, 274
Smith, T., 160, 195, 241, 251
Smith, W.E., 263, 275
Snow, C.E., 21, 22, 23, 44, 260, 272
Sochor, E.E., 148, 198
Souberman, E., 69, 198, 276
Spache, G., 147, 198
Speer, J.R., 195
Speidel, G., 308
Shepard, L.A., 262, 272, 275
Spielberger, C., 334
Spindler, G., 97
Spiro, R.J., 155, 166, 191, 192, 251, 270
Spivey, N.N., 78, 99
Spurlin, J.E., 234
Squire, J.R., 68
Stahl, S., 210, 218
Stahl, S.A., 267, 275
Stallings, J., 267, 275
Stonovich, K.E., 9, 16, 105, 123, 141, 259, 260, 275
Steffenson, M.S., 292, 313
Stein, B.S., 155, 192, 196, 217, 252
Stein, N.L., 143, 193, 197
Sternberg, R.J., 274
Stetz, F.P., 263, 275
Stevens, R., 172, 197, 267, 275
Stevenson, J.A., 263, 270
Stewart, R.A., 201, 218
Stewner-Manzanares, G., 312
Sticht, T.G., 317, 325, 326, 327, 328, 333, 334
Stiggins, R.J., 73, 75, 80, 99, 100

Stoodt, B.D., 204, 218
Strauss, W., 296, 313
Straw, S.B., 267, 275
Street, B.V., 315, 334
Strickland, D.S., 20, 35, 44, 69
Sukes, R.N., 193
Sulzby, E., 23, 44
Summers, E.G., 255, 275
Sussman, M.B., 39
Sutton, C., 295, 313
Sutton, W., 18, 44
Swain, M., 305, 309
Swerts, A., 203, 217
Swing, S.R., 250, 252
Sykes, G., 195

Taft, M.L., 206, 219
Taylor, B.M., 165, 198, 222, 223, 224, 235
Taylor, B.P., 309
Taylor, D., 18, 19, 20, 22, 23, 24, 30, 36, 44
Taylor, K.K., 222, 223, 235
Teale, W.H., 18, 19, 20, 21, 22, 23, 24, 44
Teberosky, A., 51, 63, 68
Temple, C.A., 19, 44
Terry, P., 132, 144
Terwogt, M.M., 195
Teska, J.A., 28, 41
Tharp, R.G., 292, 308, 313
Thomas, A., 77, 94
Thomas, K.F., 21, 23, 44
Tierney, R.J., 20, 44, 81, 95, 162, 167, 198
Tizard, B., 26, 45
Tizard, J., 24, 28, 41, 45
Topping, K., 26, 36, 39, 41, 44, 45
Torgesen, J., 258, 275
Torgesen, J.K., 7, 16
Tough, J., 278, 281, 285, 313
Townsend, M., 193
Trabasso, T., 143, 193, 197
Trites, R.L., 272
Trueba, H.T., 308, 311, 312
Turbill, J., 92, 95
Twyford, C.W., 310, 312
Tyler, S.J., 122

Ulsh, F., 30, 43
Unger, D.G., 39

Upton, A., 319, 331, 334
Urquhart, A.H., 218, 308

Vacca, J.L., 204, 219
Vacca, R.T., 204, 219
Valencia, S., 74, 77, 84, 87, 100, 263, 275
van Dijk, T.A., 164, 195, 222, 235
Van Roekel, J., 96
Vavrus, L.G., 194
Vellutino, F.R., 258, 259, 275, 276
Venezky, R.L., 11-12, 16, 90, 95
Ventriglia, L., 278, 282, 284, 290, 313
Vinsonhaler, J.F., 96, 262, 263, 276
Visser, T., 195
Vojir, C.P., 262, 275
von Behren, B., 31, 39
Vosniadou, S., 158, 198
Vukelich, C., 29, 45
Vye, N.J., 155, 192, 217
Vygotsky, L.S., 19, 45, 50, 69, 181, 185, 198, 268, 276

Wabigoani, W., 34, 45
Wagner, B., 21, 42
Wagner, C.C., 262, 276
Wagner, D.A., 39
Wagoner, S.A., 157, 160, 195, 199, 241, 243, 251, 252
Wahl, A., 22, 35, 45
Walberg, H.J., 26, 37, 45
Wall, A.E., 123
Wallace, C., 279, 282, 306, 313
Waller, T.G., 13, 16, 122, 238, 251
Walls, L., 30, 44
Walters, K., 34, 45, 306, 313
Wang, W.S., 313
Warren, S., 176, 197
Washburne, C., 260, 274
Waters, G., 257, 272
Waxman, H.C., 293, 312
Weaver, P.A., 13, 16, 95, 123, 143, 144, 252, 271
Webb, N.M., 89, 99

Weber, E.M., 100
Weinshank, A.B., 262, 276
Weinstein, G., 305, 313
Weintraub, S., 255, 276
Weiss, P.B., 80, 97
Weitzman, R., 334
Wellman, H.M., 159, 197
Wells, G., 278, 313
Wells, R., 25, 45
Wertsch, J., 217
Wesselman, R., 194
White, K., 25, 45
Wiggins, G., 75, 100
Wilde, S., 54, 60, 64, 68
Wilkinson, I.A.G., 15, 60, 68, 122, 143
Williams, G., 147, 199
Williams, J.P., 112, 122, 162, 199
Williams, P.L., 99
Willows, D.M., 258, 276
Wilson, S.M., 176, 199
Winne, P.H., 174, 176, 199
Winograd, P.N., 159, 161, 162, 163, 199, 222, 223, 235, 246, 251, 252
Wittenberg, S., 34, 45
Wittrock, M.C., 192, 198, 223, 235, 275
Wixson, K.K., 74, 85, 100, 148, 182, 195, 196, 246, 252
Wolf, D.P., 76, 100
Wolf, K., 81, 100
Wolf, M., 258, 276
Wolf, W., 147, 199
Wolfendale, S., 26, 36, 39, 41, 44, 45
Wong-Fillmore, L., 278, 282, 283, 285, 313
Wonnacott, C.A., 161, 166, 197
Woodward, V.A., 18, 19, 22, 41

Yopp, H.K., 203, 219
Ysseldyke, J.E., 268, 276
Yussen, S.R., 241, 252

Zetusky, W., 257, 274
Ziemba, J., 34, 45
Zubrick, A., 23, 45
Zurn, M.R., 300, 313
Zutell, J., 97

Subject Index

Note: "Mc" is alphabetized as "Mac." An "f" following a page number indicates that the reference may be found in a figure; a "t," that it may be found in a table.

ACADEMIC AMERICAN ENCYCLOPEDIA: 203
ACTION RESEARCH: 5-6, 7, 15; advantages of, 5
ACTIVITIES: parent/child, 35
ACTIVITY PACKETS: 31
ACTIVITY SHEETS: 30; parent, 33
ADAPTIVE ACTIONS: 176
ADD PROGRAM. *See* Auditory Discrimination in Depth (ADD) program
ADMINISTRATORS: as reading instruction authorities, 79; standardized tests favored by, 84. *See also* School boards; School districts
ADULTS: reading ability of U.S., 325-326; teaching reading-disabled, 314-334
ADVISORS: parents as school, 27
AFFIXES: 136
AFRICAN-AMERICANS. *See* Blacks
ALLARD, HARRY: 23
ALMANACS: 203
ALPHABET: 321, 322, 325. *See also* Letters
ALTERNATIVE REPRESENTATIONS: 176
ANALOGIES: use of, 185, 190
ARGUMENT (type of noun): 206
ARMY, U.S.: reading programs for, 327-328, 333
ARTIFICIAL INTELLIGENCE: 58
ARTS: and portfolio contents, 75-76; whole language and, 65
ATLASES: 203
ATTENTION, SELECTIVE: 130-133; automaticity theory and, 129-130
ATWELL, NANCIE: 92
AUDIENCE, SENSE OF: 65
AUDIO RECORDINGS: as text alternative, 201
AUDITORY DISCRIMINATION IN DEPTH (ADD) PROGRAM: 321-322
AUSTRALIA: learning techniques in, 30; whole language theory in, 54, 67

BASAL READERS: 57, 65, 126, 168; dominance of, 60-62, 116, 146, 171; inadequacies of, 73; inference stressed in, 165; KEEP and, 292; LEP students and, 290; oral reading emphasized in, 238-239; phonics-related revision of, 119; for reading disabled, 270; school investment in, 62; skills orientation of, 146-148; teacher misuse of, 61
BECOMING A NATION OF READERS (Commission on Reading): 9, 112, 113, 114, 115, 117, 125
BEGINNING LITERACY AND YOUR CHILD (Silvern & Silvern): 35
BIAS: subjective test evaluation and, 87
BIBLIOGRAPHIES: of children's books, 32
BILINGUAL EDUCATION: 278; tests used in, 303. *See also* ESL (English as a second language) students; Limited English proficiency (LEP) students

BLACKS: and basal readers, 90; speech patterns of, 90; writing problems of, 91
BLENDING: 127, 258; phonemic, 267; phonics and, 117-118, 120
BLOCK DIAGRAMS: for structural analysis, 319
BLOOM'S TAXONOMY: 214
BOLDFACE: 320
BOOK BANKS: 33
BOOK CHAPTERS: journal publication vs., 13-14
BOOK KITS: 30
BOOK LANGUAGE: 20
BOOKLISTS: 78, 82; teacher-provided, 30
BOOK REVIEWS: student, 82
BOOKS: Big, 296; class, 297; early reading ability and, 18-19; predictable, 54-55, 66, 295; taped, 296, 307f
BRAIN: reading and, 254, 256
BRAINSTORMING: semantic webs and, 297; thematic approach and, 301
BREAKS (main clauses): 205
BRIDGING: 296-297
BRITAIN. *See* Great Britain
BUMPER STICKERS: reading education–related, 32

CALIFORNIA: language arts assessment in, 78; literacy assessment in, 72; writing assessment in, 85. *See also* San Diego
CAMBODIAN (lang.): 284
CANADA: English as "native" language in French section of, 304; whole language in, 55. *See also* Manitoba; Nova Scotia
CANTONESE (lang.): 280; programs in English and, 33-34
CAPER. *See* Children and Parents Enjoying Reading
CAPITALIZATION: beginning writers and, 19
CAT IN THE HAT, THE (Seuss): 119
CAUSE AND EFFECT: 168, 221, 230
CERTIFICATION, TEACHER: 81
CHALKBOARDS: home, 19
CHALL, JEANNE: 112, 125, 254, 256, 269
CHANTS: as LEP reader resource, 295
CHARTS: 302. *See also* Flow charts
CHART STORIES: language experience approach and, 298
CHECKLISTS: for literacy assessment, 304
CHICAGO, UNIVERSITY OF: 57
CHILDREN: learning-delayed, 30. *See also* Students
CHILDREN AND PARENTS ENJOYING READING (CAPER): 31
CHINESE (lang.): 111, 280, 284. *See also* Cantonese; Mandarin
CHUNKING, SEMANTIC: 319, 320
CITY COLLEGE OF NEW YORK: 31-32

CLASSROOM(S): LEP, 280 (see also Teachers: of LEP students); management of, 173, 285; parents in, 27, 29 (see also Parent resource rooms); skill-based, 48; whole language, 52-53, 54, 62, 64-67. See also School; Teachers

CLAUSES: LEP student problems with, 288

CLINICS: parent reading, 31

CLOZE PROCEDURE: 303, 304

CODE(S): 103-109, 121, 321; defined, 103. See also Decoding

COGNITION: knowledge, reading, and, 323-326

COGNITIVE MEDIATIONAL PARADIGM: 174-175

COHESION ANALYSIS: schema theory and, 63

COHESIVE TIES: 205

COLLABORATION: among LEP students and peers, 285

COLOR: instructional use of, 320

COMMENTARY: parental, 29

COMMENT BOOKLETS: 31

COMMISSION ON READING: 9, 10, 112. See also Becoming a Nation of Readers

COMMUNICATION: essence of, 278; failure of, 279; knowledge and, 323, 325. See also Language; Writing

COMPARE/CONTRAST: 221

COMPOSITIONS: 81, 304; assessment of, 78-79

COMPREHENSIBLE INPUT: 282, 306; output and, 290

COMPREHENSION CURRICULUM: 148, 154, 162, 163, 168-169, 170-172, 187; teaching of, 171-191

COMPREHENSION, READING: 129, 145-199, 291-294; adjustment of, 159-162; automaticity and, 137; of degrees of text importance, 162-165; monitoring of, 157-159, 243-245, 246, 249, 267; reading instruction and, 201; of words (see Word recognition)

COMPUTERS: as LEP student resource, 300

CONFERENCES: proceedings of research-related, 14; student-teacher, 300

CONFORMITY: whole language vs., 49. See also Convention

CONJUNCTIONS: 205

CONNECTICUT: literacy assessment in, 72. See also New Haven

CONSONANTS: 113; explicit phonics and, 117

CONTENT, TEXT: comprehension of, 307f, 325; ESL students and, 302; in reading programs, 200-219

CONVENTION: learning conditioned by, 64-65. See also Conformity

COOK COUNTY (ILL.) NORMAL SCHOOL: 57

COOKING: as beginning reader resource, 35

CREATING READERS AND WRITERS (Glazer): 35

CRITICAL LITERACY: assessment of, 83

CRITICISM: student, 302; whole language and literary, 58

CUES: 185, 190; ESL students and language, 284; inadvertent, 240-241; prosodic, 138; reading, 107; in story reading, 295; to unfamiliar vocabulary, 290

CURRICULUM(-A): comprehension (see Comprehension curriculum); skills-oriented, 146-148, 168; whole language approach to, 58-59

DEARBORN, WALTER: 111

DEBATE: student, 75

DECODING: 6, 10, 101-123, 239, 288, 315, 321, 323, 325; automatic, 124-144; comprehension and, 130-133; defined, 127, 128; difficulty of, 132; by ESL students, 294, 307f; by LEP students, 286-287, 288, 289, 298; mnemonics and, 322; reading difficulty and, 105; in remedial reading, 269. See also Code(s); Matthew effect; Word attack; Word recognition

DEWEY, JOHN: 49, 57, 62; whole language and, 58

DIAGRAMS: 327; word (see Webbing, Semantic). See also Block diagrams

DIALECT: black, 90

DIALOGUES: student-teacher, 180

DICTIONARIES: as vocabulary resource, 210

DIFFERENCES: whole language approach to human, 49

DIGITS: memory and, 258

DIGRAPHS: 136

DISCOURSE ANALYSIS: 58, 63

DISCOURSE COMPETENCE: 279, 282, 294, 303

DISCRIMINABILITY: 88

DOT-TO-DOT DRAWINGS: 175

DOWD, ELWOOD P.: 2, 3

DYNAMIC ASSESSMENT: 80

DYSLEXIA: 266

ECHO READING: 296

EDITING: with LEP students, 299

EDUCATION FOR ALL HANDICAPPED CHILDREN ACT: 254

EMOTIONAL MALADJUSTMENT: reading disability and, 254

ENCYCLOPEDIA BRITANNICA: 203, 204

ENCYCLOPEDIAS: 203

ENGLAND. See Great Britain

ENGLISH (lang.): limited proficiency in (see limited English proficiency [LEP] students); mechanics of, 288; oral, 281; as a second language (see ESL [English as a second language] students); singularity of, 91; and Spanish compared, 91; translations from, 302

ERIC: 14

ERROR DETECTION: 243-244

ESL (ENGLISH AS A SECOND LANGUAGE) STUDENTS: 277-313; challenge to, 284; university-level, 293. See also Limited English proficient (LEP) students

ETHNOGRAPHY: and whole language research, 63

ETR. See Experience-Text Relationship

EXHIBITION CONCEPT: 90

EXPERIENCE(S): metacognitive, 242-245; teacher reliance on, 3-4, 6, 7

EXPERIENCE-TEXT RELATIONSHIP (ETR): 296-297
EXPERIMENTS, SCIENCE: as text alternative, 201
EXPERTS: teacher reliance on, 4-5, 6, 7
EYE MOVEMENT: reading facility and, 137-138

FACT: opinion vs., 302
FEEDBACK: parental, 36
FERNALD APPROACH: 266
FIELD TRIPS: as text alternative, 201
FIX-UP STRATEGY. *See* Comprehension, reading: adjustment of
FLESCH, RUDOLPH: 111, 125
FLOW CHARTS: 319, 327; knowledge-base-related, 331
FLUENCY, READING: 124-144; defined, 126-127
FOCUS-GROUP DISCUSSIONS: 36
FOX HILL READING PROJECT: 31
FOX IN SOCKS (Seuss): 119
FRENCH (lang.): 304
FRUSTRATION LEVEL: of reading, 268
FRY READABILITY GRAPH: 203
FUNDAMENTALISM, EDUCATIONAL: vs. rationality, 60
FUND-RAISERS: parent/school, 35-36

GAMES, EDUCATIONAL: 28, 29, 30, 31
GEISEL, THEODOR SEUSS. *See* Seuss, Dr.
GENERALIZABILITY THEORY: 89
GEORGIA: promotion guidelines mandated in, 61
GLENCOE/McGRAW-HILL: 328
GLOSSARIES: 210
GOLDEN NOTEBOOK, THE (Lessing): 129
GRAMMAR: 325; beginning writers and, 19; invention and, 64; whole language approach to, 51. *See also* Discourse analysis
GRAMMATICAL COMPETENCE: 279, 303
GRAPHEMES: 287
GRAPHICS: ESL students and, 302; as reading aid, 163; and speech contrasted, 314. *See also* Block diagrams; Charts; Diagrams; Dot-to-dot drawings; Graphs; Illustrations; Picture books; Pictures; Schematics; Tree structures
GRAPHICS TECHNOLOGY: 314, 315, 316-333
GRAPHS: 302, 318
GRAY, WILLIAM S.: 110, 125
GREAT BRITAIN: early readers in, 108; LEP students in, 285-286; reading techniques in, 28-29, 31; science instruction in, 77; student assessment in, 77; whole language in, 55
GROCERY SHOPPING: reading abilities enhanced while, 35
GUIDES: prereading, 206, 207f; teachers' (*see* Teachers' manuals)

HAITIAN (lang.): 284
HANDWRITING: whole language approach to, 51
HARINGEY READING PROJECT: 28
HARVEY (film): 2

HAWAIIANS: 292, 296
HEADINGS: instructional use of text, 223, 228, 229
HEALTH: reading disability and, 254
HEBREW (lang.): 129
HELPING YOUR CHILD BECOME A READER (Roser): 35
HIGHLIGHTING: 320
HISPANICS: 290; reading abilities of, 25, 32; writing problems of, 91. *See also* ESL (English as a second language) students; Mexican-Americans
HMONG (lang.): 305
HOLISM: LEP student and classroom, 285
HOME: reading begun in, 17-45. *See also* Scaffolding
HOME-SCHOOL PROGRAMS: district-initiated, 32-34; parents and, 26-34
HOMEWORK RESOURCE ACTIVITIES: 33
HOP ON POP (Seuss): 119
HOW CAN I PREPARE MY YOUNG CHILD FOR READING? (Grinnell): 35
HUEY, E.: 125
HUMANISM: technoscience and, 56-57, 59

IBM: writing programs of, 300
IDENTIFICATION, WORD. *See* Word recognition
ILLINOIS: reading assessment in, 85; testing programs of, 74, 77
ILLINOIS, UNIVERSITY OF: Center for the Study of Reading at, 9
ILLITERACY, ADULT: 314-334
ILLUSTRATIONS: 302
INCONSISTENCIES: recognizing written, 157-158
INDEPENDENT READING: 268
INDEXES: 319
INDIVIDUAL READING INVENTORIES: 289
INFERENCE(S): drawing of, 151t, 152t, 154, 155, 161, 165-166, 179, 203, 230, 247, 267; ESL students and, 284; "fix-up," 244; of teacher's goals, 177
INFORMAL READING INVENTORIES: 79-80
INFORMATION: reader synthesis of, 163-165; teacher-provided, 183
INFORMATION PROCESSING SKILLS TEXTS: 330, 331, 333
INSTRUCTIONAL LEVEL: of reading, 268
INTEGRATED READING PERFORMANCE RECORD: 76
INTERNATIONAL READING ASSOCIATION: as beginning-reader resource, 35
INTERVENTION ASSESSMENT: 264
INTERVIEWS, STUDENT: 86
IN THE MIDDLE: WRITING, READING, AND LEARNING WITH ADOLESCENTS (Atwell): 92
IOWA READING COMPREHENSION SUBTEST: 105
IOWA TEST OF BASIC SKILLS: 210
IRRELEVANCIES: rejection of, 164
ITALIAN (lang.): 284
ITALICS: 320

JAPANESE (lang.): 284

JOB TRAINING PARTNERSHIP ACT (JTPA): 326
JOURNAL OF EDUCATIONAL RESEARCH: 13
JOURNAL OF READING BEHAVIOR: 13
JOURNALS: ESL student, 307f; LEP student, 289; publication in, 13-14; student, 299
JTPA. *See* Job Training Partnership Act
JUNEAU, ALASKA: district case studies in, 78

KAMEHAMEHA EARLY EDUCATION PROJECT (KEEP): 292
KANA (lang.): 111
KANJI (lang.): 111
KEEP. *See* Kamehameha Early Education Project
KEY CONTENT CARDS: 298
KINDERGARTNERS: LEP, 282-283, 284, 300; reading by, 106; testing of in Georgia, 61
KNOWLEDGE: cognition, reading, and, 323-326; communication and, 323, 325; domain-specific, 163; metacognitive, 237-242, 306, 325; memory and, 324, 324f, 325, 328; metalinguistic, 306; prior (*see* Prior knowledge); representation of, 324; types of, 325
KNOWLEDGE BASES: 328-333

LAB. *See* Language Assessment Battery
LANGUAGE(S): cultural variations among, 280-281; interactive, 304; internalization of, 50; invention of, 64; and literacy learning, 278-279; meaning and, 278-279; reasons for, 50; sociolinguistic aspects of, 279; thinking and, 51. *See also* Print; Sound(s); Vocabulary; Whole language; Words
LANGUAGE ARTS: assessed in California, 78; in Great Britain, 77; whole language and, 65
LANGUAGE ASSESSMENT BATTERY (LAB): 303
LANGUAGE ASSESSMENT SCALE (LAS): 303
LANGUAGE EXPERIENCE APPROACH (LEA): 58, 297-299, 306; ESL students and, 307f
LAO (lang.): 305
LAS. *See* Language Assessment Scale
LD. *See* Learning disability
LEA. *See* Language experience approach
LEARNING: assessment of, 80; "catch-up," 106; language as central to, 50-51
LEARNING BY DOING: 52
LEARNING DISABILITY (LD): 254, 261-262, 266; research on, 255-256
LEARNING TO READ: THE GREAT DEBATE (Chall): 112, 125
LECTURES: as text alternative, 201
LEP STUDENTS. *See* Limited English proficient students
LESSING, DORIS: 129
LESSON PLANS: 281
LETTERS (alphabetic characters): discrimination among, 12; formation of, 19; memory and, 258; sounds and, 103-104, 106, 108-109, 114-118, 120-121, 127, 128, 287-288, 321

(*see also* Decoding; Language(s); Phonemes; Phonics; Pronunciation; Words); substitution of, 118; words and, 106, 107-108, 115-119, 120-121, 128, 132. *See also* Alphabet; Consonants; Digraphs; Words
LETTERS (missives): children's contributions to parents, 22; writing of, 65
LETTER STRINGS: 105
LIBRARY: as beginning reader resource, 29, 34, 35; family visits to, 27; use of, 147. *See also* School library
LIMITED ENGLISH PROFICIENT (LEP) STUDENTS: 279-283, 284-291, 293-295, 298-299, 300, 305, 307-308; adult, 300; college-level, 288; and computers, 300; and content comprehension, 302; LEA and, 298-299; learner strategies of, 284-285; and letter/sound correspondences, 287-288; strategies of, 284, 286, 288; and vocabulary comprehension, 293; and whole language theory, 301. *See also* ESL (English as a second language) students
LINGUISTIC COMPETENCE: 294
LINGUISTICS: 279
LINGUISTIC STRATEGY: with LEP students, 289
LISTING: 221
LITERACY: adult, 314-334; assessment of, 70-100, 303-304; critical (*see* Critical literacy); emergent, 18; functional, 280; graphics technology and, 317-323; at home, 22; joys of, 171; LEP students and, 281; in non-English native language, 304-306
"LITERACY CLUB": 63
LITERATURE: basalization of, 66
LITERATURE LOGS: 76, 81, 85
LOOK-BACK STRATEGY: 160, 242
LOOK-SAY APPROACH: 104

McCLOSKEY, R.: 102
MAIL: children and family, 22
MAILING LISTS: of research organizations, 14
MAINE: reading assessment in, 85; reading tests in, 77
MAIN IDEAS: isolation of, 162, 168, 169, 175, 223, 247, 267
MAKE WAY FOR DUCKLINGS (McCloskey): 102, 103, 120
MANDARIN (lang.): 280
MANITOBA: whole language in, 55
MANN, HORACE: 125
MAPS: 302; mind, 319; as reading comprehension resource, 223, 225; semantic, 76, 82, 290, 318; story, 230-231, 302; word (*see* Webbing, semantic)
MARSHALL, JAMES: 23
MARYLAND: metacognitive knowledge assessed in, 24
MASSACHUSETTS: reading tests in, 77
MATHEMATICS: problem-centered approach to, 173; spatiality and, 318; story problems in,

298; as taught in Great Britain, 77; whole language and, 65
MATRICES: 327; classification and, 319; vocabulary, 212, 213f
MATTHEW EFFECT: 105
MEANING: 202; blockages to, 180-181; decoding and, 128-129; decontextualization of, 306; language and, 278-279; reading and, 149, 322-323; words and, 6, 132, 260, 264, 267, 268; writing and, 322-323. *See also* Comprehension, reading
MEMORIZATION: 204; deemphasized, 172; test-related, 74
MEMORY: failure of, 240; knowledge and, 324, 324f, 325, 328; vocabulary comprehension and, 290; whole-word strategy and, 289
MEMORY ICONS: 329
MENTALLY HANDICAPPED CHILDREN: repeated reading and, 139-141
METACOGNITION: 157, 158, 160, 176-177, 236-242; defined, 237. *See also* Knowledge: metacognitive
METAPHORS: 185, 190
MEXICAN-AMERICANS: 289-290
MEXICO CITY: reading techniques in, 51
MICHIGAN: reading assessment in, 85; testing programs in, 74, 77
MICHIGAN READING ASSOCIATION: 85
MICHIGAN STATE UNIVERSITY: 262; Institute for Research on Teaching at, 9
MINNESOTA, UNIVERSITY OF: 136
MINORITIES: and performance tests, 90; progress of, 87; reading prowess among, 25; and summarization, 247. *See also* Blacks; ESL (English as a second language) students; Hawaiians; Hispanics; Native Americans; Mexican-Americans
MISCONCEPTION: 156
MISCUE ANALYSIS: 51, 58, 86
MISS NELSON IS MISSING (Allard/Marshall): 23
MNEMONICS: 321, 322
MODELING, TEACHER: 183-184, 299
MULTIPLE CHOICE QUESTIONS: 303

NAEP. *See* National Assessment of Educational Progress
NAEYC. *See* National Association for the Education of Young Children
NARRATIVE: invention and, 64
NATIONAL ASSOCIATION FOR THE EDUCATION OF YOUNG CHILDREN (NAEYC): 61
NATIONAL ASSESSMENT OF EDUCATIONAL PROGRESS (NAEP): 72, 331, 333; gleanings of, 86; and 1992 reading test, 75; and testing, 77; U.S. government and, 76; and writing of minorities, 91
NATIONAL COUNCIL OF TEACHERS OF ENGLISH (NCTE): 92
NATIONAL INSTITUTE OF EDUCATION: 112
NATIONAL WRITING PROJECT: 81

NATIVE AMERICANS: writing of, 64
NAVY, U.S.: education program for, 332f-333
NCTE. *See* National Council of Teachers of English
NEATNESS: 175
NEW HAMPSHIRE: literacy assessment in, 78-79
NEW HAVEN, CONN.: reading program in, 33
NEWSLETTERS: class, 35; school, 35; teacher-to-parent, 30, 33
NEWSPAPERS: class, 297; reading-related articles in local, 33
NEW ZEALAND: beginning reader patterns in, 261; early readers in, 106; learning techniques in, 30; whole language in, 55, 67
NORTHWEST REGIONAL EDUCATIONAL LABORATORY (NWREL): 78
NOTETAKING: 302
NOVA SCOTIA: whole language in, 55
NURSERY RHYMES: as beginning reader resource, 108, 119
NWREL. *See* Northwest Regional Educational Laboratory

OPEN EDUCATION: 58
OPEN-ENDED PORTFOLIO COMPONENTS: 84, 85
ORAL LANGUAGE: 323, 325; ESL students and, 307f; graphic representation of, 321-322
ORAL READING: 80, 135, 142, 147, 238-239, 262; fluency in, 267; by reading disabled, 264; and silent reading contrasted, 135. *See also* Reading aloud
ORANGE COUNTY, FLA.: district case studies in, 78
ORTHOGRAPHY: 54
ORTON-GILLINGHAM APPROACH: 266
OUTLINES, GRAPHIC: 318
OUTLINING: 302

PACT PROJECT. *See* Parents, Children, and Teachers Project
PALS. *See* Principles of Adult Literacy System
PARAPHRASING: 302
PARENT RESOURCE ROOMS: 33
PARENTS: bilingual, 279; as classroom resource, 27, 31, 33; expectations of, 24-25; as "first teachers," 37; LEP, 280; of LEP students, 306; whole language and, 6
PARENTS ASSISTANCE PROGRAM: 32
PARENTS, CHILDREN, AND TEACHERS (PACT) PROJECT: 29
PARENTS ENCOURAGE PUPILS (PEP): 30
PARKER, FRANCIS: 57
PEERS: ESL students and, 307f; LEP students and, 285, 286; reading students and, 191
PENMANSHIP. *See* Handwriting
PEP. *See* Parents Encourage Pupils
PERFORMANCE: assessment of reading, 75, 76, 84, 87-91
PHONEMES: 112; analysis of, 267; graphemes and, 287; identification of, 106; segmentation of, 109. *See also* Blending: phonemic

PHONEMIC AWARENESS: 108-109, 120, 121; explicit phonics and, 113; implicit phonics and, 113

PHONICS: 60, 101, 104-105, 111-121, 125, 146, 315, 321, 322; drill-centered, 110; explicit, 112, 113-114, 117, 121; goal of, 105; implicit, 112-113, 114, 116-117; LEP students and, 288, 290; nature of, 110; and sight word method contrasted, 105; story reading and, 114-116, 119-120. *See also* Letters; Phonemes; Sound(s)

PHONOGRAMS: 105, 113; consonants and, 118

PHONOLOGICAL AWARENESS: 267

PHRASES: decoding of, 288

PIAGET, JEAN: 46, 58, 63

PICTURE BOOKS: for LEP readers, 291

PICTURES: 323

PITTSBURGH, PENN.: district case studies in, 78

PLANNING, TEACHER: 178-181

PLR. *See* Primary Language Record

POETRY: reading-related use of, 30, 295

POLITICS: education and, 60, 61. *See also* Administrators

PORTFOLIOS: 72; student (*see* Student portfolios); teacher, 92

PORTUGUESE (lang.): 284

POSTTESTS: 213

PREDICTABILITY: as beginning reader assist, 54-55. *See also* Books: predictable

PREP. *See* Preparing Refugees for Elementary Programs

PREPARING REFUGEES FOR ELEMENTARY PROGRAMS (PREP): 299

PREPRIMERS: 102

PRESCHOOLERS: "accidental" teaching of, 36-37; language learning of, 281; print recognized by, 51; reading by, 106. *See also* Kindergartners

PRESCHOOL READINESS OUTREACH PROGRAM (PROP): 29

PREVIEWING: 302

PRIMARY LANGUAGE RECORD (PLR): 77

PRINCIPLES OF ADULT LITERACY SYSTEM (PALS): 300

PRINT: awareness of, 58; comprehending, 106-109, 121; conceptualization of, 303, 307f; functional uses of, 307f; graphics technology and, 317; recognition of, 103; sound to, 288; talk and, 170. *See also* Letters; Sentences; Words

PRIOR KNOWLEDGE: 166, 204, 206-210; of ESL readers, 292; knowledge bases and, 330; of LEP students, 285; reading comprehension and, 154-157; of reading-disabled adults, 316; and reading to learn, 318; and text cues, 176; and text importance, 163. *See also* Misconception

PROBLEM/SOLUTION PATTERNS: 221

PROBLEM SOLVING: whole language and, 65

PROCESS-FOLIOS: 76

PROCESS-PRODUCT RESEARCH: 172-173

PROCESS WRITING: 58

PROFILE INFORMATION: 88

PROGRESSIVE EDUCATION: 58

PROGRESS POINTS: 30

PROMPTING: 185, 204

PRONOUNS: ambiguous, 205; LEP student problems with, 288

PRONUNCIATION: 110, 113; approximate, 117; and LEP students, 282

PROP. *See* Preschool Readiness Outreach Program

PSYCHOLOGY AND PEDAGOGY OF READING, THE (Huey): 125

PSYCHOMETRIC THEORY: 88

PUBLISHERS, TEXTBOOK: and basal readers, 61; misplaced simplification by, 204; and tests, 73, 75; and whole language, 66

PUNCTUATION: beginning writers and, 19; invented, 64

PUNISHMENT: of poor readers, 25

QUALITY TIME: family reading as part of, 22

QUESTIONS: answering, 161; detail, 21; inferential, 21; predictive, 21; and remedial reading, 267; student-generated, 166-168, 170; teacher-generated, 180, 188. *See also* Self-questioning

QUESTIONS PARENTS ASK ABOUT READING: 33

READABILITY: 54

READERS: disabled, 253-276. *See also* Students

READER'S DIGEST: phonics endorsed by, 60

READING: cognition, knowledge, and, 323-326; development of skilled, 189; drawing and, 19; environmental influences on, 10; functional context approach to, 328-333; goal of, 127; at home, 141; indexes of expert, 153-154; individualized, 58; mechanics of, 24; oral (*see* Oral reading); prosodic, 138; psycholinguistic theory of, 54; recreational, 146; remedial, 266-270; repeated (*see* Repeated reading); schema-interactive model of, 202-203; shared (*see* Shared reading); silent (*see* Silent reading); vocational approach to teaching, 326-328; work-type, 146; writing and, 19, 177, 190, 322-323

READING ADVISORY BOARDS: parents on, 33

READING ALOUD: 20-21, 28, 32, 35; at home, 26; by visiting teenagers, 34; value of, 106. *See also* Oral reading

READING CLUB: CCNY-sponsored, 31-32

READING DISABILITY: 253-276; adult, 314-334; causes of, 256-261; contrastive research into, 258-259; diagnosis of, 261-265; teachers central to remediation of, 269. *See also* ESL (English as a second language) students; limited English proficient (LEP) students

"READING FAMILIES OF THE MONTH": 30

READING PROCESSES: 10

READING RECIPES: 33

READING RECOVERY: 80
READING REFORM FOUNDATION: phonics endorsed by, 60
READING RESEARCH QUARTERLY: 13
READING TO DO: 317-318, 327, 330, 333
READING TO LEARN: 317, 318, 327, 330, 333
READ TO SUCCEED: 33
"REAL" WRITING: assessment of, 71
RECALL: cues, 107; students and text, 222
RECIPROCAL TEACHING: 159, 165, 180, 224-225
REDUNDANCIES: identification of, 164
REGULATION STRATEGY. *See* Comprehension, reading: adjustment of
REINFORCEMENT: importance of positive, 36
REPAIR STRATEGY. *See* Comprehension, reading: adjustment of
REPEATED READING: 137-141, 143; in tandem, 139
REPORT WRITING: invention and, 64
REQUIRED PORTFOLIO COMPONENTS: 84, 85
REREADING: importance of parent, 24
RESEARCH, READING: constraints on, 63; funding of, 12; instruction-oriented, 9; pitfalls of, 53; process-oriented, 9; subthemes of, 8-9, 11; teacher use of, 1-2; volume of, 8, 11-12, 14-15
RESOURCE MATERIALS: whole language, 66
RESPONSIVE ELABORATION: 176
RHYMING: 108
ROLE PLAYING: 304; by ESL students, 284; PREP and, 298
RUSSELL AWARD FOR DISTINGUISHED RESEARCH: 92

SAMPLE LESSONS: diagnostic use of, 264
SAN DIEGO, CALIF.: bilingual classrooms in, 304-305
SCAFFOLDING: 23-24, 185, 190
SCHEMA THEORY: 58, 148-153, 174; cohesion analysis, 63; and ESL readers, 291
SCHEMATICS: and structural analysis, 319
SCHOOL: home and, 17-18 (*see also* Home-school programs); parents at (*see* Parents: as classroom resource). *See also* Classroom(s); Teachers
SCHOOL BOARDS: student letters to, 89-90
SCHOOL DISTRICTS: literacy assessment by, 78-79; restrictive thrust of, 80
SCHOOL LIBRARY: parent use of, 35
SCHWA: 113
SCIENCE: reconceptualization of, 58; as taught in Great Britain, 77; whole language and, 65
SCIENTIFIC METHOD: action research and, 5
SEATWORK: 175-176
SELF-EXPLORATION: reading and, 21
SELF-QUESTIONING: student, 231
SEMANTIC CONTINGENCY: 23
SEMIOTIC: language as, 50
SENIOR CITIZENS: as reading tutors, 34
SENTENCES: completion of, 258; decoding of, 288; interconnectedness of, 279; processing of,

267
SEQUENCING: 168
SESAME STREET: 106
SEUSS, DR. (pseud. Geisel, Theodor Seuss): 108, 119
SHARED READING: 296; ESL students and, 307f
SIGHT WORD METHOD: 104, 110-111; and phonics contrasted, 105
SIGHT WORDS: 262; LEA and, 298; recognition of, 104
SILENT READING: 146, 239, 296; and oral reading contrasted, 135. *See also* Uninterrupted Sustained Silent Reading (USSR)
SITUATED LEARNING: 80
SKILLS: and strategies contrasted, 169
SKILL SHEETS: 188
SKIMMING: 302
SOCIAL STUDIES: whole language and, 65
SOCIOLINGUISTIC COMPETENCE: 279, 280, 282, 294, 303
SONGS: as LEP reader resource, 295
SOUND(S): in explicit phonics, 113-114; in implicit phonics, 112-113; isolation of, 113; letters and, 103-104, 106, 108-109, 114-118, 120-121, 127, 128, 287-288, 321 (*see also* Decoding; Language(s); Phonemes; Phonics; Pronunciation; Words); relation of print to, 288; symbols and, 127, 128, 287 (*see also* Letters); words and, 108, 109, 114-118, 120-121, 127, 292 (*see also* Phonics; Pronunciation). *See also* Language(s); Syllables
SPANISH (lang.): 278, 283, 284, 296, 299, 304-305. *See also* ESL (English as a second language) students; Limited English proficient (LEP) students
SPECIAL EDUCATION: 261; reading disability and, 254
SPELLING: beginning writers and, 19; difficulties in English, 287; invented, 19, 54, 60, 64, 109; reading disability and, 264; as road to reading skill, 125; self-learned, 54; whole language approach to, 51
SQ3R: 223, 228, 318, 330; ESL students and, 302
STANDARDIZATION: alternative assessment techniques vs., 93
STANDARDIZED TESTS: 70-75, 76, 80, 84, 87, 89, 94; criterion-related, 303; dominance of, 60, 61, 91; LEP students and, 303; negative aspects of, 71, 73-74, 93; norm-related, 303; vs. performance assessment, 88; for reading disabled, 263-265; teacher judgment vs. results of, 84; "teaching to," 71, 74; and trial lessons contrasted, 265; weaknesses of, 263
STANFORD TEACHER ASSESSMENT PROJECT: Elementary Literacy Study of, 81-82
STATES: literary assessment and, 71-76, 77. *See also* United States; individual states by name
STEWART, JAMES: 2
STORIES: LEP students and, 295; phonics-related

revision of, 119; student, 297

STORY GRAPHS: 82

STRATEGIC COMPETENCE: 279, 282, 303

STRATEGIES: 245-250; cognitive, 284; content learning and, 248-249; defined, 245; for LEP students, 289; metacognitive, 284; socioaffective, 285

STRUCTURAL ANALYSIS: graphics technology and, 319

STRUCTURAL ORGANIZERS: 223, 225-227

STUDENT PORTFOLIOS: 75-76, 78-79, 80-91, 93; adaptability of, 81; bilingual, 91; contents of, 84; district assessment of, 78; in Vermont, 77. *See also* Primary Language Record (PLR); Process-folios

STUDENTS: academically at-risk, 173; ESL (*see* ESL students); LEP (*see* Limited English proficient students); late starters, 106; motivation to read, 181-182; self-regulated, 182

STUDENT TEACHERS: portfolios and, 92

SUITABILITY (assessment criterion): 88

SUMMARIES: 164-165, 302; hierarchical, 223-225; by minority students, 247; structural organizers and, 226

SUMMER: reading practice during, 30

SUPERORDINATION: 164, 222

SUSTAINED SILENT READING. *See* Uninterrupted sustained silent reading (USSR)

SWEDEN: early readers in, 106

SYLLABLES: 109; identification of, 105, 136

SYMBOLS: sounds and, 127, 128, 287. *See also* Letters

TABLES OF CONTENTS: 319; knowledge bases and, 330

TAPE RECORDING: repeated reading and, 139. *See also* Books: taped

TEACHERS: effectiveness of, 172-173; of ESL students, 278, 282, 292, 295, 299, 307f (*See also* Bridging; Webbing, semantic); hierarchical position of, 92; of learning disabled, 266; of LEP students, 281, 282-283, 285-286, 287, 289, 290-291, 293, 295, 306, 308; as mediators, 176, 178, 179, 185; of reading disabled, 265, 267, 268-270 (*see also* Trial lessons); research techniques for, 1; as ultimate assessors, 94; whole language, 49, 50, 51-53, 54-56, 59, 64, 65-67. *See also* Classroom(s); Curriculum (-a); Reciprocal teaching; School; Students; Student teachers; Tests

TEACHERS' MANUALS: 65; for basal readers, 126; as limiting, 57; whole language vs., 58

TEACHING: as ongoing art, 188

TECHNOLOGY: defined, 317

TEENAGERS: as home-visiting readers, 34

TELEVISION: as reader resource, 35, 106; reading while watching, 238

TEST OF ENGLISH AS A FOREIGN LANGUAGE (TOEFL): 303

TESTS: 270; achievement, 173; criterion-referenced, 72, 73; diagnostic, 269-270; marking systems for, 303; multiple choice, 78 (*see also* Standardized tests); norm-referenced, 72, 73; psychometric aspects of, 73; standardized (*see* Standardized tests); student faithfulness to, 202; techniques of, 303, 307f; timed, 303

TEXAS: standardized tests in, 74

TEXTBOOKS: design of, 11; elaborative, 204; for LEP students, 288-289

TEXT STRUCTURE: 220-235

THAI (lang.): 305

THAILAND: English classes in, 305-306

THEMES, INSTRUCTIONAL: 303-306, 307f

THERE'S A WOCKET IN MY POCKET (Seuss): 119

THESAURUSES: 210

THINK-ALOUD STRATEGIES: 302, 304

THORNDIKE'S LAWS OF LEARNING: 57

TIME ORDER: 221

TOEFL. *See* Test of English as a Foreign Language

TONGUE TWISTERS: as reading resource: 119

TOPIC SENTENCES: 164, 318, 325. *See also* Main ideas

TRAINEES, VOCATIONAL: reading needs of, 326-328

TRANSLATIONS: from first language into English, 302

TREE STRUCTURES: 318, 319

TRIAL LESSONS: 264-265, 270

TUTORS: children as, 241-242; parents as, 30, 33

"TV PICKS OF THE WEEK": 30

UNDERLINING: 320

UNINTERRUPTED SUSTAINED SILENT READING (USSR): 183

UNITED KINGDOM. *See* Great Britain

UNITED STATES: educational mandate of, 76; whole language in, 55. *See also* Army, U.S.; Navy, U.S.; States; individual states by name

UNITIZING: 135, 136

USSR. *See* Uninterrupted Sustained Silent Reading

VANCOUVER, B.C.: reading program in, 33-34

VERBAL EFFICIENCY THEORY: 138

VERBAL FACILITY: 241

VERBS: use of in instruction, 214, 215t-216t

VERMONT: reading assessment techniques in, 71-72, 77-78, 85-86

VERTICAL ARRANGEMENT: 147

VIDEOTAPES: as reading resource, 32, 201

VIETNAMESE (lang.): 280

VOCABULARY: 281; comprehension of, 293; context and, 290, 291; development of, 10; ESL students and, 284, 297, 307; hierarchical, 212, 212f; LEP students and, 282, 283, 290-291; PREP and, 299; as reading ability index, 210-212; reading as builder of, 105; sight word, 104; technical, 212; test, 303. *See*

also Words
VYGOTSKY, L.S.: 46, 50, 58, 62, 63

WALES: reading techniques in, 31
WEBBING, SEMANTIC: 297, 301
WHOLE LANGUAGE: 46-69, 125, 138, 146, 170, 300, 301, 315; and LEP students, 289-290; obstacles faced by, 49; opposition to, 66; research and, 52, 66-67
WHY JOHNNY CAN'T READ (Flesch): 111, 125
WISCONSIN: reading programs in, 32-33
WORD ATTACK: 104, 105
WORD LISTS: 30
WORD PLAY: at-home, 108
WORD RECOGNITION: 12, 104, 127, 128, 132, 134f, 135-138, 139-141, 142, 146, 260, 263, 267, 269, 279, 315; LEP students and, 287-290; as verification technique, 294. *See also* Decoding; Unitizing
WORDS: analysis of, 262, 264 (*see also* Word recognition); building of, 118; decoding of (*see* Decoding; Word recognition); looking up unfamiliar, 24; letters and, 106, 107-108, 115-119, 120-121, 128, 132; meanings of, 6, 132, 260, 264, 267, 268; memory and, 258; recognition of (*see* Word recognition); repetition of, 205; segmentation of, 258;

semantic aspects of (*see* Webbing, semantic); "shared," 7; skipping of, 259 (*see also* Skimming); sounds and, 108-109, 114-118, 120-121, 127, 292 (*see also* Phonics; Pronunciation); whole language approach to, 51. *See also* Communication; Language(s); Letters; Literacy; Phonemes; Print; Reading; Sentences; Syllables; Symbols; Vocabulary; Writing
WORKBOOKS: 169, 178, 179, 331, 333
WORKSHEETS: 177, 188; student view of, 175
WORKSHOPS: district-wide reading, 32; "make and take," 33; parent-teacher, 31; reading, 30
WORLD BOOK: 203
WRITING: computer-assisted, 300; ESL students and, 307f; ideographic, 111; phonics and children's, 120; reading and, 19, 77, 190, 322-323. *See also* Compositions; Handwriting; Paragraphs; Sentences; Words
WRITING TO READ (IBM): 300

YEARBOOKS: as research resource, 14
YOU CAN HELP YOUR YOUNG CHILD WITH WRITING (Baghban): 35

ZONE OF PROXIMAL DEVELOPMENT (Vygotsky): 63